MCAT

BIOLOGY

2009–2010 EDITION

The Staff of Kaplan

KAPLAN PUBLISHING

New York

Published by Kaplan Publishing, a division of Kaplan, Inc.
1 Liberty Plaza, 24th Floor
New York, NY 10006

Printed in the United States of America

10 9 8 7 6 5 4 3 2 1

ISBN: 978-1-4277-9872-5

Kaplan Publishing books are available at special quantity discounts to use for sales promotions, employee premiums, or educational purposes. Please email our Special Sales Department to order or for more information at kaplanpublishing@kaplan.com, or write to Kaplan Publishing, 1 Liberty Plaza, 24th Floor, New York, NY 10006.

Planet Friendly Publishing
✔ Made in the United States
✔ Printed on Recycled Paper
GREEN EDITION
Learn more at www.greenedition.org

- Manufacturing books in the United States ensures compliance with strict environmental laws and eliminates the need for international freight shipping, a major contributor to global air pollution. Printing on recycled paper helps minimize our consumption of trees, water and fossil fuels.
- Trees Saved: 66 • Air Emissions Eliminated: 5,843 pounds
- Water Saved: 25,595 gallons • Solid Waste Eliminated: 2,605 pounds

Contents

How to Use this Book

Kaplan MCAT Biology, along with the other four books in our MCAT subject review series, brings the Kaplan classroom experience right into your home!

Kaplan has been preparing premeds for the MCAT for more than 40 years in our comprehensive courses. In the past 15 years alone, we've helped over 400,000 students prepare for this important exam and improve their chances of medical school admission.

TEACHER TIPS

Think of Kaplan's five MCAT subject books as having a private Kaplan teacher right by your side! We've created a team of the **top MCAT teachers in the country,** who have read through these comprehensive guides. On every page, they offer the same tips, advice, and Test Day insight as in their Kaplan classroom.

Pay close attention to **Teacher Tip** sidebars like this:

> **TEACHER TIP**
> Hyper- and hypotonicity are commonly tested using an RBC and the Na/K ATPase, which can control the volume of a RBC placed in a stressful environment.

When you see these, you know what you're getting the same insight and knowledge that students in Kaplan MCAT classrooms across the country receive.

HIGH-YIELD MCAT REVIEW

At the end of several chapters, you'll find a special **High-Yield Questions** spread. These questions tackle the most frequently tested topics found on the MCAT. For each type of problem, you will be provided with a step-wise technique for solving the question and key directional points on how to solve for the MCAT specifically. Included on each spread are two icons: the first, a sideways hand pointing toward equations, notes equations that you should memorize for the MCAT. The second, an open hand, indicates where in a problem you can stop without doing further calculation.

At the end of each topic you will find a "Takeaways" box, which gives a concise summary of the problem-solving approach; and a "Things to watch out for" box, which points out any caveats to the approach discussed above that usually lead to wrong answer choices. Finally, there is a "Similar Questions" box at the end so you can test your ability to apply the stepwise technique to analogous questions. You can find the answers in the Answers and Explanations section of this book.

We're confident that this guide, and our award-wining Kaplan teachers, can help you achieve your goals of MCAT success and admission into medical school!

Good luck!

EXPERT KAPLAN MCAT TEAM

Marilyn Engle

MCAT Master Teacher; Teacher Trainer; Kaplan National Teacher of the Year, 2006; Westwood Teacher of the Year, 2007; Westwood Trainer of the Year, 2007; Encino Trainer of the Tear, 2005

John Michael Linick

MCAT Teacher; Boulder Teacher of the Year, 2007; Summer Intensive Program Faculty Member

Dr. Glen Pearlstein

MCAT Master Teacher; Teacher Trainer; Westwood Teacher of the Year, 2006

Matthew B. Wilkinson

MCAT Teacher; Teacher Trainer; Lone Star Trainer of the Year, 2007

INTRODUCTION TO THE MCAT

THE MCAT

The Medical College Admission Test, affectionately known as the MCAT, is different from any other test you've encountered in your academic career. It's not like the knowledge-based exams from high school and college, whose emphasis was on memorizing and regurgitating information. Medical schools can assess your academic prowess by looking at your transcript. The MCAT isn't even like other standardized tests you may have taken, where the focus was on proving your general skills.

Medical schools use MCAT scores to assess whether you possess the foundation upon which to build a successful medical career. Though you certainly need to know the content to do well, the stress is on thought process, because the MCAT is above all else a thinking test. That's why it emphasizes reasoning, critical and analytical thinking, reading comprehension, data analysis, writing, and problem-solving skills.

The MCAT's power comes from its use as an indicator of your abilities. Good scores can open doors. Your power comes from preparation and mindset, because the key to MCAT success is knowing what you're up against. That's where this section of this book comes in. We'll explain the philosophy behind the test, review the sections one by one, show you sample questions, share some of Kaplan's proven methods, and clue you in to what the test makers are really after. You'll get a handle on the process, find a confident new perspective, and achieve your highest possible scores.

TEST TIP

The MCAT places more weight on your thought process. However, you must have a strong hold of the required core knowledge. The MCAT may not be a perfect gauge of your abilities, but it is a relatively objective way to compare you with students from different backgrounds and undergraduate institutions.

ABOUT THE MCAT

Information about the MCAT CBT is included below. For the latest information about the MCAT, visit www.kaptest.com/mcat.

MCAT CBT

Format	U.S.—All administrations on computer
	International—Most on computer with limited paper and pencil in a few isolated areas
Essay Grading	One human and one computer grader
Breaks	Optional break between each section
Length of MCAT Day	Approximately 5.5 hours
Test Dates	Multiple dates in January, April, May, June, July, August, and September
	Total of 24 administrations each year.
Delivery of Results	Within 30 days. If scores are delayed notification will be posted online at www.aamc.org/mcat
	Electronic and paper
Security	Government-issued ID
	Electronic thumbprint
	Electronic signature verification
Testing Centers	Small computer testing sites

PLANNING FOR THE TEST

As you look toward your preparation for the MCAT consider the following advice:

Complete your core course requirements as soon as possible. Take a strategic eye to your schedule and get core requirements out of the way now.

Take the MCAT once. The MCAT is a notoriously grueling standardized exam that requires extensive preparation. It is longer than the graduate admissions exams for business school (GMAT, 3½ hours), law school (LSAT, 3¼ hours) and graduate school (GRE, 2½ hours). You do not want to take it twice. Plan and prepare accordingly.

> **KAPLAN EXCLUSIVE**
>
> Go online and sign up for a local Kaplan Pre-Med Edge event to get the latest information on the test.

THE ROLE OF THE MCAT IN ADMISSIONS

More and more people are applying to medical school and more and more people are taking the MCAT. It's important for you to recognize that while a high MCAT score is a critical component in getting admitted to top med schools, it's not the only factor. Medical school admissions officers weigh grades, interviews, MCAT scores, level of involvement in extracurricular activities, as well as personal essays.

In a Kaplan survey of 130 pre-med advisors, 84 percent called the interview a "very important" part of the admissions process, followed closely by college grades (83 percent) and MCAT scores (76 percent). Kaplan's college admissions consulting practice works with students on all these issues so they can position themselves as strongly as possible. In addition, the AAMC has made it clear that scores will continue to be valid for three years, and that the scoring of the computer-based MCAT will not differ from that of the paper and pencil version.

REGISTRATION

The only way to register for the MCAT is online. The registration site is: www.aamc.org/mcat.

You will be able to access the site approximately six months before your test date. Payment must be made by MasterCard or Visa.

Go to www.aamc.org/mcat/registration.htm and download *MCAT Essentials* for information about registration, fees, test administration, and preparation. For other questions, contact:

MCAT Care Team
Association of American Medical Colleges
Section for Applicant Assessment Services
2450 N. St., NW
Washington, DC 20037
www.aamc.org/mcat
Email: mcat@aamc.org

You will want to take the MCAT in the year prior to your planned start date. For example, if you want to start medical school in Fall 2010, you will need to take the MCAT and apply in 2009. Don't drag your feet gathering information. You'll need time not only to prepare and practice for the test, but also to get all your registration work done.

ANATOMY OF THE MCAT

Before mastering strategies, you need to know exactly what you're dealing with on the MCAT. Let's start with the basics: The MCAT is, among other things, an endurance test.

If you can't approach it with confidence and stamina, you'll quickly lose your composure. That's why it's so important that you take control of the test.

The MCAT consists of four timed sections: Physical Sciences, Verbal Reasoning, Writing Sample, and Biological Sciences. Later in this section we'll take an in-depth look at each MCAT section, including sample question types and specific test-smart hints, but here's a general overview, reflecting the order of the test sections and number of questions in each.

TEST TIP

The MCAT should be viewed just like any other part of your application: as an opportunity to show the medical schools who you are and what you can do. Take control of your MCAT experience.

Physical Sciences

Time	70 minutes
Format	• 52 multiple-choice questions: approximately 7–9 passages with 4–8 questions each • approximately 10 stand-alone questions (not passage-based)
What it tests	basic general chemistry concepts, basic physics concepts, analytical reasoning, data interpretation

Verbal Reasoning

Time	60 minutes
Format	• 40 multiple-choice questions: approximately 7 passages with 5–7 questions each
What it tests	critical reading

Writing Sample

Time	60 minutes
Format	• 2 essay questions (30 minutes per essay)
What it tests	critical thinking, intellectual organization, written communication skills

Biological Sciences

Time	70 minutes
Format	• 52 multiple-choice questions: approximately 7–9 passages with 4–8 questions each • approximately 10 stand-alone questions (not passage-based)
What it tests	basic biology concepts, basic organic chemistry concepts, analytical reasoning, data interpretation

The sections of the test always appear in the same order:

Physical Sciences

[optional 10-minute break]

Verbal Reasoning

[optional 10-minute break]

Writing Sample

[optional 10-minute break]

Biological Sciences

SCORING

Each MCAT section receives its own score. Physical Sciences, Verbal Reasoning, and Biological Sciences are each scored on a scale ranging from 1–15, with 15 as the highest. The Writing Sample essays are scored alphabetically on a scale ranging from J to T, with T as the highest. The two essays are each evaluated by two official readers, so four critiques combine to make the alphabetical score.

The number of multiple-choice questions that you answer correctly per section is your "raw score." Your raw score will then be converted to yield the "scaled score"—the one that will fall somewhere in that 1–15 range. These scaled scores are what are reported to medical schools as your MCAT scores. All multiple-choice questions are worth the same amount—one raw point—and *there's no penalty for guessing*. That means that *you should always select an answer for every question, whether you get to that question or not!* This is an important piece of advice, so pay it heed. Never let time run out on any section without selecting an answer for every question.

Your score report will tell you—and your potential medical schools—not only your scaled scores, but also the national mean score for each section, standard deviation, national scoring profile for each section, and your percentile ranking.

WHAT'S A GOOD SCORE?

There's no such thing as a cut-and-dry "good score." Much depends on the strength of the rest of your application (if your transcript is first rate, the pressure to strut your stuff on the MCAT isn't as intense) and on where you want to go to school (different schools have different score expectations). Here are a few interesting statistics:

For each MCAT administration, the average scaled scores are approximately 8s for Physical Sciences, Verbal Reasoning, and Biological Sciences, and N for the Writing Sample. You need scores of at least 10–11s to be considered competitive by most medical schools, and if you're aiming for the top you've got to do even better, and score 12s and above.

You don't have to be perfect to do well. For instance, on the AAMC's Practice Test 5R, you could get as many as 10 questions wrong in Verbal Reasoning, 17 in Physical Sciences, and 16 in Biological Sciences and still score in the 80th percentile. To score in the 90th percentile, you could get as many as 7 wrong in Verbal Reasoning, 12 in Physical Sciences, and 12 in Biological Sciences. Even students who receive perfect scaled scores usually get a handful of questions wrong.

It's important to maximize your performance on every question. Just a few questions one way or the other can make a big difference in your scaled score. Here's a look at recent score profiles so you can get an idea of the shape of a typical score distribution.

TEST TIP

The percentile figure tells you how many other test takers scored at or below your level. In other words, a percentile figure of 80 means that 80 percent did as well or worse than you did, and that only 20 percent did better.

TEST TIP

The raw score of each administration is converted to a scaled score. The conversion varies with administrations. Hence, the same raw score will not always give you the same scaled score.

Physical Sciences		
Scaled Score	Percent Achieving Score	Percentile Rank Range
15	0.1	99.9–99.9
14	1.2	98.7–99.8
13	2.5	96.2–98.6
12	5.1	91.1–96.1
11	7.2	83.9–91.0
10	12.1	71.8–83.8
9	12.9	58.9–71.1
8	16.5	42.4–58.5
7	16.7	25.7–42.3
6	13.0	12.7–25.6
5	7.9	04.8–12.6
4	3.3	01.5–04.7
3	1.3	00.2–01.4
2	0.1	00.1–00.1
1	0.0	00.0–00.0
Scaled Score Mean = 8.1 Standard Deviation = 2.32		

Verbal Reasoning		
Scaled Score	Percent Achieving Score	Percentile Rank Range
15	0.1	99.9–99.9
14	0.2	99.7–99.8
13	1.8	97.9–99.6
12	3.6	94.3–97.8
11	10.5	83.8–94.2
10	15.6	68.2–83.7
9	17.2	51.0–68.1
8	15.4	35.6–50.9
7	10.3	25.3–35.5
6	10.9	14.4–25.2
5	6.9	07.5–14.3
4	3.9	03.6–07.4
3	2.0	01.6–03.5
2	0.5	00.1–01.5
1	0.0	00.0–00.0
Scaled Score Mean = 8.0 Standard Deviation = 2.43		

Writing Sample		
Scaled Score	Percent Achieving Score	Percentile Rank Range
T	0.5	99.9–99.9
S	2.8	94.7–99.8
R	7.2	96.0–99.3
Q	14.2	91.0–95.9
P	9.7	81.2–90.9
O	17.9	64.0–81.1
N	14.7	47.1–63.9
M	18.8	30.4–47.0
L	9.5	21.2–30.3
K	3.6	13.5–21.1
J	1.2	06.8–13.4
		02.9–06.7
		00.9–02.8
		00.2–00.8
		00.0–00.1
75th Percentile = Q 50th Percentile = O 25th Percentile = M		

Biological Sciences		
Scaled Score	Percent Achieving Score	Percentile Rank Range
15	0.1	99.9–99.9
14	1.2	98.7–99.8
13	2.5	96.2–98.6
12	5.1	91.1–96.1
11	7.2	83.9–91.0
10	12.1	71.8–83.8
9	12.9	58.9–71.1
8	16.5	42.4–58.5
7	16.7	25.7–42.3
6	13.0	12.7–25.6
5	7.9	04.8–12.6
4	3.3	01.5–04.7
3	1.3	00.2–01.4
2	0.1	00.1–00.1
1	0.0	00.0–00.0
Scaled Score Mean = 8.2 Standard Deviation = 2.39		

WHAT THE MCAT REALLY TESTS

It's important to grasp not only the nuts and bolts of the MCAT, so you'll know *what* to do on Test Day, but also the underlying principles of the test so you'll know *why* you're doing what you're doing on Test Day. We'll cover the straightforward MCAT facts later. Now it's time to examine the heart and soul of the MCAT, to see what it's really about.

THE MYTH

Most people preparing for the MCAT fall prey to the myth that the MCAT is a straightforward science test. They think something like this:

"It covers the four years of science I had to take in school: biology, chemistry, physics, and organic chemistry. It even has equations. OK, so it has Verbal Reasoning and Writing, but those sections are just to see if we're literate, right? The important stuff is the science. After all, we're going to be doctors."

Well, here's the little secret no one seems to want you to know: The MCAT is not just a science test; it's also a thinking test. This means that the test is designed to let you demonstrate your thought process, not only your thought content.

The implications are vast. Once you shift your test-taking paradigm to match the MCAT modus operandi, you'll find a new level of confidence and control over the test. You'll begin to work with the nature of the MCAT rather than against it. You'll be more efficient and insightful as you prepare for the test, and you'll be more relaxed on Test Day. In fact, you'll be able to see the MCAT for what it is rather than for what it's dressed up to be. We want your Test Day to feel like a visit with a familiar friend instead of an awkward blind date.

THE ZEN OF MCAT

Medical schools do not need to rely on the MCAT to see what you already know. Admission committees can measure your subject-area proficiency using your undergraduate coursework and grades. Schools are most interested in the potential of your mind.

In recent years, many medical schools have shifted pedagogic focus away from an information-heavy curriculum to a concept-based curriculum. There is currently more emphasis placed on problem solving, holistic thinking, and cross-disciplinary study. Be careful not to dismiss this important point, figuring you'll wait to worry about academic trends until you're actually in medical school. This trend affects you right now, because it's reflected in the MCAT. Every good tool matches its task. In this case the tool is the test, used to measure you and other candidates, and the task is to quantify how likely it is that you'll succeed in medical school.

Your intellectual potential—how skillfully you annex new territory into your mental boundaries, how quickly you build "thought highways" between ideas, how confidently and creatively you solve problems—is far more important to admission committees than your ability to recite Young's modulus for every material known to man. The schools assume they can expand your knowledge base. They choose applicants carefully because expansive knowledge is not enough to succeed in medical school or in the profession. There's something more. It's this "something more" that the MCAT is trying to measure.

Every section on the MCAT tests essentially the same higher-order thinking skills: analytical reasoning, abstract thinking, and problem solving.

Most test takers get trapped into thinking they are being tested strictly about biology, chemistry, etc. Thus, they approach each section with a new outlook on what's expected. This constant mental gear-shifting can be exhausting, not to mention counterproductive. Instead of perceiving the test as parsed into radically different sections, you need to maintain your focus on the underlying nature of the test: It's designed to test your thinking skills, not your information-recall skills. Each test section thus presents a variation on the same theme.

WHAT ABOUT THE SCIENCE?

With this perspective, you may be left asking these questions: "What about the science? What about the content? Don't I need to know the basics?" The answer is a resounding "Yes!" You must be fluent in the different languages of the test. You cannot do well on the MCAT if you don't know the basics of physics, general chemistry, biology, and organic chemistry. We recommend that you take one year each of biology, general chemistry, organic chemistry, and physics before taking the MCAT, and that you review the content in this book thoroughly. Knowing these basics is just the beginning of doing well on the MCAT. That's a shock to most test takers. They presume that once they recall or relearn their undergraduate science, they are ready to do battle against the MCAT. Wrong! They merely have directions to the battlefield. They lack what they need to beat the test: a copy of the test maker's battle plan!

You won't be drilled on facts and formulas on the MCAT. You'll need to demonstrate ability to reason based on ideas and concepts. The science questions are painted with a broad brush, testing your general understanding.

TAKE CONTROL: THE MCAT MINDSET

In addition to being a thinking test, as we've stressed, the MCAT is a standardized test. As such, it has its own consistent patterns and idiosyncrasies that can actually work in your favor. This is the key to why test preparation works. You have the opportunity to familiarize yourself with those consistent peculiarities, to adopt the proper test-taking mindset.

The following are some overriding principles of the MCAT Mindset that will be covered in depth in the chapters to come:

- Read actively and critically.
- Translate prose into your own words.

TEST TIP

Don't think of the sections of the MCAT as unrelated timed pieces. Each is a variation on the same theme, because the underlying purpose of each section and of the test as a whole is to evaluate your thinking skills. Memorizing formulas won't boost your score. Understanding fundamental scientific principles will.

TEST TIP

Those perfectionist tendencies that make you a good student and a good medical school candidate may work against you in MCAT Land. If you get stuck on a question or passage, move on. Perfectionism is for medical school—not the MCAT. Moreover, you don't need to understand every word of a passage before you go on to the questions—what's tripping you up may not even be relevant to what you'll be asked.

- Save the toughest questions for last.
- Know the test and its components inside and out.
- Do MCAT-style problems in each topic area after you've reviewed it.
- Allow your confidence to build on itself.
- Take full-length practice tests a week or two before the test to break down the mystique of the real experience.
- Learn from your mistakes—get the most out of your practice tests.
- Look at the MCAT as a challenge, the first step in your medical career, rather than as an arbitrary obstacle.

That's what the MCAT Mindset boils down to: Taking control. Being proactive. Being on top of the testing experience so that you can get as many points as you can as quickly and as easily as possible. Keep this in mind as you read and work through the material in this book and, of course, as you face the challenge on Test Day.

Now that you have a better idea of what the MCAT is all about, let's take a tour of the individual test sections. Although the underlying skills being tested are similar, each MCAT section requires that you call into play a different domain of knowledge. So, though we encourage you to think of the MCAT as a holistic and unified test, we also recognize that the test is segmented by discipline and that there are characteristics unique to each section. In the overviews, we'll review sample questions and answers and discuss section-specific strategies. For each of the sections—Verbal Reasoning, Physical/Biological Sciences, and the Writing Sample—we'll present you with the following:

- **The Big Picture**
  You'll get a clear view of the section and familiarize yourself with what it's really evaluating.

- **A Closer Look**
  You'll explore the types of questions that will appear and master the strategies you'll need to deal with them successfully.

- **Highlights**
  The key approaches to each section are outlined, for reinforcement and quick review.

TEST EXPERTISE

The first year of medical school is a frenzied experience for most students. In order to meet the requirements of a rigorous work schedule, students either learn to prioritize and budget their time or else fall hopelessly behind. It's no surprise, then, that the MCAT, the test specifically designed to predict success in the first year of medical school, is a high-speed, time-intensive test. It demands excellent time-management skills as well as that sine qua non of the successful physician—grace under pressure.

It's one thing to answer a Verbal Reasoning question correctly; it's quite another to answer several correctly in a limited time frame. The same goes for Physical and Biological Sciences—it's a whole new ball game once you move from doing an individual passage at your leisure to handling a full section under actual timed conditions. You also need to budget your time for the Writing Sample, but this section isn't as time sensitive. Nevertheless when it comes to the multiple-choice sections, time pressure is a factor that affects virtually every test taker.

So when you're comfortable with the content of the test, your next challenge will be to take it to the next level—test expertise—which will enable you to manage the all-important time element of the test.

THE FIVE BASIC PRINCIPLES OF TEST EXPERTISE

On some tests, if a question seems particularly difficult you'll spend significantly more time on it, as you'll probably be given more points for correctly answering a hard question. Not so on the MCAT. Remember, every MCAT question, no matter how hard, is worth a single point. There's no partial credit or "A" for effort. Moreover because there are so many questions to do in so little time, you'd be a fool to spend 10 minutes getting a point for a hard question and then not have time to get a couple of quick points from three easy questions later in the section.

Given this combination—limited time, all questions equal in weight—you've got to develop a way of handling the test sections to make sure you get as many points as you can as quickly and easily as you can. Here are the principles that will help you do that:

TEST TIP

For complete MCAT success, you've got to get as many correct answers as possible in the time you're allotted. Knowing the strategies is not enough. You have to perfect your time-management skills so that you get a chance to use those strategies on as many questions as possible.

TEST TIP

In order to meet the stringent time requirements of the MCAT, you have to cultivate the following elements of test expertise:

- Feel free to skip questions.
- Learn to recognize and seek out questions you can do.
- Use a process of answer elimination.
- Remain calm.
- Keep track of time.

1. FEEL FREE TO SKIP AROUND

One of the most valuable strategies to help you finish the sections in time is to learn to recognize and deal first with the questions that are easier and more familiar to you. That means you must temporarily skip those that promise to be difficult and time-consuming, if you feel comfortable doing so. You can always come back to these at the end, and if you run out of time, you're much better off not getting to questions you may have had difficulty with, rather than not getting to potentially feasible material. Of course, because there's no guessing penalty, always put an answer to every question on the test, whether you get to it or not. (It's not practical to skip passages, so do those in order.)

This strategy is difficult for most test takers; we're conditioned to do things in order. But give it a try when you practice. Remember, if you do the test in the exact order given, you're letting the test makers control you. But you control how you take this test. On the other hand, if skipping around goes against your moral fiber and makes you a nervous wreck—don't do it. Just be mindful of the clock, and don't get bogged down with the tough questions.

2. LEARN TO RECOGNIZE AND SEEK OUT QUESTIONS YOU CAN DO

Another thing to remember about managing the test sections is that MCAT questions and passages, unlike items on the SAT and other standardized tests, are not presented in order of difficulty. There's no rule that says you have to work through the sections in any particular order; in fact, the test makers scatter the easy and difficult questions throughout the section, in effect rewarding those who actually get to the end. Don't lose sight of what you're being tested for along with your reading and thinking skills: efficiency and cleverness.

Don't waste time on questions you can't do. We know that skipping a possibly tough question is easier said than done; we all have the natural instinct to plow through test sections in their given order. But it just doesn't pay off on the MCAT. The computer won't be impressed if you get the toughest question right. If you dig in your heels on a tough question, refusing to move on until you've cracked it, well, you're letting your ego get in the way of your test score. A test section (not to mention life itself) is too short to waste on lost causes.

> **TEST TIP**
>
> Every question is worth exactly one point, but questions vary dramatically in difficulty level. Given a shortage of time, work on easy questions and then move on to the hard ones.

> **TEST TIP**
>
> Don't let your ego sabotage your score. It isn't easy for some of us to give up on a tough, time-consuming question, but sometimes it's better to say "uncle." Remember, there's no point of honor at stake here, but there are MCAT points at stake.

3. USE A PROCESS OF ANSWER ELIMINATION

Using a process of elimination is another way to answer questions both quickly and effectively. There are two ways to get all the answers right on the MCAT. You either know all the right answers, or you know all the wrong answers. Because there are three times as many wrong answers, you should be able to eliminate some if not all of them. By doing so you either get to the correct response or increase your chances of guessing the correct response. You start out with a 25 percent chance of picking the right answer, and with each eliminated answer your odds go up. Eliminate one, and you'll have a 33⅓ percent chance of picking the right one, eliminate two, and you'll have a 50 percent chance, and, of course, eliminate three, and you'll have a 100 percent chance. Increase your efficiency by actually crossing out the wrong choices on the screen using the strikethrough feature. Remember to look for wrong-answer traps when you're eliminating. Some answers are designed to seduce you by distorting the correct answer.

4. REMAIN CALM

It's imperative that you remain calm and composed while working through a section. You can't allow yourself to become so rattled by one hard reading passage that it throws off your performance on the rest of the section. Expect to find at least one killer passage in every section, but remember, you won't be the only one to have trouble with it. The test is curved to take the tough material into account. Having trouble with a difficult question isn't going to ruin your score—but getting upset about it and letting it throw you off track will. When you understand that part of the test maker's goal is to reward those who keep their composure, you'll recognize the importance of not panicking when you run into challenging material.

5. KEEP TRACK OF TIME

Of course, the last thing you want to happen is to have time called on a particular section before you've gotten to half the questions. Therefore, it's essential that you pace yourself, keeping in mind the general guidelines for how long to spend on any individual question or passage. Have a sense of how long you have to do each question, so you know when you're exceeding the limit and should start to move faster.

So, when working on a section, always remember to keep track of time. Don't spend a wildly disproportionate amount of time on any one question or group of questions. Also, give yourself 30 seconds or so at the end of each section to fill in answers for any questions you haven't gotten to.

SECTION-SPECIFIC PACING

Let's now look at the section-specific timing requirements and some tips for meeting them. Keep in mind that the times per question or passage are only averages; there are bound to be some that take less time and some that take more. Try to stay balanced. Remember, too, that every question is of equal worth, so don't get hung up on any one. Think about it: If a question is so hard that it takes you a long time to answer it, chances are you may get it wrong anyway. In that case, you'd have nothing to show for your extra time but a lower score.

VERBAL REASONING

Allow yourself approximately eight to ten minutes per passage and respective questions. It may sound like a lot of time, but it goes quickly. Keep in mind that some passages are longer than others. On average, give yourself about three or four minutes to read and then four to six minutes for the questions.

PHYSICAL AND BIOLOGICAL SCIENCES

Averaging over each section, you'll have about one minute and 20 seconds per question. Some questions, of course, will take more time, some less. A science passage plus accompanying questions should take about eight to nine minutes, depending on how many questions there are. Stand-alone questions can take anywhere from a few seconds to a minute or more. Again, the rule is to do your best work first. Also, don't feel that you have to understand everything in a passage before you go on to the questions. You may not need that deep an understanding to answer questions, because a lot of information may be extraneous. You should overcome your perfectionism and use your time wisely.

WRITING SAMPLE

You have exactly 30 minutes for each essay. As mentioned in discussion of the 7-step approach to this section, you should allow approximately five minutes to prewrite the essay, 23 minutes to write the essay, and two minutes to proofread. It's important that you budget your time, so you don't get cut off.

COMPUTER-BASED TESTING STRATEGIES

ARRIVE AT THE TESTING CENTER EARLY

Get to the testing center early to jump-start your brain. However, if they allow you to begin your test early, decline.

> **TEST TIP**
>
> For Verbal Reasoning, here are some of the important time techniques to remember:
>
> - Spend eight to ten minutes per passage
> - Allow about three to four minutes to read and four to six minutes for the questions

> **TEST TIP**
>
> Some suggestions for maximizing your time on the science sections:
>
> - Spend about eight to nine minutes per passage
> - Maximize points by doing the questions you can do first
> - Don't waste valuable time trying to understand extraneous material

USE THE MOUSE TO YOUR ADVANTAGE

If you are right-handed, practice using the mouse with your left hand for Test Day. This way, you'll increase speed by keeping the pencil in your right hand to write on your scratch paper. If you are left-handed, use your right hand for the mouse.

KNOW THE TUTORIAL BEFORE TEST DAY

You will save time on Test Day by knowing exactly how the test will work. Click through any tutorial pages and save time.

PRACTICE WITH SCRATCH PAPER

Going forward, always practice using scratch paper when solving questions because this is how you will do it on Test Day. Never write directly on a written test.

GET NEW SCRATCH PAPER

Between sections, get a new piece of scratch paper even if you only used part of the old one. This will maximize the available space for each section and minimize the likelihood of you running out of paper to write on.

REMEMBER YOU CAN ALWAYS GO BACK

Just because you finish a passage or move on, remember you can come back to questions about which you are uncertain. You have the "marking" option to your advantage. However, as a general rule minimize the amount of questions you mark or skip.

MARK INCOMPLETE WORK

If you need to go back to a question, clearly mark the work you've done on the scratch paper with the question number. This way, you will be able to find your work easily when you come back to tackle the question.

LOOK AWAY AT TIMES

Taking the test on computer leads to faster eye-muscle fatigue. Use the Kaplan strategy of looking at a distant object at regular intervals. This will keep you fresher at the end of the test.

PRACTICE ON THE COMPUTER

This is the most critical aspect of adapting to computer-based testing. Like anything else, in order to perform well on computer-based tests you must practice. Spend time reading passages and answering questions on the computer. You often will have to scroll when reading passages.

PART I
SUBJECT REVIEW

CHAPTER 1

THE CELL

The cell is the fundamental unit of all living things. Every function in biology involves a process that occurs within cells or at the interface between cells. Therefore, to understand biology, you need to appreciate the structure and function of the different parts of the cell (the organelles) as well as the properties that define the plasma membrane that surrounds the cell.

CELL THEORY

The cell was not discovered or studied in detail until the development of the microscope in the 17 century. Since then much more has been learned, and a unifying theory known as the **Cell Theory** has been proposed.

The Cell Theory may be summarized as follows:

- All living things are composed of cells.
- The cell is the basic functional unit of life.
- Cells arise only from pre-existing cells.
- Cells carry genetic information in the form of **DNA.** This genetic material is passed from parent cell to daughter cell.

TEACHER TIP

Know these points: The MCAT likes to test what sorts of systems could be considered "cells."

METHODS AND TOOLS

There are many tools available to study the cell and its structures. Three primary methods are **microscopy, autoradiography,** and **centrifugation.**

A. MICROSCOPY

Of the many tools used by scientists to study cells, the microscope is the most basic. **Magnification** is the increase in apparent size of an object. **Resolution** is the differentiation of two closely situated objects.

1. Compound Light Microscope

A compound light microscope uses two lenses or lens systems to magnify an object. The total magnification is equal to the product of the eyepiece magnification (usually 10×) and the magnification of the selected objective lens (usually 4×, 10×, 20×, or 100×). The chief components of the microscope are the **diaphragm,** the **coarse adjustment knob,** and the **fine adjustment knob** (see Figure 1.1).

- The diaphragm controls the amount of light passing through the specimen.
- The coarse adjustment knob roughly focuses the image.
- The fine adjustment knob sharply focuses the image.

In general, the compound light microscope is used in the observation of nonliving specimens. Light microscopy requires contrast between cells and cell structures; such contrast is obtained through staining techniques that result in cell death. Various stains and dyes may be used for light microscopy. For example, the dye hematoxylin reveals the distribution of **DNA** and **RNA** within a cell due to its affinity for negatively charged molecules.

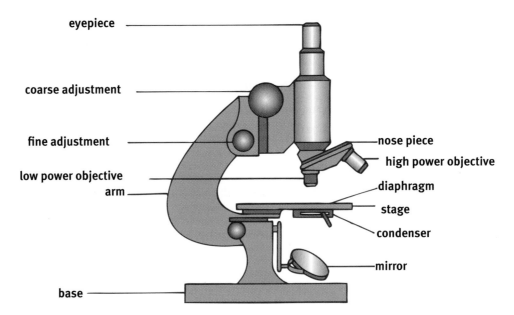

Figure 1.1. Compound Light Microscope

2. Phase Contrast Microscope

A phase contrast microscope is a special type of light microscope that permits the study of living cells. Differences in refractive index are used to produce contrast between cellular structures. This technique does not kill the specimen.

3. Electron Microscope

An electron microscope uses a beam of electrons to allow a thousand-fold higher magnification than is possible with light microscopy. Unfortunately, examination of living specimens is not possible because of the preparations necessary for electron microscopy; tissues must be fixed and sectioned and, sometimes, stained with solutions of heavy metals.

B. AUTORADIOGRAPHY

This technique uses radioactive molecules to trace and identify cell structures and biochemical activity. Cells are exposed to a radioactive compound for a brief, measured period of time (enough time for it to be incorporated into the cell). They are incubated, fixed at various intervals, and processed for microscopy. Each preparation is covered with a film of photographic emulsion. The preparations must be kept in the dark for several days while the radioactive compound decays. The emulsion is then developed; dark silver grains reveal the distribution of radioactivity within the specimen. Autoradiography can be used to study protein synthesis: Labeling amino acids with radioactive isotopes allows the pathways of protein synthesis to be examined. Similar techniques are used to study the mechanisms of DNA and RNA synthesis.

C. CENTRIFUGATION

Differential centrifugation can be used to separate cells or mixtures of cells without destroying them in the process. At lower speeds, cell mixtures separate into layers on the basis of cell type. Spinning fragmented cells at high speeds in the centrifuge will cause their components to sediment at different levels in the test tube on the basis of their respective densities. For example, centrifugation of a **eukaryotic** cell sediments high-density **ribosomes** at the bottom of the test tube, while low-density **mitochondria** and **lysosomes** remain at the top.

MCAT SYNOPSIS

Prokaryotes	Eukaryotes
Bacteria	Protists, fungi, plants, animals
Cell wall present in all prokaryotes	Cell wall present in fungi and plants only
No nucleus	Nucleus
Ribosomes (subunits = 30S and 50S)	Ribosomes (subunits = 40S and 60S)
No membrane-bound organelles	Membrane-bound organelles

PROKARYOTES VS. EUKARYOTES

Cells can be structurally categorized into two distinct groups, **prokaryotic** and **eukaryotic. Viruses** occupy a unique category and are not technically considered cells because they are not capable of living independently.

A. PROKARYOTES

Prokaryotes, which include **bacteria** and **cyanobacteria** (blue-green algae), are unicellular organisms with a simple cell structure. Prokaryotic cells have an outer cell membrane but do not contain any membrane-bound organelles. There is no true nucleus; the genetic material consists of a single circular molecule of DNA concentrated in an area of the cell called the **nucleoid** region. In addition, there may be smaller rings of DNA called **plasmids,** consisting of just a few genes. Plasmids replicate independently of the main chromosome, and often contain genes that allow the prokaryote to survive adverse conditions. Plasmids are one mechanism, for example, of imparting resistance to antibiotics.

Bacteria have a **cell wall,** a **cell membrane, cytoplasm,** ribosomes (somewhat different from those found in eukaryotes), and sometimes **flagella** (also different from those in eukaryotes) that are used for locomotion. Respiration occurs at the cell membrane (see Figure 1.2).

B. EUKARYOTES

All multicellular organisms and all nonbacteria unicellular organisms are composed of eukaryotic cells. A typical eukaryotic cell is bounded by a cell membrane and contains cytoplasm. Cytoplasm contains **organelles** suspended in a semifluid medium called the **cytosol.** The genetic material consists of linear strands of DNA organized into **chromosomes** and located within a membrane-enclosed organelle called the **nucleus.** Although both animal and plant cells are eukaryotic, they differ from each other. **Centrioles,** located in the centrosome area, are found in animal cells but not in plant cells (see Figure 1.3).

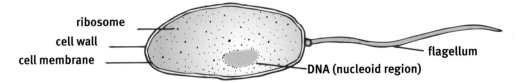

ribosome
cell wall
cell membrane
flagellum
DNA (nucleoid region)

Figure 1.2. Prokaryotic Cell

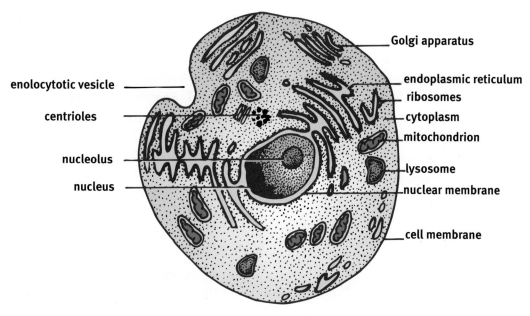

Figure 1.3. Eukaryotic Cell

EUKARYOTIC ORGANELLES

Cytosol is the fluid component of the cytoplasm and consists of an aqueous solution containing free proteins, nutrients, and other solutes. The **cytoskeleton,** which is composed of **microtubules, microfilaments, intermediate fibers,** and other accessory proteins, is also found in the cytosol. These proteinaceous filaments give the cell its shape and anchor the organelles. They also function in cell maintenance and aid in intracellular transport. The cell membrane surrounds the cell and regulates passage of materials in both directions.

The organelles are specialized structures of unique form and function. They include the nucleus, ribosomes, **endoplasmic reticulum, Golgi apparatus, vesicles, vacuoles,** lysosomes, **microbodies,** mitochondria, chloroplasts, and centrioles.

A. CELL MEMBRANE

The cell membrane (plasma membrane) encloses the cell and is composed of a **phospholipid bilayer.** Phospholipids have both a hydrophilic (polar) phosphoric acid and a hydrophobic (nonpolar) fatty acid region. In a lipid bilayer, the hydrophilic regions are found on the exterior surfaces of the membrane whereas the hydrophobic regions are found on the interior of the membrane (see Figure 1.4).

TEACHER TIP

The ability of different molecules to traverse a membrane is critical to cells. The cell must be able to allow nutrients and required compounds in, while preventing bacteria, viruses, and harmful compounds from entering.

25

This phospholipids bilayer structure allows the cell membrane to regulate the passage of material and molecules in and out of the cell and exhibits **selective permeability.** Selective permeability means that the cell membrane allows some compounds/molecules to pass through freely, where others are prohibited or regulated. Specifically, small nonpolar (hydrophobic) molecules generally pass through freely (diffuse) across the cell membrane. In contrast, charged ions and large molecules such as proteins and complex carbohydrates do not diffuse freely. They may require carrier proteins to help carry them across the cell membrane.

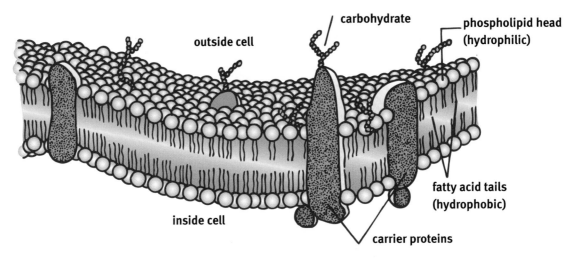

Figure 1.4. Fluid Mosaic Model

According to the generally accepted fluid mosaic model, the cell membrane consists of a phospholipids bilayer with proteins embedded throughout. The lipids and many of the proteins can move freely within the membrane. Cholesterol molecules are often embedded in the hydrophobic interior and contribute to the cell membrane's fluidity. Proteins interspersed throughout the membrane may be partially or completely embedded in the bilayer; one or both ends of the protein may extend beyond the membrane on either side. Such proteins can play a role in cell adhesion by forming junctions with proteins on adjacent cells. Transport proteins are membrane-spanning proteins that allow certain ions and polar molecules to pass through the lipid bilayer. Cell adhesion molecules (CAMs) are proteins that contribute to cell recognition and adhesion, and are particularly important during development.

Receptors are complex proteins or glycoproteins generally embedded in the membrane with sites that bind to specific molecules in the cell's external environment. The receptor may carry the molecule into the cell via **pinocytosis** or it may signal across the membrane and into the cell via a second messenger (see chapter 11).

TEACHER TIP

We will have more to say about receptors later; they may be tested in many ways including membrane trafficking, isomerism, specificity, and binding kinetics.

B. NUCLEUS

The nucleus controls the activities of the cell, including cell division. It is surrounded by a **nuclear membrane, or envelope,** which is a double membrane that maintains a nuclear environment distinct from that of the cytoplasm. Interspersed throughout the nuclear membrane are **nuclear pores** that allow selective two-way exchange of materials between the nucleus and the cytoplasm. The nucleus contains the DNA, which is complexed with structural proteins called **histones** to form chromosomes. The **nucleolus** is a dense structure in the nucleus where ribosomal RNA (rRNA) synthesis occurs.

C. RIBOSOMES

Ribosomes are the sites of protein production and are synthesized by the nucleolus (see chapter 14). Ribosomes consist of two subunits, one large and one small; each subunit is composed of rRNA and proteins. **Free ribosomes** are found in the cytoplasm, while **bound ribosomes** line the outer membrane of the endoplasmic reticulum.

D. ENDOPLASMIC RETICULUM

The endoplasmic reticulum (**ER**) is a network of membrane-enclosed spaces connected at points with the nuclear membrane. ER with ribosomes lining its outer surface is known as **rough ER (RER)** and ER without ribosomes is known as **smooth ER.**

KAPLAN EXCLUSIVE

Rough ER—makes protein for secretion and intracellular transport.

Smooth ER—lipid synthesis and detoxification.

In general, ER is involved in the transport of materials throughout the cell, especially those materials destined to be secreted from the cell. Smooth ER is involved in lipid synthesis and the detoxification of drugs and poisons, while rough ER is involved in protein synthesis. Proteins synthesized by the bound ribosomes cross into the cisternae of the RER, where they undergo chemical modification. The proteins then cross into smooth ER, where they are secreted into cytoplasmic vesicles and transported to the Golgi apparatus.

TEACHER TIP

The ER is like a factory. It produces all the products that the cell puts out.

E. GOLGI APPARATUS

The Golgi apparatus consists of a stack of membrane-enclosed sacs. The Golgi receives vesicles and their contents from smooth ER, modifies them (e.g., glycosylation), repackages them into vesicles, and distributes them. The Golgi is particularly active in the distribution of newly synthesized materials to the cell surface. **Secretory vesicles,** produced by the Golgi, release their contents to the cell's exterior by the process of **exocytosis.**

F. VESICLES AND VACUOLES

Vesicles and vacuoles are membrane-bound sacs involved in the transport and storage of materials that are ingested, secreted, processed, or digested by the cell. Vacuoles are larger than vesicles and are more likely to be found in plant cells.

G. LYSOSOMES

Lysosomes are membrane-bound vesicles that contain hydrolytic enzymes involved in intracellular digestion. These enzymes are maximally effective at a pH of 5 and therefore need to be enclosed within the lysosome—an acidic environment distinct from the neutral pH of the cytosol. Lysosomes fuse with endocytotic vacuoles, thereby breaking down the material ingested by the cell. Lysosomes also aid in renewing a cell's own components by breaking down the old ones and releasing their molecular building blocks into the cytosol for reuse. A cell in an injured or dying tissue may "commit suicide" by rupturing the lysosome membrane and releasing its hydrolytic enzymes, which will digest cellular contents; this process is referred to as **autolysis.**

H. MICROBODIES

Microbodies are membrane-bound organelles specialized as containers for metabolic reactions. Two important types of microbodies are **peroxisomes** and **glyoxysomes.** Peroxisomes contain oxidative enzymes that catalyze a class of reactions in which hydrogen peroxide is produced by the transfer of hydrogen from a substrate to oxygen. Peroxisomes break fats down into smaller molecules that can be used for fuel, and are also used in the liver to detoxify compounds harmful to the body, such as alcohol. Glyoxysomes are usually found in fat tissue of germinating seedlings. They are used by the seedling to convert fats into sugars until the seedling is mature enough to produce its own supply of sugars by photosynthesis.

I. MITOCHONDRIA

Mitochondria are the sites of aerobic respiration within the cell and hence the suppliers of energy. Each mitochondrion is bound by an outer and an inner phospholipid bilayer membrane. The outer membrane is smooth and acts as a sieve, allowing molecules through on the basis of size. The area between the inner and outer membranes is known as the **intermembrane space.** The inner membrane has many convolutions called **cristae** and a high protein content that includes the proteins of the electron transport chain. The area bounded by the inner membrane is known as the mitochondrial **matrix** and is the site of many of the reactions in cell respiration (see chapter 3). Mitochondria are different from the other organelles in that they are **semiautonomous**; i.e., they contain their own DNA (which is circular) and ribosomes, which enable them to produce some of their own proteins and to self-replicate by **binary fission.** Mitochondria are believed by many to have been early prokaryotic cells that evolved a symbiotic relationship with the ancestors of eukaryotic cells.

J. CELL WALL

Many eukaryotic cells such as plant cells and fungi are surrounded by a tough outer cell wall that protects the cell from external stimuli and desiccation. Animal cells are **not** surrounded by a cell wall.

K. CENTRIOLES

Centrioles are a specialized type of microtubule (see below) involved in spindle organization during cell division and are **not** bound by a membrane. Animal cells usually have a pair of centrioles that are oriented at right angles to each other and lie in a region called the **centrosome.** Plant cells do **not** contain centrioles.

L. CYTOSKELETON

The cytoskeleton gives the cell mechanical support, maintains its shape, and functions in cell motility. It is composed of microtubules, microfilaments, and intermediate filaments.

Microtubules are hollow rods made up of polymerized **tubulins** that radiate throughout the cell and provide it with support. Microtubules provide a framework for organelle movement within the cell. Centrioles, which direct the separation of chromosomes during cell division, are composed of microtubules (see chapter 4). **Cilia** and flagella are specialized arrangements of microtubules that extend from certain cells and are involved in cell motility.

TEACHER TIP

FUN FACT: Mitochondria are only inherited from the mother. That means if a woman has a genetic defect in one of her mitochondrial genes, she will pass it on to all of her children; conversely, a man cannot pass it on to *any* of his children.

Microfilaments are solid rods of **actin,** involved in cell movement as well as support. Muscle contraction, for example, is based on the interaction of actin with **myosin** in muscle cells (see chapter 6). Microfilaments move materials across the plasma membrane, for instance, in the contraction phase of cell division, and in amoeboid movement.

Intermediate filaments are a collection of fibers involved in maintenance of cytoskeletal integrity. Their diameters fall between those of microtubules and microfilaments.

MOVEMENT ACROSS THE CELL MEMBRANE

Substances can move into and out of cells in various ways. Some methods occur passively, without energy, while others are active and require energy expenditure (ATP).

A. SIMPLE DIFFUSION

Simple diffusion is the net movement of dissolved particles down their concentration gradients—from a region of higher concentration to a region of lower concentration. This is a passive process (see Figure 1.5). **Osmosis** is the simple diffusion of water from a region of lower solute concentration to a region of higher solute concentration. If a membrane is impermeable to a particular solute, then water will flow across the membrane until the differences in the solute concentrations have been equilibrated. Differences in the concentration of substances to which the membrane is impermeable affect the direction of osmosis. When the cytoplasm of the cell has a lower solute concentration than the extracellular medium, the medium is said to be **hypertonic** to the cell and water will flow out, causing the cell to shrink. When the cytoplasm of a cell has a higher solute concentration than the extracellular medium, the medium is said to be **hypotonic** to the cell and water will flow in, causing the cell to swell; if too much water flows in, the cell may **lyse.** When the solute concentrations inside and outside the cell are equal, the cell and the medium are said to be **isotonic,** and there is no net flow of water in either direction (see Figure 1.6).

B. FACILITATED DIFFUSION

Facilitated diffusion (passive transport) is the net movement of dissolved particles down their concentration gradient with the help of carrier molecules. This process, like simple diffusion, does not require energy (see Figure 1.5).

C. ACTIVE TRANSPORT

Active transport is the net movement of dissolved particles against their concentration gradient with the help of transport proteins. Unlike diffusion, active transport requires energy (see Figure 1.5). Active transport is required to maintain membrane potentials in specialized cells such as neurons (see chapter 12).

BRIDGE

Diffusion is the biological version of a ball rolling down a hill—down its potential energy gradient. Active transport is the biological equivalent of pushing a ball up a hill; energy, in the form of ATP, must be expended and work is performed.

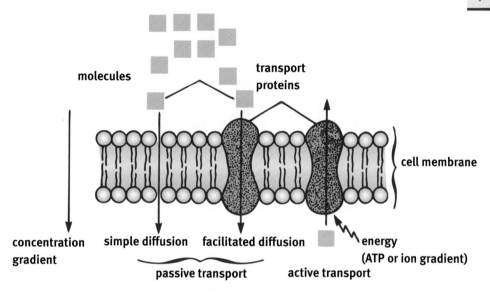

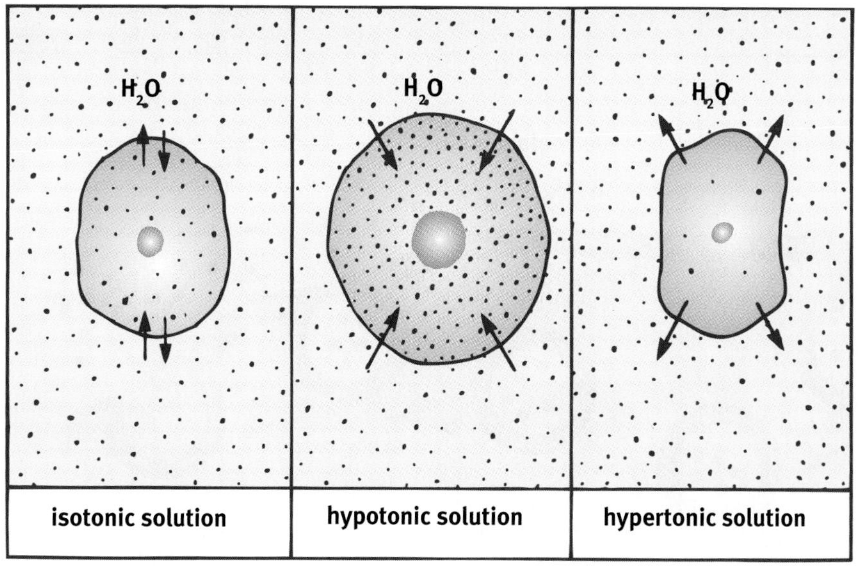

Figure 1.5. Movement Across Memberances

EXCLUSIVE

Notice how the "O" in Hyp–o–tonic looks like a swollen cell.

Figure 1.6. Osmosis

MCAT SYNOPSIS

Types of transport:

Passive diffusion
- Down gradient
- No carrier
- No energy required

Facilitated diffusion
- Down gradient
- Carrier
- No energy required

Active transport
- Against gradient
- Carrier
- Energy required

D. ENDOCYTOSIS

Endocytosis is a process in which the cell membrane invaginates, forming a vesicle that contains extracellular medium (see Figure 1.7). Pinocytosis is the ingestion of fluids or small particles, and **phagocytosis** is the engulfing of large particles. Particles may first bind to receptors on the cell membrane before being engulfed.

E. EXOCYTOSIS

In exocytosis, a vesicle within the cell fuses with the cell membrane and releases its contents to the outside. Fusion of the vesicle with the cell membrane can play an important role in cell growth and intercellular signalling (see Figure 1.7). Note that in both endocytosis and exocytosis, the material never actually crosses through the cell membrane.

Table 1.1: Movement Across the Cell Membrane

	Diffusion	Osmosis	Facilitated Transport	Active Transport
Concentration Gradient	High ⟶ Low	High ⟶ Low	High ⟶ Low	Low ⟶ High
Membrane Protein Required	No	No	Yes	Yes
Energy Required	NO—this is a PASSIVE process	NO—this is a PASSIVE process	NO—this is a PASSIVE process	YES—this is a ACTIVE process. Requires ATP
Type of Molecule/s Transported	Small nonpolar (O_2, CO_2, etc . . .)	H_2O	Large nonpolar (e.g. glucose)	Polar molecules or ions (e.g. Na^+, Cl^-, K^+, etc . . .)

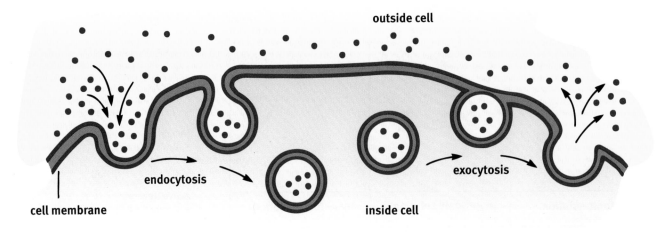

Figure 1.7. Endocytosis and Exocytosis

TISSUES

Tissues are groups of morphologically and functionally related cells. The four basic types of tissue found in the body are **epithelial, connective, nervous,** and **muscle.**

A. EPITHELIAL TISSUE

Epithelial tissue covers the surfaces of the body and lines the cavities, protecting them against injury, invasion, and desiccation. Epithelium is also involved in absorption, secretion, and sensation.

B. CONNECTIVE TISSUE

Connective tissue is involved in body support and other functions. Specialized connective tissues include bone, cartilage, tendons, ligaments, adipose tissue, and blood.

C. NERVOUS TISSUE

Nervous tissue is composed of specialized cells called neurons that are involved in the perception, processing, and storage of information concerning the internal and external environments (see chapter 12).

D. MUSCLE TISSUE

Muscle tissue has a great contractile capability and is involved in body movement. The three types of vertebrate muscle tissue are **skeletal** muscle, **cardiac** muscle, and **smooth** muscle (see chapter 6).

VIRUSES

Viruses are unique acellular structures composed of nucleic acid enclosed by a protein coat. Viruses range in size from 20–300 mm. In contrast, prokaryotes are 1–10 mm and eukaryotic cells are 10–100 mm. The nucleic acid can be either linear or circular, and has been found in four varieties: single-stranded DNA, double-stranded DNA, single-stranded RNA, and double-stranded RNA. The protein coat, or **capsid,** is composed of many protein subunits and may be enclosed by a membranous envelope.

> ### TEACHER TIP
> KEY POINT: Exo– and endocytosis allow the cell to "compartmentalize" certain functions, creating specific environments favorable to reactions such as digestion.

> ### CLINICAL CORRELATE
> Diseases caused solely by viruses include the common cold, measles, mumps, chicken pox, croup, polio, influenza, hepatitis, and AIDS. Fighting viruses with drugs is trickier than fighting bacteria because the viruses actually live inside host cells, and viruses don't have any organelles of their own. To date, the few antiviral medications that exist work by interfering with enzymatic reactions involved in viral replication. More success in combating viruses has been achieved through vaccination. Of the diseases listed above, vaccines currently exist for measles, mumps, chicken pox, polio, influenza, and hepatitis.

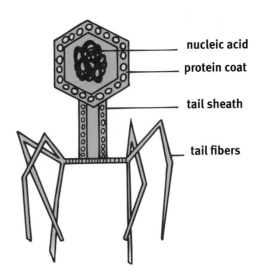

nucleic acid

protein coat

tail sheath

tail fibers

Figure 1.8. Bacteriophage

Viruses are **obligate intracellular parasites**; i.e., they can express their genes and reproduce only within a living host cell, because they lack the structures necessary for independent activity and reproduction. A virus attaches itself to a host cell and injects its nucleic acid, taking control of protein synthesis within the cell. The viral genome replicates itself many times, produces new protein coats, and assembles new **virions** that leave the host cell in search of new hosts. Viruses that exclusively infect bacteria are called **bacteriophages.** The bacteriophage injects its nucleic acid into a bacterial cell; the phage capsid does not enter the cell (see chapter 14).

PRACTICE QUESTIONS

1. A new laboratory has just finished constructing an autoradiography developing room. It wishes to test the equipment with a control experiment. If radiolabeled antibodies against estrogen receptors are added to an antibody-permeable common eukaryotic cell line, where should the fluorescence appear on autoradiography?

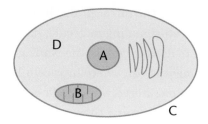

   A. A—nucleus
   B. B—mitochondrion
   C. C—cell membrane
   D. D—cytoplasm

2. A cancer researcher has developed a new radioactive antibody to identify the organizational structure of eukaryotic microtubules more precisely during the cell cycle. What other cellular structures might this antibody label?

   A. Flagella of spermatozoa
   B. Actin filaments of muscle cells
   C. Prokaryotic cilia
   D. Nuclear pores

3. A patient is brought to the ER after an occupational exposure to toxic compound X, a substance which is metabolized by the liver. A biopsy of the liver would likely show which of the following?

   A. Hypochromic rough endoplasmic reticulum
   B. Hyperplasia with nuclear irregularities
   C. Proliferation of the smooth endoplasmic reticulum
   D. Cell wall breakdown with early stages of cell death

4. The drug colchicine blocks microtubule polymerization without destruction of the tubulin monomers. Its ability to interfere with cellular motility, specifically that of pro-inflammatory immune cells, makes colchicine useful in the treatment of gout. Which of the following is a possible mechanism of action of colchicine?

   A. Stabilization of centrioles
   B. Binding the tubulin polymerization site
   C. Hydrolase activity at the tubulin polymerization site
   D. Increasing tubulin production

5. An investigator hypothesizes that a trial cancer drug interferes with protein folding after protein synthesis. In order to test its effects, a radiolabeled version of Drug A was added to a culture of cells. Of the following cellular locations, which would likely be identified upon autoradiography?

   A. Nucleus and endoplasmic reticulum
   B. Endoplasmic reticulum
   C. Cytoplasm and endoplasmic reticulum
   D. Nucleus and Golgi apparatus

6. Lactose intolerance results in diarrhea caused from an influx of lactose due to the absence of certain brush border enzymes that break down lactose. On the other hand, secretory diarrhea can be caused by pathogens (i.e., cholera), which pump chloride ions (Cl^-) into the gastrointestinal lumen. Which of the following statements is true about these processes?

   I. Lactose is osmotically active, creating a diffusion gradient into the lumen.
   II. The movement of chloride ions in secretory diarrhea creates a hypotonic lumen.
   III. Lactose can be absorbed in the absence of brush border enzymes.

   A. I
   B. I and II
   C. I and III
   D. I, II, and III

7. Antidiuretic hormone (ADH, aka vasopressin) increases the permeability of the collecting ducts of the nephron to water. Which of the following statements is correct about the ensuing process?

   A. Water channels allow water to move down its gradient and into the nephron, diluting the urine.
   B. Water channels actively pump water against its gradient out of the nephron, concentrating the urine.
   C. Water channels allow electrolytes and water to move down their gradient and out of the nephron, without changing the tonicity of the urine.
   D. Water channels allow water to move down its gradient and out of the nephron, concentrating the urine.

8. Which of the following statements about membrane carrier proteins is true?

   A. Carrier proteins transport molecules against their diffusion gradient.
   B. Small nonpolar molecules often require carrier proteins to cross the cell membrane.
   C. Carrier proteins allow large polar molecules to cross the cell membrane.
   D. Carrier protein transport is required for steroid transport into the cell.

9. Increases in the intracellular levels of cyclic-AMP, a cell-signaling molecule, have been shown to down-regulate the Na/K pump. An experiment is run where intracellular electrolytes are monitored while cyclic-AMP is depleted from cells and then replenished. Which of the following accurately depicts the levels of *intracellular* electrolytes during this experiment in response to cAMP replenishing?

   A. Increase in $[Na^+]$ and decrease in $[K^+]$
   B. Increase in $[Na^+]$ and increase in $[K^+]$
   C. Decrease in $[Na^+]$ and decrease in $[K^+]$
   D. Decrease in $[Na^+]$ and increase in $[K^+]$

10. An antiport is a type of membrane protein that is involved in *secondary active transport*, where the movement of one molecule *against* its diffusion gradient is coupled to the movement of another molecule *down* its diffusion gradient.

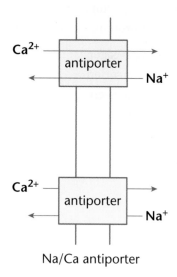

Na/Ca antiporter

Given the information provided, which of the following statements is true?

A. Secondary active transport differs from active transport in that it requires ATP.
B. In the Na/Ca^{2+} antiporter, calcium moves from an area of low concentration to high concentration, and sodium moves from an area of low concentration to high concentration.
C. The Na/K pump is an antiporter.
D. Antiporters take advantage of the diffusion gradient of one molecule in order to transport another molecule.

11. Scientists discover a new disease that causes a defect in all connective tissues. Which of the following would likely be unaffected by this disease?

A. Tendons
B. Epidermis
C. Bone
D. Blood

12. Lysozyme is a free enzyme found in solution and secretions such as teardrops and mucus. It is also believed to be present in storage vesicles within immune cells. Which of the following is a probable mechanism explaining the presence of lysozyme in both secretions and immune cells?

A. Lysozyme is manufactured in immune cells and then released into body fluids via exocytosis.
B. Lysozyme is manufactured in the extracellular space and is engulfed by immune cells via phagocytosis.
C. Lysozyme is manufactured in immune cells and then released into body fluids via endocytosis.
D. Lysozyme is manufactured in all cells and is permanently sequestered in storage vesicles.

13. ATP-binding cassette (ABC) transporters are a large family of transmembrane proteins that transport a wide variety of products across the cell membrane. They have been shown to play an important role in some forms of drug resistance, where they transport large drug molecules against their diffusion gradient out of tumor cells. Which of the following likely describes the type of movement facilitated by ABC transporters?

A. Simple diffusion
B. Facilitated diffusion
C. Exocytosis
D. Active transport

14. With the discovery of deep sea hydrothermal vents in the 20th century, hundreds of new species were cataloged. If a team of scientists wanted to quickly identify a unicellular organism from a hydrothermal vent as either a prokaryote or eukaryote, what characteristics would be important to look for via light microscopy?

  I. Cell wall
 II. Nucleus
III. Ribosomal subunit sizes

A. I
B. I and II
C. II and III
D. I, II and III

15. In the search for a vaccine against the human immunodeficiency virus (HIV), researchers were faced with a major problem: Certain HIV envelope proteins that are heavily glycosylated interfere with their detection by the immune system. The organelle within the host cell that is primarily responsible for glycosylation of proteins is also responsible for

A. storage of glycogen.
B. aerobic respiration.
C. production of secretory vesicles.
D. protein synthesis.

CHAPTER 2

ENZYMES

Enzymes are protein catalysts that accelerate reactions, such as those in metabolic pathways, by reducing the initial energy (**activation energy**) necessary for them to proceed. The enzyme does not change the equilibrium point of a reaction; it changes only the rate at which it is attained. During the course of reactions, the enzymes themselves are neither consumed nor changed. Most enzyme reactions are reversible; the product synthesized by an enzyme can also be decomposed by the same enzyme. Figure 2.1 compares an uncatalyzed reaction with an enzymatically catalyzed reaction. The activation energy of the catalyzed reaction is lower, yet the overall **change in free energy** (ΔG) of the two reactions remains the same.

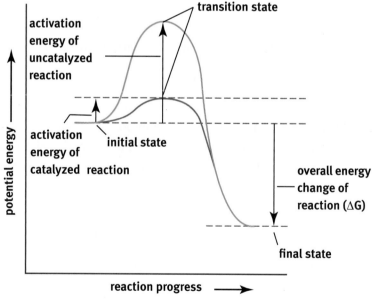

Figure 2.1. Reaction Coordinate

TEACHER TIP

Enzymes very often break down or create molecules (H_2O_2, OCl^-) that would be very damaging to the cell if they were released into the cytoplasm. Recall from the last chapter how cells deal with these reactive species, which are necessary for certain reactions.

ENZYME SPECIFICITY

Enzymes are very selective; they may catalyze only one reaction or one specific class of closely related reactions. Urease, for example, selectively catalyzes the breakdown of urea. (Note that the suffix *ase* generally denotes an enzyme.) Chymotrypsin, on the other hand, selectively catalyzes the hydrolysis of specific types of peptide bonds, enabling it to catalyze the hydrolysis of more than one type of peptide (see chapter 7).

The molecule upon which an enzyme acts is called the **substrate.** There is an area on each enzyme to which the substrate bonds to form an **enzyme-substrate complex.** This area, the **active site,** has a three-dimensional shape into which the substrate fits and is held at a particular orientation. There are two models describing the formation of an enzyme-substrate complex: the **lock and key theory** and the **induced fit hypothesis.**

A. THE LOCK AND KEY THEORY

This theory holds that the spatial structure of an enzyme's active site (lock) is exactly complementary to the spatial structure of its substrate (key). Their 3-D configurations are such that the active site and the substrate fit together, forming an enzyme-substrate complex.

B. THE INDUCED FIT HYPOTHESIS

The induced fit hypothesis describes the active site of an enzyme as having some flexibility of shape. When the appropriate substrate comes in contact with the active site, the conformation of the active site changes such that it surrounds the substrate, creating a close fit (see Figure 2.2). A substrate of the wrong shape will not induce a conformational change in the enzyme's active site, thereby preventing the formation of an enzyme-substrate complex.

Studies suggest that the induced fit hypothesis is more plausible than the lock and key theory, and induced fit is currently more widely accepted.

Table 2.1. Activation Energy

1. LOWER the ACTIVATION ENERGY
2. INCREASE the RATE OF THE REACTION
3. DO NOT alter the equilibrium constant
4. ARE NOT CHANGED OR CONSUMED in the reaction (This means that they will appear in both the reactants and products.)
5. Enzymes are pH and temperature sensitive, with optimal activity at specific pH ranges and temperatures
6. DO NOT affect the overall ΔG of the reaction
7. Are SPECIFIC for a particular REACTION or CLASS of REACTIONS

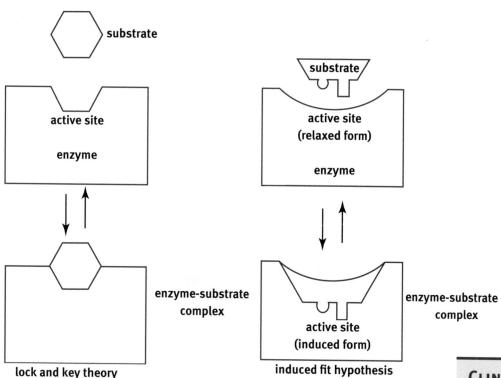

Figure 2.2. Models for Enzyme-Substrate Interactions

COFACTORS

Many enzymes require the incorporation of a nonprotein molecule to become catalytically active. These molecules, called **cofactors,** can aid in binding the substrate to the enzyme or in stabilizing the enzyme in an active conformation. An enzyme devoid of its necessary cofactor is called

CLINICAL CORRELATE

Deficiencies in vitamin cofactors can result in devastating disease. Thiamin is an important cofactor for several enzymes involved in cellular metabolism and nerve conduction. Thiamin deficiency, often seen in alcoholics, results in a disease known as Wernicke-Korsokoff syndrome. In this disorder, patients suffer from a variety of neurological deficits, including delirium, balance problems, and in severe cases, the inability to form new memories.

an **apoenzyme** and is catalytically inactive, while an enzyme containing its cofactor is called a **holoenzyme.** Cofactors can be bound to their enzymes by weak noncovalent interactions or by strong covalent bonds. Tightly bound cofactors are called **prosthetic groups.**

Two important types of cofactors are metal cations (e.g., Zn^{2+}, Fe^{2+}) and small organic groups (e.g., biotin). These latter organic cofactors are called **coenzymes.** Most coenzymes cannot be synthesized by the body and are obtained from the diet as vitamin derivatives. Lack of a particular vitamin can impair the action of its corresponding enzyme and lead to disease.

TEACHER TIP

Vitamins come in 2 major classes: fat and water soluble. This is important to consider in digestive diseases, where different parts of the GI tract may be affected by different disease processes. Loss of parts of the GI tract may cause various vitamin deficiencies.

ENZYME KINETICS

The rate of an enzyme-catalyzed reaction is related to a number of factors, including the concentrations of both the enzyme and the substrate, and environmental variables such as temperature and pH.

A. EFFECTS OF CONCENTRATION

The concentrations of substrate [S] and enzyme [E] during the course of a reaction greatly affect the reaction rate. When the concentration of the substrate is low compared to that of the enzyme, many of the active sites are unoccupied and the reaction rate is low. Initial increases in the substrate concentration (at constant enzyme concentration) lead to proportional increases in the rate of the reaction because unoccupied active sites on the enzyme readily bind to the additional substrate. However, once most of the active sites are occupied, the reaction rate levels off, regardless of further increases in substrate concentration. At high concentrations of substrate, the reaction rate approaches its **maximal velocity, V_{max}.** At this point, increases in substrate concentration will no longer increase reaction rate (see Figure 2.3.)

According to the Michaelis-Menten model proposed in 1913, an enzyme-substrate complex, ES, is formed at rate k_1 from enzyme E and substrate S. The ES complex can either dissociate into E and S at rate k_2, or form product P at rate k_3. The relationship between the three rates is defined by the **Michaelis constant, K_m,** as $\dfrac{(k_2 + k_3)}{k_1}$, or the ratio of the breakdown of the ES complex to its formation.

TEACHER TIP

MM kinetics may not be your favorite topic to learn but *know these kinetics thoroughly*. They are one of the most commonly appearing MCAT topics.

$$E + S \underset{k_2}{\overset{k_1}{\rightleftharpoons}} ES_{\frac{1}{2}} \overset{k_3}{\longrightarrow} E + P$$

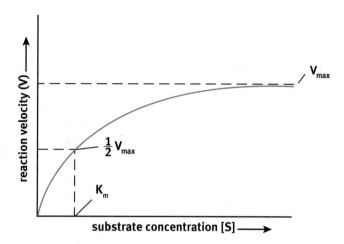

Figure 2.3. Michaelis-Menten Model

When the reaction rate is equal to ½ V_{max}, K_m = [S] and can be understood as the point at which half of the enzyme's active sites are filled (see Figure 2.3). When [S] is less than K_m, changes in substrate concentration greatly affect the reaction rate. In contrast, at high concentrations of substrate, [S] is larger than K_m, and V approaches V_{max}.

B. EFFECTS OF TEMPERATURE

Rates of enzyme-catalyzed reactions tend to double for every 10°C increase in temperature until their optimal temperature is reached. For most enzymes operating in the human body, the optimal temperature is 37°C. At higher temperatures, enzymes become denatured: their 3-D structure is destroyed and the enzyme becomes nonfunctional. Enzymes that are partially denatured can sometimes regain their activity upon being cooled (see Figure 2.4).

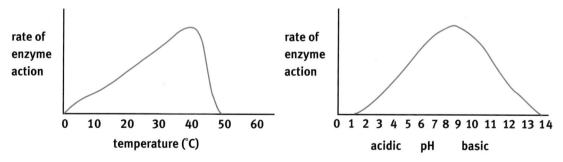

Figure 2.4. Effects of Temperature and pH on Enzyme Activity

C. EFFECTS OF pH

For each enzyme there is also an optimal pH above and below which enzymatic activity declines. Maximal activity of many human enzymes occurs around pH 7.4 (7.35–7.45), which is the pH of most body fluids and tissues. Plueral fluid is an exception and has a standard pH closer to 7.6. The other exceptions include pepsin, which works best in the highly acidic conditions of the stomach (pH = 2), and pancreatic enzymes, which work optimally in the alkaline conditions of the small intestine (pH = 8.5).

REGULATION OF ENZYMATIC ACTIVITY

The regulation of enzymatic activity is accomplished in a number of ways, most notably through allosteric effects and inhibitory interactions.

A. ALLOSTERIC EFFECTS

An **allosteric enzyme** has at least one active or catalytic site and at least one separate regulatory site. Often, these enzymes possess a quarternary structure. An allosteric enzyme oscillates between two configurations—an active state capable of catalyzing a reaction, and an inactive state that cannot. An interaction between an allosteric enzyme and a **regulator** (a molecule other than the substrate that binds to the enzyme) can stabilize either configuration, depending on the type of regulator involved. There are two types of regulators—**allosteric inhibitors** and **allosteric activators.** An inhibitor prevents an enzyme from binding to its substrate by stabilizing the inactive conformation, whereas an activator stabilizes the active configuration, promoting the formation of enzyme-substrate complexes.

Another allosteric effect involves increased affinity of an enzyme for its substrate. Sometimes the binding of a regulator at the allosteric site, or the binding of substrate at one of the enzyme's active sites, may stimulate the other active sites on the enzyme to bind more efficiently by increasing their affinity for the substrate. This type of cooperation is not unique to allosteric enzymes. Hemoglobin is composed of four subunits, each with its own oxygen-binding site; the binding of oxygen at one subunit increases the affinity for oxygen at the remaining three active sites (see chapter 9).

B. INHIBITION

An enzyme's activity may be regulated by one of the products of the reactions it catalyzes, or by a substance that binds to the enzyme and inhibits it from binding substrate. These interferences with enzymatic activity

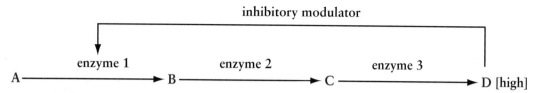

Figure 2.5. Negative Feedback

can be categorized as **feedback inhibition, competitive inhibition,** and **noncompetitive inhibition.**

1. Feedback Inhibition

Many biological reactions are regulated by feedback inhibition mechanisms, in which the end product of a sequence of enzymatic reactions becomes an allosteric modulator (in this case, an inhibitor) of one of the preceding enzymes in the sequence. In the reaction sequence shown, (Figure 2.5), product D is an inhibitory modulator for enzyme 1. Thus, when the concentration of D reaches some critical level, virtually all enzyme 1 molecules are inhibited and production of B (and thus of C and D) is halted. The process is sometimes reversible and can be instantaneous; as D levels decrease, enzyme 1 inhibition decreases, and A is again converted to B. This feedback process allows organisms to avoid overproduction of metabolites. (For an additional discussion of feedback inhibition see chapter 11.)

> **TEACHER TIP**
>
> This process is widely used in all biological organisms. Its opposite (feed-forward activation) is rarely used, though we will see a special example with estrogen and the menstrual cycle when we study reproduction.

2. Competitive Inhibitors

Competitive inhibitors compete with the substrate directly by binding to the active site of the enzyme. The active site of an enzyme is specific for a particular substrate or class of substrates. However, it is possible for molecules that are structurally similar to the substrate to bind to the active site of the enzyme. If this similar molecule is present in a concentration comparable to the concentration of the substrate, it will compete with the substrate for bonding sites on the enzyme and it will interfere with enzyme activity. This is known as competitive inhibition because the enzyme is inhibited by the inactive substrate, or competitor, so called because it *competes* with the substrate for the active site. Competitive inhibition is reversible with increased concentrations of substrate.

> **TEACHER TIP**
>
> Inhibition is commonly tested in an experimental passage. If you add more substrate and inhibition decreases (i.e., enzymatic activity goes back up), you know you are dealing with competitive inhibition. If inhibition remains the same (i.e., no change in enzymatic activity), you're dealing with noncompetitive inhibition.

3. Noncompetitive Inhibitors

A noncompetitive inhibitor is a substance that forms strong covalent bonds with an enzyme and consequently may not be displaced by the addition of excess substrate. Therefore, noncompetitive inhibition is irreversible. A noncompetitive inhibitor may be bonded at, near, or remote from the active site. This is an example of allosteric inhibition. Noncompetitive inhibition can be overcome by increasing the concentration of the enzyme.

INACTIVE ENZYMES

A **zymogen** is an enzyme that is secreted in an inactive form. The zymogen is cleaved under certain physiological conditions to the active form of the enzyme. Important examples of zymogens include pepsinogen, trypsinogen, and chymotrypsinogen, which are cleaved in the digestive tract to yield the active enzymes pepsin, trypsin, and chymotrypsin, respectively (see chapter 7).

PRACTICE QUESTIONS

1. Which of the following best represents the amount of energy conserved through using an enzyme for the reaction depicted in the following graph?

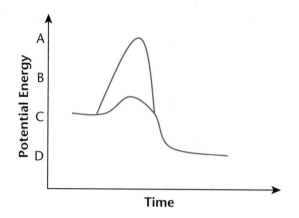

A. A – B

B. A + B

C. B – C

D. B + D

2. In the equation below, substrate C is an allosteric inhibitor to enzyme 1. Which of the following is another mechanism caused by substrate C?

A ⟶ enzyme 1 ⟶ B ⟶ enzyme 2 ⟶ C

A. Competitive inhibition

B. Irreversible inhibition

C. Feedback enhancement

D. Negative feedback

3. Which of the following would initiate a competitive inhibition of the production of substrate C in the metabolic pathway shown below?

A ⟶ enzyme 1 ⟶ B ⟶ enzyme 2 ⟶ C
⟶ enzyme 3 ⟶ D

A. Allosteric inhibition of enzyme 1

B. Allosteric inhibition of enzyme 3

C. Substrate D fits into the active site of enzyme 3

D. Substrate D fits into the active site of enzyme 1

4. When lactase hydrolyzes milk sugars, which of the following occurs?

A. Lactase retains its structure after the reaction.

B. Lactose retains its structure after the reaction.

C. Lactase increases the activation energy of the reaction.

D. Lactose decreases the activation energy of the reaction.

5. In a chemical reaction that they mediate, what are enzymes' function?

A. Change the potential energy level of the reaction

B. Change the potential energy levels of the products

C. Change the activation energy of the reaction

D. Change the enzyme energy levels of the reaction

6. Bonding between atoms within an enzyme such as trypsin is best described as

A. peptide.

B. saccharide.

C. ionic.

D. Van der Waals.

7. Which organelle is likely to contain extra protection, such as a double membrane?

A. Golgi body

B. Endoplasmic reticulum

C. Lysosome

D. Ribosome

8. Lipase does all of the following EXCEPT

A. break down lipids.

B. speed up the rate of fatty acid production.

C. slow down the rate of glycerol production.

D. increase its rate of activity with higher lipid concentrations.

9. In the graph below, which of the following best describes the chemical activity depicted by region "X" ?

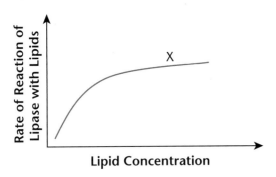

A. Active sites on lipase enzymes are all occupied by lipids.

B. Lipase concentration decreases with the rate of the reaction.

C. Lipid concentration increases with the rate of the reaction.

D. Active sites on lipid molecules are all occupied by lipase.

10. Which of the following is true of the amino acids of an active site found in a hemoglobin molecule?

A. They are all found on the primary protein chains.

B. They are all found on the secondary protein chains.

C. They are found on different tertiary chains.

D. They are found within the carboxylic acid groups on the chains.

11. In any enzyme-mediated chemical reaction, which of the following applies?

A. It is always endergonic.

B. It is always exergonic.

C. The overall energy change of the reaction is the same as the uncatalyzed version.

D. The overall energy change of the reaction is never the same as the uncatalyzed version.

12. An allosteric interaction with enzyme "X" will always

A. inhibit the activity of enzyme "X."

B. enhance the activity of enzyme "X."

C. block the substrate from the active site.

D. change the shape of enzyme "X."

CHAPTER 3

CELLULAR METABOLISM

Cellular metabolism is the sum total of all chemical reactions that take place in a cell. These reactions can be generally categorized as either **anabolic** or **catabolic.** Anabolic processes are energy-requiring, involving the biosynthesis of complex organic compounds from simpler molecules. Catabolic processes release energy as they break down complex organic compounds into smaller molecules. The metabolic reactions of cells are coupled so that energy released from catabolic reactions can be harnessed to fuel anabolic reactions.

TRANSFER OF ENERGY

A. THE FLOW OF ENERGY

The ultimate energy source for living organisms is the sun. **Autotrophic** organisms, such as green plants, convert sunlight into **bond energy** stored in the bonds of organic compounds (chiefly glucose) in the anabolic process of **photosynthesis.** Autotrophs do not need an exogenous supply of organic compounds. **Heterotrophic** organisms obtain their energy catabolically, via the breakdown of organic nutrients that must be ingested. Figure 3.1 is an energy flow diagram for biological systems; note that some energy is dissipated as heat at every stage.

> **TEACHER TIP**
>
> Link to Physics: Remember that no machine—even a biological one—is perfectly efficient. Primarily, this energy will be lost in the form of heat.

Glucose plays an essential role in the energetics of cell metabolism. The production of glucose ($C_6H_{12}O_6$) by autotrophs involves the breaking of C–O and O–H bonds in CO_2 and H_2O, and the forming of C–H, C–O, C–C, and O–H bonds in glucose. The net reaction of photosynthesis:

$$6CO_2 + 6H_2O + \text{Energy} \longrightarrow \underset{\text{glucose}}{C_6H_{12}O_6} + 6O_2$$

Heterotrophic organisms metabolize glucose and other organic molecules to release the stored bond energies. The net reaction of glucose catabolism, which is essentially the reversal of photosynthesis, is:

$$\underset{\text{glucose}}{C_6H_{12}O_6} + 6O_2 \longrightarrow 6CO_2 + 6H_2O + \text{Energy}$$

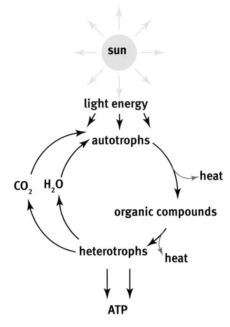

Figure 3.1. Energy Flow in Biological Systems

B. ENERGY CARRIERS

During metabolism, the cell uses various molecular carriers, such as **ATP** and the coenzymes **NAD⁺, NADP⁺,** and **FAD,** to shuttle energy between reactions.

1. ATP

ATP, or **adenosine triphosphate,** is the cell's main energy currency. Through its formation and degradation, cells have a quick way of releasing and storing energy. ATP is synthesized during glucose catabolism. ATP is composed of the nitrogenous base adenine, the sugar ribose, and three weakly linked phosphate groups. The energy of ATP is stored in the covalent bonds attaching these phosphate groups, often referred to as high-energy bonds.

Hydrolysis of ATP to **ADP (adenosine diphosphate)** and **P_i (inorganic phosphate)** releases stored bond energy that the cell can use

TEACHER TIP

Why are these bonds high energy? Because the large number of negative charges in close proximity requires a good deal of energy to keep coupled.

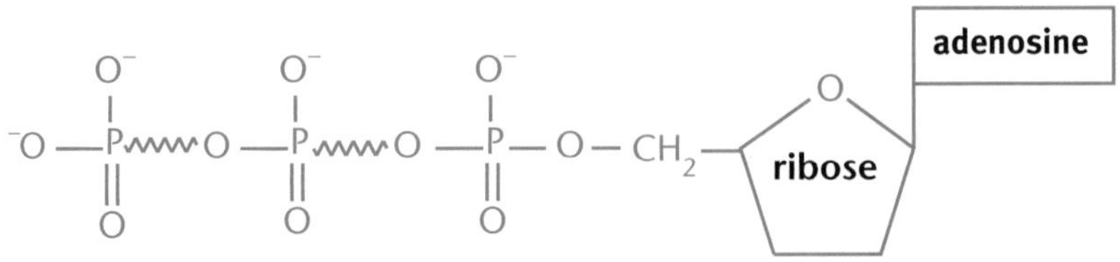

Figure 3.2. ATP

in metabolic processes. Approximately 7 kcal of energy are released per mole of ATP. This provides energy for **endergonic** (endothermic) reactions such as muscle contraction, motility, and the active transport of substances across plasma membranes. ATP may also be hydrolyzed into **AMP (adenosine monophosphate)** and **PP$_i$ (pyrophosphate)**:

$$\text{ATP} \longrightarrow \text{ADP} + \text{P}_i + 7 \text{ kcal/mole}$$

$$\text{ATP} \longrightarrow \text{AMP} + \text{PP}_i + 7 \text{ kcal/mole}$$

Alternatively, ADP and P$_i$ combine to form ATP; in this way the cell regenerates its ATP supply. This process requires energy (supplied by the degradation of glucose):

$$\text{ADP} + \text{P}_i + 7 \text{ kcal/mole} \longrightarrow \text{ATP}$$

2. NAD$^+$, NADP$^+$, and FAD

A second mechanism by which the cell stores chemical energy is in the form of **high potential electrons.** Electrons are transferred as **hydride ions (H:$^-$)** or as pairs of hydrogen atoms. During glucose oxidation, hydrogen atoms are removed. Most of these are accepted by the carrier coenzymes **NAD$^+$ (nicotinamide adenine dinucleotide), FAD (flavin adenine dinucleotide),** and **NADP$^+$ (nicotinamide adenine dinucleotide phosphate).** These molecules transport the high-energy electrons of the hydrogen atoms to a series of carrier molecules on the inner mitochondrical membrane that are collectively known as the **electron transport chain.**

Oxidation refers to the loss of an electron. NAD$^+$, NADP$^+$, and FAD are referred to as oxidizing agents because they cause other molecules to lose electrons and undergo oxidation. In the process, they themselves undergo **reduction**; that is, they gain electrons. For example, when NAD$^+$ accepts electrons in the form of a hydride ion it is reduced to **NADH,** while the donating molecule is oxidized. Likewise, when FAD accepts electrons in the form of hydrogen atoms, it is reduced to **FADH$_2$.** In their reduced forms, NADH, NADPH, and FADH$_2$ all behave as reducing agents. NADH transfers its electrons to another electron acceptor (e.g., the first carrier of the electron transport chain), thereby reducing it, and in the process NADH is oxidized back to NAD$^+$. NADPH is found in plant, not animal, cells. Thus, these coenzymes temporarily store and release energy in the form of electrons through their successive oxidations and reductions.

MCAT SYNOPSIS

In general, NAD$^+$, NADP$^+$, and FAD are all *reduced* during catabolic processes; their reduced forms (NADH, NADPH, and FADH$_2$) are *oxidized* during anabolic processes

TEACHER TIP

Link to Gen. Chem.: Hydride ions are one of the strongest reducing agents that you'll see on the exam. Remember lithium aluminum hydride and sodium borohydride.

MCAT SYNOPSIS

Animal cells store energy in high potential electrons in NADH and FADH$_2$.

TEACHER TIP

These redox reactions do not themselves produce usable energy. Rather they create high energy elections that can then be passed to a final acceptor (oxygen). That, in turn, is coupled to ATP generation.

oxidized form   reduced form

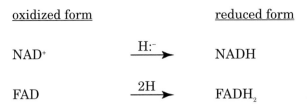

Figure 3.3. Reduction of NAD$^+$ and FAD

GLUCOSE CATABOLISM

The degradative oxidation of glucose occurs in two stages, **glycolysis** and **cellular respiration.**

A. GLYCOLYSIS

The first stage of glucose catabolism is glycolysis. Glycolysis is a series of reactions that lead to the oxidative breakdown of glucose into two molecules of **pyruvate** (the ionized form of pyruvic acid), the production of ATP, and the reduction of NAD$^+$ into NADH. All of these reactions occur in the cytoplasm and are mediated by specific enzymes. The glycolytic pathway is outlined below in Figure 3.4.

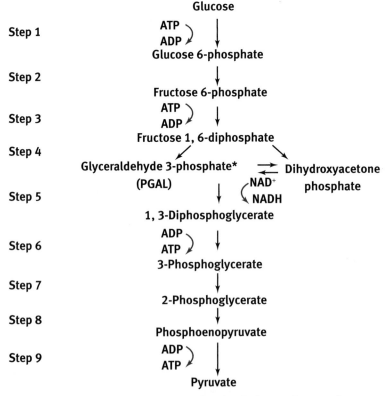

*NOTE: Steps 5–9 occur twice per molecule of glucose (see text).

Figure 3.4. Glycolysis

TEST TIP

You do *not* need to memorize the individual reactions of glycolysis for the MCAT. You will need to memorize them in medical school.

TEACHER TIP

You *do* need to know the net input and output of these reactions. Also, know that this reaction is ANAEROBIC. It can occur in the absence of oxygen.

---

1. Glycolytic Pathway

Note that at step 4, fructose 1, 6-diphosphate is split into 2 three-carbon molecules: **dihydroxyacetone phosphate** and **glyceraldehyde 3-phosphate (PGAL).** Dihydroxyacetone phosphate is isomerized into PGAL so that it can be used in subsequent reactions. Thus, 2 molecules of PGAL are formed per molecule of glucose, and all of the subsequent steps occur twice for each glucose molecule.

From 1 molecule of glucose (a six-carbon molecule), 2 molecules of pyruvate (a three-carbon molecule) are obtained. During this sequence of reactions, 2 ATP are used (in steps 1 and 3) and 4 ATP are generated (two in step 6, and two in step 9). Thus, there is a net production of 2 ATP per glucose molecule. This type of phosphorylation is called **substrate level phosphorylation,** because ATP synthesis is directly coupled with the degradation of glucose without the participation of an intermediate molecule such as NAD^+. One NADH is produced per PGAL, for a total of 2 NADH per glucose.

> **TEACHER TIP**
>
> Know these numbers; they are commonly tested.

The net reaction for glycolysis is:

$$\text{Glucose} + 2\text{ADP} + 2\text{P}_i + 2\text{NAD}^+ \longrightarrow$$
$$2\text{Pyruvate} + 2\text{ATP} + 2\text{NADH} + 2\text{H}^+ + 2\text{H}_2\text{O}$$

This series of reactions occurs in both prokaryotic and eukaryotic cells. However, at this stage, much of the initial energy stored in the glucose molecule has not been released and is still present in the chemical bonds of pyruvate. Depending on the capabilities of the organism, pyruvate degradation can proceed in one of two directions. Under **anaerobic** conditions (in the absence of oxygen), pyruvate is reduced during the process of fermentation. Under **aerobic** conditions (in the presence of oxygen), pyruvate is further oxidized during cell respiration in the mitochondria.

> **TEACHER TIP**
>
> Know the difference between *total* and *net output.* Glycolysis results in an output of 4 ATP but the net output is 2 ATP, as 2 ATP are required to drive the process.

B. CELLULAR RESPIRATION—ANAEROBIC

Cellular respiration can be described as aerobic or anaerobic.

2. Fermentation

NAD^+ must be regenerated for glycolysis to continue in the absence of O_2. This is accomplished by reducing pyruvate into **ethanol** or **lactic acid.** Fermentation refers to all of the reactions involved in this process—glycolysis and the additional steps leading to the formation of ethanol or lactic acid. Fermentation produces only 2 ATP per glucose molecule.

> **BRIDGE**
>
> The conversion of acetaldehyde to ethanol is a typical reduction reaction of an aldehyde to an alcohol.

a. Alcohol fermentation

Alcohol fermentation commonly occurs only in yeast and some bacteria. The pyruvate produced in glycolysis is decarboxylated to become acetaldehyde, which is then reduced by the NADH generated in step 5 of glycolysis to yield ethanol.

In this way, NAD^+ is regenerated and glycolysis can continue.

$$\text{Pyruvate (3C)} \xrightarrow{\quad CO_2 \quad} \text{Acetaldehyde (2C)} \xrightarrow[\quad NADH + H^+ \quad\to\quad NAD^+ \quad]{} \text{Ethanol (2C)}$$

TEACHER TIP

This regeneration of usable intermediates from lactic acid once oxygen has been restored is known as the Cori cycle and it occurs in the liver.

b. Lactic acid fermentation

Lactic acid fermentation occurs in certain fungi and bacteria and in human muscle cells during strenuous activity. When the oxygen supply to muscle cells lags behind the rate of glucose catabolism, the pyruvate generated is reduced to lactic acid. As in alcohol fermentation, the NAD^+ used in step 5 of glycolysis is regenerated when pyruvate is reduced. In humans, lactic acid may accumulate in the muscles during exercise, causing a decrease in blood pH that leads to muscle fatigue. Once the oxygen supply has been replenished, the lactic acid is oxidized back to pyruvate and enters cellular respiration. The amount of oxygen needed for this conversion is known as **oxygen debt.**

$$\text{Pyruvate (3C)} \xrightarrow[\quad NADH + H^+ \quad\to\quad NAD^+ \quad]{} \text{Lactic acid (3C)}$$

C. CELLULAR RESPIRATION—ANAEROBIC

Cellular respiration is the most efficient catabolic pathway used by organisms to harvest the energy stored in glucose. Whereas glycolysis yields only 2 ATP per molecule of glucose, cellular respiration can yield 36–38 ATP. Cellular respiration is an aerobic process; oxygen acts as the final acceptor of electrons that are passed from carrier to carrier during the final stage of glucose oxidation. The metabolic reactions of cell respiration occur in the eukaryotic mitochondrion and are catalyzed by reaction-specific enzymes. Cellular respiration can be divided into three stages: **pyruvate decarboxylation,** the **citric acid cycle,** and the **electron transport chain.**

TEACHER TIP

KEY POINT: Remember that glucose has six carbons. None of these are lost during glycolysis. All are passed though to pyruvate decarboxylation and the TCA cycle where they are lost in the form of CO_2.

1. Pyruvate Decarboxylation

The pyruvate formed during glycolysis is transported from the cytoplasm into the mitochondrial matrix where it is decarboxylated; i.e., it loses a CO_2, and the acetyl group that remains is transferred to **coenzyme A** to form **acetyl CoA.** In the process, NAD⁺ is reduced to NADH.

$$\text{Pyruvate (3 C)} + \text{Coenzyme A} \xrightarrow{\quad NAD^+ \quad NADH + H^+ \quad} \text{Acetyl CoA (2C)}$$

2. Citric Acid Cycle

The citric acid cycle is also known as the **Krebs cycle** or the **tricarboxylic acid cycle (TCA cycle).** The cycle begins when the two-carbon acetyl group from acetyl CoA combines with **oxaloacetate,** a four-carbon molecule, to form the six-carbon **citrate.** Through a complicated series of reactions, 2 CO_2 are released, and oxaloacetate is regenerated for use in another turn of the cycle (Figure 3.5).

For each turn of the citric acid cycle 1 ATP is produced by substrate level phosphorylation via a GTP intermediate. In addition, electrons

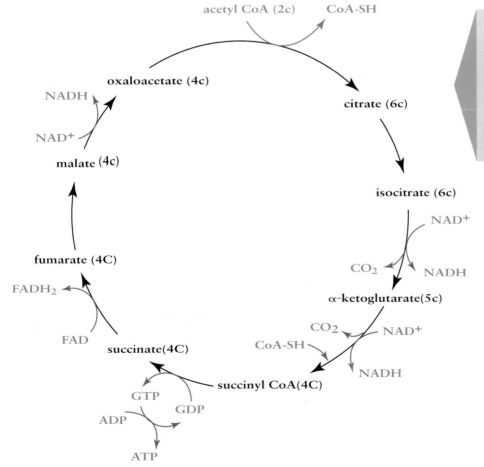

TEACHER TIP

You do *not* need to know the eight intermediates of the TCA cycle. You should know that the major purpose of this cycle is to generate high-energy intermediates that can be used to make ATP. Note that some ATP is generated from GTP directly. This is known as substrate level phosphorylation.

Figure 3.5. Citric Acid Cycle

are transferred to NAD^+ and FAD, generating NADH and $FADH_2$, respectively. These coenzymes then transport the electrons to the electron transport chain, where more ATP is produced via **oxidative phosphorylation.** Studying the cycle, we can do some bookkeeping; keep in mind that for each molecule of glucose, 2 pyruvates are decarboxylated and channeled into the citric acid cycle.

$$2 \times 3 \text{ NADH} \longrightarrow 6 \text{ NADH}$$
$$2 \times 1 \text{ FADH}_2 \longrightarrow 2 \text{ FADH}_2$$
$$2 \times 1 \text{ GTP (ATP)} \longrightarrow 2 \text{ ATP}$$

The net reaction of the citric acid cycle per glucose molecule is:

$$2\text{Acetyl CoA} + 6\text{NAD}^+ + 2\text{FAD} + 2\text{ATP} + 2\text{P}_i + 4\text{H}_2\text{O} \longrightarrow$$
$$4\text{CO}_2 + 6\text{NADH} + 2\text{FADH}_2 + 2\text{ATP} + 4\text{H}^+ + 2\text{CoA}$$

3. Electron Transport Chain

a. Electron transfer

The electron transport chain **(ETC)** is a complex carrier mechanism located on the inside of the inner mitochondrial membrane. During oxidative phosphorylation, ATP is produced when high energy potential electrons are transferred from NADH and $FADH_2$ to oxygen by a series of carrier molecules located in the inner mitochondrial membrane. As the electrons are transferred from carrier to carrier, free energy is released, which is then used to form ATP. Most of the molecules of the ETC are **cytochromes,** electron carriers that resemble hemoglobin in the structure of their active site. The functional unit contains a central iron atom, which is capable of undergoing a reversible redox reaction; that is, it can be alternatively reduced and oxidized.

FMN (flavin mononucleotide) is the first molecule of the ETC. It is reduced when it accepts electrons from NADH, thereby oxidizing NADH to NAD^+. Sequential redox reactions continue to occur as the electrons are transferred from one carrier to the next; each carrier is reduced as it accepts an electron and is then oxidized when it passes it on to the next carrier.

The last carrier of the ETC, **cytochrome a_3,** passes its electron to the final electron acceptor, O_2. In addition to the electrons, O_2 picks up a pair of hydrogen ions from the surrounding medium, forming water.

$$2\text{H}^+ + 2\text{e}^- + \frac{1}{2}\text{O}_2 \longrightarrow \text{H}_2\text{O}$$

MCAT SYNOPSIS

Energy checkpoint:

2ATP	(from glycolysis)
2NADH	(from glycolysis)
2NADH	(from decarboxylation of pyruvate)
6NADH	(TCA cycle)
2FADH$_2$	(TCA cycle)
2ATP	(TCA cycle)

TEACHER TIP

KEY POINT: Oxygen is the final electron acceptor in the ETC and the result is the formation of a water molecule.

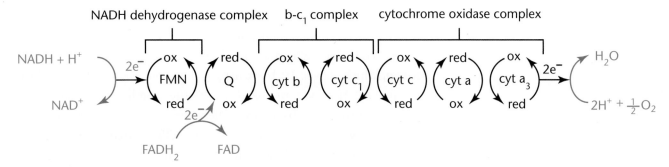

Figure 3.6. Electron Transport Chain

Without oxygen, the ETC becomes backlogged with electrons. As a result, NAD^+ cannot be regenerated and glycolysis cannot continue unless lactic acid fermentation occurs. Likewise, ATP synthesis comes to a halt if respiratory poisons such as **cyanide** or **dinitrophenol** enter the cell. Cyanide blocks the transfer of electrons from cytochrome a_3 to O_2. Dinitrophenol uncouples the electron transport chain from the proton gradient established across the inner mitochondrial membrane.

b. ATP generation and the proton pump

The electron carriers are categorized into three large protein complexes: **NADH dehydrogenase,** the **b-c_1 complex,** and **cytochrome oxidase.** There are energy losses as the electrons are transferred from one complex to the next; this energy is then used to synthesize 1 ATP per complex. Thus, an electron passing through the entire ETC supplies enough energy to generate 3 ATP. NADH delivers its electrons to NADH dehydrogenase complex, so that for each NADH, 3 ATP are produced. However, $FADH_2$ bypasses the NADH dehydrogenase complex and delivers its electrons directly to **carrier Q (ubiquinone),** which lies between the NADH dehydrogenase and b-c_1 complexes. Therefore, for each $FADH_2$, there are only two energy drops, and only 2 ATP are produced.

The operating mechanism in this type of ATP production involves coupling the oxidation of NADH to the phosphorylation of ADP. The coupling agent for these two processes is a **proton gradient** across the inner mitochondrial membrane, maintained by the ETC. As NADH passes its electrons to the ETC, free hydrogen ions (H^+) are released and accumulate in the mitochondrial matrix. The ETC pumps these ions out of the matrix, across the inner mitochondrial membrane, and into the intermembrane space at each of the three protein complexes. The continuous translocation of H⁺ creates a positively charged acidic environment in the intermembrane space. This electrochemical gradient generates a **proton-motive force,** which drives H⁺ back across the inner membrane and into the matrix. However, to pass through the membrane (which is impermeable to ions), the H⁺ must flow through specialized channels provided by enzyme complexes called **ATP synthetases.** As the H⁺ pass through the ATP synthetases, enough energy is released to allow for the phosphorylation of ADP to ATP. The coupling of the oxidation of NADH with the phosphorylation of ADP is called **oxidative phosphorylation.**

C. REVIEW OF GLUCOSE CATABOLISM

It is important to understand how all of the events described above are interrelated. Figure 3.7 is a eukaryotic cell with a mitochondrion magnified for detail.

<table>
<tr><td colspan="2">**MCAT Synopsis**</td></tr>
<tr><td>Event</td><td>Location</td></tr>
<tr><td>Glycolysis</td><td>Cytoplasm</td></tr>
<tr><td>Fermentation</td><td>Cytoplasm</td></tr>
<tr><td>Pyruvate to Acetyl CoA</td><td>Mitochondrial matrix</td></tr>
<tr><td>TCA cycle</td><td>Mitochondrial matrix</td></tr>
<tr><td>Electron transport chain</td><td>Inner mitochondrial membrane</td></tr>
</table>

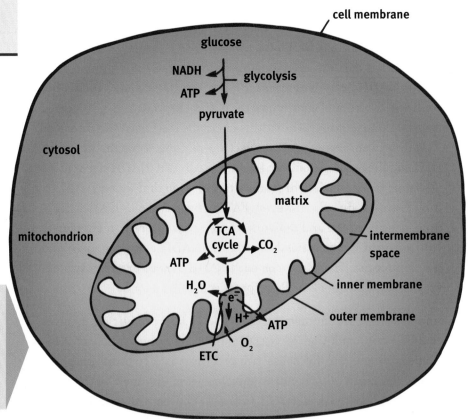

Figure 3.7. Schematic of Glucose Catabolism

To calculate the net amount of ATP produced per molecule of glucose we need to tally the number of ATP produced by substrate level phosphorylation and the number of ATP produced by oxidative phosphorylation.

1. Substrate Level Phosphorylation

Degradation of 1 glucose molecule yields a net of 2 ATP from glycolysis and 1 ATP for each turn of the citric acid cycle. Thus, a total of 4 ATP are produced by substrate level phosphorylation.

2. Oxidative Phosphorylation

Two pyruvate decarboxylations yield 1 NADH each for a total of 2 NADH. Each turn of the citric acid cycle yields 3 NADH and 1 $FADH_2$, for a total of 6 NADH and 2 $FADH_2$ per glucose molecule. Each $FADH_2$ generates 2 ATP, as previously discussed. Each NADH generates 3 ATP except for the 2 NADH that were reduced during glycolysis; these NADH cannot cross the inner mitochondrial membrane and must transfer their electrons to an intermediate carrier molecule, which delivers the electrons to the second carrier protein complex, Q. Therefore, these NADH generate only 2 ATP per glucose. So the 2 NADH of glycolysis yield 4 ATP, the other 8 NADH yield 24 ATP, and the 2 $FADH_2$ produce 4 ATP, for a total of 32 ATP by oxidative phosphorylation.

The total amount of ATP produced during eukaryotic glucose catabolism is therefore 4 via substrate level phosphorylation plus 32 via oxidative phosphorylation, for a total of 36 ATP. (For prokaryotes the yield is 38 ATP, because the 2 NADH of glycolysis don't have any mitochondrial membranes to cross and therefore don't lose energy.) See Table 3.1 for a summary of eukaryotic ATP production.

> **TEACHER TIP**
> This ATP is actually made in the form of GTP, which is energetically equivalent.

> **MCAT SYNOPSIS**
> In an ANAEROBIC environment, eukaryotic cells can generate only 2 net ATP; in an AEROBIC environment, these cells can generate a net of 36 ATP!

Table 3.1. Eukaryotic ATP Production per Glucose Molecule

Glycolysis		
2 ATP invested (steps 1 and 3)	−2	ATP
4 ATP generated (steps 6 and 9)	+4	ATP (substrate)
2 NADH × 2 ATP/NADH (step 5)	+4	ATP (oxidative)
Pyruvate Decarboxylation		
2 NADH × 3 ATP/NADH	+ 6	ATP (oxidative)
Citric Acid Cycle		
6 NADH × 3 ATP/NADH	+18	ATP (oxidative)
2 $FADH_2$ × 2 ATP/$FADH_2$	+ 4	ATP (oxidative)
2 GTP × 1 ATP/GTP	+ 2	ATP (substrate)
Total	**+136**	**ATP**

TEACHER TIP

The body's ability to use a variety of energy sources is the basis for different fad diets. Regardless of the intake, though, the same three types of intermediate molecules (carbohydrates, proteins, and fats) are used to run the body.

CLINICAL CORRELATE

Diabetic ketoacidosis (DKA) occurs when diabetics (primarily insulin dependent) fail to take their insulin. The blood glucose levels accumulate and the cells are, ironically, starved for glucose because there is no insulin. As a result, their bodies resort to the breakdown of fats, which produces β-ketoacids, eventually resulting in a coma, as they build up in the bloodstream.

ALTERNATE ENERGY SOURCES

When glucose supplies run low, the body uses other energy sources. These sources are used by the body in the following preferential order: other carbohydrates, fats, and proteins. These substances are first converted to either glucose or glucose intermediates, which can then be degraded in the glycolytic pathway and TCA cycle.

A. CARBOHYDRATES

Disaccharides are hydrolyzed into monosaccharides, most of which can be converted into glucose or glycolytic intermediates. Glycogen stored in the liver can be converted, when needed, into glucose 6-phosphate, a glycolytic intermediate.

B. FATS

Fat molecules are stored in adipose tissue in the form of triglyceride. When needed, they are hydrolyzed by lipases to fatty acids and glycerol, and are carried by the blood to other tissues for oxidation. Glycerol can be converted into PGAL, a glycolytic intermediate. A fatty acid must first be "activated" in the cytoplasm; this process requires 2 ATP. Once activated, the fatty acid is transported into the mitochondrion and taken through a series of **beta-oxidation cycles** that convert it into two-carbon fragments, which are then converted into acetyl CoA. Acetyl CoA then enters the TCA cycle. With each round of β-oxidation of a saturated fatty acid, 1 NADH and 1 $FADH_2$ are generated.

Of all the high-energy compounds used in cellular respiration, fats yield the greatest number of ATP per gram. This makes them extremely efficient energy storage molecules. Thus, while the amount of glycogen stored in humans is enough to meet the short-term energy needs of about a day, the stored fat reserves can meet the long-term energy needs for about a month.

C. PROTEINS

The body degrades amino acids (the building blocks of proteins) only when there is not enough carbohydrate available. Most amino acids undergo a **transamination** reaction in which they lose an amino group to form an α-keto acid. The carbon atoms of most amino acids are converted into acetyl CoA, pyruvate, or one of the intermediates of the citric acid cycle. These intermediates enter their respective metabolic pathways, allowing cells to produce fatty acids, glucose, or energy in the form of ATP.

METABOLIC MAP

Below is a diagram illustrating the relationship between fats, protein, and carbohydrate catabolism. Note where the products of fats and protein catabolism feed into the reactions of carbohydrate catabolism.

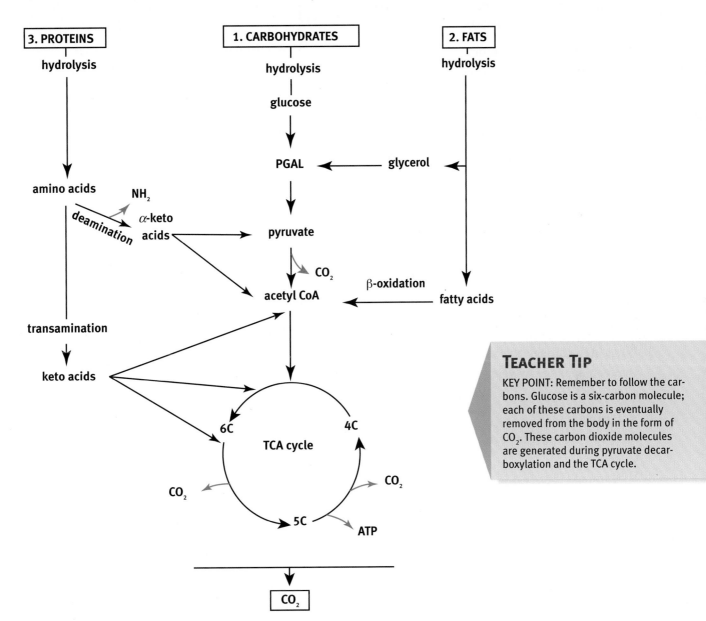

TEACHER TIP

KEY POINT: Remember to follow the carbons. Glucose is a six-carbon molecule; each of these carbons is eventually removed from the body in the form of CO_2. These carbon dioxide molecules are generated during pyruvate decarboxylation and the TCA cycle.

Figure 3.8. Nutrient Metabolism

PRACTICE QUESTIONS

1. Red blood cells (RBC) metabolize glucose anaerobically due to the absence of mitochondria. Which process is of primary importance to provide energy for RBCs?

   A. Electron transport chain
   B. Oxidative phosphorylation
   C. Citric acid (Krebs) cycle
   D. Glycolysis

2. Which part of the process of catabolism of glucose can be referred to as respiratory and accounts for the greatest portion of oxygen use by the body, producing the highest amount of ATP?

   A. Pyruvate decarboxylation
   B. Electron transport chain
   C. Glycolysis
   D. Citric acid (Krebs) cycle

3. What is the alternative product to lactic acid that can be made by yeast in the absence of oxygen?

   A. Pyruvate
   B. Acetyl CoA and lactate
   C. Glucose
   D. Ethanol

4. A researcher is staining cells with a fluorescent marker, which binds to the enzyme pyruvate dehydrogenase to experimentally verify its location. This enzyme catalyzes the reaction shown below. Theoretically, the fluorescence is expected at which location?

   **Alcohol
   Dehydrogenase**

   Ethanol $\longrightarrow$ Acetaldehyde

   A. Cytoplasm
   B. Inner membrane of mitochondria
   C. Matrix of mitochondria
   D. Rough endoplasmic reticulum

5. β-ketoacids detected in a patient's urine signal the catabolism of

   A. fats.
   B. proteins.
   C. carbohydrates.
   D. nucleic acids.

6. ATP consists of the base adenine, ribose, and three phosphates. It is structurally similar to which of the following?

   A. Phospholipid
   B. Amino acid
   C. Nucleic acid
   D. Monosaccharide

7. In the process of breaking down amino acids, which of the following groups must be detached before the amino acid can enter the citric acid cycle?

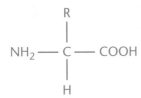

A. R-radical group of amino acid
B. COOH-carboxylic group of amino acid
C. H-proton of amino acid
D. NH$_2^-$ amino group

8. For which of the following situations is anaerobic glycolysis of primary importance?

  I. Oxygen supply is limited to the tissue.

  II. Glucose supply is limited.

  III. Tissues have few or no mitochondria.

A. I, II and III
B. I and III
C. I only
D. I and II

9. As lactic acid accumulates in the skeletal muscle during intense exercise, all of the following must be taking place EXCEPT

A. oxidative phosphorylation.
B. pyruvate conversion to lactate.
C. intracellular pH decreas.
D. anaerobic glycolysis.

10. Lipitor, one of the "statin" medications, competitively inhibits one of the rate-limiting steps in cholesterol synthesis. It can be inferred that

A. Lipitor binds at a site different from where the substrate binds.
B. Lipitor binds to the active site of the enzyme.
C. Lipitor binds to cholesterol.
D. None of the above

11. Phosporylation of glucose to glucose 6-phosphate is catalyzed by the enzyme hexokinase. As glucose 6-phosphate accumulates, it inhibits hexokinase activity. This is an example of what kind of activity?

A. Hormonal regulation
B. Negative feedback
C. Positive feedback loop
D. Parasympathetic regulation

12. How many lactate molecules are generated for each glucose molecule entering anaerobic glycolysis?

A. 3
B. 1
C. 4
D. 2

13. What molecule enters the tricarboxylic acid cycle in a cell?

A. Glucose
B. Acetyl CoA
C. NAD$^+$
D. Malate

14. What high-energy molecule is responsible for the production of most ATP as it passes its electrons along the electron transport chain?

A. $FADH^2$

B. NADH

C. GTP

D. Cytochrome a

15. According to the table below, one molecule of Acetyl CoA produces:

High-Energy Molecules Produced	ATP Conversion
3NADH	NADH $\longrightarrow$ 3ATP
FADH$_2$	FADH$_2$ $\longrightarrow$ 2ATP
GTP	GTP $\longrightarrow$ ATP

What is the total amount of ATP yielded by the catabolism of one glucose molecule via the Krebs cycle?

A. 6 ATP

B. 12 ATP

C. 24 ATP

D. 36 ATP

16. In which part of glucose catabolism is CO_2 produced?

A. Tricarboxylic acid cycle

B. Electron transport chain

C. Phosphorylation

D. Glycolysis

CHAPTER 4

REPRODUCTION

Reproduction is the process by which an organism perpetuates itself and its species, ensuring the precise duplication of genetic material and its representation in successive generations. Reproduction can be divided into three topics: **cell division, asexual reproduction,** and **sexual reproduction.**

CELL DIVISION

Cell division is the process by which a cell doubles its organelles and cytoplasm, replicates its DNA, and then divides in two. For unicellular organisms, cell division is a means of reproduction, while for multicellular organisms it is a method of growth, development, and replacement of worn-out cells. Prokaryotes and eukaryotes differ in their means of cell division.

Prokaryotes divide by a process called **binary fission** (a type of asexual reproduction). The single DNA molecule attaches to the plasma membrane during replication and duplicates, while the cell continues to grow in size. The cell membrane pinches inward, splitting the cell into two equal halves, with each daughter cell receiving a complete copy of the original chromosome.

Eukaryotic cell division is more complicated than binary fission because cells must duplicate and equally distribute chromosomes, organelles, and cytoplasm to both daughter cells. Eukaryotic **somatic,** or **autosomal,** cells contain the diploid number of chromosomes characteristic of its species, which is designated as **2N (N** is the number of chromosomes found in a **haploid** cell, or **gamete).** The diploid number for humans is 46, and the haploid number is 23; 23 chromosomes are inherited from each parent.

The life cycle of a eukaryotic cell can be broken down into four distinct stages collectively known as the **cell cycle.**

TEACHER TIP

KEY POINT: In autosomal cells, division results in two identical (genetically) daughter cells. In germ line cells, the daughters are NOT equivalent.

A. THE CELL CYCLE

The four stages of the cell cycle are designated as **G_1, S, G_2,** and **M.** The first three stages of the cell cycle are **interphase** stages, that is, they occur between cell divisions. The fourth stage, **mitosis,** includes the actual cell division.

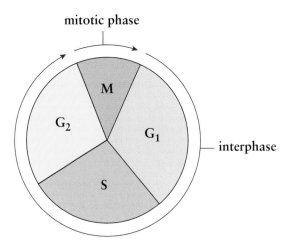

Figure 4.1. The Cell Cycle

1. Interphase

This is by far the longest part of the cell cycle. A cell normally spends at least 90 percent of the cycle in interphase.

a. G1 stage (presynthetic gap)

This stage is one of intense biochemical activity and growth. The cell doubles in size and new organelles such as mitochondria, ribosomes, endoplasmic reticulum, and centrioles are produced. A typical cell proceeds through the G_1 stage, passing a **restriction point,** after which it is committed to continue through the rest of the cell cycle and divide. However, some cells, including specialized skeletal muscle cells and nerve cells, never pass this point, instead entering a nondividing phase sometimes referred to as **G_0.**

b. S stage (synthesis)

In the synthetic stage each chromosome is replicated so that during division, a complete copy of the genome can be distributed to both daughter cells. After replication, the chromosomes, consist of two identical **sister chromatids** held together at a central region called the **centromere.** The ends of the chromosome are called the **telomeres.** Note that after DNA replication, the cell still contains the diploid number (2N) of chromosomes, but because each chromosome now consists of two chromatids, cells entering G_2 actually contain twice as much DNA as cells in G_1.

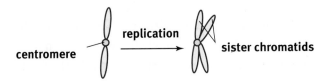

Figure 4.2. Chromosome Replication

c. G_2 stage (postsynthetic gap)

The cell continues to grow in size, while assembly of new organelles and other cell structures continues.

2. M Stage (Mitotic Stage)

This stage consists of mitosis and **cytokinesis**. Mitosis is the division and distribution of the cell's DNA to its two daughter cells such that each cell receives a complete copy of the original genome. Cytokinesis refers to the division of cytoplasm that follows.

a. Mitosis

During interphase, the nucleus is membrane-bound and clearly visible, and one or more nucleoli may be observed. Individual chromosomes are not visible under a light microscope because they are active and uncoiled. The DNA appears granular and is called **chromatin.** As mitosis begins, the chromosomes coil up, condense, and become visible under high-power microscopy. This coiling facilitates their movement during the later stages of mitosis.

Chromosome movement is dependent on certain cytoplasmic organelles. The centrioles, which are typically found in pairs, are cylindrical organelles located outside of the interphase nucleus in an area referred to as the **centrosome.** During the first stage of mitosis, the centrioles, which have already replicated, migrate to opposite poles of the cell, and a system of **spindle fibers** composed of microtubules and associated proteins appears near each pair of centrioles. The spindle fibers radiate outward from the centrioles, forming structures called **asters.** The asters extend toward the center of the nucleus, forming the **spindle apparatus.** The movement of chromosomes toward opposite poles of the cell during the later stages of mitosis is caused by the shortening of the spindle apparatus.

Although mitosis is a continuous process, four stages are discernible: **prophase, metaphase, anaphase,** and **telophase.**

- **Prophase**

  The chromosomes condense, the centriole pairs separate and move toward opposite poles of the cell, and the spindle apparatus forms between them. The nuclear membrane dissolves, allowing spindle fibers to enter the nucleus, while the nucleoli become less distinct or disappear. **Kinetochores,** with attached **kinetochore fibers,** appear at the chromosome centromere.

- **Metaphase**

  The centriole pairs are now at opposite poles of the cell. The kinetochore fibers interact with the fibers of the spindle apparatus to align the chromosomes at the **metaphase plate** (equatorial plate), which is equidistant to the two poles of the spindle fibers.

- **Anaphase**

  The centromeres now split, so that each chromatid has its own distinct centromere, thus allowing the sister chromatids to separate. The telomeres are the last part of the chromatids to separate. The sister chromatids are pulled toward the opposite poles of the cell by the shortening of the kinetochore fibers.

- **Telophase**

  The spindle apparatus disappears. A nuclear membrane forms around each set of chromosomes and the nucleoli reappear. The chromosomes uncoil, resuming their interphase form. Each of the two new nuclei has received a complete copy of the genome identical to the original genome and to each other. Cytokinesis occurs.

See Figure 4.3 for a summary of mitosis.

b. Cytokinesis

Near the end of telophase, the cytoplasm divides into two daughter cells, each with a complete nucleus and its own set of organelles. In animal cells, a cleavage furrow forms; the cell membrane indents along the equator of the cell and finally pinches through the cell, separating the two nuclei.

The life cycle of a cell is not an arbitrary series of events; cell division is a specified sequence of events dictated by the nucleus. For example, a typical somatic cell is programmed to divide between 20 and 50 times and then die. As mentioned earlier, some cells, such as

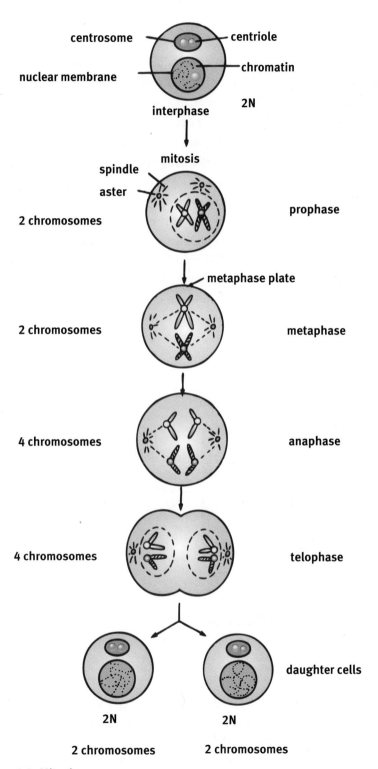

Figure 4.3. Mitosis

CLINICAL CORRELATE

Cancer cells are cells in which mitosis has gone wild. The challenge of cancer therapy (chemotherapy) is to kill cancer cells without destroying the body's normal cells. Because cancer cells typically divide faster than normal cells, most chemotherapeutic agents work by targeting rapidly dividing cells. They do so by a variety of mechanisms such as inhibiting DNA synthesis or affecting spindle formation or function.

TEACHER TIP

KEY POINT: The MCAT loves to test the differences between mitosis and meiosis. Be sure to note that the diploid number is maintained throughout mitosis, whereas the process of meiosis results in haploid cells.

muscle and nerve cells, never divide at all. Cancer cells can divide indefinitely; they do not respond to the control mechanisms that normally regulate cell division.

ASEXUAL REPRODUCTION

Asexual reproduction is the production of offspring without fertilization. New organisms are formed by division of a single parent cell. Offspring are essentially genetic carbon copies of their parent cells. Thus, except for random mutations, the offspring are genetically identical to the parent cells. The different types of asexual reproduction are **binary fission, budding, regeneration,** and **parthenogenesis.**

A. BINARY FISSION

Binary fission is a simple form of asexual reproduction seen in prokaryotes. The circular chromosome replicates and a new plasma membrane and cell wall grow inward along the midline of the cell, dividing it into two equally sized cells, each containing a duplicate of the parent chromosome. A very similar process occurs in some primitive eukaryotic cells.

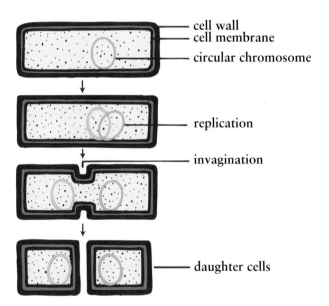

Figure 4.4. Binary Fission

B. BUDDING

Budding is the replication of the nucleus followed by unequal cytokinesis. The cell membrane pinches inward to form a new cell that is smaller in size but genetically identical to the parent cell and which subsequently grows to adult size. The new cell may separate immediately from the parent or it may remain attached to it, develop as an outgrowth, and separate at a later stage. Budding occurs in hydra and yeast.

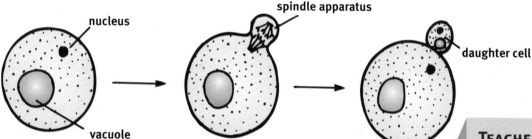

nucleus

spindle apparatus

daughter cell

vacuole

Figure 4.5. Budding

C. REGENERATION

Regeneration is the regrowth of a lost or injured body part. Replacement of cells occurs by mitosis. Some lower animals such as hydra and starfish have extensive regenerative capabilities. If a starfish loses an arm, it can regenerate a new one; the severed arm may even be able to regenerate an entire body, as long as the arm contains a piece of an area called the central disk. Salamanders and tadpoles can generate new limbs. The extent of regeneration depends on the nerve damage to the severed body part. In adult birds and mammals, regeneration is usually limited to the healing of tissues, although some internal organs, such as the liver, have considerable regenerative capabilities as long as part of the organ remains viable.

D. PARTHENOGENESIS

Parthenogenesis is the development of an unfertilized egg into an adult organism. This process occurs naturally in certain lower organisms. For example, in most species of bees and ants, the males develop from unfertilized eggs, and several species of all-female, parthenogenetic salamander exist. The eggs of some higher organisms can be induced to develop parthenogenetically (although the process does not occur naturally), with the resulting embryos surviving for variable lengths of time. Frog eggs have been induced to develop into tadpoles, and unfertilized rabbit eggs have been stimulated to develop into adult rabbits. Because the organism develops from a haploid cell, all of its cells will be haploid.

SEXUAL REPRODUCTION

Sexual reproduction differs from asexual reproduction in that there are two parents involved, and the end result is genetically unique offspring. Sexual reproduction occurs via the fusion of two gametes—specialized sex cells produced by each parent. **Meiosis** is the process whereby these

TEACHER TIP

Binary fission results in two cells of equal size, whereas budding results in cells of unequal size. Both cases, however, give rise to genetically identical cells.

TEACHER TIP

In fact, liver transplants can now be done from living donors. Only part of the liver is removed and transplanted. The donor's liver will enlarge in both the donor and recipient until it reaches the appropriate size.

TEACHER TIP

Unlike asexual reproduction, the offspring will be genetically unique from either of the parents—who are also genetically unique from one another.

sex cells are produced. Meiosis is similar to mitosis in that a cell duplicates its chromosomes before undergoing the process. However, mitosis preserves the diploid number of the cell, while meiosis halves it, resulting in haploid cells. Furthermore, mitosis comprises one division resulting in two diploid cells, while meiosis comprises two divisions resulting in four haploid gametes. Somatic cells undergo mitosis, while specialized cells called **gametocytes** undergo meiosis. During fertilization, two haploid gametes fuse, restoring the diploid number.

A. MEIOSIS

As in mitosis, the gametocyte's chromosomes are replicated during the S phase of the cell cycle and the centrioles replicate at some point during interphase. The first round of division (meiosis I) produces two intermediate daughter cells. The second round of division (meiosis II), similar to mitosis, involves the separation of the sister chromatids, resulting in four genetically distinct haploid gametes. Each meiotic division has the same four stages as mitosis.

1. Meiosis I

a. Prophase I

The chromatin condenses into chromosomes, the spindle apparatus forms, and the nucleoli and nuclear membrane disappear. **Homologous chromosomes** (chromosomes that code for the same traits, one inherited from each parent), come together and intertwine in a process called **synapsis.** Because at this stage each chromosome consists of two sister chromatids, each synaptic pair of homologous chromosomes contains four chromatids and is, therefore, often called a **tetrad.** Sometimes chromatids of homologous chromosomes break at corresponding points and exchange equivalent pieces of DNA; this process is called **crossing over.** Note that crossing over occurs between homologous chromosomes and not between sister chromatids of the same chromosome. (The latter are identical, so crossing over would not produce any change.) Those chromatids involved are left with an altered but structurally complete set of genes. The chromosomes remain joined at points called **chiasmata** where the crossing over occurred. Such **genetic recombination** can "unlink" **linked genes** (see chapter 13), thereby increasing the variety of genetic combinations that can be produced via gametogenesis. Recombination among chromosomes results in increased genetic diversity within a species. Note that sister chromatids are no longer identical after recombination has occurred (see Figure 4.6).

MCAT FAVORITE

Remember that MITOSIS occurs in all of the cells of the body that divide. MEIOSIS occurs only in the sex cells (a.k.a., "germ cells" or gametocytes) found in the reproductive system (the testes and ovaries).

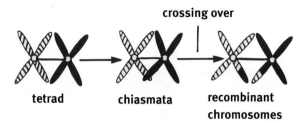

Figure 4.6. Synapsis

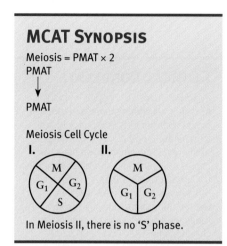
b. Metaphase I

Homologous pairs (tetrads) align at the equatorial plane, and each pair attaches to a separate spindle fiber by its kinetochore.

c. Anaphase I

The homologous pairs separate and are pulled to opposite poles of the cell. This process is called **disjunction,** and it accounts for a fundamental **Mendelian law** (see chapter 13). During disjunction, each chromosome of paternal origin separates (or disjoins) from its homologue of maternal origin, and either chromosome can end up in either daughter cell. Thus, the distribution of homologous chromosomes to the two intermediate daughter cells is random with respect to parental origin. Each daughter cell will have a unique pool of **alleles** (genes coding for alternative forms of a given trait; e.g., yellow flowers or purple flowers) from a random mixture of maternal and paternal origin.

d. Telophase I

A nuclear membrane forms around each new nucleus. At this point each chromosome still consists of sister chromatids joined at the centromere. The cell divides (by cytokinesis) into two daughter cells, each of which receives a nucleus containing the haploid number of chromosomes. Between cell divisions there may be a short rest period, or **interkinesis,** during which the chromosomes partially uncoil.

2. Meiosis II

This second division is very similar to mitosis, except that meiosis II is not preceded by chromosomal replication.

a. Prophase II

The centrioles migrate to opposite poles and the spindle apparatus forms.

CLINICAL CORRELATE

If, during anaphase I or II of meiosis, homologous chromosomes (anaphase I) or sister chromatids (anaphase II) fail to separate (nondisjunction), then one of the resulting gametes will have two copies of a particular chromosome and the other gamete will have no copies. Subsequently, during fertilization, the resulting zygote may have one too many or one too few copies of the chromosome. Note that nondisjunction can affect both the autosomal chromosomes (e.g., trisomy 21; Down's syndrome) and the sex chromosomes (Klinefelter's; Turner's).

MCAT SYNOPSIS

1) Sex cells
2) Diploid ⟶ Haploid
   2N ⟶ 1N
3) 4 daughter cells in males (except in females; there is only 1 daughter cell)

TEACHER TIP

In females, the other cells generated contain genetic material but they are incapable of undergoing fertilization and creating a zygote.

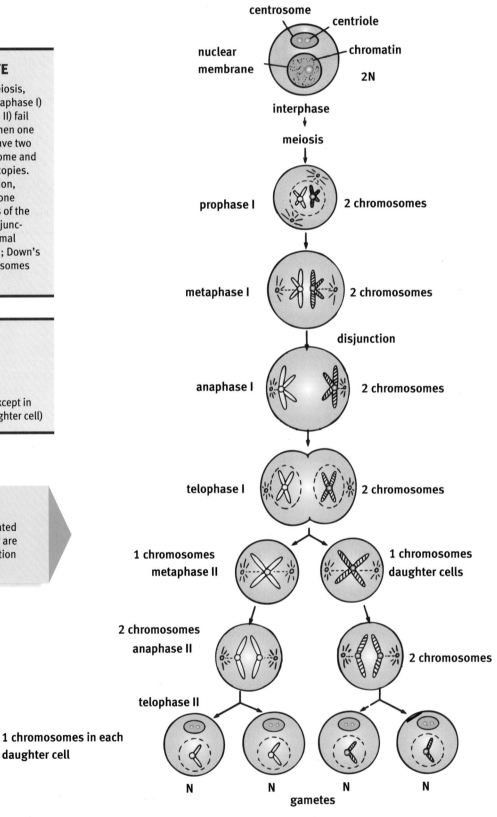

Figure 4.7. Meiosis

b. Metaphase II

The chromosomes line up along the equatorial plane. The centromeres divide, separating the chromosomes into pairs of sister chromatids.

c. Anaphase II

The sister chromatids are pulled to opposite poles by the spindle fibers.

d. Telophase II

A nuclear membrane forms around each new (haploid) nucleus. Cytokinesis follows and two daughter cells are formed. Thus, by the completion of meiosis II, four haploid daughter cells are produced per gametocyte. (In women, only one of these becomes a functional gamete.)

The random distribution of chromosomes in meiosis, coupled with crossing over in prophase I, enables an individual to produce gametes with many different genetic combinations. Thus, as opposed to asexual reproduction, which produces identical offspring, sexual reproduction produces genetic variability in offspring. The possibility of so many different genetic combinations is believed to increase the capability of a species to evolve and adapt to a changing environment.

B. HUMAN SEXUAL REPRODUCTION

Human reproduction is a highly complex process involving not only sexual intercourse between male and female but also interactions between the reproductive and endocrine systems within the body. Children are the product of fertilization—the fusion of **sperm** and **egg** (the gametes) in the female reproductive tract. The gametes are produced in the primary reproductive organs, or **gonads.**

1. Male Reproductive Anatomy

The male gonads, called the **testes,** contain two functional components: the **seminiferous tubules** and the **interstitial cells (cells of Leydig).** Sperm are produced in the highly coiled seminiferous tubules, where they are nourished by **Sertoli cells.** The interstitial cells, located between the seminiferous tubules, secrete **testosterone** and other **androgens** (male sex hormones) (see chapter 11). The testes are located in an external pouch called the **scrotum,** which maintains testes temperature 2–4°C lower than body temperature, a condition essential for sperm survival. Sperm pass from the seminiferous tubules into the coiled tubules of the **epididymis.** Here they acquire

MCAT SYNOPSIS

Mitosis	Meiosis
2N → 2N	2N → N
Occurs in all dividing cells	Occurs in sex cells only
Homologous chromosomes don't pair up	Homologous chromosomes pair up at metaphase plate forming tetrads
No crossing over	Crossing over can occur

MCAT SYNOPSIS

To remember the pathway of sperm, think SEVEN UP.
Seminiferous tubules
Epididymus
Vas deferens
Ejaculatory duct
(Nothing)
Urethra
Penis

TEACHER TIP

Common MCAT topic: Enzymes have a temperature range in which they maximally work. Consider what this means in terms of enzymes, which work in the testes.

motility, mature, and are stored until **ejaculation.** During ejaculation they travel through the **vas deferens** to the ejaculatory duct and then to the **urethra.** The urethra passes through the **penis** and opens to the outside at its tip. In males, the urethra is a common passageway for both the reproductive and excretory systems.

Sperm is mixed with **seminal fluid** as it moves along the reproductive tract; seminal fluid is produced by three glands: the **seminal vesicles,** the **prostate gland,** and the **bulbourethral glands.** The paired seminal vesicles secrete a fructose-rich fluid that serves as an energy source for the highly active sperm. The prostate gland releases an alkaline milky fluid that protects the sperm from the acidic environment of the female reproductive tract. Finally, the bulbourethral glands secrete a small amount of viscous fluid prior to ejaculation; the function of this secretion is not known. Seminal fluid aids in sperm transport by lubricating the passageways through which the sperm will travel. Sperm plus seminal fluid is known as **semen.**

> **CLINICAL CORRELATE**
>
> In older males, the prostate often enlarges. Because it surrounds the urethra, this commonly results in urinary frequency and urgency.

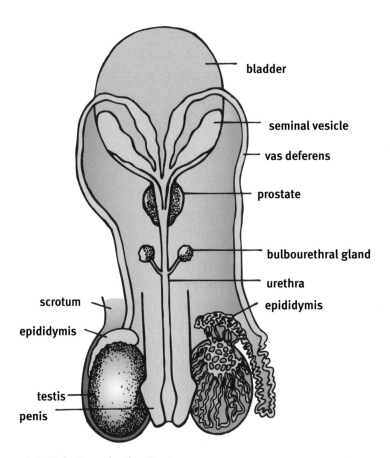

Figure 4.8. Male Reproductive Tract

2. Spermatogenesis

Spermatogenesis, or sperm production, occurs in the seminiferous tubules. Diploid cells called **spermatogonia** differentiate into diploid cells called **primary spermatocytes,** which undergo the first meiotic division to yield two haploid **secondary spermatocytes** of equal size; the second meiotic division produces four haploid **spermatids** of equal size. Following meiosis, the spermatids undergo a series of changes leading to the production of mature sperm, or **spermatozoa,** which are specialized for transporting the sperm nucleus to the egg, or **ovum.** The mature sperm is an elongated cell with a head, neck, body, and tail. The head consists almost entirely of the nucleus. The tail (flagellum) propels the sperm, while mitochondria in the neck and body provide energy for locomotion. A caplike structure called the **acrosome,** derived from the Golgi apparatus, develops over the anterior half of the head. The acrosome contains enzymes needed to penetrate the tough outer covering of the ovum. After a male has reached sexual maturity, approximately three million primary spermatocytes begin to undergo spermatogenesis per day, the maturation process taking a total of 65–75 days.

3. Female Reproductive Anatomy

The female gonads, called the **ovaries,** produce eggs **(ova),** and secrete the hormones estrogen and progesterone (see chapter 11). The ovaries are found in the abdominal cavity, below the digestive system. The ovaries consist of thousands of **follicles**; a follicle is a multilayered sac of cells that contains, nourishes, and protects an immature ovum. It is actually the follicle cells that produce estrogen. Once a month, an immature ovum is released from the ovary into the abdominal cavity and drawn into the nearby **fallopian tube.** The inner surface of the fallopian tube is lined with cilia that create currents that move the ovum into and along the tube. Each fallopian tube opens into the upper end of a muscular chamber called the **uterus,** which is the site of fetal development. The lower, narrow end of the uterus is called the **cervix.** The cervix connects with the **vaginal canal,** which is the site of sperm deposition during intercourse and is also the passageway through which a baby is expelled during childbirth. The external female genitalia is referred to as the **vulva.** Note that in the mammalian (placental) female, the reproductive and excretory systems are distinct from one another; i.e., the urethra and the vagina are not connected.

MCAT SYNOPSIS

spermatogonia (2N)

↓

1° spermatocytes (2N)
      meiosis I
↓
2° spermatocytes (N)
      meiosis II
↓
spermatids (N)

↓

spermatozoa (N)

TEACHER TIP

Spermatogenesis in males is a 1:4 division whereas in females it is 1:1.

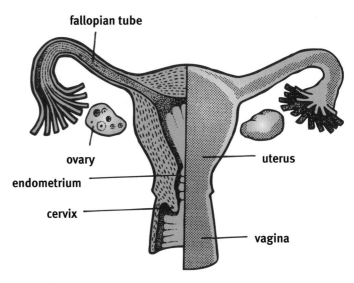

Figure 4.9. Female Reproductive Tract

4. Oogenesis

Oogenesis, which is the production of female gametes, occurs in the ovarian follicles. At birth, all of the immature ova, known as **primary oocytes,** that a female will produce during her lifetime are already in her ovaries. Primary oocytes are diploid cells that form by mitosis in the ovary. After menarche (the first time a female gets her period), one primary oocyte per month completes meiosis I, yielding two daughter cells of unequal size—a **secondary oocyte** and a small cell known as a **polar body.** The secondary oocyte is expelled from the follicle during ovulation. Meiosis II does not occur until fertilization. The oocyte cell membrane is surrounded by two layers of cells; the inner layer is the **zona pellucida,** the outer layer is the **corona radiata.** Meiosis II is triggered when these layers are penetrated by a sperm cell, yielding two haploid cells—a mature ovum and another polar body. (The first polar body may also undergo meiosis II; eventually, the polar bodies die.) The mature ovum is a large cell containing a lot of cytoplasm, RNA, organelles, and nutrients needed by a developing embryo.

Women ovulate approximately once every four weeks (except during pregnancy and, usually, lactation) until menopause, which typically occurs between the ages of 45 and 50. During menopause, the ovaries become less sensitive to the hormones that stimulate follicle development (FSH and LH), and eventually they atrophy. The remaining follicles disappear, estrogen and progesterone levels greatly decline, and ovulation stops. The profound changes in hormone levels are often

MCAT Synopsis

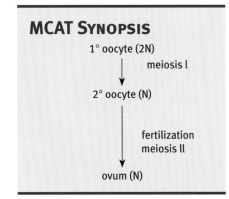

1° oocyte (2N)

meiosis I

2° oocyte (N)

fertilization
meiosis II

ovum (N)

Teacher Tip

Sometimes the egg will implant in the fallopian tube instead of the uterus. This condition is known as an *ectopic pregnancy* and is a medical emergency due to the risk of rupture and hemorrhage as the zygote enlarges.

accompanied by physiological and psychological changes that persist until a new balance is reached.

5. Fertilization

An egg can be fertilized during the 12–24 hours following ovulation. Fertilization occurs in the lateral, widest portion of the fallopian tube. Sperm must travel through the vaginal canal, cervix, uterus, and into the fallopian tubes to reach the ovum. Sperm remain viable and capable of fertilization for one to two days following intercourse.

The first barrier that the sperm must penetrate is the corona radiata. Enzymes secreted by the sperm aid in penetration of the corona radiata. The acrosome is responsible for penetrating the zona pellucida; it releases enzymes that digest this layer, thereby allowing the sperm to come into direct contact with the ovum cell membrane. Once in contact with the membrane, the sperm forms a tubelike structure called the **acrosomal process,** which extends to the cell membrane and penetrates it, fusing the sperm cell membrane with that of the ovum. The sperm nucleus now enters the ovum's cytoplasm. It is at this stage of fertilization that the ovum completes meiosis II.

The acrosomal reaction triggers a **cortical reaction** in the ovum, causing calcium ions to be released into the cytoplasm; this, in turn, initiates a series of reactions that result in the formation of the **fertilization membrane.** The fertilization membrane is a hard layer that surrounds the ovum cell membrane and prevents multiple fertilizations. The release of Ca^{2+} also stimulates metabolic changes within the ovum, greatly increasing its metabolic rate. This is followed by the fusion of the sperm nucleus with the ovum nucleus to form a diploid zygote. The first mitotic division of the zygote soon follows (see chapter 5).

6. Multiple Births

a. Monozygotic (identical) twins

Monozygotic twins result when a single zygote splits into two embryos. If the splitting occurs at the two-cell stage of development, the embryos will have separate chorions and separate placentas; if it occurs at the blastula stage, then the embryos will have only one chorionic sac and will therefore share a placenta and possibly an amnion (see chapter 5). Occasionally the division is incomplete, resulting in the birth of "Siamese" twins, which are attached at some point on the body, often sharing limbs and/or organs. Monozygotic twins are genetically identical, because they develop from the same

> **TEACHER TIP**
>
> Identical twins are commonly used to study the interaction between genes and the environment. Because they have the same genetic complement, they can be studied to see how much of an effect the environment has in contributing to a certain condition (e.g., schizophrenia).

zygote. Monozygotic twins are therefore of the same sex, blood type, and so on.

b. Dizygotic (fraternal) twins

Dizygotic twins result when two ova are released in one ovarian cycle and are fertilized by two different sperm. The two embryos implant in the uterine wall individually, and each develops its own placenta, amnion, and chorion (although the placentas may fuse if the embryos implant very close to each other). Fraternal twins share no more characteristics than any other siblings, because they develop from two distinct zygotes.

PRACTICE QUESTIONS

1. How many chromatids does a eukaryotic somatic cell inherit from each parent?

   A. N
   B. 2N
   C. 4N
   D. ½N

2. Cytokinesis is the process by which a cell's cytoplasm splits into two equal parts to form two daughter cells. Disproportionate splitting of the cytoplasm is a natural phenomenon of

   A. binary fission, the asexual reproduction seen in prokaryotes.
   B. parthogenesis.
   C. nothing; unequal cytokinesis never occurs.
   D. the reproductive cycle of yeast.

3. At what point does crossing over between sister chromatids occur?

   A. During prophase of meiosis
   B. During prophase of mitosis
   C. During anaphase II of meiosis
   D. It does not occur in meiosis

4. In order to amplify the DNA sequence indicated below, which of the following primers would you use?

   5' GGCTAAGATCTGAATTTTCCAAG …

   TTGGGCAATAATAATGTAGCGCCTT 3'

   A. Primer 1:
      5' GGCTAAGATCTGAATTTTCCAAG 3'
      Primer 2:
      5' AAGGCGCTACATTATTATTGCCCAA 3'
   B. Primer 1:
      5' GAACCTTTTAAGTCTAGAATCGG
      Primer 2:
      5' AACCCGTTATTATTACATCGCGGAA 3'
   C. Primer 1:
      5' CCGATTCTAGACTTAAAAGGTTC 3'
      Primer 2:
      5' TTCCGCGATGTAATAATAACGGGTT 3'
   D. Primer 1:
      5' GAACCTTTTAAGTCTAGAATCGG 3'
      Primer 2:
      5' TTCCGCGATGTAATAATAACGGGTT 3'

5. The following sequence of genetic code is taken from the middle of a protein. Referring to the genetic code table provided below, what is the amino acid sequence for the protein produced by the following gene? Assume that the coding frame starts at the first nucleotide.

5' TCTAGCCTGAACTAATGC 3'
3' AGATCGGACTTGATTACG 5'

ISOLEUCINE	ATT, ATC, ATA
LEUCINE	CTT, CTC, CTA, CTG, TTA, TTG
VALINE	GTT, GTC, GTA, GTG
PHENYLALANINE	TTT, TTC
METHIONINE	ATG
CYSTEINE	TGT, TGC
ALANINE	GCT, GCC, GCA, GCG
GLYCINE	GGT, GGC, GGA, GGG
PROLINE	CCT, CCC, CCA, CCG
THREONINE	ACT, ACC, ACA, ACG
SERINE	TCT, TCC, TCA, TCG, AGT, AGC
TYROSINE	TAT, TAC
TRYPTOPHAN	TGG
GLUTAMINE	CAA, CAG
ASPARAGINE	AAT, AAC
HISTIDINE	CAT, CAC
GLUTAMIC ACID	GAA, GAG
ASPARTIC ACID	GAT, GAC
LYSINE	AAA, AAG
ARGININE	CGT, CGC, CGA, CGG, AGA, AGG
STOP CODONS	TAA, TAG, TGA

A. Amino—Ala Leu Val Gln Ala Ser—Carboxy
B. Carboxy—Ala Leu Val Gln Ala Ser—Amino
C. Amino—Ser Ser Leu Asp Leu Cys—Carboxy
D. Amino—Arg Ser Asp Leu Iso Thr—Carboxy

6. Polymorphism refers to an instance in nature in which two or more distinct phenotypes exist in a species. A polymorphic Simple Sequence Repeat (SSR) marker from four individuals is amplified via PCR. The products yield the following gel:

Which of the following statements is not possible?

A. Individuals B and C are the parents of individuals A and D.
B. Individuals A and D are the parents of individuals B and C.
C. Individuals A and B are the parents of individuals C and D.
D. Individuals A and C are related.

7. The process by which DNA replicates is considered "semiconservative." Semiconservative refers to the fact that

A. if radiolabeled DNA of bacterial strain A is introduced to a culture of unlabeled bacteria strain B, descendants of the strain will have more DNA contributed from A than from B.
B. in DNA replication, one strand of the newly synthesized DNA will be a complement of the original parental strand, and one strand will be an exact replica of the original parental strand.
C. in DNA replication, half of each strand of newly synthesized DNA is a complement of the original parental strand, but half of each strand of newly synthesized DNA is an exact replica of the original parental strand.
D. DNA strands are antiparallel and the two strands of the replicated DNA are complements of one another.

8. Which of the following graphs accurately represents LH levels during the female menstrual cycle?

A.
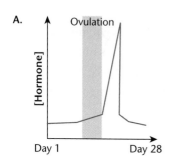

B.
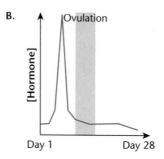

C.
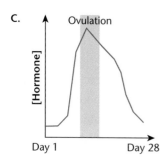

D.
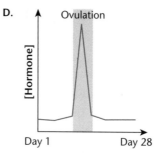

9. DHT or dihydroxytestosterone is a hormone secreted by the embryonic testes, which stimulates the development of male external genitalia. If compound A breaks down DHT, what would be the primary effect of introducing high levels of compound A to an embryo in the early stages of development?

A. The embryo would develop into a fetus lacking external genitalia.

B. The embryo would develop into a fetus with female external genitalia.

C. The embryo would be unable to complete development into a fetus.

D. The embryo would develop into a fetus with both female and male external genitalia.

10. Mullerian-inhibiting substance is secreted by embryonic Sertoli cells. Based on this fact, which of the following statements must be false?

A. Mullerian ducts develop into male sex accessory ducts.

B. Mullerian ducts develop into female sex accessory ducts.

C. Female sex accessory ducts are the default condition.

D. Wolffian ducts develop into male sex accesory ducts.

11. Spermatogenesis and spermiogenesis are the two processes by which immature male germ cells—also known as spermatogonium—produce sperm.

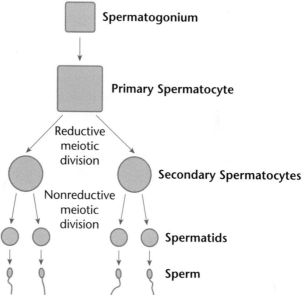

If four male germ cells undergo spermatogenesis and spermiogenesis, what will they produce?

A. 8 (2N) sperm

B. 8 (N) sperm

C. 16 (N) sperm

D. 16 (½N) sperm

12. Down syndrome, also known as trisomy 21, results from a chromosomal abnormality wherein all cells have an extra copy of the 21st chromosome. Mosaic Down syndrome is a specific case in which some, but not all, cells have an extra copy of the 21st chromosome. Which of the following could possibly cause full Down syndrome, where all cells are affected?

A. Disruption of anaphase in mitosis
B. Disruption of telophase in mitosis
C. Disruption of anaphase II in meiosis
D. Duplication event involving chromosome 21

13. In which of the following situations would male infertility be readily apparent without additional testing?

A. Blockage of the seminiferous tubules
B. Blockage of the bulbourethral gland
C. Blockage of the urethra
D. Blockage of the vas deferens

14. Though fraternal twins share their mother's womb and are born only seconds apart, they are no more genetically similar to one another than normal, non-twin siblings. Which of the following is a reasonable explanation for fraternal twins?

A. A zygote splits into two embryos at the two-cell stage of development.
B. A zygote splits into two embryos at the blastula stage of development.
C. Two ova are released in one ovarian cycle and are fertilized by two different sperm.
D. Two ova are released in one ovarian cycle and are fertilized by the same sperm.

15. Mary had an infection which caused large amounts of scarring, blocking her fallopian tubes. Which of the following statements is true?

A. Ovulation will occur less frequently.
B. Urination will become impossible.
C. Fertilization will be less likely.
D. Menstruation will become impossible.

16. In what location are male sperm stored?

A. Vas deferens
B. Seminiferous tubules
C. Sertoli cells
D. Epididymis

17. Your friend gives you one brown and one black guinea pig for your birthday. You know that in this particular species of guinea pig, coat color is controlled by one gene. You also know that this gene has one dominant allele and one recessive allele. After mating the two guinea pigs, you find that you have two black and two brown offspring. What can you conclude?

A. One guinea pig is homozygous and one is heterozygous.
B. Both guinea pigs are homozygous.
C. Both guinea pigs are heterozygous.
D. It is impossible to determine from the information given if any of the above are true.

18. Estradiol and estrogen can bind to the same steroid receptors. However, when estradiol and estrogen are present in equal concentrations, a larger proportion of the estradiol is found bound to the receptors. Which of the following would increase the amount of estrogen bound to the receptors?

A. Introducing an estrogen analog
B. Introducing an estradiol analog
C. Increasing the concentration of estradiol
D. Increasing the concentration of estrogen

FETAL CIRCULATION

Fetal lungs are supplied with only enough blood to nourish the lung tissue itself because fetal lungs do not function prior to birth. Obstruction of which fetal structure would cause an increase in blood supply to fetal lungs?

1) Identify the unique structures involved in fetal circulation.

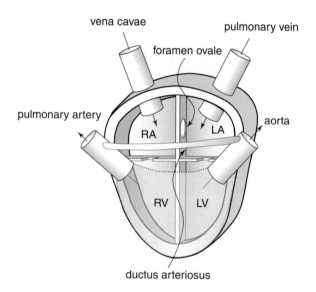

Fetal circulation differs from adult circulation in several important ways. The major difference is that in fetal circulation, blood is oxygenated in the placenta because, as the question states, fetal lungs are nonfunctional before birth. The fetal circulatory route contains three shunts that divert blood flow away from the developing fetal liver and lungs. The umbilical vein carries oxygenated blood from the placenta to the fetus. The blood bypasses the fetal liver by way of a shunt called the ductus venosus, before converging with the inferior vena cava. The inferior and superior vena cavae return deoxygenated blood to the right atrium. Because the oxygenated blood from the umbilical vein mixes with the deoxygenated blood of the vena cavae, the blood entering the right atrium is only partially oxygenated. Most of this blood bypasses the pulmonary circulation and enters the left atrium directly from the right atrium by way of the foramen ovale, a shunt that diverts blood away from the right ventricle and pulmonary artery. The remaining blood in the right atrium empties into the right ventricle and is pumped to the lungs via the pulmonary artery. Most of this blood is shunted directly from the pulmonary artery to the aorta via the ductus arteriosus, diverting even more blood away from the fetal lungs.

2) Examine the normal flow of blood to fetal lungs.

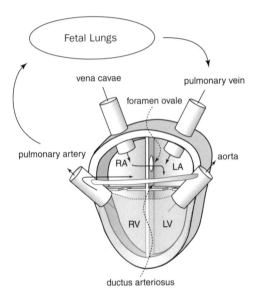

In the fetus, the pulmonary arteries carry oxygenated blood to the lungs, though this blood is by no means saturated with oxygen. The blood that is delivered to the lungs is further deoxygenated there because the blood unloads its oxygen to the fetal lungs, which need it for proper development. Remember, gas exchange does not occur in the fetal lungs—it occurs in the placenta. The deoxygenated blood then returns to the left atrium via pulmonary veins. Despite the fact that this blood mixes with the partially oxygenated blood that crossed over from the right atrium (via the foramen ovale) before being pumped into the systemic circulation by the left ventricle, the blood delivered via the aorta has an even lower partial pressure of oxygen than the blood that was delivered to the lungs. Deoxygenated blood is returned to the placenta via the umbilical arteries.

---

3) Determine which structure is most critical in bypassing fetal lungs.

The ductus arteriosus and foramen ovale shunt blood from the pulmonary arteries to the systemic circulation, bypassing the lungs. Obstruction of either structure would cause an increase in blood supply to the fetal lungs because all of the blood pumped into the pulmonary arteries by the right ventricle would then have to flow through the lungs—there would be no place else for it to go.

Remember: There are three important shunts that divert blood flow in the fetus: the ductus venosus, the foramen ovale, and the ductus arteriosus.

CHAPTER 5

EMBRYOLOGY

Embryology is the study of the development of a unicellular zygote into a complete multicellular organism. In the course of nine months, a unicellular human zygote undergoes cell division, cellular differentiation, and morphogenesis in preparation for life outside the uterus. Much of what is known about mammalian development stems from the study of less complex organisms such as sea urchins and frogs.

EARLY DEVELOPMENTAL STAGES

A. CLEAVAGE

Early embryonic development is characterized by a series of rapid mitotic divisions known as **cleavage.** These divisions lead to an increase in cell number without a corresponding growth in cell protoplasm, i.e., the total volume of cytoplasm remains constant. Thus, cleavage results in progressively smaller cells, with an increasing ratio of nuclear-to-cytoplasmic material. Cleavage also increases the surface-to-volume ratio of each cell, thereby improving gas and nutrient exchange. An **indeterminate cleavage** is one that results in cells that maintain the ability to develop into a complete organism. Identical twins are the result of an indeterminate cleavage (see chapter 4). A **determinate cleavage** results in cells whose future **differentiation** pathways are determined at an early developmental stage. Differentiation is the specialization of cells that occurs during development.

The first complete cleavage of the zygote occurs approximately 32 hours after fertilization. The second cleavage occurs after 60 hours, and the third cleavage after approximately 72 hours, at which point the eight-celled embryo reaches the uterus. As cell division continues, a solid ball of embryonic cells, known as the **morula,** is formed. **Blastulation** begins when the morula develops a fluid-filled cavity called the **blastocoel,** which by the fourth day becomes a hollow sphere of cells called the **blastula.** The mammalian blastula is called a **blastocyst** (see Figure 5.1) and consists of two cell groups: the **inner cell mass,** which protrudes

> **TEACHER TIP**
>
> FUN FACT: Morula is a Latin word meaning *mulberry*, which is what the developing ball of cells looks like at this early point in time.

into the blastocoel, and the **trophoblast,** which surrounds the blastocoel and later gives rise to the chorion.

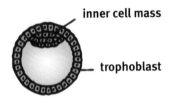

Figure 5.1. Mammalian Blastocyst

B. IMPLANTATION

The embryo implants in the uterine wall during blastulation, approximately five to eight days after fertilization. The uterus is prepared for implantation by the hormone progesterone (see chapter 11), which causes glandular proliferation in the **endometrium**—the mucosal lining of the uterus. The embryonic cells secrete proteolytic enzymes that enable the embryo to digest tissue and implant itself in the endometrium. Eventually, maternal and fetal blood exchange materials at this site, later to be the location of the placenta.

C. GASTRULATION

Once implanted, cell migrations transform the single cell layer of the blastula into a three-layered structure called a **gastrula.** In the sea urchin, gastrulation begins with the appearance of a small invagination on the surface of the blastula. An inpocketing forms as cells continue to move toward the invagination, eventually eliminating the blastocoel. The result is a two-layered cup, with a differentiation between an outer cellular layer—the **ectoderm,** and an inner cellular layer—the **endoderm.** The newly formed cavity of the two-layered gastrula is called the **archenteron,** and later develops into the gut. The opening of the archenteron is called the **blastopore.** (In organisms classified as **deuterostomes,** such as humans, the blastopore is the site of the future anus, whereas in organisms classified as **protostomes,** the blastopore is the site of the future mouth.) Proliferation and migration of cells into the space between the ectoderm and the endoderm gives rise to a third cell layer, called the **mesoderm.** These three **primary germ layers** are responsible for the differential development of the tissues, organs, and systems of the body at later stages of growth.

- **Ectoderm**—integument (including the epidermis, hair, nails, and epithelium of the nose, mouth, and anal canal), the lens of the eye, and the nervous system.

- **Endoderm**—epithelial linings of the digestive and respiratory tracts (including the lungs), and parts of the liver, pancreas, thyroid, and bladder.

- **Mesoderm**—musculoskeletal system, circulatory system, excretory system, gonads, connective tissue throughout the body, and portions of digestive and respiratory organs.

> **TEACHER TIP**
>
> KEY POINT: The MCAT commonly tests the adrenal glands in the context of germ layers. The adrenal cortex is derived from the mesoderm, *but* the adrenal medulla is derived from the ectoderm because it contains some nervous tissue.

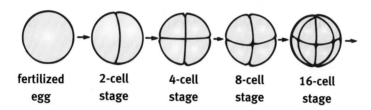

fertilized egg → 2-cell stage → 4-cell stage → 8-cell stage → 16-cell stage →

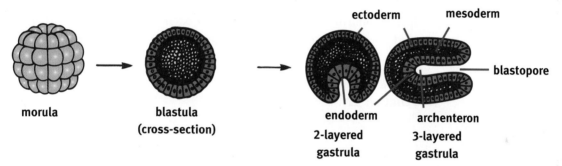

morula → blastula (cross-section) → endoderm / ectoderm / 2-layered gastrula → archenteron / mesoderm / blastopore / 3-layered gastrula

Figure 5.2. Amphibian Cleavage and Gastrulation

Despite the fact that all embryonic cells are derived from a single zygote and therefore have the same DNA, cells and tissues differentiate to perform unique and specialized functions. Most of this differentiation is accomplished through selective transcription of the genome. As the embryo develops, different tissue types express different genes. Most of the genetic information within any given cell is never expressed.

Induction is the influence of a specific group of cells (sometimes known as the **organizer**) on the differentiation of another group of cells. Induction is most often mediated by chemical substances (**inducers**) passed from the organizer to adjacent cells. In development of the eyes, lateral outpocketings from the brain (optic vesicles) grow out and touch the overlying ectoderm. The optic vesicle induces the ectoderm to thicken and form the lens placode. The lens placode then induces the optic vesicle to flatten and invaginate inward, forming the optic cup. The optic cup then induces the lens placode to invaginate and form the cornea and lens. Experiments with frog embryos show that if this ectoderm is transplanted to the trunk (after the optic vesicles have grown out), a lens will develop in the trunk. If, however, the ectoderm is transplanted before the outgrowth of the optic vesicles, it will not form a lens.

D. NEURULATION

By the end of gastrulation, regions of the germ layers begin to develop into a rudimentary nervous system; this process is known as **neurulation.** A rod of mesodermal cells, called the **notochord,** develops along the long-itudinal axis just under the dorsal layer of ectoderm. The notochord has an inductive effect on the overlying ectoderm, causing it to bend inward and form a groove along the dorsal surface of the embryo. The dorsal ectoderm folds on either side of the groove; these **neural folds** grow upward and finally fuse, forming a closed tube. This is the **neural tube,** which gives rise to the brain and spinal cord **(central nervous system).** Once the neural tube is formed, it detaches from the surface ectoderm. The cells at the tip of each neural fold are called the **neural crest** cells. These cells migrate laterally and give rise to many components of the **peripheral nervous system,** including the sensory ganglia, autonomic ganglia, adrenal medulla, and Schwann cells (see chapter 12).

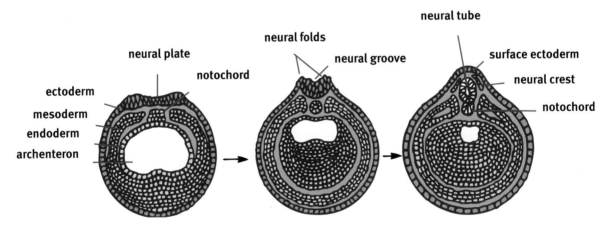

Figure 5.3. Neurulation

FETAL RESPIRATION

The growing **fetus** (the embryo is referred to as a fetus after eight weeks of **gestation**) receives oxygen directly from its mother through a specialized circulatory system. This system not only supplies oxygen and nutrients to the fetus, but removes carbon dioxide and metabolic wastes as well. The two components of this system are the **placenta** and the **umbilical cord,** which both develop in the first few weeks following fertilization.

The placenta and the umbilical cord are outgrowths of the four extra-embryonic membranes formed during development: the **amnion, chorion, allantois,** and **yolk sac.** The amnion is a thin, tough membrane containing a watery fluid called **amniotic fluid.** Amniotic fluid acts as a shock absorber of external and localized pressure from uterine contractions during **labor.** Placenta formation begins with the chorion, a membrane that completely surrounds the amnion. About two weeks after fertilization the chorion extends villi into the uterine wall. These **chorionic villi** become closely associated with endometrial cells, developing into the spongy tissue of the placenta. A third membrane, the allantois, develops as an outpocketing of the gut. The blood vessels of the allantoic wall enlarge and become the **umbilical vessels,** which will connect the fetus to the developing placenta. The yolk sac, the site of early development of blood vessels, becomes associated with the umbilical vessels. At some point the allantois and yolk sac are enveloped by the amnion, forming the primitive **umbilical cord,** which is the initial connection between the fetus and the placenta. The mature umbilical cord consists of the umbilical vessels, which developed from the allantoic vessels, surrounded by a jellylike matrix. As the embryo grows, it remains attached to the placenta by the umbilical cord, which permits it to float freely in the amniotic fluid.

The placenta is the site of nutrition, respiration, and waste disposal for the fetus. Water, glucose, amino acids, vitamins, and inorganic salts diffuse across maternal capillaries into fetal blood. **Fetal hemoglobin (Hb-F)** has a greater affinity for oxygen than does adult hemoglobin **(Hb-A)**; consequently, oxygen preferentially diffuses into fetal blood. Concurrently, metabolic wastes and carbon dioxide diffuse in the opposite direction—from fetal blood into maternal blood. Note that the circulatory systems of the mother and the fetus are not directly connected, so maternal and fetal blood do not mix. As can be seen in Figure 5.5, all exchange of material between maternal and fetal blood vessels occurs in the placenta via diffusion.

TEACHER TIP

KEY POINT: Though the fetus gets its nutrients and oxygen from the mother, there is no actual mixing of the blood supplies. Instead, the placenta allows for the close proximity of the fetal and maternal blood stream so that diffusion can occur.

TEACHER TIP

The fetal blood supply is opposite in terms of oxygenation. The umbilical artery carries DEOXYGENATED blood and the umbilical vein carries OXYGENATED blood.

MCAT SYNOPSIS

Remember, gas exchange in the fetus occurs across the placenta. Fetal lungs do not become functional until birth.

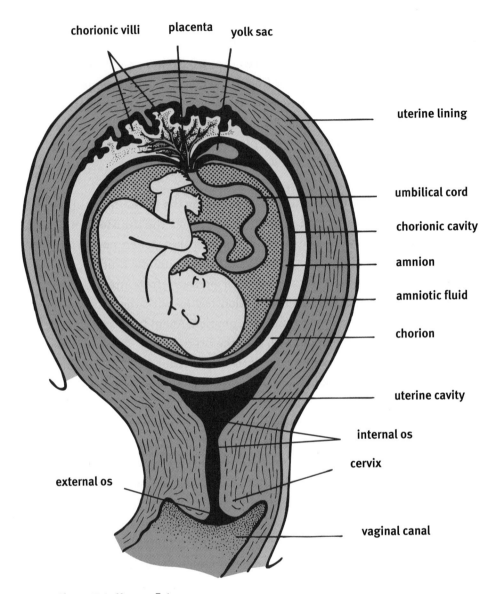

chorionic villi   placenta   yolk sac

uterine lining

umbilical cord

chorionic cavity

amnion

amniotic fluid

chorion

uterine cavity

internal os

cervix

external os

vaginal canal

Figure 5.4. Human Fetus

In addition to nutritive and respiratory functions, the placenta offers the fetus some immunological protection by preventing the diffusion of foreign matter (e.g., bacteria) into fetal blood. However, the placenta is permeable to viruses, alcohol, and many drugs and toxins, all of which can adversely affect fetal development. The placenta also functions as an endocrine gland, producing the hormones progesterone, estrogen, and human chorionic gonadotropin (HCG)—all of which are essential for maintaining a pregnancy (see chapter 11). The presence of HCG in urine is the simplest test for pregnancy.

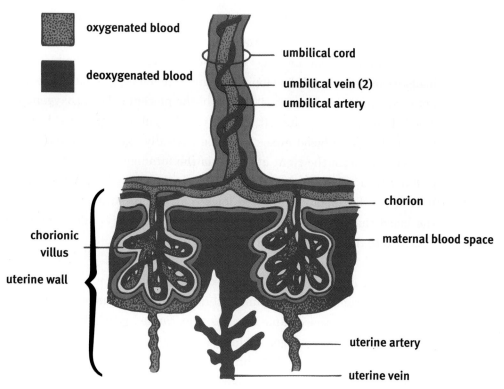

oxygenated blood

deoxygenated blood

umbilical cord

umbilical vein (2)

umbilical artery

chorion

chorionic villus

maternal blood space

uterine wall

uterine artery

uterine vein

Figure 5.5. Placenta

FETAL CIRCULATION

Fetal circulation differs from adult circulation in several important ways. The major difference is that in fetal circulation, blood is oxygenated in the placenta (because fetal lungs are nonfunctional prior to birth), while in adult circulation, blood is oxygenated in the lungs. In addition, the fetal circulatory route contains three shunts that divert blood flow away from the developing fetal liver and lungs. The **umbilical vein** carries oxygenated blood from the placenta to the fetus. The blood bypasses the fetal liver by way of a shunt called the **ductus venosus,** before converging with the inferior vena cava. The inferior and superior venae cavae return deoxygenated blood to the right atrium. Because the oxygenated blood from the umbilical vein mixes with the deoxygenated blood of the venae cavae, the blood entering the right atrium is only partially oxygenated. Most of this blood bypasses the pulmonary circulation and enters the left atrium directly from the right atrium by way of the **foramen ovale,** a shunt that diverts blood away from the pulmonary arteries. The remaining blood in the right atrium empties into the right ventricle and is pumped into the pulmonary artery. Most of this blood is shunted directly from the pulmonary artery to the aorta via the **ductus arteriosus,** diverting

MCAT SYNOPSIS

A small amount of blood must reach the pulmonary circulation in order to nourish the developing fetal lungs.

TEACHER TIP

These three bypasses are all closed in the adult. If they remain patent (open), they can lead to severe hemodynamic problems.

even more blood away from the lungs. This means that in the fetus, the pulmonary arteries carry partially oxygenated blood to the lungs. The blood that does reach the lungs is further deoxygenated as the blood unloads its oxygen to the developing lungs. Remember, gas exchange does not occur in the fetal lungs—it occurs in the placenta. The deoxygenated blood then returns to the left atrium via the pulmonary veins. Despite the fact that this blood mixes with the partially oxygenated blood that crossed over from the right atrium (via the foramen ovale) before being pumped into the systemic circulation by the left ventricle, the blood delivered via the aorta has an even lower partial pressure of oxygen than the blood that was delivered to the lungs. This deoxygenated blood is returned to the placenta via the **umbilical arteries.**

In contrast, in adult circulation, deoxygenated blood enters the right atrium, the right ventricle pumps this blood to the lungs via the pulmonary arteries (those same arteries that carried partially oxygenated blood in the fetus), and gas exchange occurs in the lungs. Oxygenated blood is returned to the left atrium via the pulmonary veins (those same veins that carried deoxygenated blood in the fetus), and the left ventricle pumps the blood into circulation via the aorta. (For a more complete discussion of adult circulation, see chapter 9.)

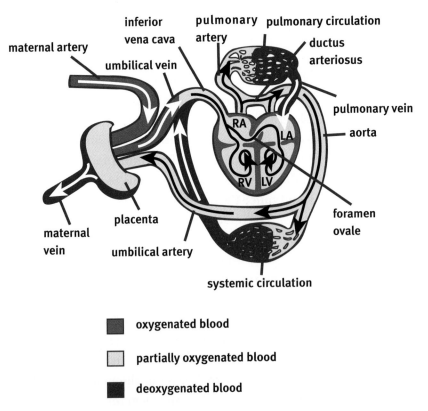

Figure 5.6. Fetal Circulation

After birth, a number of changes occur in the circulatory system as the fetus adjusts to breathing on its own. The lungs expand with air and rhythmic breathing begins. Resistance in the pulmonary blood vessels decreases, causing an increase in blood flow through the lungs. When umbilical blood flow stops, blood pressure in the inferior vena cava decreases, causing a decrease in pressure in the right atrium. In contrast, left atrial pressure increases due to increased blood flow from the lungs. Increased left atrial pressure coupled with decreased right atrial pressure causes the foramen ovale to close. In addition, the ductus arteriosus constricts and later closes permanently. The ductus venosus degenerates over a period of time, completely closing in most infants three months after birth. The infant begins to produce adult hemoglobin, and by the end of the first year of life little fetal hemoglobin can be detected in the blood.

GESTATION

Human pregnancy, or gestation, is approximately nine months (266 days), and can be subdivided into three **trimesters.** The primary developments that occur during each trimester are described below.

A. FIRST TRIMESTER

During the first weeks, the major organs begin to develop. The heart begins to beat at approximately 22 days, and soon afterward, the eyes, gonads, limbs, and liver start to form. By five weeks the embryo is 10 mm in length; by six weeks the embryo has grown to 15 mm. The cartilaginous skeleton begins to turn into bone by the seventh week (see chapter 6). By the end of eight weeks, most of the organs have formed, the brain is fairly developed, and the embryo is referred to as a fetus. At the end of the third month, the fetus is about 9 cm long.

B. SECOND TRIMESTER

During the second trimester, the fetus does a tremendous amount of growing. It begins to move around in the amniotic fluid, its face appears human, and its toes and fingers elongate. By the end of the sixth month, the fetus is 30–36 cm long.

C. THIRD TRIMESTER

The seventh and eighth months are characterized by continued rapid growth and further brain development. During the ninth month, antibodies are transported by highly selective active transport from the mother to the fetus for protection against foreign matter. The growth rate slows and the fetus becomes less active, as it has less room to move about.

TEACHER TIP

Understanding why blood flows from the right atrium to the left in the fetus may seem more like a physics concept—and it is. But it is commonly tested in the Biology section as well. This is a common MCAT trend—topics which are applicable to both the Physics section and the Biology section.

TEACHER TIP

Advances in medicine have allowed babies to be born as early as 24 weeks, which is far short of a normal 39. Though these children may live, there are often severe consequences given that fetal development isn't complete at 24 weeks. These problems are most apparent in the respiratory system where the amount of surfactant is insufficient.

BIRTH

Childbirth is accomplished by labor, a series of strong uterine contractions. Labor can be divided into three distinct stages. In the first stage, the cervix thins out and dilates, and the amniotic sac ruptures, releasing its fluids. During this time contractions are relatively mild. The second stage is characterized by rapid contractions, resulting in the birth of the baby, followed by the cutting of the umbilical cord. During the final stage, the uterus contracts, expelling the placenta and the umbilical cord.

PRACTICE QUESTIONS

1. During meiosis, haploid cells are created from diploid parent cells. The process occurs only in sexual reproduction, and it involves two complete division cycles. At what stage of mitotic division do the recently condensed chromosomes align in the equatorial region of the cell, in preparation for separation?

   A. Anaphase
   B. Telophase
   C. Metaphase
   D. Prophase

2. At what stage does dormancy occur in primary oocytes?

   A. Metaphase I
   B. Prophase II
   C. Metaphase II
   D. Prophase I

3. What is the origin of mitochondrial DNA?

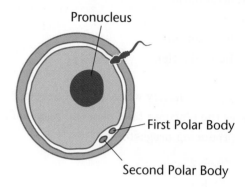

   A. Equal paternal and maternal DNA
   B. Random combination of paternal and maternal DNA
   C. Paternal only
   D. Maternal only

4. Gonadotropin-releasing hormone (GnRH) is synthesized by hypothalamic neurosecretory cells, which in turn stimulates the release of two ovarian stimulating hormones, follicle-stimulating hormone (FSH) and lutenizing hormone (LH). FSH and LH are produced by which of the following?

   A. Ovaries
   B. Adrenal gland
   C. Anterior pituitary
   D. Posterior pituitary

5. Which of the following cells is capable of prolonged dormancy?

   A. First polar body
   B. Primary oocyte
   C. Second polar body
   D. Secondary oocyte

6. The process by which one of the two copies of X-chromosomes in mammalian females becomes inactivated is called

A. attenuation.
B. attrition.
C. lyonization.
D. hybridization.

7. At approximately what week of development does the placenta take over the responsibility of producing progesterone?

A. Week 2
B. Week 4
C. Week 6
D. Week 8

8. You are scheduled to assist in a delivery today and the chief resident wants to find out if you understand the different types of twins. You mention dizygotic and you're asked to clarify what that means. You say that dizygotic twins are

A. the fertilization of one secondary oocyte by one sperm.
B. twins genetically identical.
C. one blastocyst that split.
D. twins not genetically identical.

9. Which pharyngeal arch exists only transiently during embryonic development?

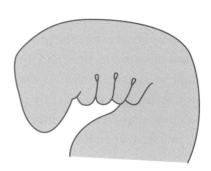

A. III
B. IV
C. V
D. VI

10. The three germ layers will give rise to all the tissues and organs of the body. The mesoderm layer will eventually develop which of the following?

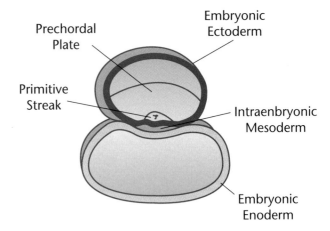

A. Central nervous system
B. Pituitary gland
C. Heart
D. Thyroid and parathyroid glands

11. In fetal circulation, through which shunt does the majority of oxygenated-enriched blood reach the systemic circulation?

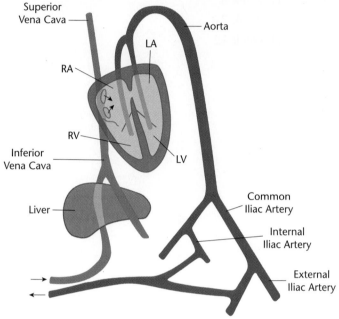

A. Ductus arteriosus
B. Ductus venosus
C. Foramen ovale
D. Umbilical arteries

12. One of the first signs of gastrulation is the formation of the

A. notochord.
B. tertiary chorionic villi.
C. primitive streak.
D. neural tube.

13. Somites are derived from which intraembryonic mesoderm layer?

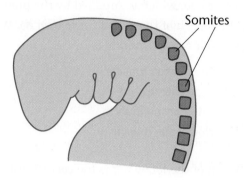

A. Paraxial mesoderm
B. Lateral mesoderm
C. Intraembryonic somatic mesoderm
D. Intraembryonic visceral mesoderm

14. Intraembryonic coelom divides the lateral mesoderm into two distinctive layers, the intraembryonic somatic mesoderm and intra embryonic visceral mesoderm. By the fourth week of development, the intraembryonic coelom becomes the

A. kidneys and gonads.
B. body cavities.
C. cartilage and bone.
D. nucleus pulposus.

15. During embryological development, which organ system is the first to reach a functional state?

A. Nervous system
B. Cardiovascular system
C. Respiratory system
D. Skeletal system

16. All the extrinsic muscles of the tongue are supplied by the hypoglossal nerve (CN XII) except one, which is supplied by the pharyngeal branch of the vagus nerve (CN X). Which extrinsic tongue muscle is it?

A. Genioglossus muscle
B. Hyoglossus muscle
C. Palatoglossus muscle
D. Styloglossus muscle

17. Which of the following is the correct order of hematopoiesis by embryonic organs?

A. Liver, thymus, spleen, bone marrow
B. Liver, spleen, thymus, bone marrow
C. Thymus, liver, spleen, bone marrow
D. Thymus, spleen, liver, bone marrow

18. By what week of development can phenotypic sexual differentiation first be recognized?

A. Week 1
B. Week 6
C. Week 7
D. Week 12

CHAPTER 6

MUSCULOSKELETAL SYSTEM

The musculoskeletal system forms the basic internal framework of the vertebrate body. Muscles and bones work in close coordination to produce voluntary movement. In addition, bone and muscle perform a number of other independent functions.

SKELETAL SYSTEM

The skeleton functions primarily as the physical support of an organism. In contrast to the external skeleton (**exoskeleton**) of arthropods, vertebrates have an internal skeleton, or **endoskeleton.** The mammalian skeleton is divided into the **axial** and **appendicular** skeletons. The axial skeleton is the basic framework of the body, consisting of the skull, the vertebral column, and the rib cage. The appendicular skeleton consists of the limb bones and the pelvic and pectoral girdles. In addition to providing the lever upon which skeletal muscles act during locomotion, the skeleton surrounds and protects delicate organs such as the brain and the spinal cord. Furthermore, skeletal bone marrow houses much of the body's blood-forming elements.

The two major components of the skeleton are **cartilage** and **bone.**

TEACHER TIP

FUN FACT: An adult human has 206 bones. Over 100 of these are in the feet and hands.

CARTILAGE

Cartilage is a type of connective tissue that is softer and more flexible than bone. It is made of a firm but elastic matrix called **chondrin,** which is secreted by specialized cells called **chondrocytes.** Cartilage is the principal component of embryonic skeletons in higher animals. During mammalian development, however, much of it hardens and calcifies into bone. Cartilage is retained in adults in places where firmness and flexibility are needed. For example, in humans, the external ear, the nose, the walls of the larynx and trachea, and the skeletal joints contain cartilage. Most cartilage is avascular (i.e., contains no blood or lymph vessels) and is devoid of nerves; it receives nourishment from capillaries located in nearby connective tissue and bone via diffusion through the surrounding fluid.

TEACHER TIP

Cartilage continues to grow throughout life. This is why the noses and ears of many older individuals seem larger than the other features on the face.

BONE

Bone is a specialized type of mineralized connective tissue that has the ability to withstand physical stress. Ideally designed for body support, bone tissue is hard and strong, while at the same time, somewhat elastic and lightweight.

A. MACROSCOPIC BONE STRUCTURE

There are two basic types of bone: **compact bone** and **spongy bone.** Compact bone is dense bone that does not appear to have any cavities when observed with the naked eye. Spongy bone, also called **cancellous bone,** is much less dense, and consists of an interconnecting lattice of bony spicules (trabeculae); the cavities in between the spicules are filled with **yellow** and/or **red bone marrow.** Yellow marrow is inactive and infiltrated by adipose tissue; red marrow is involved in blood cell formation (see chapter 9).

The bones of the appendages, the **long bones,** are characterized by a cylindrical shaft called a **diaphysis** and dilated ends called **epiphyses.** The diaphysis is primarily compact bone surrounding a cavity containing bone marrow. The epiphyses are spongy bone surrounded by a thin layer of compact bone. The **epiphyseal plate** is a disk of cartilaginous cells separating the diaphysis from the epiphysis and is the site of longitudinal growth. A fibrous sheath called the **periosteum** surrounds the long bone and is the site of attachment to muscle tissue. Some periosteum cells differentiate into bone-forming cells.

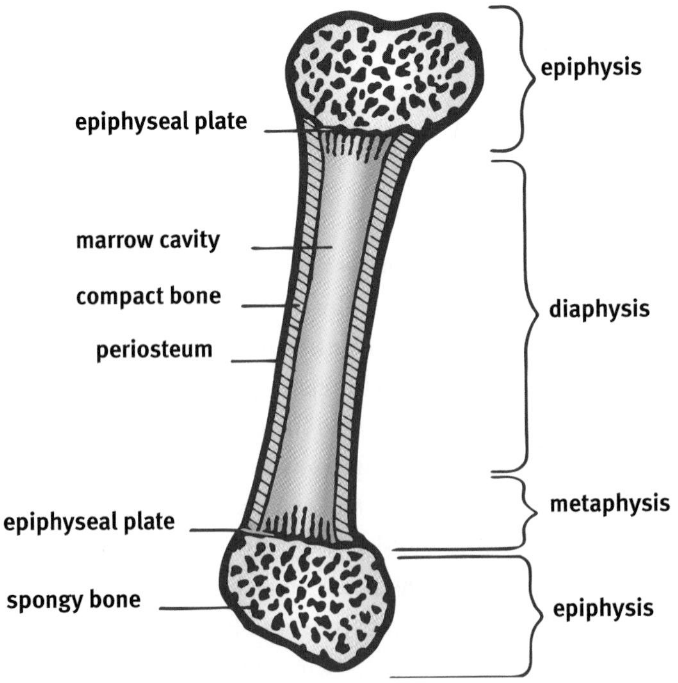

TEACHER TIP

The epiphyseal plates seal as a result of the effects of sex hormones (testosterone in males and estrogen in females). Thus, growth continues through puberty until around the age of 25, when the process is complete, Most of the growth, however, is done between the onset of puberty and the age of 18.

Figure 6.1. Long Bone

B. MICROSCOPIC BONE STRUCTURE

Compact bone is a dense, hardened **bone matrix,** which contains both organic and inorganic components. The organic components include proteins (principally collagen fibers and glycoproteins), while the inorganic components include calcium, phosphate, and hydroxide (which combine and harden to form **hydroxyapatite crystals**), as well as sodium, potassium, and magnesium ions. The association of hydroxyapatite crystals with collagen fibers gives bone its characteristic strength.

The bony matrix is deposited in structural units called **osteons (Haversian systems).** Each osteon consists of a central microscopic channel called a **Haversian canal,** surrounded by a number of concentric circles of bony matrix called **lamellae.** There are blood vessels, nerve fibers, and lymph in the Haversian canals, vascularizing and innervating bone tissue. Interspersed within the matrix are spaces called **lacunae,** which house mature bone cells called **osteocytes.** Osteocytes are involved in bone maintenance. Radiating from each lacuna are a number of minute canals called **canaliculi.** The canaliculi interconnect with each other and with the Haversian canals, allowing for exchange of nutrients and wastes (see Figure 6.2).

> **MCAT SYNOPSIS**
>
> Don't forget that bone is much more dynamic than you might think. Bone is both vascular and innervated. The bone's blood supply can become infected after an injury (a disease known as osteomyelitis) and if you break a bone, it will hurt (a lot). In addition, remember that bone is in a dynamic equilibrium between being broken down (by osteoCLASTS) and being built up (by osteoBLASTS.) This is known as bone remodeling.

> **TEACHER TIP**
>
> We know from our MCAT synopsis that bone growth is dynamic. The benefit of this is it allows for remodeling as different stresses in the environment impinge on the body.

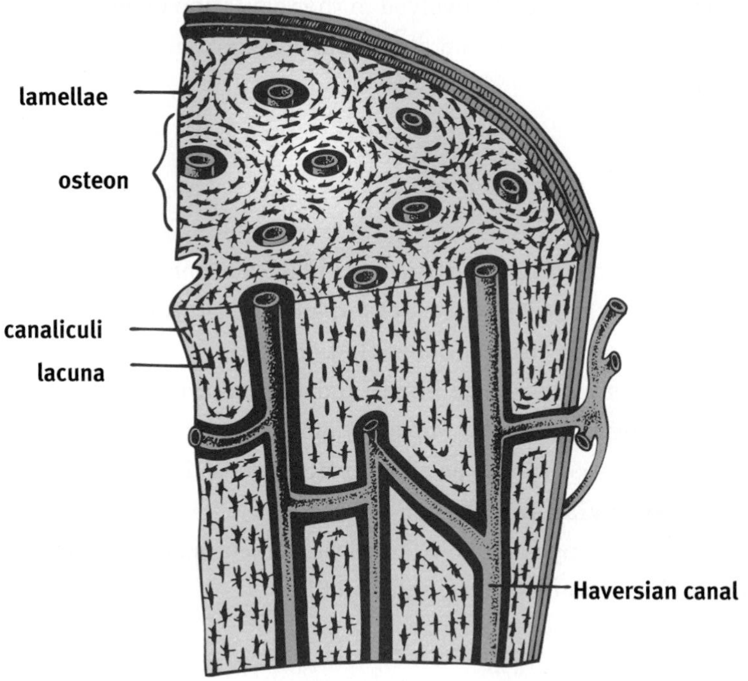

Figure 6.2. Microscopic Bone Structure

Two other types of cells found in bone tissue are **osteoblasts** and **osteoclasts.** Osteoblasts synthesize and secrete the organic constituents of the bone matrix; once they have become surrounded by their matrix, they mature into osteocytes. Osteoclasts are large, multinucleated cells involved in **bone resorption.**

C. BONE FORMATION (OSSIFICATION)

Bone formation occurs by either **endochondral ossification** or by **intramembranous ossification.** In endochondral ossification, existing cartilage is replaced by bone. Long bones arise primarily through endochondral ossification. In intramembranous ossification, **mesenchymal** (embryonic, undifferentiated) connective tissue is transformed into, and replaced by, bone.

D. BONE REMODELING

Bone matrix is dynamic; i.e., it is continuously and simultaneously degraded and reformed. During **bone reformation,** inorganic ions (e.g., calcium and phosphate) are absorbed from the blood for use in bone formation; in the process of **bone resorption** (degradation), these ions are released into the blood. These two processes are collectively known as **bone remodeling.** Vitamin D and hormones such as parathyroid hormone and calcitonin are all involved in the regulation of bone remodeling (see chapter 11). Bone use and stress during exercise are also factors in bone remodeling.

JOINTS

Joints are connective tissue structures that join bones together. Bones that do not move relative to each other, such as skull bones, are held in place by **immovable joints.** Bones that do move relative to one another are held together by **movable joints** and are additionally supported and strengthened by **ligaments.** Movable joints consist of a **synovial capsule,** which encloses a **joint cavity (articular cavity).** Movement is facilitated by **synovial fluid,** which lubricates the joint, and by **articular cartilage** on the opposing bone surfaces, which is smooth and reduces tension during movement (see Figure 6.3).

CLINICAL CORRELATE

Osteoporosis is the most common bone disease in the United States. Affecting primarily post-menopausal women, osteoporosis causes hundreds of thousands of hip fractures annually. Osteoporosis is caused by loss of bone mass; it is thought to be the result of increased osteoclast resorption and some concomitant slowing of bone formation. It is believed that estrogen helps prevent osteoporosis by inhibiting osteoclast activity.

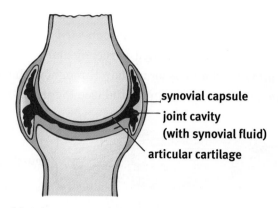

synovial capsule
joint cavity
(with synovial fluid)
articular cartilage

Figure 6.3. Movable Joint

MUSCULAR SYSTEM

Muscle tissue consists of bundles of specialized contractile fibers held together by connective tissue. There are three morphologically and functionally distinct types of muscle in mammals: **skeletal muscle, smooth muscle,** and **cardiac muscle.**

Table 6.1. Skeletal Muscle

Smooth Muscle	Cardiac Muscle	Skeletal Muscle
• Nonstriated	• Striated	• Striated
• 1 nucleus per cell	• 1–2 nuclei per cell	• Multinucleated cells
• Involuntary/Autonomic nervous system	• Involuntary/Autonomic nervous system	• Voluntary/Somatic nervous system
• Smooth continuous contractions	• Strong forceful contractions	• Strong forceful contractions

SKELETAL MUSCLE

Skeletal muscle is responsible for voluntary movements and is innervated by the **somatic nervous system** (see chapter 12). A muscle is a bundle of parallel fibers. Each fiber is a multinucleated cell created by the fusion of several mononucleate embryonic cells. The nuclei are usually found at the periphery of the cell. Embedded in the fibers are filaments called **myofibrils,** which are further divided into contractile units called **sarcomeres.** The myofibrils are enveloped by a modified endoplasmic reticulum that stores calcium ions and is called the **sarcoplasmic reticulum.** The cytoplasm of a muscle fiber is called **sarcoplasm,** and the cell membrane is called the **sarcolemma.** The sarcolemma is capable of propagating an action potential (see chapter 12), and is connected to a system of **transverse tubules (T system)** oriented perpendicularly to the myofibrils. The T system provides channels for ion flow throughout the muscle fibers, and can also propagate an action potential (see Figure 6.4).

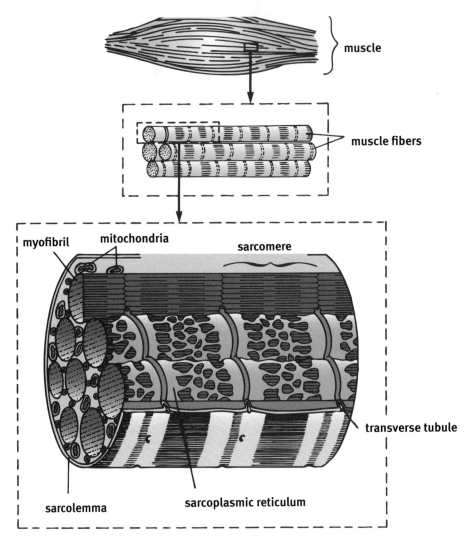

Figure 6.4. Skeletal Muscle

TEACHER TIP

The MCAT requires you to be able to apply what you have learned. Think about what types of muscles would be red versus white. When would you want to be able to use fast or slow twitch fibers?

Skeletal muscle has striations of light and dark bands, and is therefore also referred to as **striated** muscle. Skeletal muscle fibers can be characterized as either red or white. **Red fibers** (slow-twitch fibers) have a high **myoglobin** content (a protein resembling hemoglobin) and many mitochondria. They derive their energy primarily from aerobic respiration and are capable of sustained and vigorous activity. **White fibers** (fast-twitch fibers) are anaerobic and therefore contain less myoglobin and fewer mitochondria than red fibers. White fibers have a greater rate of contraction than red fibers; however, white fibers fatigue more easily.

THE SARCOMERE

A. STRUCTURE

The sarcomere is composed of **thin** and **thick filaments.** The thin filaments are chains of globular **actin** molecules associated with two other proteins, **troponin** and **tropomyosin.** The thick filaments are composed of organized bundles of **myosin** molecules; each myosin molecule has a head region and a tail region.

Electron microscopy reveals that the sarcomere is organized as follows: **Z lines** define the boundaries of a single sarcomere and anchor the thin filaments. The **M line** runs down the center of the sarcomere. The **I band** is the region containing thin filaments only. The **H zone** is the region containing thick filaments only. The **A band** spans the entire length of the thick filaments and any overlapping portions of the thin filaments. Note that during contraction, the A band is not reduced in size, while the H zone and I band are.

> **MCAT SYNOPSIS**
>
> H-Band = Myosin only
> I-Band = Actin only
> A-Band = Entire myosin fiber

> **TEACHER TIP**
>
> Z lines, I band, and H zone all get smaller or closer together during contraction because they are defined relative to one another. The A band remains constant because it is defined as the total length of the thick fibers, regardless of state of contraction.

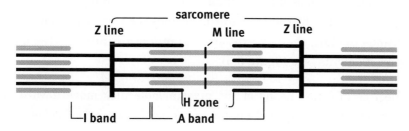

Figure 6.5. Sarcomere

B. CONTRACTION

1. Initiation

Muscle contraction is stimulated by a message from the somatic nervous system sent via a **motor neuron.** The link between the **nerve terminal (synaptic bouton)** and the sarcolemma of the muscle fiber is called the **neuromuscular junction.** The space between the two is known as the **synapse,** or **synaptic cleft.** Depolarization of the motor neuron results in the release of **neurotransmitters** (e.g., acetylcholine) from the nerve terminal. The neurotransmitter diffuses across the synaptic cleft and binds to special receptor sites on the sarcolemma. If enough of these receptors are stimulated, the permeability of the sarcolemma is altered and an **action potential** is generated (see chapter 12). The action

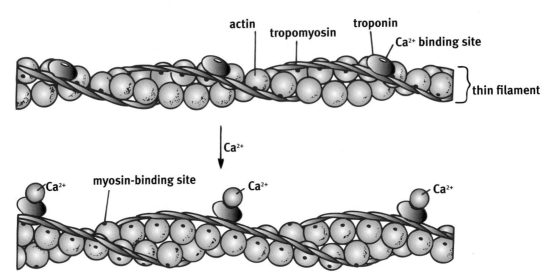

Figure 6.6. Thin Filament

potential then quickly spreads through the transverse tubules to sequentially contract the entire muscle with spontaneous synchronization.

2. Shortening of the Sarcomere

Once an action potential is generated, it is conducted along the sarcolemma and the T system, and into the interior of the muscle fiber. This causes the sarcoplasmic reticulum to release Ca^{2+} into the sarcoplasm. The Ca^{2+} binds to the troponin molecules, causing the tropomyosin strands to shift, thereby exposing the **myosin-binding sites** on the actin filaments (see Figure 6.6).

The free globular heads of the myosin molecules move toward and then bind to the exposed binding sites on the actin molecules, forming actin-myosin cross-bridges. In creating these cross-bridges, the myosin pulls on the actin molecules, drawing the thin filaments toward the center of the H zone and shortening the sarcomere (see Figure 6.7). ATPase activity in the myosin head provides the energy for the powerstroke that results in the dissociation of the myosin head from the actin. (An ATPase is an enzyme that hydrolyzes ATP.) The myosin returns to its original position and is now free to bind to another actin molecule and repeat the process, thus further pulling the thin filaments towards the center of the H zone.

3. Relaxation

When the sarcolemmic receptors are no longer stimulated, the Ca^{2+} is pumped back into the sarcoplasmic reticulum. The products of ATP hydrolysis are released from the myosin head, a new ATP binds to the

MCAT FAVORITE

When the muscle contracts—the H and I bands are eliminated.

MCAT SYNOPSIS

Think of tropomyosin as the chaperone responsible for protecting actin's binding sites from the advances of the myosin head. In the presence of Ca^{2+}, troponin changes its conformation and moves tropomyosin away from its guard position, thereby allowing myosin to bind to actin and the action to begin.

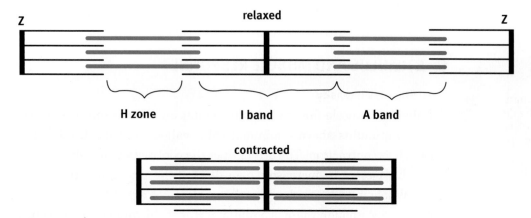

Z relaxed Z

H zone | I band | A band

contracted

Figure 6.7. Contraction

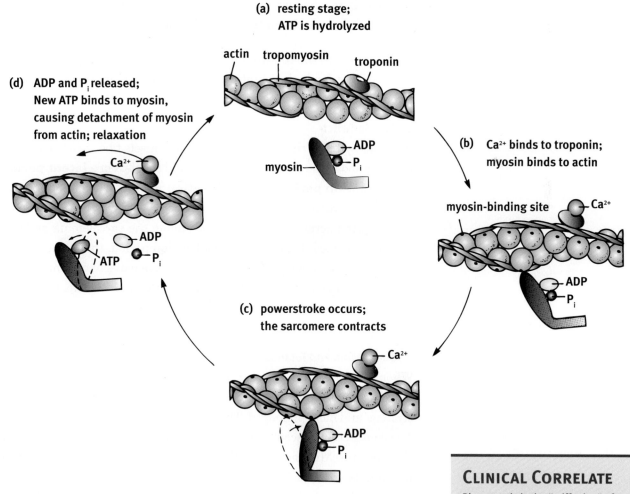

(a) resting stage;
ATP is hydrolyzed

actin tropomyosin troponin

(d) ADP and P$_i$ released;
New ATP binds to myosin,
causing detachment of myosin
from actin; relaxation

myosin

Ca^{2+}

ADP
P$_i$

(b) Ca^{2+} binds to troponin;
myosin binds to actin

ADP
ATP
P$_i$

myosin-binding site Ca^{2+}

ADP
P$_i$

(c) powerstroke occurs;
the sarcomere contracts

Ca^{2+}

ADP
P$_i$

Figure 6.8. ATPase Activity

CLINICAL CORRELATE

Rigor mortis is the "stiffening" of muscles after death. This results from the lack of ATP to relax the muscle.

head, resulting in the dissociation of the myosin from the thin filament, and the sarcomere returns to its original width.

C. STIMULUS AND MUSCLE RESPONSE

1. Stimulus Intensity

Individual muscle fibers generally exhibit an **all-or-none response**; only a stimulus above a minimal value called the **threshold value** can elicit contraction. The strength of the contraction of a single muscle fiber cannot be increased, regardless of the strength of the stimulus. Whole muscle, on the other hand, does not exhibit an all-or-none response. Although there is a minimal threshold value needed to elicit a muscle contraction, the strength of the contraction can increase as stimulus strength is increased by involving more fibers. A maximal response is reached when all of the fibers have reached the threshold value and the muscle contracts as a whole.

Tonus refers to the continual low-grade contractions of muscle, which are essential for both voluntary and involuntary muscle contraction. Even at rest, muscles are in a continuous state of tonus.

2. Simple Twitch

A simple twitch is the response of a single muscle fiber to a brief stimulus at or above the threshold stimulus and consists of a **latent period,** a **contraction period,** and a **relaxation period.** The latent period is the time between stimulation and the onset of contraction. During this time lag, the action potential spreads along the sarcolemma and Ca^{2+} ions are released. Following the contraction period, there is a brief relaxation period in which the muscle is unresponsive to a stimulus; this period is known as the **absolute refractory period.** This is followed by a **relative refractory period,** during which a greater-than-normal stimulus is needed to elicit a contraction (see Figure 6.9).

3. Summation and Tetanus

When the fibers of a muscle are exposed to very frequent stimuli, the muscle cannot fully relax. The contractions begin to combine, becoming stronger and more prolonged. This is known as **frequency summation.** The contractions become continuous when the stimuli are so frequent that the muscle cannot relax. This type of contraction is known as **tetanus** and is stronger than a simple twitch of a single fiber. If tetanization is prolonged, the muscle will begin to fatigue (see Figure 6.9).

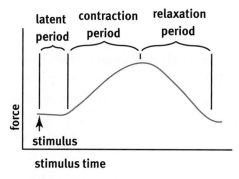

simple twitch (single fiber)

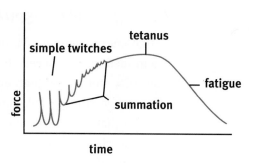

summation and tetanus (whole muscle)

Figure 6.9. Simple Twitch and Summation/Tetanus

SMOOTH MUSCLE

Smooth muscle is responsible for involuntary actions and is innervated by the **autonomic nervous system** (see chapter 12). Smooth muscle is found in the digestive tract, bladder, uterus, and blood vessel walls, among other places. Smooth muscle cells possess one centrally located nucleus. While smooth muscle cells also contain actin and myosin filaments, these filaments lack the organization of skeletal sarcomeres; consequently, smooth muscles lack the striations of skeletal muscle.

As in skeletal muscle, smooth muscle contractions result from the sliding of actin and myosin over one another and are regulated by an influx of calcium ions. However, smooth muscle contractions are slower and are capable of being sustained longer than skeletal muscle contractions. Smooth muscle typically has both inhibitory and excitatory synapses that regulate contraction via the nervous system. Smooth muscle also has the property of reflexively contracting without nervous stimulation; this is called **myogenic** activity.

CARDIAC MUSCLE

The muscle tissue of the heart is composed of cardiac muscle fibers. These fibers possess characteristics of both skeletal and smooth muscle fibers. As in skeletal muscle, actin and myosin filaments are arranged in sarcomeres, giving cardiac muscle a striated appearance. However, cardiac muscle cells generally have only one or two centrally located nuclei. Cardiac muscle is innervated by the autonomic nervous system, which serves only to modulate its inherent beat, because cardiac muscle, like smooth muscle, is myogenic (see chapter 9).

MCAT SYNOPSIS

Skeletal Muscle
- Striated
- Voluntary
- Somatic innervation
- Many nuclei per cell
- Ca^{2+} required for contraction

Cardiac Muscle
- Striated
- Involuntary
- Autonomic innervation
- One to two nuclei per cell
- Ca^{2+} required for contraction

Smooth Muscle
- Nonstriated
- Involuntary
- Autonomic innervation
- One nucleus per cell
- Ca^{2+} required for contraction

TEACHER TIP

The MCAT loves to test the fact that smooth muscle exhibits myogenic activity. Striated muscle requires descending input from the nervous system. Smooth muscle, however, will contract even without this input. Of course, the nervous system can regulate smooth muscle as well.

ENERGY RESERVES

A. CREATINE PHOSPHATE

High-energy compounds, such as fatty acids, glycogen, and glucose, can be degraded in muscle cells to produce ATP. In addition, energy can be temporarily stored in a high-energy compound called **creatine phosphate.** During resting periods, creatine phosphate is produced via a reaction that transfers a high-energy phosphate group from ATP to creatine. During exercise, the reaction proceeds in reverse, resynthesizing ATP from creatine phosphate and ADP, thus replenishing the ATP supply without the need for additional oxygen.

$$\text{creatine} + \text{ATP} \rightleftarrows \text{creatine phosphate} + \text{ADP}$$

B. MYOGLOBIN

Myoglobin is a hemoglobin-like protein found in muscle tissue. Myoglobin has a high O_2 affinity; it binds to O_2 from the bloodstream and holds onto it. During strenuous exercise, when muscle cells rapidly run out of available O_2, myoglobin releases its O_2. In this way, myoglobin acts as an additional oxygen reserve for active muscle. However, during strenuous exercise, the oxygen supply to muscles may be insufficient to meet its energy demands, despite the extra O_2 supplied by myoglobin. During this period the muscle obtains additional energy via anaerobic respiration, resulting in the build-up of lactic acid (see chapter 3).

CONNECTIVE TISSUE

The major function of connective tissue is to bind and support other tissue. Connective tissue is a sparsely scattered population of cells contained in an amorphous ground substance which may be liquid, jelly-like, or solid. **Loose connective tissue** is found throughout the body. It binds epithelium to underlying tissues and is the packing material that holds organs in place. It contains proteinaceous fibers of three types: **collagenous fibers,** which are composed of collagen and have great tensile strength; **elastic fibers,** which are composed of elastin and endow connective tissue with resilience; and **reticular fibers,** which are branched, tightly woven fibers that join connective tissue to adjoining tissue. There are two major cell types in loose connective tissue: **fibroblasts,** which secrete substances that are components of extracellular fibers, and **macrophages,** which engulf bacteria and dead cells via phagocytosis.

FLASHBACK

Remember, in the absence of oxygen, pyruvate is reduced to lactic acid in the cytoplasm, and the TCA cycle and electron transport chain do not come into play. Lactic acid build-up is responsible for the "feel the burn" stage of vigorous exercise. See chapter 3.

TEACHER TIP

This acid can be converted back into energy-producing intermediates once sufficient levels of oxygen become available. This process occurs in the liver and is known as the Cori cycle.

Dense connective tissue is connective tissue with a very high proportion of collagenous fibers. The fibers are organized into parallel bundles that give the fibers great tensile strength. Dense connective tissue forms **tendons,** which attach muscle to bone, and **ligaments,** which hold bones together at the joints.

MUSCLE-BONE INTERACTIONS

Locomotion is dependent on interactions between the skeletal and muscular systems. If a given muscle (including associated joints) is attached to two bones, contraction of the muscle will cause only one of the two bones to move. The end of the muscle attached to the stationary bone is called the **origin**; in limb muscles it corresponds to the **proximal end.** The end of the muscle attached to the bone that moves during contraction is called the **insertion**; in limb muscles, the insertion corresponds to the **distal end.**

Often muscles work in antagonistic pairs; one relaxes while the other contracts. Such is the case in the arm, where the biceps and triceps work antagonistically. When you move your hand toward your shoulder, the biceps contract and the triceps relax; when you move your hand down again, the biceps relax and the triceps contract (see Figure 6.10). There are also **synergistic muscles,** which assist the principal muscles during movement.

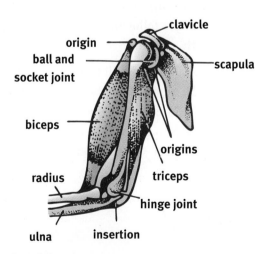

Figure 6.10. Muscles of the Upper Arm

A **flexor** muscle will contract to decrease the angle of a joint, whereas an **extensor muscle** will contract to straighten the joint. An **abductor** moves a part of the body away from the body's midline; an **adductor** moves a part of the body toward the midline.

PRACTICE QUESTIONS

1. Cartilage and bone have various differences. Which of the following scenarios would be expected given the known differences?

   A. Bone fractures heal more quickly than ruptured tendons.
   B. Bone fractures heal more slowly than ruptured tendons.
   C. Bone fractures bleed less than ruptured tendons.
   D. Bone fractures heal at the same rate as ruptured tendons.

2. Which cell layer gives rise to the skeletal system?

   A. Ectoderm
   B. Mesoderm
   C. Endoderm
   D. Epithelial cell layer

3. Which of the following is the most important element involved in muscle contraction?

   A. Iron
   B. Magnesium
   C. Phosphate
   D. Calcium

4. The bone marrow serves several functions. Which of the following cell types is derived from the bone marrow?

   A. Lymphocyte
   B. Epithelial
   C. Neuron
   D. Keratinocyte

5. A long-distance runner has exhausted the stores of glycogen in her liver, and the stores in the muscle are running low. She is forced to rely on anaerobic metabolism at the end of her workout. How many ATPs will she produce in this anaerobic state, compared to an aerobic state?

   A. 2 versus 38
   B. 36 versus 38
   C. 15 versus 38
   D. 1 versus 38

6. A patient with elevated parathyroid hormone may be expected to show signs of which of the following?

   A. Rheumatoid arthritis
   B. Osteoporosis
   C. Migraine
   D. Ankle sprain

7. In death, the production of ATP ceases. Which of the following findings will be present in this state?

   A. Muscles will be stiff and rigid.
   B. Muscles will be relaxed but not contracted.
   C. Muscles will be contracted but not relaxed.
   D. Muscles will be completely flaccid and able to be relaxed and contracted.

8. Storage of calcium and phosphate in the bones requires absorption of calcium from the intestinal track and by the kidneys from blood filtrate. Vitamin D plays an important role in this process of absorption; it is ingested and is also made in the skin. What two organs are responsible for activating vitamin D once it is present in the body?

A. Brain and lungs
B. Lungs and intestine
C. Kidney and liver
D. Liver and lungs

9. The musculoskeletal system depends upon input from the nervous system to drive its activities. Smooth muscle is innervated by which of the following systems?

A. Autonomic nervous system
B. Somatic nervous system
C. Parasympathetic but not sympathetic nervous system
D. Sympathetic but not parasympathetic nervous system

10. Weight lifting causes skeletal muscles to increase in size. By what process does this primarily occur?

A. Hypertension
B. Hyperplasia
C. Hypertrophy
D. Hyperextension

11. In the figure below, which band of the sarcomere does not change length during muscle contraction?

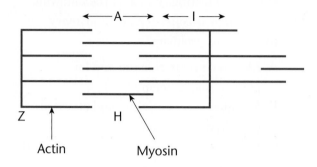

A. Z
B. I
C. H
D. A

12. Excitatory estrogen receptors have been recently found on osteoblasts. During menopause, there is a sharp decrease in the amount of estrogen production. Which of the following can be expected?

A. Decrease in the ratio of osteoclast/osteoblast activity
B. Increase in the ratio of osteoclast/osteoblast activity
C. Increase in the ratio of osteoblast/osteoclast activity
D. No change in the ratio of osteoblast/osteoclast activity

13. A patient has recently been diagnosed with primary hyperparathyroidism. The physician sends his blood to the lab for routine electrolyte testing. Which of the following lab findings is consistent with primary hyperparathyroidism?

A. Elevated serum calcium and low parathyroid hormone level

B. Elevated serum calcium and elevated parathyroid hormone level

C. Low serum calcium and low parathyroid hormone level

D. Low serum calcium and elevated parathyroid hormone level

CHAPTER 7

DIGESTION

Digestion consists of the degradation of large molecules into smaller molecules that can be absorbed into the bloodstream and used directly by cells. **Intracellular digestion** occurs within the cell, usually in membrane-bound vesicles. **Extracellular digestion** refers to a digestive process that occurs outside of the cell, within a lumen or tract. Mammals have a one-way digestive tract known as the **alimentary canal**. Mammalian digestive tracts tend to be complex and are organized into regions specialized for the digestion and absorption of specific nutrients.

The human digestive tract begins with the **oral cavity** and continues with the **pharynx,** the **esophagus,** the **stomach,** the **small intestine,** and the **large intestine** (see Figure 7.1). Accessory organs, such as the **salivary glands,** the **pancreas,** the **liver,** and the **gall bladder,** also play essential roles in the digestive process.

Most body surfaces (e.g., the skin and lungs, and the linings of the nose, mouth, esophagus, stomach, and intestines) are covered or lined by continuous sheets of epithelial cells. Epithelial cells are joined tightly together, facilitating their ability to act as a barrier against mechanical injury, invading organisms, and fluid loss. The free surface of epithelium is exposed to air or liquid and may be ciliated. The inner surface is attached to underlying connective tissue by a **basement membrane.**

THE ORAL CAVITY

The oral cavity (the mouth) is where mechanical and chemical digestion of food begins. Mechanical digestion is the breakdown of large food particles into smaller particles through the biting and chewing action of teeth (mastication). While mechanical digestion does not lead to changes in the molecular composition of food, the total surface area of the food is increased, allowing for faster and more efficient enzymatic action. **Chemical digestion** refers to the enzymatic breakdown of macromolecules into smaller molecules and begins in the mouth when the salivary glands secrete saliva. Saliva lubricates food to facilitate swallowing and

TEACHER TIP

The individual molecules that the body can absorb will be discussed in detail later. The big-picture concept to keep in mind is that all foods are broken down into simple sugars, amino acids and peptides, and fats.

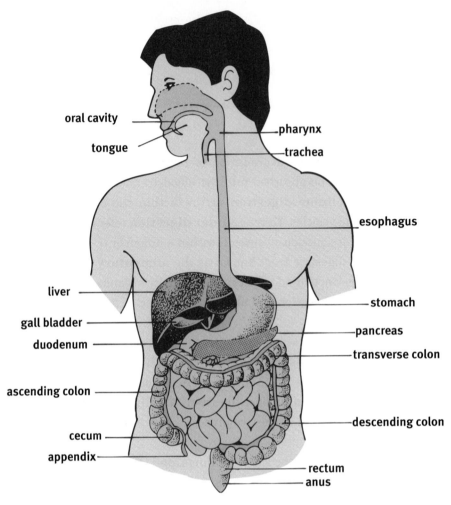

Figure 7.1. Human Digestive Tract

provides a solvent for food particles. Saliva is secreted in response to a nervous reflex triggered by the presence of food in the oral cavity. Saliva contains the enzyme salivary amylase (ptyalin), which hydrolyzes starch into simple sugars. However, since food does not remain in the mouth for long, only a small portion of starch is hydrolyzed there. The muscular tongue, containing the taste buds, manipulates the food, rolls it into a ball called a bolus, and pushes the bolus into the pharynx.

THE PHARYNX

The pharynx is the cavity that leads food from the mouth into the esophagus. The pharynx also functions in respiration as the passageway through which air enters the trachea. During swallowing, the opening of the trachea is covered by a flap called the **epiglottis,** thereby preventing food particles from being aspirated into the lungs.

THE ESOPHAGUS

The esophagus is the muscular tube leading from the pharynx to the stomach. Food is moved down the esophagus by rhythmic waves of involuntary muscular contractions called **peristalsis.** When a wave of peristalsis spreads down the esophagus, a specialized ring of muscle in the lower esophagus opens, allowing food to enter the stomach. Following the peristaltic wave, this muscle, called the **lower esophageal sphincter** or **cardiac sphincter,** returns to its normal closed state, thus preventing the regurgitation of stomach contents into the esophagus.

THE STOMACH

The stomach, a large, muscular organ located in the upper abdomen, stores and partially digests food. The walls of the stomach are lined by the thick gastric mucosa, which contains the **gastric glands** and **pyloric glands.** The gastric glands are stimulated by nervous impulses from the brain, which responds to the sight, taste, and/or smell of food. The gastric glands are composed of three types of secretory cells: **mucous cells, chief cells,** and **parietal cells.** Mucous cells secrete mucus, which protects the stomach lining from the harshly acidic juices (pH = 2) present in the stomach. **Gastric juice** is composed of the secretions of the chief cells and the parietal cells. Chief cells secrete **pepsinogen,** the zymogen of the protein-hydrolyzing enzyme **pepsin.** The chief cells also secrete intrinsic factor, which plays a role in the absorption of vitamin B^{12}. Parietal cells secrete **hydrochloric acid (HCl).** HCl kills bacteria, dissolves the intercellular "glue" holding food tissues together, and facilitates the conversion of pepsinogen to pepsin. Pepsin hydrolyzes specific peptide bonds to yield polypeptide fragments. The pyloric glands secrete the hormone **gastrin** in response to the presence of certain substances in food. Gastrin stimulates the gastric glands to secrete more HCl and also stimulates muscular contractions of the stomach, which churn food. This churning produces an acidic, semifluid mixture of partially digested food known as **chyme.**

At the junction of the stomach and the small intestine is the muscular **pyloric sphincter,** which regulates the passage of chyme from the stomach into the small intestine via alternating contractions and relaxations. Although nutrient absorption occurs in the small intestine, alcohol and certain drugs (e.g., aspirin) can be directly absorbed into the systemic circulation through capillaries in the stomach wall.

MCAT SYNOPSIS

The initial contraction of the upper esophagus is voluntary; however, once irritated, the involuntary peristalsis proceeds. This is why we can cough up food when it "feels" like we are about to choke.

TEACHER TIP

Weakness in the lower esophageal sphincter can lead to classical "heartburn" after eating.

CLINICAL CORRELATE

Zollinger-Ellison syndrome is a rare disease resulting from a gastrin-secreting tumor (gastrinoma). Typically, the tumor is found in the pancreas. As you would expect, the excess gastrin stimulates an increase in HCl production in the stomach. Not surprisingly, the most notable feature of ZE is the presence of severe, intractable ulcer disease.

THE SMALL INTESTINE

Chemical digestion is completed in the small intestine. The small intestine is divided into three sections: the **duodenum,** the **jejunum,** and the **ileum.** In order to maximize the surface area available for digestion and absorption, the intestine is extremely long (greater than six meters in length) and highly coiled. In addition, numerous fingerlike projections called **villi** extend out of the intestinal submucosa, and tiny cytoplasmic projections called **microvilli** project from the surface of the individual cells lining the villi (see Figure 7.2). The total surface area of the small intestine is approximately 300 m^2.

A. DIGESTIVE FUNCTIONS

Most digestion in the small intestine occurs in the duodenum, where the secretions of the intestinal glands, pancreas, liver, and gall bladder mix together with the acidic chyme entering from the stomach. The presence of chyme triggers hormonal release, which in turn stimulates and regulates the secretions of the small intestine and its accessory organs.

CLINICAL CORRELATE

Severe narrowing of the pyloric sphincter can result in a condition known as pyloric stenosis. Most commonly seen in infants, the hallmark symptom of pyloric stenosis is projectile vomiting. In addition, a mass can often be palpated in the belly and peristaltic waves may be visible across the baby's abdomen. Pyloric stenosis can be surgically corrected.

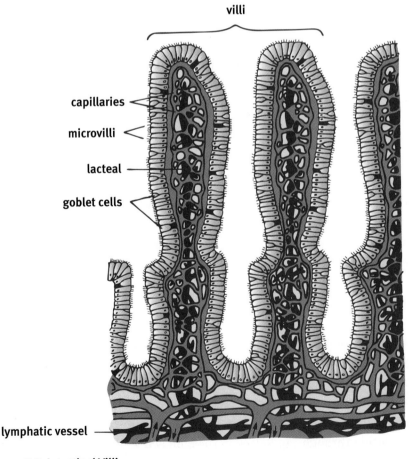

villi

capillaries

microvilli

lacteal

goblet cells

lymphatic vessel

Figure 7.2. Intestinal Villi

The intestinal mucosa secretes enzymes that hydrolyze carbohydrates into monosaccharides, such as **maltase, lactase,** and **sucrase,** and **peptidases,** which hydrolyze dipeptides and oligo peptides. The hormone **secretin** is released by the duodenum in response to the acidity of chyme, stimulating the pancreas to secrete **pancreatic juice.** The enzymes of the small intestine function optimally at a slightly basic pH and are denatured by acid; pancreatic juice is an alkaline fluid (due to a high concentration of bicarbonate) that helps neutralize the acidity of chyme and contains enzymes that digest carbohydrates, proteins, and lipids. **Trypsinogen** is a proteolytic zymogen secreted by the pancreas and is converted to its active form, **trypsin,** by an enzyme called **enterokinase** (secreted by the intestinal glands). Trypsin then converts another pancreatic zymogen, **chymotrypsinogen,** to its active form, **chymotrypsin.** Each of these enzymes cleaves specific peptide bonds within proteins, producing polypeptide fragments. The pancreas also secretes **carboxypeptidase** (also secreted as a zymogen and activated by trypsin). Proteolytic enzymes in the pancreatic juice break down proteins into dipeptides and oligopeptides. Then, similar to the hydrolysis of carbohydrates, the intestinal mucosa breaks these compounds into amino acids by secreting amino peptidase.

The hormone **CCK (cholecystokinin)** is secreted into the bloodstream by the duodenum in response to the presence of chyme. CCK stimulates the secretion of pancreatic enzymes and the release of **bile.** Bile is an alkaline fluid synthesized and secreted by the liver, stored and concentrated in the gall bladder, and released into the duodenum. Bile is composed of bile salts, bile pigments, and cholesterol. Bile salts are molecules with a water-soluble region on one end and a fat-soluble region on the other. This structure, similar to that of detergents, allows bile salts to emulsify, i.e. dissolve, fat globules and to surround and maintain these particles in finely dispersed complexes called **micelles,** which are soluble in aqueous media. This process is called the **emulsification** of fat and exposes more of the lipids' surface area to the actions of **lipases,** which hydrolyze molecules of fat into glycerol and fatty acids. The amount of bile released is proportional to the amount of fat ingested. If the chyme is particularly fatty, the duodenum releases the hormone **enterogastrone,** which inhibits stomach peristalsis, thus slowing down the release of chyme into the small intestine (fats take a longer time to digest than the other macromolecules).

In addition to hormonal regulation, the digestive processes are also stimulated by the **parasympathetic nervous system** and inhibited by the **sympathetic nervous system** (See chapter 12).

TEACHER TIP

These enzymes are key to proper digestion. Only simple sugars (monosaccharides) can be absorbed by the gut. Without these enzymes, the sugars will either pass through the body unchanged or be digested by bacteria in the colon.

CLINICAL CORRELATE

Lactose intolerance results from the absence of lactase. Hence, lactose passes to the colon undigested. This results in the symptoms experienced by those with this deficiency.

TEACHER TIP

Having trouble keeping the sections of the small intestine in order? Just think of the stock market. The major index—Dow Jones Industrials—is in the same order as the small intestine—duodenum, jejunum, ileum.

MCAT SYNOPSIS

We've now reviewed two important "good" functions of cholesterol: contributor to the fluidity of cell membranes (chapter 1) and key component of bile. More to come . . .

B. ABSORPTIVE FUNCTIONS

The majority of nutrient absorption occurs across the walls of the jejunum and the ileum (a small amount of absorption occurs in the duodenum). Monosaccharides are absorbed via active transport and facilitated diffusion into the epithelial cells lining the villi; amino acids are absorbed into the epithelium via active transport. Monosaccharides, amino acids, and small fatty acids diffuse directly into the intestinal capillaries and enter portal circulation via the **hepatic portal vein.** Larger fatty acids, glycerol, and cholesterol diffuse into the mucosal cells; the fatty acids and glycerol recombine to form triglycerides, which, along with phosphoglycerides and cholesterol, are packaged into protein-coated droplets called **chylomicrons.** The chylomicrons are secreted into tiny lymph vessels within the villi called **lacteals,** which lead into the lymphatic system; the lymphatic system converges with venous blood at the thoracic duct located in the neck. The chylomicrons are processed in the bloodstream and delivered to the liver. They are repackaged there and released into the bloodstream as LDLs, VLDLs, and HDLs (lipoproteins or proteins complexed with lipids).

Vitamins and minerals are also absorbed in the small intestine. The fat-soluble vitamins (A, D, E, and K) are absorbed along with fats, and most water-soluble vitamins (e.g., the vitamin B complexes and vitamin C) are absorbed via simple diffusion into the circulatory system. Approximately seven liters of fluid enter the small intestine every day; the majority of it is absorbed through the walls of the small intestine.

THE LARGE INTESTINE

TEACHER TIP

KEY POINT: Although the large intestine reabsorbs massive amounts of water, it is the kidneys that actually regulate total body water. More on this process later.

The large intestine is approximately 1.5 m long and consists of six parts: the **cecum,** the **ascending colon, transverse colon, descending colon, sismoid colon,** and the **rectum.** The cecum is a blind outpocketing at the junction of the small and large intestines. At the tip of the cecum is a small, fingerlike projection called the **appendix.** The appendix is a **vestigial structure** (see chapter 15) containing lymphoid tissue that is often surgically removed if it becomes infected. The colon functions in the absorption of salts and the absorption of any water not already absorbed by the small intestine. If digested matter moves through the colon too quickly, too little water is absorbed, causing diarrhea and dehydration. Alternatively, if movement through the bowels is too slow, too much water is absorbed, causing constipation. The rectum stores **feces,** which consist of bacteria (particularly **E. coli**), water, undigested food, and unabsorbed

Table 7.1. Digestive Enzymes

Nutrient	Enzyme	Site of Production	Site of Function	Function
Carbohydrates	Salivary amylase (Ptyalin)	Salivary glands	Mouth	Hydrolyzes starch to maltose
	Pancreatic amylase	Pancreas	Small intestine	Hydrolyzes starch to maltose
	Maltase	Intestinal glands	Small intestine	Hydrolyzes maltose to two glucose molecules
	Sucrase	Intestinal glands	Small intestine	Hydrolyzes sucrose to glucose and fructose
	Lactase	Intestinal glands	Small intestine	Hydrolyzes lactose to glucose and galactose
Proteins	Pepsin (secreted as pepsinogen)	Gastric glands	Stomach	Hydrolyzes specific peptide bonds
	Trypsin (secreted as trypsinogen)	Pancreas	Small intestine	Hydrolyzes specific peptide bonds Converts chymotrypsinogen to chymotry
	Chymotrypsin (secreted as chymotrypsinogen)	Pancreas	Small intestine	Hydrolyzes specific peptide bonds
	Carboxy-peptidase	Pancreas	Small intestine	Hydrolyzes terminal peptide bond at carboxyl end
	Aminopeptidase	Intestinal glands	Small intestine	Hydrolyzes terminal peptide bond at amino end
	Dipeptidases	Intestinal glands	Small intestine	Hydrolyzes pairs of amino acids
	Enterokinase	Intestinal glands	Small intestine	Converts trypsinogen to trypsin
Lipids	Bile*	Liver	Small intestine	Emulsifies fat
	Lipase	Pancreas	Small intestine	Hydrolyzes lipids

*Note that bile is NOT an enzyme.

digestive secretions (e.g., enzymes and bile). The **anus** is the opening through which wastes are eliminated and is separated from the rectum by two sphincters that regulate elimination.

ACCESSORY ORGANS

A. LIVER

The liver has many functions such as storage of glycogen, gluconeogenesis, conversion of ammonia to urea, lipid metabolism, synthesis of the majority of proteins in the human blood stream, detoxification of drugs and their metabolites in the blood stream, and production and secretion of bile into the gastrointestinal tract to emulsify fats.

TEACHER TIP

Though the gallbladder stores bile, it isn't completely necessary for life. High fat diets commonly result in formation of stones or sludge within the gallbladder or cystic duct. If this blockage cannot be cleared, the gallbladder may have to be removed. This is known as a cholecystectomy.

TEACHER TIP

Many of the digestive enzymes could be fairly damaging to the body. Thus, they are often secreted as inactive precursors (zymogens).

B. GALLBLADDER

The gall bladder is primarily responsible for the storage and secretion of excess bile.

C. PANCREAS

The pancreas has both exocrine and endocrine function. The endocrine function of the pancreas arises from its production of insulin and glucagons, and somatostatin primarily relates to glucose metabolism. In contrast, the exocrine function of the pancreas refers to its secretions of bicarbonate and digestive enzymes such as trypsin, chymotrypsin, enterokinase, amylase, and lipase into the small intestine for digestion.

SUMMARY OF DIGESTION

Digestion begins in different parts of the digestive tract for each of the three classes of macromolecules. Carbohydrate digestion begins in the mouth; protein digestion begins in the stomach; and lipid digestion begins in the small intestine. Table 7.1 is a summary of the digestive enzymes.

PRACTICE QUESTIONS

1. The digestive system has two main functions: breaking down large food molecules into small molecules and absorption of these small molecules, minerals, and water into the body. There are four major activities of the gastrointestinal tract which will accomplish these two main functions. Which of the following is not one of the activities?

   A. Propulsion
   B. Secretion
   C. Opsonization
   D. Digestion

2. What is the correct linear arrangement of the gastrointestinal tract?

   A. Mouth, trachea, stomach, duodenum, anus
   B. Mouth, trachea, jejunum, large intestine, anus
   C. Mouth, esophagus, jejunum, duodenum, anus
   D. Mouth, esophagus, duodenum, ileum, anus

3. The autonomic nervous system of the gastrointestinal tract has both extrinsic and intrinsic components. The extrinsic system is comprised of the sympathetic and parasympathetic innervations, while the intrinsic system is comprised of the enteric nervous system. The parasympathetic nervous system of the gastrointestinal tract is supplied by both the vagus nerve (CN X) and the pelvic nerve. Which portion of the gastrointestinal tract is not supplied by the vagus nerve?

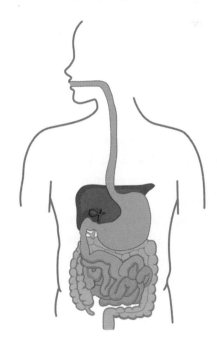

   A. Transverse colon
   B. Stomach wall
   C. Small intestine
   D. Ascending colon

4. Which subdivision of the gastrointestinal wall contains the main blood vessels of the gastrointestinal tract?

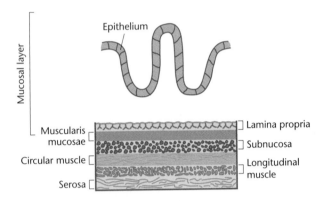

A. Mucosal layer
B. Muscularis mucosae
C. Lamina propria
D. Submucosal layer

5. An apparently healthy newborn develops excessive vomiting and abdominal distension a few hours after birth. The vomitus contains bile. Radiographic examination shows a gas-filled stomach and dilated, gas-filled small bowel loops, but no air is present in the large intestine. A diagnosis of a congenital obstruction of the small bowel is made. Where is the obstruction most likely to be located?

A. Jejunum
B. Duodenum
C. Ileum
D. Appendix

6. Which of the following is not a function of cholecystokinin (CCK)?

A. Stimulation of gallbladder contraction
B. Inhibition of H^+ secretion
C. Secretion of pancreatic HCO_3^-
D. Inhibition of gastric emptying

7. Chief cells located in the stomach secrete inactive pepsinogen. Which of the following is required to start the conversion process of pepsinogen into its active form, pepsin?

A. HCO_3^-
B. H_2CO_3
C. HCl
D. $CaCl_2$

8. Hirschsprung's disease, or congenital aganglionic megacolon, is a disease in which a portion of the colon lacks ganglion cells in the myenteric plexus. What is a likely symptom of this disease?

A. Diarrhea
B. Weight loss due to malabsorption
C. Constipation
D. Dehydration

9. During embryonic development, structures within the abdomen undergo numerous rotations before attaining their final abdominal position. With the stomach as the central point, a structure that is attached posterior to the stomach would find itself where in relation to the stomach after the final rotation?

A. Posterior to the stomach
B. Right of the stomach
C. Anterior to the stomach
D. Inferior to the stomach

10. What process is required to convert primary bile acids into secondary bile acids?

A. Conjugation
B. Dehydroxylation
C. Dehydration
D. Methylation

11. Which amino acid is used to conjugate secondary bile acids, thereby forming bile salts?

A. Arginine
B. Carnitine
C. Glycine
D. Phenylalanine

12. Which of the following is not a function of bile acid?

A. Cholesterol elimination
B. Cholesterol solubilization
C. Absorption of vitamins B_1, B_2, B_6, B_{12}, and C
D. Lipid emulsification

13. Saliva is secreted from acinar cells within the salivary glands. It is then modified by ductal cells within the glands, causing the once isotonic solution to become hypotonic. Acinar cells also secrete other products into saliva, such as enzymes required for initial digestion of lipids and starch. What enzyme found in saliva is also secreted by the pancreas?

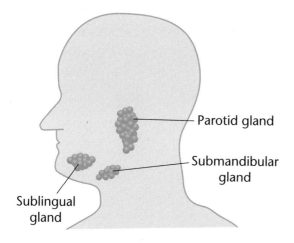

Parotid gland

Submandibular gland

Sublingual gland

A. Pepsin
B. Chymotrypsin
C. Amylase
D. Trypsin

14. The pancreas contains groups of hormone-producing cells known as islets of Langerhans. Some of these cells produce insulin, while others produce glucagon. There is a third cluster of cells which have the ability to inhibit the secretion of both insulin and glucagon. This paracrine hormone is known as:

A. aldosterone.
B. somatostatin.
C. vasopressin.
D. cholecystokinin.

15. Cholecystokin (CCK) is secreted into the duodenum in response to the presence of fat and protein in the intestine. CCK inhibits further gastric emptying, while enhancing the digestive process within the duodenum. Other digestive products are secreted into the intestine due to CCK EXCEPT

A. pancreatic lipase.
B. hepatic bile.
C. somatostatin.
D. chymotrypsin.

16. Starch is a polysaccharide carbohydrate composed of numerous glucose monosaccharides joined together by glycosidic bonds. In which part of the digestive tract does the digestion of starch begin?

A. Stomach
B. Duodenum
C. Mouth
D. Jejunum

17. Where does final disaccharide digestion and absorption take place?

A. Stomach
B. Jejunum
C. Mouth
D. Sigmoid colon

18. The abdominal aorta is the largest artery in the abdominal cavity. Three major branches of the abdominal aorta are considered to be the main sources of blood to the abdomen and abdominal organs. Which one of these branches is not a major blood source to the abdomen?

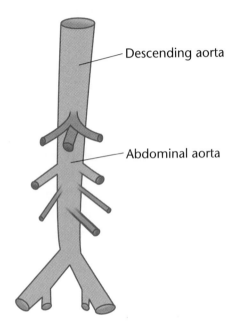

Descending aorta

Abdominal aorta

A. Superior mesenteric artery
B. Inferior mesenteric artery
C. Common iliac
D. Celiac trunk

DIGESTIVE SYSTEM

In the gastric phase of digestion, food in the stomach, particularly the presence of amino acids and peptides, causes G cells to secrete gastrin, which in turn stimulates parietal cells. Gastrin secretion is normally inhibited once acidic chyme, with a pH less than 3, reaches the duodenum. What physiological condition would be the result of a gastrin-secreting tumor?

1) Determine the role of gastrin in the stomach.
According to the question stem, gastrin stimulates parietal cells when food is present in the stomach. Parietal cells secrete HCl, and therefore gastrin is a physiological agonist of HCl secretion. Once the chyme reaches a certain acidity (pH < 3) and moves into the small intestine, gastrin secretion is inhibited and therefore HCl secretion is decreased.

2) Determine the role of HCl in the stomach.
In the stomach, HCl is necessary for the proper function of pepsin because the proper pH for pepsin is between 1 and 3.

3) Examine what occurs when acidic chyme reaches the small intestine.
Once the chyme moves into the small intestine, the pH needs to be increased in order to reach the optimal pH (≈ 8) for pancreatic proteases and lipases. Therefore, gastrin release is inhibited and the pancreas is stimulated to secrete bicarbonate in order to neutralize the acid. The pancreas also releases hydrolytic enzymes such as amylase, trypsinogen, chymotrypsinogen, and pancreatic lipases.

4) Examine the effect of a gastrin-secreting tumor.
A gastrin-secreting tumor will secrete gastrin at all times and will not be inhibited by normal feedback mechanisms such as the presence of chyme in the small intestine. This gastrin will continually stimulate parietal cells to produce HCl. This excess of acid will move with the chyme into the small intestine. Normal amounts of bicarbonate will be released; however, this is not enough to neutralize such an excess of HCl effectively.

5) Determine the effects of an acidic environment in the small intestine.
Pancreatic juices require a less acidic environment than do stomach enzymes. If the environment in the small intestine is too acidic, then pancreatic secretions will be unable to function normally. While proteins and carbohydrates are partially digested before they reach the small intestine, fats do not begin digestion until they reach the duodenum. If pancreatic lipases are unable to

KEY CONCEPTS

Digestive enzymes

Pancreatic enzymes

Pancreas

Duodenum

Gastric acid

TAKEAWAYS

Having a good understanding of the normal digestive system provides a strong basis for evaluating the effects of abnormalities that may occur within the system.

THINGS TO WATCH OUT FOR

An acidic duodenal pH will affect the functioning ability of all of the pancreatic enzymes, but protein absorption can still occur because proteins are digested in the stomach. Carbohydrate digestion does not rely on pancreatic secretions. Absorption can still occur because carbohydrates begin digestion in the mouth and continue to be broken down by maltase and sucrase in the intestinal brush border.

function due to an excessively acidic environment, they will not be able to digest lipids. This hypersecretion of gastrin will lower the pH of the duodenum so that pancreatic lipases are inactivated. This will result in the malabsorption of lipids, also known as steatorrhea.

Remember: *The pH levels of the stomach and the small intestine affect the ability of enzymes to function properly.*

SIMILAR QUESTIONS

1) A patient with a peptic ulcer takes a large overdose of antacid. This would affect the activity of what enzyme?

2) Pancreatic ductal cells secrete bicarbonate, which is moved into the intestinal lumen. What would be the physiological results if these ductal cells were destroyed by an autoimmune disorder?

3) Pancreatitis is a disease that prevents the pancreas from being able to produce adequate amounts of lipase enzymes. What will be the physiological results of this disease?

OSMOSIS

The sodium potassium pump is an ATPase that pumps 3 Na$^+$ out of the cell and 2 K$^+$ into the cell for each ATP hydrolyzed. Cells can use the pump to help maintain cell volume. What would most likely happen to the rate of ATP consumption if a cell were moved to a hypertonic environment?

1) Determine the relationship between two solutions to predict the flow of water.

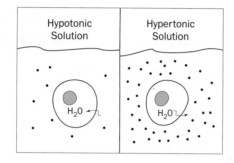

A hypertonic environment means that the environment is more concentrated than the cell is. Note that you can similarly express this condition by stating that the cell is hypotonic to the environment. A hypotonic solution is one that is less concentrated than the solution to which it is being compared.

The cell is being moved into a hypertonic environment, which means that the environment is more concentrated with solutes than the interior of the cell. Thus, we can predict that water will flow out of the cell.

2) Given the flow of water, determine how the biological function in question will be affected.

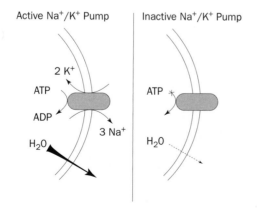

Water will flow out of the cell, thus decreasing cell volume. To counter this effect, ATP consumption will decrease to maintain cell volume.

KEY CONCEPTS

Hypertonic solution

Hypotonic solution

Sodium potassium pump

TAKEAWAYS

Questions that involve osmosis are usually combined with other biology topics (particularly kidney function) to create a multistep solution. The key is to have a solid understanding of what hypertonic and hypotonic mean, and how the terms can be used interchangeably to describe the same state.

THINGS TO WATCH OUT FOR

Some students presume that the scenario presented will eventually return to equilibrium and may actually predict that ATP consumption will decrease and then increase. However, the question stem does not speak of a return to equilibrium. Be wary of trying to read too much into the question.

The sodium potassium pump moves in two potassium ions as it moves out three sodium ions. The net effect is to decrease cell solute concentration as the cell loses one ion per each pump. The pump is dependent upon ATP consumption; therefore, relative to its current rate of ATP consumption, an increase in consumption will decrease cell volume whereas a decrease in consumption will increase cell volume.

SIMILAR QUESTIONS

1) Antidiuretic hormone (ADH) directly increases the ability of the blood to reabsorb water from the nephron. If an individual's blood becomes hypotonic with respect to the filtrate, would ADH secretion increase or decrease?

2) The reabsorption of water from the filtrate increases as the concentration of the interstitial fluid increases. Using the terms "hypertonic" and "hypo-osmotic," describe the relationship between the interstitial fluid and the filtrate as well as the relationship between the filtrate and the interstitial fluid.

3) Alcohol and caffeine block the activity of ADH, a hormone that increases the ability of the blood to reabsorb water from the filtrate. An individual drinks a large coffee in the morning, and when he goes to the restroom finds that his urine is nearly colorless. Was the urine produced hypotonic, isotonic, or hypertonic to the blood?

RESPIRATION

Respiration is a broad term referring to the exchange of gases between an organism and its external environment, the transport of these gases within the organism, and the diffusion of gases into and out of cells. (Cellular respiration, discussed in chapter 3, refers to the role that these gases play in generating energy at the cellular level.) Aerobic organisms exchange CO_2 generated during cellular respiration for O_2 obtained from the external environment. Higher vertebrates have developed respiratory systems whereby gas exchange occurs at a single **respiratory surface,** the **lungs.**

ANATOMY

In the human respiratory system, air enters the lungs after traveling through a series of respiratory airways, as outlined in Figure 8.1. Air enters the respiratory tract through the **external nares** (nostrils) and then travels through the nasal cavities, where it is filtered by mucous and nasal hairs. It then passes through the pharynx and into a second chamber called the **larynx.** Ingested food also passes through the pharynx en route to the esophagus. To ensure that food does not accidentally enter the larynx and induce choking, a piece of tissue called the epiglottis covers the glottis (the opening to the larynx) during swallowing, thereby channeling food into the esophagus (see chapter 7). Air passes from the larynx into the cartilaginous **trachea,** which divides into two bronchi, one entering the right lung, the other entering the left. Both the trachea and bronchi are lined by ciliated epithelial cells, which filter and trap particles inhaled along with the air. The bronchi repeatedly branch into smaller bronchi, the terminal branches of which are called **bronchioles.** Each bronchiole is surrounded by clusters of small air sacs called **alveoli.** Gas exchange between the lungs and the circulatory system occurs across the very thin walls of the alveoli. Each alveolus is coated with a thin layer of liquid containing **surfactant** and is surrounded by an extensive network of capillaries. Surfactant lowers the surface tension of the alveoli and facilitates gas exchange across the membranes. Three hundred million alveoli provide approximately 100 m² of moist respiratory surface for gas exchange.

TEACHER TIP

The mouth and nose serve several important purposes in breathing. They allow for dirt and particulate matter to be removed from the air, and they warm and humidify the air before it reaches the lungs.

Following gas exchange, air rushes back through the respiratory pathway and is exhaled.

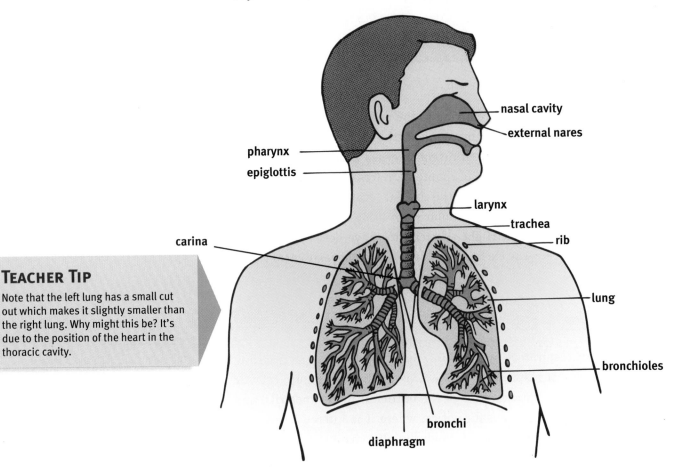

TEACHER TIP

Note that the left lung has a small cut out which makes it slightly smaller than the right lung. Why might this be? It's due to the position of the heart in the thoracic cavity.

Figure 8.1. Respiratory System

VENTILATION

Ventilation of the lungs (breathing) is the process by which air is inhaled and exhaled. The purpose of ventilation is to take in oxygen from the atmosphere and eliminate carbon dioxide from the body. The ventilating mechanism is dependent upon pressure changes in the **thoracic cavity,** the body cavity that contains the heart and lungs. The thoracic cavity is separated from the abdominal cavity by a muscle known as the **diaphragm** and is bounded on the sides by the chest wall. The lungs are surrounded by membranes called the **visceral pleura** and the **parietal pleura.** The space between the two pleura, the **intrapleural space,** contains a thin layer of fluid (see Figure 8.2). The pressure differential between the intrapleural space and the lungs (which is essentially atmospheric pressure) prevents the lungs from collapsing.

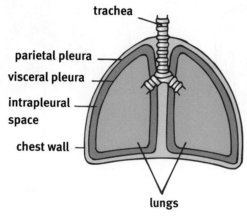

Figure 8.2. Thoracic Cavity (neutral position)

A. STAGES OF VENTILATION

1. Inhalation

During inhalation, the diaphragm contracts and flattens, and the **external intercostal muscles** contract, pushing the rib cage and chest wall up and out. This causes the thoracic cavity to increase in volume. This volume increase, in turn, reduces the intrapleural pressure, causing the lungs to expand and fill with air. This is referred to as **negative-pressure breathing** because air is drawn in by a vacuum.

BRIDGE

Remember, Boyle's law says that the pressure and volume of gases are inversely related. This is the principle underlying negative-pressure breathing.

2. Exhalation

Exhalation is generally a passive process. The lungs and chest wall are highly elastic and tend to recoil to their original positions following inhalation. The diaphragm and external intercostal muscles relax and the chest wall pushes inward. The consequent decrease in thoracic cavity volume causes the air pressure in the intrapleural space to increase. This causes the lungs to deflate, forcing air out of the alveoli. During forced exhalation, the **internal intercostal muscles** contract, pulling the rib cage down. Surfactant reduces the high surface tension of the fluid lining the alveoli, preventing alveolar collapse during exhalation.

TEACHER TIP

KEY POINT: Inhalation and exhalation are different processes in terms of energy expenditure. Muscle contraction is required to create the negative pressure in the thoracic cavity that makes air rush in during inspiration. Expiration during calm states is entirely due to elastic recoil of the lungs and musculature. Of course, during more active states, the muscles can be used to force air out and speed the process of ventilation.

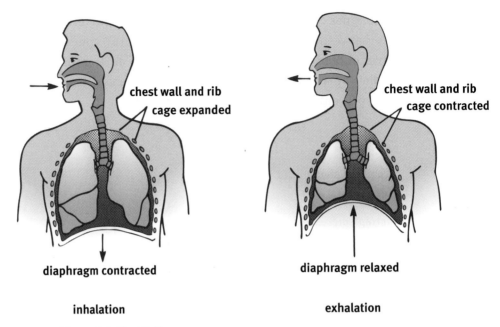

chest wall and rib cage expanded

chest wall and rib cage contracted

diaphragm contracted

diaphragm relaxed

inhalation

exhalation

Figure 8.3. Ventilation

B. CONTROL OF VENTILATION

Ventilation is regulated by neurons (referred to as **respiratory centers**) located in the **medulla oblongata,** whose rhythmic discharges stimulate the intercostal muscles and/or the diaphragm to contract. These neural signals can be modified by **chemoreceptors** (e.g., in the aorta), which respond to changes in the pH and the partial pressure of CO_2 in the blood. For example, when the partial pressure of CO_2 rises, the medulla oblongata stimulates an increase in the rate of ventilation.

To a limited extent, ventilation can be consciously controlled by the cerebrum. However, if a person tries to hold his breath indefinitely, the high concentration of CO_2 in the blood will stimulate the medulla oblongata to "override" this conscious attempt and stimulate inhalation. Hyperventilation (deep, rapid breathing) lowers the partial pressure of CO_2 in the blood below normal; chemoreceptors sense this and send signals to the respiratory center, which temporarily inhibits breathing.

LUNG CAPACITIES AND VOLUMES

An instrument called a **spirometer** measures the amount of air normally present in the respiratory system and the rate at which ventilation occurs. The maximum amount of air that can be forcibly inhaled and exhaled from the lungs is called the **vital capacity.** The amount of air normally inhaled and exhaled with each breath is called the **tidal volume.** The residual volume is the air that always remains in the lungs, preventing the alveoli from collapsing. The **expiratory reserve volume** is the volume of air that can still be forcibly exhaled following a normal exhalation (see Figure 8.4). **Total lung capacity** is equal to the vital capacity plus the residual volume.

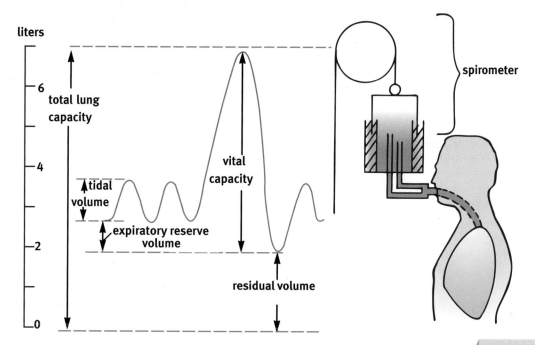

Figure 8.4. Spirometer

GAS EXCHANGE

A dense network of minute blood vessels called the pulmonary capillaries surrounds the alveoli. Gas exchange occurs by diffusion across these capillary walls and those of the alveoli; gases move from regions of higher partial pressure to regions of lower partial pressure. Blood enters the pulmonary capillaries in a deoxygenated state and thus has a lower partial pressure of O_2 than does the inhaled air in the alveoli. Hence, O_2 diffuses down its gradient into the capillaries where it binds with hemoglobin and returns to the heart via the pulmonary veins. In contrast, the partial pressure of CO_2 in the capillaries is greater than that of the inhaled alveolar air; thus CO_2 diffuses from the capillaries into the alveoli, where it is subsequently released into the external environment during exhalation (see Figure 8.5).

TEACHER TIP

KEY POINT: A certain volume of air, called residual volume, can *never* be removed from the lungs during normal breathing processes.

MCAT SYNOPSIS

O_2 in the alveoli flows down its partial pressure gradient from the alveoli into the pulmonary capillaries where it can bind to hemoglobin for transport. Meanwhile, CO_2 flows down its partial pressure gradient from the capillaries into the alveoli for expiration.

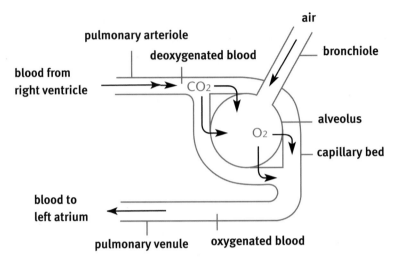

Figure 8.5. Gas Exchange

At high altitudes, the partial pressure of O_2 in the atmosphere declines, making it more difficult to get sufficient oxygen to diffuse into the capillaries. The body can compensate for these conditions in a variety of ways, such as by increasing the rate of ventilation (hyperventilation) and by increasing the production of red blood cells to carry more oxygen (polycythemia). In addition, the affinity of hemoglobin for oxygen decreases to facilitate unloading of oxygen in tissues, and there is greater vascularization of the peripheral tissues.

PRACTICE QUESTIONS

1. The uncoupling agent 2, 4-dinitrophenol dissociates the proton gradient from the electron transport chain. Administration of 2, 4-dinitrophenol would have which of the following effects?

   A. Increase in NADH concentrations within the mitochondria
   B. Increase followed by a decrease in NADH concentrations
   C. Decrease in NADH concentrations within the mitochondria
   D. Decrease followed by an abrupt increase in NADH concentrations

2. A man breathes 12 times per minute with a tidal volume of 500 ml and an inspiratory reserve volume of 300 ml. His son breathes 8 times per minute with a tidal volume of 300 ml and an inspiratory reserve volume of 600 ml. Who has greater total minute ventilation?

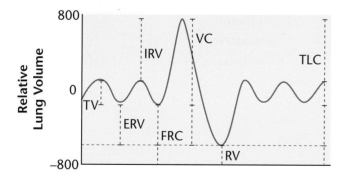

   A. Man
   B. Son
   C. Total ventilations are equal
   D. Cannot calculate minute ventilation from this data

3. Death from muscular dystrophy is often due to poor ventilation. What anatomical defect is responsible for this failure to ventilate?

   A. Damaged cardiac muscle
   B. Inadequate intercostal muscle function
   C. Narrowed trachea
   D. Poorly compliant lung tissue

4. A scientist is interested in creating an artificial surfactant to decrease surface tension on the alveoli of the lung. It is believed that this surfactant will decrease the electric recoil of the lungs. Surfactant A is made with 80 percent lipid, 10 percent water, and 10 percent protein. Surfactant B is made of 65 percent lipids and 35 percent water. Surface tension for sample A is 37 dynes/cm, while surface tension for sample B is 52 dynes/cm. What most likely accounts for the difference?

   A. Greater degree of hydrophobicity in sample A due to the presence of more lipid
   B. Greater degree of hydrophobicity in sample B
   C. Presence of protein in sample A
   D. Rate of respiration of subjects

5. When traveling to higher altitudes, the respiratory system adapts to maintain adequate oxygenation, i.e., minute ventilation (the product of respiratory rate and tidal volume). Comparing the respirations of a person at 7,000 feet to that of a person at sea level will reveal

   A. a lower respiratory rate at 7,000 feet as compared to sea level.
   B. a higher respiratory rate at 7,000 feet as compared to sea level.
   C. a higher respiratory rate at 3,000 feet as compared to sea level.
   D. the same respiratory rate at both altitudes.

6. Minute ventilation is the product of the respiratory rate and the tidal volume (volume in each breath of inspired air). How will increased minute ventilation impact the pH of arterial blood?

A. Increases pH
B. Decreases pH
C. There will be no change in pH
D. An initial increase, followed by sharp decrease

7. In the figure below, what line represents the oxygen dissociation curve during exercise?

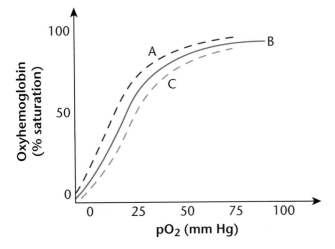

A. A
B. B
C. C
D. D

8. Pulmonary fibrosis is a disease process that results in replacement of the lung parenchyma (alveoli), which is normally very compliant, with fibrous scar tissue that is dense and cartilaginous. There is no known cure. As patients with pulmonary fibrosis progress, which of the following would be expected observations?

A. Increased lung volume with hyperoxygenation
B. Decreased lung volume with hyperoxygenation
C. Increased lung volume with hypoxia
D. Decreased lung volume with hypoxia

9. What element is crucial to proper functioning of hemoglobin?

A. Copper
B. Iron
C. Manganese
D. Selenium

10. Where is the respiratory drive centered?

A. Forebrain
B. Midbrain
C. Brainstem
D. Cerebellum

11. Under normal conditions, air is driven into the respiratory system via

A. positive airway pressure.
B. negative intrapleural pressure.
C. positive intrapleural pressure.
D. functional reserve capacity.

12. Via what route is unoxygenated blood driven from the right ventricle of the heart to the lung for oxygenation?

A. Pulmonary arteries
B. Pulmonary veins
C. Aorta
D. Foramen ovale

13. CO_2 is transported in the blood via all the following forms, EXCEPT

A. acetyl CoA.
B. dissolved in plasma.
C. carbamino compounds.
D. bicarbonate.

14. Blood in the pulmonary veins is rich in which of the following?

A. Oxyhemoglobin
B. Lactic acid
C. Chyme
D. Hemoglobin

KEY CONCEPTS

Respiratory system

Alveoli

Oxygen exchange

Physiological dead space

Anatomical dead space

Alveolar dead space

TAKEAWAYS

The respiratory system is intimately linked to the circulatory system. Oxygen is delivered to tissues, and CO_2 is removed from tissues and ultimately removed from the lungs through capillaries.

THINGS TO WATCH OUT FOR

Under resting conditions, alveolar oxygen equilibrates with the arterial blood of the pulmonary capillary. This is considered a perfusion-limited exchange. Underconditions of exercise, the partial pressures of oxygen do not equilibrate along the length of the pulmonary capillary and the partial pressure gradient is maintained.

RESPIRATORY SYSTEM

The volume of the lungs that does not participate in gas exchange is considered physiological dead space. There are two types of dead space that are seen at rest: anatomical and alveolar. Anatomical dead space is in the conducting areas, such as the mouth and trachea, where oxygen enters the respiratory system but does not contact alveoli. Alveolar dead space is the area in the alveoli that does contact air but lacks sufficient circulation to participate in gas exchange. How can physiological dead space be reduced?

1) Examine each type of dead space separately

Anatomical dead space refers to the air that remains in the mouth and trachea with every breath. Because the size and length of the mouth and trachea are set and relatively unchangeable, it is unlikely that physiological dead space can be decreased through the anatomical dead space.

Alveolar dead space involves alveoli that contact air but do not participate in gas exchange. Because the alveoli are normal, they are capable of participating in gas exchange under the right conditions; therefore, alveolar dead space can be reduced.

---

2) Review the method of gas exchange at the tissues and in the lungs.

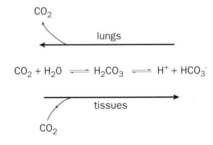

In the normal lung, O_2 will diffuse from alveolar air into the pulmonary capillary. When the partial pressures of O_2 in alveolar air and capillary blood equilibrate, the diffusion stops. Normally this occurs before the blood in the pulmonary capillary passes out of the lungs and is considered perfusion-limited gas exchange. This O_2 is bound to hemoglobin and is taken and released to the tissues. CO_2 is produced by the tissues and diffuses into capillary blood, where it is carried to the lungs as HCO_3^-. At the lungs, the reaction is reversed and CO_2 is exhaled.

---

3) Determine why some alveoli do not participate in gas exchange.

There is not sufficient blood flow through the capillaries of these "dead space" alveoli to induce them to participate in gas exchange. There must be blood flow in order for gas exchange to occur.

---

4) Determine how to increase blood flow through the lungs.

If pulmonary blood flow were increased, then more alveoli would be perfused with blood and would therefore participate in gas exchange. Increasing pulmonary blood flow would require increasing the output of the right ventricle. Cardiac output increases during exercise because there is an increased heart rate and increased venous return due to skeletal muscle activity. Therefore, exercise would increase the amount of pulmonary blood flow. This increased flow of blood through the lungs would recruit more alveoli for gas exchange and therefore reduce alveolar and physiological dead space.

Remember: Gas exchange occurs between alveolar air and the pulmonary capillaries. In order to increase the number of alveoli being used for gas exchange, the amount of pulmonary blood available for gas exchange must also be increased.

SIMILAR QUESTIONS

1) What is the result if blood flow to the left lung is completely blocked by a pulmonary embolism?

2) If an area of the lung is not ventilated due to an obstruction, what is the partial pressure of oxygen (Po_2) of the pulmonary capillary in that area?

3) At what point will the diffusion of air from the alveoli to the capillary stop?

CHAPTER 9

CIRCULATION

Higher organisms rely on a complex **cardiovascular system** to transport respiratory gases, nutrients, and wastes to and from cells. A secondary circulatory system, the **lymphatic system,** collects excess body fluids and returns them to the cardiovascular circulation.

THE CARDIOVASCULAR SYSTEM

The human cardiovascular system is composed of a muscular four-chambered **heart,** a network of **blood vessels,** and the **blood** itself. The right side of the heart pumps deoxygenated blood into the lungs via the pulmonary arteries. Oxygenated blood returns from the lungs to the left side of the heart via the pulmonary veins. It is then pumped into the **aorta,** which branches into a series of arteries. The arteries branch into arterioles, and then into microscopic capillaries. Exchange of gases, nutrients, and cellular waste products occurs via diffusion across capillary walls. The capillaries then converge into venules, and eventually into veins, leading deoxygenated blood back toward the right side of the heart. Blood returning from the lower body and extremities enters the heart via the **inferior vena cava,** while deoxygenated blood from the upper head and neck region flows through the **jugular vein** and into the **superior vena cava,** which also leads into the right atrium of the heart. The blood then flows to the right ventricle through the tricuspid valve. From the right ventricle, the blood goes to the pulmonary artery and is pumped to the lungs to be oxygenated (see chapter 8). The blood then returns from the lungs to the left atrium via the pulmonary veins. The left atrium then pumps the blood to the left ventricle through the mitral valve. Finally, the blood enters systemic circulation as it enters the aorta from the left ventricle. Oxygenated blood is supplied to heart muscle by the **coronary arteries.** The first branches off the aorta; **the coronary veins** and **coronary sinus** return deoxygenated blood to the right side of the heart.

In systemic circulation there are three special circulatory routes, referred to as **portal systems,** in which blood travels through *two* capillary beds before returning to the heart. There is a portal system in the

> **TEACHER TIP**
>
> Link to Physics: The heart and blood vessels are analogous to a pair of pumps that are linked in series. The right heart is a low-pressure system that sends blood to the lungs, whereas the left heart is a high pressure system that sends blood to the body.

liver (hepatic portal circulation), in the kidneys (see chapter 10), and in the brain (hypophyseal portal circulation; see chapter 11).

A. THE HEART

The heart is the driving force of the circulatory system. The right and left halves can be viewed as two separate pumps: The right side of the heart pumps deoxygenated blood into pulmonary circulation (toward the lungs), while the left side pumps oxygenated blood into systemic circulation (throughout the body). The two upper chambers are called **atria** and the two lower chambers are called ventricles. The atria are thin-walled, while the **ventricles** are extremely muscular. The left ventricle is more muscular than the right ventricle because it is responsible for generating the force that propels systemic circulation and because it pumps against a higher resistance.

TEACHER TIP

Because the right heart only pumps to the lungs, which are quite close, it can operate at lower pressures; consequently the right heart is not as muscled as the left. The left heart, responsible for the body, is more well-developed and can pump more strongly to move blood through the vasculature.

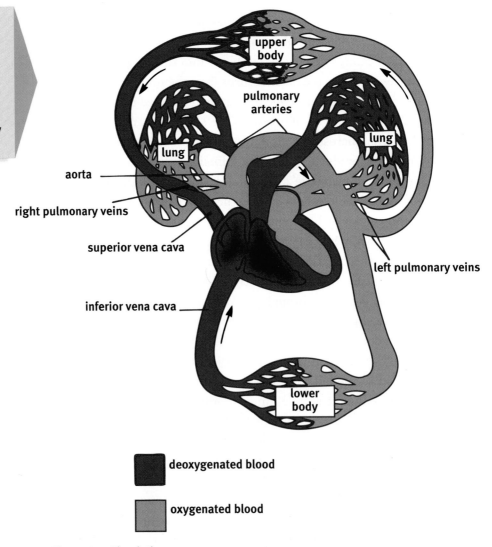

Figure 9.1. Circulation

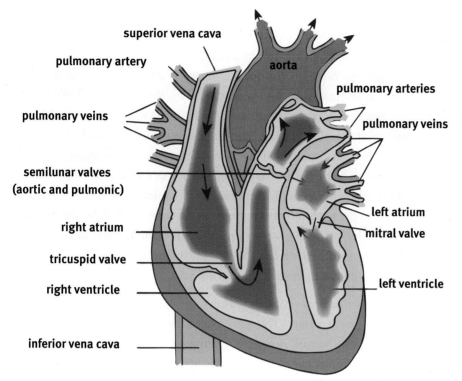

superior vena cava

pulmonary artery

aorta

pulmonary arteries

pulmonary veins

pulmonary veins

**semilunar valves
(aortic and pulmonic)**

left atrium

mitral valve

right atrium

tricuspid valve

right ventricle

left ventricle

inferior vena cava

Figure 9.2. Human Heart

1. Valves

The **atrioventricular valves,** located between the atria and ventricles on both sides of the heart, prevent backflow of blood into the atria. The valve on the right side of the heart has three cusps and is called the **tricuspid valve.** The valve on the left side of the heart has two cusps and is called the **mitral valve.** The **semilunar valves** have three cusps and are located between the left ventricle and the aorta (the aortic valve) and between the right ventricle and the pulmonary artery (the pulmonic valve).

2. Contraction

a. Phases

The heart's pumping cycle is divided into two alternating phases, **systole** and **diastole,** which together make up the **heartbeat.** Systole is the period during which the ventricles contract. Diastole is the period of cardiac muscle relaxation during which blood drains into all four chambers. **Cardiac output** is defined as the total volume of blood the left ventricle pumps out per minute. Cardiac output = **heart rate** (number of heartbeats per minute) × **stroke volume** (volume of blood pumped out of the left ventricle per contraction).

b. Mechanism and control

Cardiac muscle (see chapter 6) contracts rhythmically without stimulation from the nervous system, producing impulses that spread through its internal conducting system. An ordinary cardiac contraction originates in, and is regulated by, the **sinoatrial (SA) node** (the **pacemaker**), a small mass of specialized tissue located in the wall of the right atrium. The SA node spreads impulses through both atria, stimulating them to contract simultaneously. The impulse arrives at the **atrioventricular (AV) node,** which conducts slowly, allowing enough time for atrial contraction and for the ventricles to fill with blood. The impulse is then carried by the **bundle of His (AV bundle),** which branches into the right and left bundle branches and through the **Purkinje fibers** in the walls of both ventricles, generating a strong contraction.

The **autonomic nervous system** (see chapter 12) modifies the rate of heart contraction. The parasympathetic system innervates the heart via the **vagus nerve** and causes a decrease in the heart rate. The sympathetic system innervates the heart via the cervical and upper thoracic ganglia and causes an increase in the heart rate. The adrenal medulla exerts hormonal control via epinephrine (adrenaline) secretion, which causes an increase in heart rate (see chapter 11).

CLINICAL CORRELATE

The heart's electrical impulses can be detected on the body's surface by placing electrodes on the skin on opposite sides of the heart. A recording of these currents is called an electrocardiogram (a.k.a., ECG or EKG). Electrocardiograms are incredibly powerful tools for assessing the status of a patient's heart. A normal EKG is shown below.

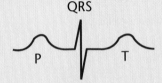

QRS

P   T

Because depolarization will precede cardiac muscle contraction, the electrical spokes of the EKG occur just before a cardiac contractile event. The P wave occurs immediately before the atria contract and the QRS complex occurs just before the ventricles contract. The T wave represents ventricular repolarization.

TEACHER TIP

Cardiac muscle is a hybrid of smooth muscle and striated muscle. It can beat without descending input due to the presence of the SA node, AV node, and Purkinje; however, much like we saw earlier with smooth muscle, this rate can be affected by the descending input.

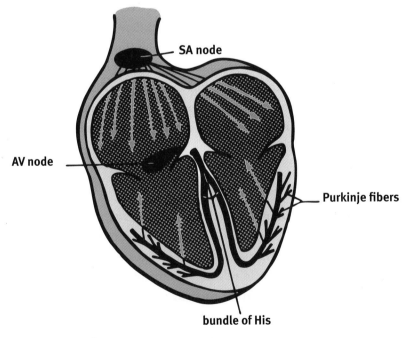

Figure 9.3. Contraction

B. BLOOD VESSELS

The three types of blood vessels are arteries, veins, and capillaries. **Arteries** are thickly-walled, muscular, elastic vessels that transport oxygenated blood away from the heart—except for the pulmonary arteries, which transport deoxygenated blood from the heart to the lungs. **Veins** are relatively thinly walled, inelastic vessels that conduct deoxygenated blood towards the heart—except for the pulmonary veins, which carry oxygenated blood from the lungs to the heart. Much of the blood flow in veins depends on their compression by skeletal muscles during movement, rather than on the pumping of the heart. Venous circulation is often at odds with gravity; thus larger veins, especially those in the legs, have valves that prevent backflow. **Capillaries** have very thin walls composed of a single layer of endothelial cells across which respiratory gases, nutrients, enzymes, hormones, and wastes can readily diffuse. Capillaries have the smallest diameter of all three types of vessels; red blood cells must often travel through them single file.

TEACHER TIP

When the valves break down in larger veins, the blood begins to pool rather than return to the heart. This is commonly seen in many individuals as varicose veins.

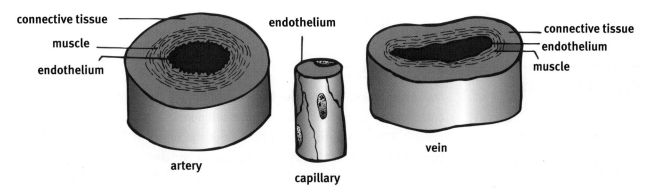

Figure 9.4. Blood Vessels

C. BLOOD PRESSURE

Blood pressure is the force per area that blood exerts on the walls of the blood vessels. Blood pressure is measured by an instrument called a **sphygmomanometer** (a.k.a., "blood pressure cuff") and is expressed as systolic pressure/diastolic pressure. As blood flows through the circulatory system from artery to capillary, blood pressure gradually drops, due to friction between blood and the walls of the vessels, and to the increase in cross-sectional area afforded by the numerous capillary beds (see Figure 9.5).

BRIDGE

In Physics pressure is defined as force/area. This holds true for blood pressure as well.

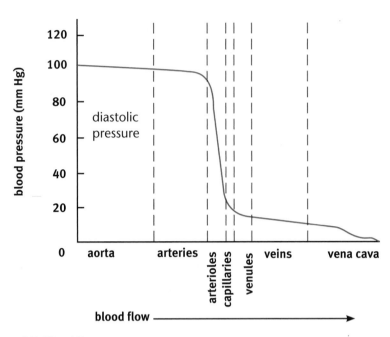

Figure 9.5. Blood Pressure

BLOOD

A. COMPOSITION

On the average, the human body contains 4–6 liters of blood. Blood has both liquid (55 percent) and cellular components (45 percent; formed elements). **Plasma** is the liquid portion of the blood. It is an aqueous mixture of nutrients, salts, respiratory gases, wastes, hormones, and blood proteins (e.g., immunoglobulins, albumin, and fibrinogen). The cellular components of the blood are **erythrocytes, leukocytes,** and **platelets.**

1. Erythrocytes (red blood cells)

Erythrocytes are the oxygen-carrying components of blood. An erythrocyte contains approximately 250 million molecules of **hemoglobin,** each of which can bind up to four molecules of oxygen. Adult hemoglobin consists of 2β chains and 2α chains. Erythrocytes have a distinct biconcave, disklike shape, which gives them both increased surface area for gas exchange and greater flexibility for movement through those tiny capillaries. Erythrocytes are formed from stem cells in the bone marrow, where they lose their nuclei, mitochondria, and membranous organelles. Because erythrocytes lack mitochondria, they are anaerobic and obtain their ATP via glycolysis alone. Once mature, erythrocytes circulate in the blood for about 120 days, after which they are phagocytized by special cells in the spleen and liver. There are about 5 million erythrocytes per one mm³ of blood.

2. Leukocytes (white blood cells)

Leukocytes arise from stem cells in the marrow of long bones. Leukocytes are larger than erythrocytes and have protective functions. The number of leukocytes in the blood varies widely; there are normally 5,000–10,000 leukocytes per one mm^3 of blood, but this number substantially increases when the body is battling an infection. There are three types of leukocytes: **granular leukocytes, lymphocytes,** and **monocytes.**

Granular leukocytes are nonspecific and attack general invading pathogens, such as bacteria or parasites. Granular leukocytes (**neutrophils, basophils,** and **eosinophils**) play key roles in inflammation, allergic reactions, pus formation, and the destruction of invading bacteria and parasites. Neutrophiles predominantly fight bacterial infections, where eosmophiles are associated with parasitic infections. Basophiles are responsible for allergies and allergic reactions through the release of histamine.

Lymphocytes play an important role in the **immune response**; they are produced in the lymph nodes, tonsils, spleen, appendix, thymus, and bone marrow and are involved in the production of **antibodies.** As a result, lymphocytes are involved in the specific immune response against a specific invading pathogen. For example, if you have antibodies against influenza virus, you can still be infected with another strain. The two types of lymphocytes are **B lymphocytes** and **T lymphocytes.** Monocytes are involved in the nonspecific immune response. They phagocytize foreign matter and organisms such as bacteria. Some monocytes migrate from the blood to tissue, where they mature into stationary cells called **macrophages.** Macrophages have greater phagocytic capability than monocytes.

TEACHER TIP

HIV causes a loss of a certain subset of T cells known as helper T cells (CD4+). While this alone is not particularly detrimental to the organism, a loss of these cells prevents activation of other lymphocytes and generation of an immune response. This is why people infected with HIV are more susceptible to disease.

3. Platelets

Platelets are cell fragments approximately 2–3 μm in diameter and are also formed in the bone marrow. Platelets lack nuclei and function in clot formation. There are about 250,000–500,000 platelets per one mm^3 of blood.

CLINICAL CORRELATE

Anasarca is a condition of generalized edema in the tissues. It is caused by very low albumin concentration in the blood, i.e. low osmotic pressure in the capillary at the venule end.

B. BLOOD ANTIGENS

Erythrocytes have characteristic cell-surface proteins (**antigens**). Antigens are macromolecules that are foreign to the host organism and trigger an immune response. The two major groups of red blood cell antigens are the **ABO group** and the **Rh factor.**

TEACHER TIP

You are almost guaranteed to see at least one question on blood groups. It is critical that you learn how the system works (A/B codominant).

1. ABO Group

There are four ABO blood groups, **A, B, AB,** and **O**; see Table 9.1.

Table 9.1

Blood Type	Antigen in Red Blood Cell	Antibodies Produced
A	A	anti-B
B	B	anti-A
AB (universal recipient)	A and B	none
O (universal donor)	none	anti-A and anti-B

It is extremely important during blood transfusions that donor and recipient blood types be appropriately matched. The aim is to avoid transfusion of red blood cells that will be clumped ("rejected") by antibodies (proteins in the immune system that bind specifically to antigens) present in the recipient's plasma. The rule of blood matching is as follows: If the donor's antigens are already in the recipient's blood, no clumping occurs. Type AB blood is termed the **"universal recipient,"** as it has neither anti-A nor anti-B antibodies. Type O blood is considered to be the **"universal donor"**; it will not elicit a response from the recipient's immune system because it does not possess any surface antigens (see chapter 13 for further discussion of ABO blood groups).

CLINICAL CORRELATE

When an Rh⁻ woman delivers an Rh⁺ fetus, she stands a good chance of being exposed to the baby's Rh⁺ blood cells. This may lead to the development of antibodies against the Rh antigen, which can cause problems (erythroblastosis fetalis) with future Rh⁺ pregnancies. This problem can be avoided in most cases by giving the mother Rh immune globulin (RhoGAM) immediately after delivery. Administration of immune globulin (which is a type of passive immunization) will suppress the development of active immunity on the mother's part, preventing the production of antibodies to the Rh antigen.

2. Rh Factor

The Rh factor is another antigen that may be present on the surface of red blood cells. Individuals may be Rh⁺, possessing the Rh antigen, or Rh⁻, lacking the Rh antigen. Consideration of the Rh factor is particularly important during pregnancy. An Rh⁻ woman can be sensitized by an Rh⁺ fetus if fetal red blood cells (which will have the Rh factor) enter maternal circulation during birth. If this woman subsequently carries another Rh⁺ fetus, the anti-Rh antibodies she produced when sensitized by the first birth may cross the placenta and destroy fetal red blood cells. This results in severe anemia for the fetus, known as **erythroblastosis fetalis.** Erythroblastosis is not caused by ABO blood-type mismatches between mother and fetus, because anti-A and anti-B antibodies cannot cross the placenta.

FUNCTIONS OF THE CIRCULATORY SYSTEM

Blood transports nutrients and O_2 to tissue, and wastes and CO_2 from tissue. Platelets are involved in injury repair. Leukocytes are the main component of the immune system.

A. TRANSPORT OF GASES

Erythrocytes transport O_2 throughout the circulatory system. Actually, it is the hemoglobin molecules in erythrocytes that bind to O_2. A hemoglobin molecule is composed of four polypeptide chains, each containing a prosthetic heme group. Each heme group is capable of binding to one molecule of oxygen. Thus, each hemoglobin molecule is capable of binding to four molecules of O_2. The binding of O_2 at the first heme group induces a conformational change that facilitates the binding of O_2 at the other three heme groups. Similarly, the unloading of O_2 at one heme group facilitates the unloading of O_2 at the other three heme groups. This cooperation between the heme groups is an allosteric effect (see chapter 2); this is reflected in hemoglobin's S-shaped **dissociation curve** (see Figure 9.6).

> ### TEACHER TIP
> Hemoglobin has four subunits (i.e., quaternary structure). This is what allows it to shift when oxygen binds and gives the classic sigmoidal binding curve. Myoglobin is a single subunit (i.e., no quaternary structure). Its curve is not sigmoidal. This is a concept commonly tested on the MCAT.

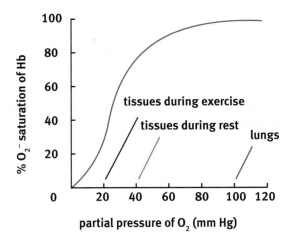

Figure 9.6. Hemoglobin Dissociation Curve

Hemoglobin also binds to CO_2. Carbon dioxide diffuses from tissue into erythrocytes, where it combines with H_2O to form carbonic acid (H_2CO_3). Carbonic acid then dissociates into a bicarbonate ion (HCO_3^-) and a hydrogen ion (H^+). The H^+ binds to the hemoglobin molecule, while HCO_3^- diffuses into the plasma. There is an allosteric relationship between the concentrations of CO_2, H^+, and O_2, known as the **Bohr effect.** According to the Bohr effect, increasing concentrations of H^+ (a decrease in pH) and CO_2 (an increase in HCO_3^-) in the blood decrease hemoglobin's O_2 affinity.

Thus, the presence of high concentrations of H^+ and CO_2 in metabolically active tissue, such as muscle, enhances the release of O_2 to this tissue. Conversely, a high concentration of O_2, as in the alveolar capillaries, promotes O_2 uptake and CO_2 release from hemoglobin. In the lungs, HCO_3^- and H^+ reassociate to form CO_2 and H_2O, which are expelled during exhalation (see chapter 8). Both formation and dissociation of carbonic acid are catalyzed by the enzyme **carbonic anhydrase.**

$$CO_2 + H_2O \underset{\text{anhydrase}}{\overset{\text{carbonic}}{\rightleftharpoons}} H_2CO_3 \rightleftharpoons H^+ + HCO_3^-$$

B. TRANSPORT OF NUTRIENTS AND WASTES

Amino acids and simple sugars are absorbed into the bloodstream at the intestinal capillaries and transported to the liver via the hepatic portal vein. After processing, they are transported throughout the body. Fats enter the lymphatic system through lymph capillaries in the small intestine and drain into the bloodstream at the large veins of the neck, thereby bypassing the liver. Throughout the body, metabolic waste products (e.g., water, urea, and carbon dioxide) diffuse into capillaries from surrounding cells; these wastes are then delivered to the appropriate excretory organs (see chapter 10).

The exchange of materials is greatly influenced by the balance between the **hydrostatic pressure** and the **osmotic pressure** of the blood and tissue fluids. The hydrostatic pressure at the arteriole end of the capillaries is greater than the hydrostatic pressure of the surrounding tissue fluids (interstitial fluid). This causes fluid to move out of the capillaries at the arteriole end. However, because blood has a higher solute concentration than the tissue fluid, osmotic pressure causes fluid to move back into the capillaries at the venule end. Proteins, such as albumin, are primarily responsible for the majority of this osmotic pressure.

As shown in Figure 9.7, the hydrostatic pressure at the arteriole end of the capillary bed is approximately 36 mm Hg, while the opposing osmotic pressure is approximately 25 mm Hg. This 11 mm Hg difference favors the hydrostatic pressure, and so there is a net flow of fluid out of the capillaries. At the venule end of the capillary bed, the osmotic pressure across the wall is greater than the hydrostatic pressure, which has dropped to 15 mm Hg. This difference tends to draw fluid into the capillaries. Hence, most of the fluid is forced out of the capillaries at the arteriole

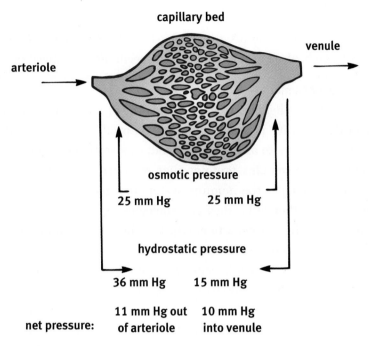

arteriole

capillary bed

venule

osmotic pressure

25 mm Hg   25 mm Hg

hydrostatic pressure

36 mm Hg   15 mm Hg

net pressure: 11 mm Hg out   10 mm Hg
                  of arteriole   into venule

Figure 9.7. Net Fluid Flow at Capillary Bed

TEACHER TIP

Note how much lower the pressure is here than in the arteries (normal 120/80). Recall that this pressure drop occurs across the arterioles and is necessary because the capillaries cannot handle higher pressure. They are only a single cell thick so that gas exchange can occur.

end and is reabsorbed by the capillaries at the venule end. The remaining fluid is transported back into the blood via the lymphatic system.

C. CLOTTING

When platelets come into contact with the exposed collagen of a damaged vessel, they release a chemical that causes neighboring platelets to adhere to one another, forming a platelet plug. Subsequently, both the platelets and the damaged tissue release the clotting factor **thromboplastin.** Thromboplastin, with the aid of its cofactors calcium and vitamin K, converts the inactive plasma protein **prothrombin** to its active form, **thrombin.** Thrombin then converts **fibrinogen** (another plasma protein) into **fibrin.** Threads of fibrin coat the damaged area and trap blood cells to form a **clot.** Clots prevent extensive blood loss while the damaged vessel heals itself. People suffering from the genetic disease **hemophilia** lack one of the agents involved in clot formation and bleed excessively, even from minor cuts and bruises (see chapter 13).

D. IMMUNOLOGICAL REACTIONS

The body has the ability to distinguish between "self" and "nonself," and to "remember" nonself entities (antigens) that it has previously encountered. These defense mechanisms are an integral part of the **immune system.** The immune system is composed of two **specific defense mechanisms**: **humoral immunity,** which involves the production of antibodies; and

TEACHER TIP

In some individuals this ability to distinguish between self and nonself is lost, resulting in a class of diseases known as auto-immune diseases. Type I diabetes is a result of auto-immunity to the beta cells of the pancreas and is an MCAT favorite.

cell-mediated immunity, which involves cells that combat fungal and viral infection. Lymphocytes are responsible for both of these immune mechanisms. The body also has a number of nonspecific defense mechanisms.

1. Humoral Immunity

One of the body's defense mechanisms is the production of antibodies. Humoral immunity is responsible for the proliferation of antibodies following exposure to antigens. Antibodies, also called **immunoglobulins** (Igs), are complex proteins that recognize and bind to specific antigens and trigger the immune system to remove them. Antibodies either attract other cells (such as leukocytes) to phagocytize the antigen, or cause the antigens to clump together (agglutinate) and form large insoluble complexes, facilitating their removal by phagocytic cells. An antibody molecule consists of four polypeptide chains—two identical **heavy chains** and two identical **light chains**—held together by disulfide linkages and noncovalent bonds. Certain regions on the chains (called **variable regions**) serve as antigen-binding sites; these sites are structured so as to bind to one specific antigen. The remaining part of the chains (the **constant regions**) aid in the process by which foreign antigens are destroyed (see Figure 9.8). There are five types of constant regions—M, A, D, G, and E—defining five classes of immunoglobulins: **IgM, IgA, IgD, IgG,** and **IgE.**

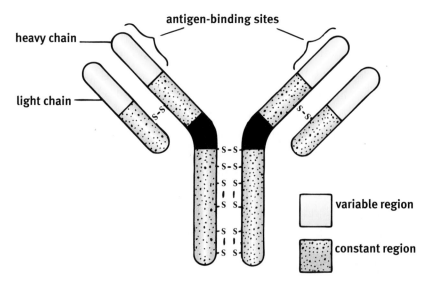

Figure 9.8. Antibody Structure

The lymphocytes involved in the humoral response are the B lymphocytes, or **B cells,** which originate in the bone marrow and differentiate in the spleen, lymph nodes, and other lymphatic organs. When exposed to a specific antigen, B lymphocytes specific for that antigen proliferate. Some of the daughter cells become **memory cells,** and others become **plasma cells (effector cells)**; this is known as the **primary response.** Plasma cells produce and release antibodies specific for the antigen. It generally takes 7–10 days for the plasma cells to generate a sufficient amount of antibody. Memory cells "remember" the antigen and are long-lived in the bloodstream, sometimes remaining there permanently. Memory cells are able to elicit a more immediate response upon subsequent exposure to the same antigen; this is referred to as the **secondary response.**

Active immunity refers to the production of antibodies during an immune response. Active immunity can be conferred by vaccination; an individual is injected with a weakened, inactive, or related form of a particular antigen, that stimulates the immune system to produce specific antibodies against it. Active immunity may require weeks to build up. **Passive immunity** involves the transfer of antibodies produced by another individual or organism. Passive immunity is acquired either passively or by injection. For example, during pregnancy, some maternal antibodies cross the placenta and enter fetal circulation, conferring passive immunity upon the fetus. Although passive immunity is acquired immediately, it is very short-lived, lasting only as long as the antibodies circulate in the blood system.

2. Cell-Mediated Immunity

The lymphocytes involved in cell-mediated immunity are T lymphocytes, or **T cells,** which develop in bone marrow and mature and proliferate in the thymus. T cells act primarily against the body's own cells that are infected by a fungus or virus. T cells differentiate into effector cells: **cytotoxic T cells** destroy antigens directly; **helper T cells** activate other B and T cells, as well as nonlymphocyte cells such as macrophages, through the secretion of **lymphokines** (e.g., interleukins); **suppressor T cells** regulate other B and T cells to decrease their activity against antigens. Some T cells differentiate into memory cells. These events constitute the primary components of a cell-mediated response. During a secondary response, these memory cells proliferate vigorously and produce a large number of cytotoxic T cells to combat the invader.

T cells play important roles in allergic reactions and in the rejection of organ transplants. Sometimes pollen or certain foods can act as antigens, stimulating the release of substances (e.g., **histamine**)

TEACHER TIP

Sometimes the organisms that cause diseases are so similar in structure that the immune system can be fooled—even for our benefit. When Edward Jenner was trying to find a treatment for smallpox, he inoculated his son with infectious particles from a different but related disease, cowpox. While the child contracted cowpox, he became immunized to smallpox due to the similarity of the two diseases!

TEACHER TIP

Recall that viruses must be inside of cells in order to replicate, thus they can often evade the immune system. One way that the immune system deals with this problem is by using cytotoxic T cells to kill virally infected cells.

responsible for allergic symptoms, such as hives and mucous membrane inflammation. Cell-mediated immunity plays an important role in transplant rejection; i.e., tissue from a donor is recognized by the recipient as foreign because the recipient's body does not recognize the antigens on the transplanted cells, and in response, cytotoxic T cells are sent out to destroy the foreign cells. In certain diseases, the body mistakenly identifies its own cells as foreign and elicits an **autoimmune** response, destroying its own cells.

3. Nonspecific Defense Mechanisms

The body employs a number of nonspecific defenses against foreign material: 1) Skin is a physical barrier against bacterial invasion. In addition, pores on the skin's surface secrete sweat, which contains an enzyme that attacks bacterial cell walls. 2) Passages (e.g., the respiratory tract) are lined with ciliated mucous-coated epithelia, which filter and trap foreign particles. 3) Macrophages engulf and destroy foreign particles. 4) The **inflammatory response** is initiated by the body in response to physical damage: injured cells release histamine, which causes blood vessels to dilate, thereby increasing blood flow to the damaged region. Granulocytes attracted to the injury site phagocytize antigenic material. An inflammatory response is often accompanied by a fever. 5) Proteins called **interferons** are produced by cells under viral attack. Interferons diffuse to other cells, where they help prevent the spread of the virus.

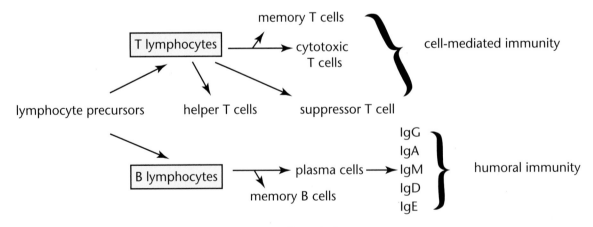

Figure 9.9. Lymphocyte Differentiation

THE LYMPHATIC SYSTEM

The lymphatic system is a secondary circulatory system distinct from cardiovascular circulation. Its vessels transport excess interstitial fluid, called **lymph,** to the cardiovascular system, thereby keeping fluid levels in the body constant. **Lymph capillaries** (lacteals) collect fats by absorbing chylomicrons in the small intestine and transporting them to cardiovascular circulation (see chapter 7). Lymph capillaries are closed at one end and lead into other lymph vessels that have valves to prevent the backflow of lymph. These lymph vessels then converge in the region of the upper chest and neck, where they drain into the large veins of the cardiovascular system. Lymph flow is regulated by contraction of neighboring skeletal muscles and rhythmic contractions of the lymphatic vessels themselves. **Lymph nodes** are swellings along lymph vessels containing phagocytic cells (leukocytes) that filter the lymph, removing and destroying foreign particles.

TEACHER TIP

Flashback to Digestion: Recall that unlike carbohydrates and proteins (amino acids), fat molecules are taken up by the lymphatics and dumped directly into the circulation. Thus, they (unlike carbohydrates and proteins) are not seen by the liver before entering the circulation.

PRACTICE QUESTIONS

1. At any given time, there is more blood in the venous system than the arterial system. Which of the following features of a vein allows this?

   A. Relative lack of smooth muscle in the wall
   B. Presence of valves
   C. Proximity of veins to lymphatic vessels
   D. Thin endothelial lining

2. Which of the following is the body's primary mechanism for buffering the blood?

   A. Fluid intake
   B. Absorption of nutrients in the gastrointestinal system
   C. Carbon dioxide produced from metabolism
   D. Reabsorption in the kidney

3. A deficiency of eosinophils would predispose the body to which of the following?

   A. Giardia
   B. Sickle cell disease
   C. Hepatitis B
   D. Influenza

4. Allergic reactions are mediated by which of the following?

   A. Granules in basophils
   B. Nucleus of eosinophils
   C. IgG of red blood cells
   D. Granules in neutrophils

5. Systolic blood pressure is the pressure at which

   A. the aortic valve is open.
   B. the mitral valve is open.
   C. the pulmonic valve is closed.
   D. venous valves are closed.

6. Diastolic blood pressure is measured when

   A. right ventricular pressure is equal to left ventricular pressure.
   B. arterial pressure equals venous pressure.
   C. ventricular pressure is less than atrial pressure.
   D. pulmonic artery pressure is equal to aortic pressure.

7. Which of the following correctly demonstrates the relationship between the parasympathetic nervous system and heart rate at rest?

   A. Administration of intravenous epinephrine increases heart rate.
   B. Blocking the sympathetic nervous system at rest does not alter the heart rate.
   C. Blocking acetylcholine receptors at rest does not alter the heart rate.
   D. Administration of intravenous acetylcholine increases the heart rate.

8. Following are the sample lab results from Rh testing in a family:

	Rh Factor
Mother	Negative
Father	Positive
1st Child	Positive

It is not known whether the mother received immunoglobulins against Rh factor (antigen D) in her first pregnancy. Based on the data above, if the mother is six months pregnant with a second child by the same father, which of the following is most likely?

A. Red blood cells of the first child are circulating within the mother.
B. The father's Rh factor protects the fetus against auto-immune attack.
C. The mother's immune system may be generating antibodies against Rh.
D. Administration of Rh immune globin at this point would provide protection to the fetus.

9. Which of the following conveys the most strength to a clot?

A. Thrombin
B. Fibrinogen
C. Platelets
D. Fibrin

10. The porto-hepatic system lies in series with the upper and lower body with respect to the heart as diagramed below.

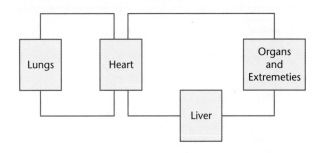

Placement of the porto-hepatic system in series serves which of the following functions?

A. Oxygenates liver tissue
B. Enhances absorption of water
C. Increases venous return to the heart
D. Filters deoxygenated blood

11. What is the half-life of epinephrine given the graph of epinephrine clearance below?

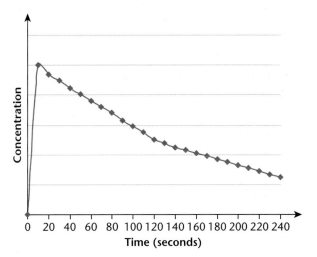

A. 60 seconds
B. 90 seconds
C. 120 seconds
D. 180 seconds

12. Which of the following is described in the graph of antibody producton below?

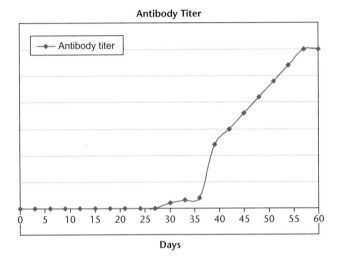

Antibody Titer

Days

A. Passive immunization

B. Exposure to a new antigen

C. Exposure to a previously recognized antigen

D. Lymphocytopenia

13. Put the following in chronological order.

1. Rearrangement of heavy and light chains

2. First exposure to antigen

3. Proliferation of B cells into memory and plasma cells

4. Binding of antibody to antigen

5. Phagocytosis

A. 2, 3, 1, 4, 5

B. 2, 1, 4, 3, 5

C. 2, 3, 4, 1, 5

D. 4, 2, 3, 1, 5

14. Pus is primarily composed of phagocytosed bacterial remnants. Which of the following would you expect to find in a microscopic sample of pus?

A. Red blood cells, white blood cells, and platelets

B. Granulocytes, monocytes, and macrophages

C. Eosinophils, basophils, and neutrophils

D. Collagen, white blood cells, and calcium

15. An acute, uncompensated drop in stroke volume would preferentially spare which of the following body parts?

A. Left-upper extremity

B. Right-upper extremity

C. Brain

D. Heart

CIRCULATION

Increased O_2 consumption in the left ventricle coupled with left ventricular hypertrophy and a heart murmur is most likely the result of what condition, and what symptoms would be seen in a patient with this condition?

1) Examine the reasons for increased O_2 consumption in the heart.

O_2 consumption in the heart increases when there is increased afterload (or increased aortic pressure), increased heart rate, increased contractility, and/or increased size of the heart.

2) Examine the reasons for left ventricular hypertrophy.

Left ventricular hypertrophy is the abnormal enlargement of the muscle of the left ventricle. This thickening occurs when the left ventricle has to work harder to generate enough force to overcome greater pressure as it is pumping (greater afterload).

3) Review the flow of blood through the heart.

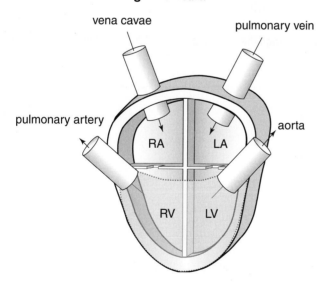

Blood travels into the right atrium through the vena cava. It moves through the tricuspid valve into the right ventricle and is then passed into the pulmonary artery, which carries it to the lungs. After leaving the lungs, blood travels through the pulmonary vein to the left atrium, then through the mitral valve into the left ventricle. The left ventricle pumps blood through the aortic valve into the aorta.

TAKEAWAYS

It's important to be able to integrate knowledge from different areas, in this case O_2 consumption, blood flow, and the pathway of the heart, when examining a question.

SIMILAR QUESTIONS

1) Where would a patient diagnosed with stenosis of the mitral valve experience the greatest increase in blood pressure?

2) If a tracer substance were injected into a patient's superior vena cava, which structure would it reach last before leaving the heart?

3) The decrease in the number of pulmonary capillaries due to the loss of functional lung tissue will most likely result in a pressure overload. Where will this overload occur?

4) Determine the cause of the heart murmur.

Heart murmurs result from turbulent blood flow through the heart, particularly through the valves. Deformities of a valve will cause blood flow through the valve to become turbulent and create a heart murmur.

5) Determine the cause of the left ventricular hypertrophy and the increased O_2 consumption.

The left ventricle thickens and uses more oxygen because it cannot easily pump the blood through the aortic valve into the aorta. Stenosis is a condition in which the leaves of a heart valve adhere to each other, decreasing the volume of blood flow through the valve. Therefore, a stenotic aortic valve would make pumping blood through the aortic valve more difficult and lead to increased O_2 consumption and left ventricular hypertrophy.

6) Determine the effects of decreased blood flow due to aortic stenosis.

If less blood can be pumped from the left ventricle into the aorta, the ability to supply the body with blood will be reduced. This can cause blood to back up into the lungs and cause shortness of breath, especially with activity, as well as chest pain. Also, because less blood will be going out to the body, weakness can result; further, because less blood will be going to the brain, fainting is also a symptom of aortic stenosis.

Remember: *Knowing the pathway that blood takes through the heart is essential!*

NORMAL OXYGEN DISSOCIATION CURVE

How does the oxygen dissociation curve of arterial blood differ from the curve for venous blood, and what accounts for this difference?

1) Review the normal oxygen dissociation curve.

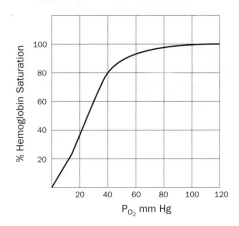

The oxygen dissociation curve shows the percent saturation of hemoglobin as a function of the partial pressure of O_2 (P_{O_2}). At P_{O_2} = 100 mm Hg, hemoglobin saturation is 100 percent, which means that four oxygen molecules are bound to the hemoglobin. At P_{O_2} = 40 mm Hg, hemoglobin is 80 percent saturated and at P_{O_2} = 25 mm Hg, hemoglobin is 50% saturated with oxygen molecules. The cooperative binding of O_2, meaning the binding of the first O_2 molecule, facilitates the binding of the next and results in a sigmoidal, or S-shaped, curve.

2) Examine how arterial blood differs from venous blood.

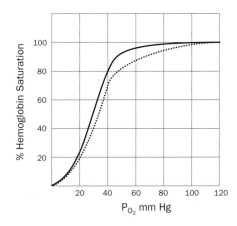

After blood passes through the lungs and into the arteries, the hemoglobin is 100 percent saturated with oxygen. The tissues of the body produce CO_2 as waste. The increase in CO_2 at the tissues decreases the pH of the tissues.

KEY CONCEPTS

Oxygen dissociation curve

Arterial blood saturation

Venous blood saturation

Right/left shift

Bohr effect

TAKEAWAYS

It is important to understand how to read the oxygen dissociation curve and how changes in the curve equate to changes in the affinity of hemoglobin for oxygen. Increases in P_{CO_2}, decreases in pH, and increases in temperature shift the curve to the right. The opposite of those, a decrease in P_{CO_2}, an increase in pH, or a decrease in temperature shift the curve to the left.

THINGS TO WATCH OUT FOR

Right shifts of the curve are more common, but don't forget the factors that shift the curve to the left.

SIMILAR QUESTIONS

1) How is the P_{50} of venous blood different from that of arterial blood?

2) How will the fetal oxygen dissociation curve differ from that of an adult?

3) How will arterial Po_2 be affected by living at a high altitude?

Increases in CO_2 or decreases in pH decrease the affinity of hemoglobin for oxygen and cause the curve to shift slightly to the right, increasing the Po_2 and facilitating the unloading of O_2 at the tissues. The tissues keep Po_2 low by consuming O_2 for aerobic metabolism, so that the O_2 diffusion gradient is maintained. In arterial blood, the hemoglobin saturation at 40 mm Hg is 80 percent, but in venous blood the Hb saturation at 40 mm Hg is 75 percent. Therefore, about 5 percent more oxygen is released. This right shift of the curve is known as the Bohr effect. An increase in temperature also causes a right shift.

At the lungs, alveolar gas has a Po_2 of 100 mm Hg. O_2 diffuses from the alveolar air into the capillaries. O_2 is bound very tightly to hemoglobin because at a Po_2 of 100 mm Hg, hemoglobin has a very high affinity for O_2. This maintains the partial pressure gradients and facilitates the diffusion of oxygen into the blood.

ABNORMAL OXYGEN DISSOCIATION CURVE

Carbon monoxide (CO) binding to hemoglobin occurs in competition with oxygen (O_2) to hemoglobin binding; hemoglobin's affinity for CO is over 200 times its affinity for O_2. However, the binding of CO at one site increases the affinity for O_2 at the remaining sites. Draw the oxygen dissociation curve for CO poisoning, measuring hemoglobin oxygen content (in units of mL O_2/dL) on the vertical axis.

1) Visualize the normal oxygen dissociation curve.

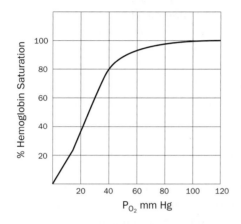

The oxygen dissociation curve shows the percent saturation of hemoglobin as a function of the partial pressure of O_2 (Po_2). At Po_2 = 100 mm Hg, hemoglobin saturation is 100 percent, which means that four oxygen molecules are bound to the hemoglobin. At Po_2 = 40 mm Hg, hemoglobin is 80 percent saturated and at Po_2 = 25 mm Hg, hemoglobin is 50 percent saturated with oxygen molecules. The cooperative binding of O_2, meaning the binding of the first O_2 molecule, facilitates the binding of the next and results in a sigmoidal, or S-shaped, curve.

2) Examine the effect that CO binding has on O_2 binding.
The question stem states that CO competes with O_2 when binding hemoglobin. Because hemoglobin affinity is 200 times greater for CO than for O_2, hemoglobin will preferentially bind CO first on a hemoglobin molecule. This will decrease the amount of O_2 that can bind to hemoglobin and therefore decrease the amount of O_2 that is in the blood.

**THINGS TO
WATCH OUT FOR**

Right shifts in the
dissociation curve (Bohr
effect) are more commonly
seen, but be prepared for
the factors that can cause
the curve to shift to the left.

3) Determine the effect that CO binding will have on the oxygen dissociation curve.

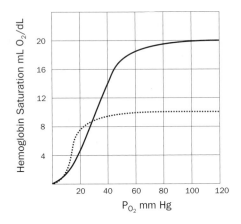

SIMILAR QUESTIONS

1) How will exercise affect the oxygen dissociation curve?

2) What type of physical reaction would high P_{CO_2} cause?

3) What would the oxygen dissociation curve look like in a patient with metabolic alkalosis?

The question stem also states that the binding of CO increases hemoglobin affinity for O_2 at the remaining sites. Any physiological factor (i.e., decreased P_{CO_2}, increased pH, or decreased temperature) that increases the affinity of hemoglobin for oxygen has the effect of shifting the curve to the left. Any physiological factor (i.e., increased P_{CO_2}, decreased pH, or increased temperature) that decreases the affinity of hemoglobin for oxygen has the effect of shifting the curve to the right. The right shift is known as the Bohr effect. However, in this case the affinity of hemoglobin for oxygen is increased and there will be a left shift in the oxygen dissociation curve. It is this left shift that makes CO poisoning so deadly; with CO bound to hemoglobin, the O_2 molecules are bound so tightly that they cannot be off-loaded at the tissues and thus asphyxia occurs.

Remember: The oxygen dissociation curve can be shifted to the left or to the right based on physiological conditions.

LYMPHATIC SYSTEM

Approximately 20 L/day of fluid filters across capillaries. Reabsorption across capillaries is approximately 16 L/day, and therefore the excess fluid must be returned to circulation by the lymphatic system. Lymphatic vessels are attached to the underlying connective tissue by fine filaments. What purpose do these filaments serve?

1) Examine the structure of lymph vessels.

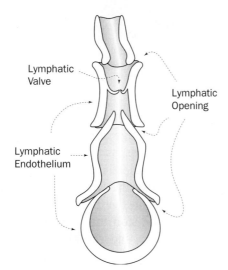

Lymphatic Valve

Lymphatic Opening

Lymphatic Endothelium

Lymphatic vessels have very thin walls that do not contain the smooth muscle that is found in arteries. Lymph vessels contain valves that ensure the unidirectional flow of lymph through the vessels. Filtrate from blood vessels, including cells and protein that have moved into the interstitial fluid compartment, is picked up by the lymphatic vessels. Lymphatic vessels called lacteals absorb fats from the gastrointestinal tract. The filtrate is moved through the system of lymphatic vessels, passing through lymph nodes where foreign particles are destroyed and removed. It rejoins blood circulation at the thoracic duct and superior vena cava.

TAKEAWAYS

The lymphatic system plays a very important role in returning fluid, cells, and proteins back to the blood stream, but it relies on the movement of skeletal muscles in order to accomplish this role.

2) Determine how interstitial fluid moves through lymph vessels.

Because lymphatic vessels do not have smooth muscle in their walls, they must rely on outside forces to move the lymph fluid through the vessels. The movement of skeletal muscles around the lymphatic vessels aids in moving lymph along, and their one-way valves prevent backflow of this fluid.

THINGS TO WATCH OUT FOR

Although the lymphatic system has some similarities with the circulatory system, lymphatic vessels are closed-ended, they do not connect in a complete circuit, and they are unidirectional.

SIMILAR QUESTIONS

1) If a patient's lymphatic channels have been obstructed by the spread of malignant tumors, what will result?

2) What physiological conditions can contribute to excess fluid in the interstitial space?

3) How does the lymphatic system return interstitial proteins to the blood?

3) Determine how interstitial fluid enters lymphatic vessels.

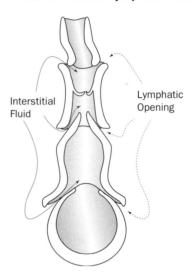

Interstitial Fluid

Lymphatic Opening

Capillaries have tight junctions between their endothelial cells. These tight junctions prevent unregulated passage of solutes in and out of the capillary lumen. Lymphatic vessels do not possess these tight junctions but rather have openings through which the interstitial fluid, complete with cells and proteins, can pass into the vessel. Because the lymph vessels are attached by fine filaments to their underlying connective tissue, skeletal muscle contraction will pull on these filaments and distort the lymphatic vessel. This distortion causes spaces to open between the endothelial cells of the vessel and allows the interstitial fluid to enter.

Remember: Lymphatic vessels differ from blood vessels in that they lack smooth muscle around the vessel and lack tight junctions between endothelial cells.

CHAPTER 10

HOMEOSTASIS

Homeostasis is the process by which a stable internal environment within an organism is maintained. Some important homeostatic mechanisms include the maintenance of a water and solute balance **(osmoregulation),** the removal of metabolic waste products **(excretion),** the regulation of blood glucose levels, and the maintenance of a constant internal body temperature **(thermoregulation).** In mammals, the primary homeostatic organs are the **kidneys,** the **liver,** the **large intestine,** and the **skin.**

THE KIDNEYS: OSMOREGULATION

The kidneys regulate the concentration of salt and water in the blood through the formation and excretion of urine. The kidneys are bean-shaped and are located behind the stomach and liver. Each kidney is composed of approximately one million units called **nephrons.**

A. STRUCTURE

The kidney is divided into three regions: the **cortex,** the **medulla,** and the **pelvis.** Blood enters the kidney through the **renal artery,** which divides into many **afferent arterioles** that run through the medulla and into the cortex (see Figure 10.1). Each afferent arteriole branches into a convoluted network of capillaries called a **glomerulus** (see Figure 10.2). Rather than converging directly into a vein, the capillaries converge into an **efferent arteriole,** which divides into a fine capillary network known as the **vasa recta.** The vasa recta enmeshes the nephron tubule and then converges into the **renal vein.** This arrangement of tandem capillary beds is a portal system (see chapter 9).

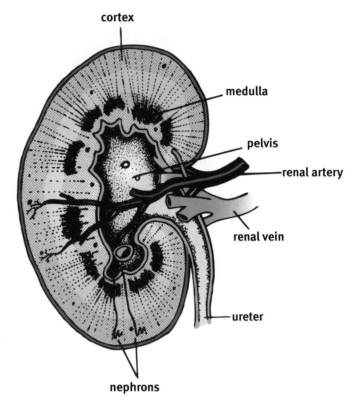

cortex

medulla

pelvis

renal artery

renal vein

ureter

nephrons

Figure 10.1. Kidney

A nephron consists of a bulb called **Bowman's capsule,** which embraces a glomerulus and leads into a long coiled tubule that is divided into five units: the **proximal convoluted tubule,** the **descending limb** of the **loop of Henle,** the **ascending limb** of the **loop of Henle,** the **distal convoluted tubule,** and the **collecting duct.** The nephron is positioned such that the loop of Henle runs through the medulla, while the convoluted tubules and Bowman's capsule are in the cortex (see Figure 10.2).

B. FUNCTION

1. Overview

Filtration, secretion, and **reabsorption** are the three processes that regulate salt and water balance in the blood.

a. Filtration

Blood pressure forces 20 percent of the blood plasma entering the glomerulus into the surrounding Bowman's capsule. The fluid and small solutes entering the nephron are called the **filtrate.** The filtrate is isotonic with blood plasma. Molecules too large to filter through the glomerulus, such as blood cells and albumin, remain in the circulatory system.

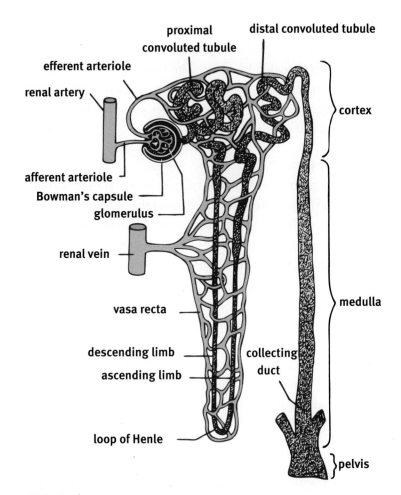

Figure 10.2. Nephron

b. Secretion

The nephron secretes substances such as acids, bases, and ions from the interstitial fluid into the filtrate by both passive and active transport. Secretion maintains blood pH, potassium concentration in the blood, and nitrogenous waste concentration in the filtrate.

c. Reabsorption

Essential substances (glucose, salts, and amino acids) and water are reabsorbed from the filtrate and returned to the blood. This results in the formation of concentrated urine, which is hypertonic to the blood.

2. Nephron Function

Through the selective permeability of its walls and the maintenance of an osmolarity gradient, the nephron reabsorbs nutrients, salts, and water from the filtrate and returns them to the body, thus maintaining the bloodstream's solute concentration.

a. Selective permeability

The walls of the proximal tubule and the descending limb of the loop of Henle are permeable to water. The walls of the lower ascending limb are permeable only to salt. In the presence of ADH, the walls of the collecting duct are permeable to water and urea but only slightly permeable to salt.

b. Osmolarity gradient

The selective permeability of the tubules establishes an **osmolarity gradient** in the surrounding interstitial fluid. By exiting and then reentering at different segments of the nephron, solutes create an osmolarity gradient, with tissue osmolarity increasing from cortex to inner medulla. The solutes that contribute to the maintenance of the gradient are urea and salt (Na^+ and Cl^-). Urea diffuses out of the collecting duct; it eventually reenters the nephron by diffusing into the ascending limb. Salt is cycled between the two limbs of the loop of Henle. Na^+ and Cl^- diffuse out of the lower half of the ascending limb, while the upper half actively pumps out Na^+ (Cl^- passively follows). This combination of passive diffusion and active transport of solutes maximizes water conservation and the excretion of urine hypertonic to the blood (see Figure 10.3).

c. Flow of filtrate

Filtrate enters Bowman's capsule and flows into the proximal convoluted tubule, where virtually all glucose, amino acids, and other important organic molecules are reabsorbed via active transport. In addition, 60–70 percent of the Na^+ in the filtrate is reabsorbed (by both active and passive mechanisms); water and Cl^- passively follow. The filtrate then flows down the descending limb into the renal medulla, where there is an increasing ionic concentration in the interstitial fluid, causing more water to diffuse out of the nephron. The filtrate flows through the ascending limb, which is impermeable to water, and then into the distal convoluted tubule. The filtrate continues through the collecting duct, where water reabsorption is under hormonal (ADH) control. The remaining filtrate, urine, is hypertonic to the blood and highly concentrated in urea and other solutes.

C. HORMONAL REGULATION

Hormonal regulation plays a key role in urine formation. Two hormones that regulate water reabsorption are **aldosterone** and **ADH.**

TEACHER TIP

Flashback to Chapter 1: The entire system under which the kidney operates is membrane transport. Both active and passive transport are used, and the extent to which they are used depends on the specific section of the nephron in question. The key point is that membrane permeability is absolutely necessary for the kidneys to work.

TEACHER TIP

KEY POINT: Water is not reabsorbed by itself. In fact, it is not usually pumped at all. The kidney moves ions (primarily Na and Cl) to create gradients that water will follow.

MCAT SYNOPSIS

The kidneys function to eliminate wastes (urea, H+) generated by metabolic activity, while reabsorbing various important substances (glucose, amino acids, sodium) for re-use by the body. Generation of a solute concentration gradient from cortex to medulla allows a considerable amount of water to be reabsorbed. Excretion of a concentrated urine serves to limit water losses from the body and helps preserve blood volume.

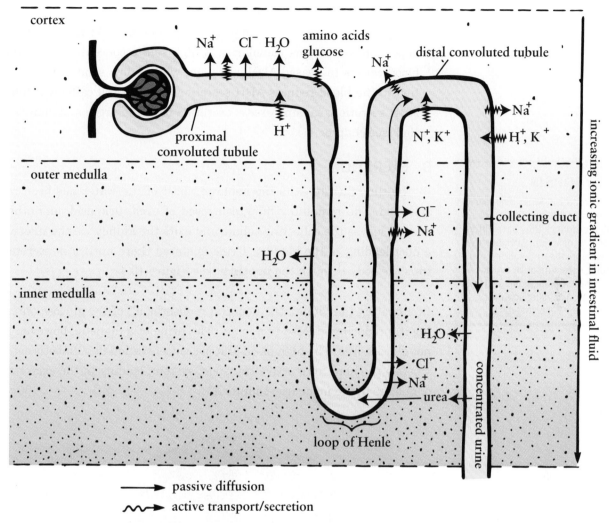

passive diffusion

active transport/secretion

Figure 10.3. Selective Permeability and Osmolarity Gradient in the Nephron

1. Aldosterone

Aldosterone, which is produced by the adrenal cortex, stimulates both the reabsorption of Na^+ from the collecting duct and the secretion of K^+. Reabsorption of Na^+ increases water reabsorption, leading to a rise in blood volume, and hence a rise in blood pressure. In a person suffering from **Addison's disease,** aldosterone is produced insufficiently or not at all. This causes overexcretion of urine with a high Na^+ concentration, which causes a considerable drop in blood pressure. Aldosterone secretion is regulated by the **renin-angiotensin system** (see chapter 11).

2. ADH (Antidiuretic Hormone)

ADH, also known as **vasopressin,** is formed in the hypothalamus and stored in the posterior pituitary. As an "antidiuretic," it causes

TEACHER TIP

It is critical to know how aldosterone and ADH exert their effects. Aldosterone directly increases sodium reabsorption and water follows. ADH makes the CCD more leaky (permeable) to water such that it will reenter the interstitium. The ultimate effect is similar but the mechanism in which they work is slightly different.

increased water reabsorption. It acts directly on the collecting duct, increasing its permeability to water. The amount of ADH produced is dependent on plasma osmolarity. A high solute concentration in the blood causes increased ADH secretion, while a low solute concentration in the blood reduces ADH secretion. Alcohol and caffeine inhibit ADH secretion, causing excess excretion of dilute urine and dehydration (see chapter 11).

D. EXCRETION

By the time filtrate exits the nephron, most of the water has been reabsorbed. The remaining fluid, composed of urea, uric acid, and other wastes, leaves the collecting tubule and exits the kidney via the **ureter,** a duct leading to the bladder. Urine is stored there until it is excreted from the body through the **urethra** (see Figure 10.4).

In a healthy individual, the nephron reabsorbs all of the glucose entering it, producing glucose-free urine. The urine of a diabetic, however, is not glucose-free. The high blood glucose concentration in a diabetic overwhelms the nephron's active transport system, leading to the excretion of glucose in the urine (see chapter 11).

> ## MCAT Synopsis
>
> While aldosterone and ADH ultimately do the same thing (increase water reabsorption in the kidney), they have different mechanisms of action: ADH directly increases water reabsorption from the nephron's collecting duct, while aldosterone indirectly increases water reabsorption by increasing sodium reabsorption from the collecting duct.

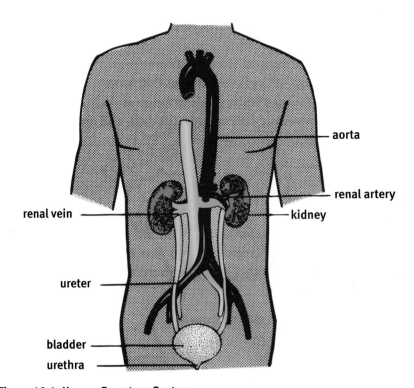

Figure 10.4. Human Excretory System

THE LIVER

The liver helps regulate blood glucose levels and produces urea. Glucose and other monosaccharides absorbed during digestion are delivered to the liver via the **hepatic portal vein** (see chapter 7). Glucose-rich blood is processed by the liver, which converts excess glucose to glycogen for storage. If the blood has a low glucose concentration, the liver converts glycogen into glucose and releases it into the blood, restoring blood glucose levels to normal. In addition, the liver synthesizes glucose from noncarbohydrate precursors via the process of **gluconeogenesis.** Glycogen metabolism is under both hormonal and nervous control (see chapter 11).

The liver is also responsible for the processing of nitrogenous wastes. Excess amino acids are absorbed in the small intestine and transported to the liver via the hepatic portal vein. There the amino acids undergo a process called **deamination,** in which the amino group is removed from the amino acid and converted into ammonia, a highly toxic compound. In a complex biochemical process, the liver combines ammonia with carbon dioxide to form urea, a relatively nontoxic compound, which is released into the blood and eventually excreted by the kidneys.

> **TEACHER TIP**
>
> KEY POINT: Recall that when we discussed cells, compartmentalization was a key way in which cells were able to carry out fairly dangerous reactions without damaging themselves. Here again in the liver, we see the compartmentalization of a damaging molecule (ammonia) and its conversion to a nontoxic intermediate (urea) which can be excreted.

The liver is also responsible for:

- Detoxification of toxins
- Storage of iron and vitamin B_{12}
- Destruction of old erythrocytes
- Synthesis of bile
- Synthesis of various blood proteins
- Defense against various antigens
- Beta-oxidation of fatty acids to ketones
- Interconversion of carbohydrates, fats, and amino acids

THE LARGE INTESTINE

The large intestine absorbs water and sodium not previously absorbed in the small intestine (see chapter 7). However, the large intestine also functions as an excretory organ for excess salts. Excess calcium, iron, and other salts are excreted into the colon and then eliminated with the feces.

THE SKIN: OSMOREGULATION AND THERMOREGULATION

A. STRUCTURE

The skin is the largest organ of the body, comprising an average of 16 percent of total body weight. The two major layers of the skin are the **epidermis** and the **dermis,** beneath which lies subcutaneous tissues, sometimes called the **hypodermis.**

The epidermis is the outermost epithelial layer and is composed of five cellular layers: the **stratum basalis (or stratum germinativum),** the **stratum spinosum,** the **stratum granulosum,** the **stratum lucidum,** and the **stratum corneum.** The deepest layer, the stratum basalis, continuously proliferates, pushing older epidermal cells outward. As the older cells reach the outermost layer (stratum corneum), they die, lose their nuclei, and transform into squames (scales) of keratin. The keratinized cells of the stratum corneum are tightly packed, serving as a protective barrier against microbial attack. Hair projects above the surface of the epithelium; sweat pores open to the surface.

The dermis can be subdivided into a layer of loose connective tissue known as the **papillary layer** and a layer of dense connective tissue known as the **reticular layer.** Within the dermis are the sweat glands, the sense organs, blood vessels, and the bulbs of hair follicles.

The **hypodermis,** composed of loose connective tissue, is abundant in fat cells and binds the outer skin layers to the body (see Figure 10.5).

B. FUNCTION

TEACHER TIP

The skin is also involved in the production of vitamin D via the effect sunlight has on it. Recall that vitamin D is critical in bone maintenance.

The skin protects the body from microbial invasion and from environmental stresses, such as dry weather and wind. Specialized epidermal cells called **melanocytes** synthesize the pigment **melanin,** which protects the body from ultraviolet light. The skin is a receptor of stimuli, such as pressure and temperature. The skin is also an excretory organ (removing excess water and salts from the body) and a thermoregulatory organ (helping control both the conservation and release of heat).

Sweat glands secrete a mixture of water, dissolved salts, and urea via sweat pores. As sweat evaporates, the skin is cooled. Thus, sweating has both an excretory and a thermoregulatory function. Sweating is under nervous control.

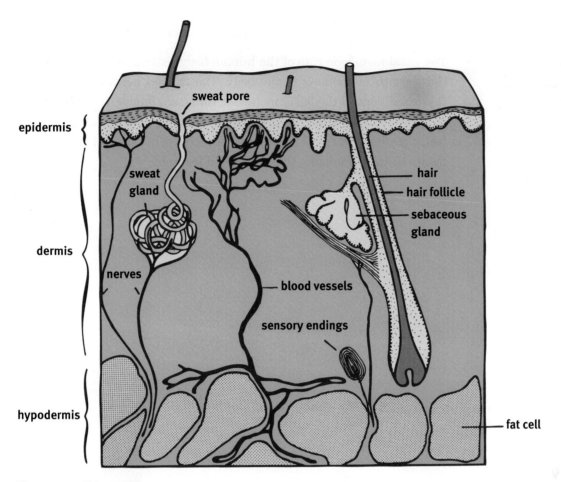

Figure 10.5. Human Skin

Subcutaneous fat in the hypodermis insulates the body. Hair entraps and retains warm air at the skin's surface. Hormones such as epinephrine can increase the metabolic rate, thereby increasing heat production. In addition, muscles can generate heat by contracting rapidly (shivering). Heat loss can be inhibited through the constriction of blood vessels in the dermis. Likewise, dilation of these same blood vessels dissipates heat.

Alternative mechanisms are used by some mammals to regulate their body temperature. For example, **panting** is a cooling mechanism that evaporates water from the respiratory passages. Most mammals have a layer of fur; fur traps and conserves heat. Some mammals exhibit varying states of **torpor** in the winter months in order to conserve energy; their metabolism, heart rate, and respiration rate greatly decrease during these months. **Hibernation** is a type of torpor during which the animal remains dormant over a period of weeks or months with body temperature maintained below normal. Animals with a constant body temperature are referred to as **homeotherms (endotherms).**

MCAT SYNOPSIS

While this chapter focuses on the homeostatic roles played by the kidney, liver, and skin, you should be aware that homeostasis is not limited to those organs; all the organs of the body are involved in one way or another in preserving physiologic equilibrium.

TEACHER TIP

Homeostasis is largely maintained automatically. This is partially done through local, organ-level effects, but the master control for homeostatic mechanisms is via the endocrine system: the topic of our next chapter and a common MCAT topic.

THYROID GLAND: THERMOREGULATION

The basal metabolic rate of the human body contributes a great deal to the warmth or coolness of the body. The thyroid hormones, primarily thyroxine, control the basal metabolic rate (see chapter 11). When there is overproduction of these hormones (hyperthyroidism), the person will feel excessively warm. When there is a decrease in the level of these hormones (hypothyroidism), the person will feel cold.

PRACTICE QUESTIONS

1. Which of the following is a normal finding in the filtrate when the glomerulus is functioning properly?

   A. Erythrocytes are in the filtrate.
   B. Albumin (69 kD) is in the filtrate.
   C. Glucose is in the filtrate.
   D. Large (larger than 69 kD) proteins are in the filtrate.

2. An increase in aldosterone will NOT cause

   A. reabsorption of Na^+ from collecting duct.
   B. an increase in blood pressure.
   C. urine with a high concentration of Na^+.
   D. urine with a low concentration of Na^+.

3. Which of the following would most likely happen after ingesting a large quantity of water quickly?

   A. Vasopressin secretion is stimulated.
   B. Vasopressin secretion is inhibited.
   C. Aldosterone production is stimulated.
   D. There is increased reabsorption of water from the collecting duct.

4. Which of the following properly traces the order of the structural pathway that filtrate follows in a nephron?

   A. Bowman's capsule, proximal convoluted tubule, loop of Henle, collecting duct
   B. Glomerulus, proximal convoluted tubule, loop of Henle, distal convoluted tubule
   C. Glomerulus, collecting duct, proximal convoluted tubule, distal convoluted tubule
   D. Bowman's capsule, distal convoluted tubule, loop of Henle, collecting duct

5. Which of the following is NOT a function of the liver?

   A. Production of bile from cholesterol
   B. Production of essential amino acids via interconversion from other amino acids
   C. Storage of vitamins and iron
   D. Production of energy by metabolizing fat

6. Which of the following is NOT a function of the epidermis?

   A. Sweat production
   B. Protection against harmful bacteria
   C. Protection against excess water loss
   D. Protection against ultraviolet radiation

7. Which of the following organs is NOT responsible for thermoregulation?

   A. Thyroid gland
   B. Skin
   C. Kidneys
   D. All of the above are responsible for thermoregulation.

8. Where in the nephron is glucose normally reabsorbed?

   A. Bowman's capsule
   B. Proximal convoluted tubule
   C. Loop of Henle
   D. Distal convoluted tubule

9. Assuming that vasopressin release is completely blocked, which of the following will occur after aldosterone release?

   A. Slight increase or no change in blood pressure due to osmoregulation of the kidneys
   B. Decrease in urine volume
   C. Decrease in Na^+ reabsorption
   D. Decrease in K^+ secretion

10. Which of the following situations would NOT result in a higher perceived temperature?

A. A patient who just finished exercising

B. Hyperthyroidism

C. Vascular disease, which results in constriction of blood vessels in the dermis

D. Overactive sweat glands

11. A patient's urine is sweet-smelling, and she has been diagnosed as diabetic. What is the most likely reason glucose appears in her urine?

A. Glucose reabsorption in the proximal convoluted tubule has stopped occurring.

B. Glucose reabsorption in the distal convoluted tubule is not occurring.

C. There is an increased secretion of glucose across the distal convoluted tubule.

D. There is an oversaturation of glucose such that glucose transporters in the proximal tubule are overwhelmed.

12. The image below illustrates the reaction of glycogenolysis, the formation of glucose from the breakdown of glycogen. Which of the following statements is true about this process?

A. This process is impaired in those with impaired kidney function.

B. The reaction is stimulated by high glucose levels in the body.

C. The reaction may result in an increased production of fat.

D. The reaction is solely under hormonal control.

13. The image below illustrates the transport of glucose and sodium from the lumen of a nephron tubule to the renal interstitium. Which of the following is true about the glucose transport depicted here?

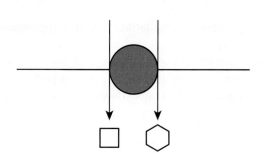

A. This transport occurs at the distal convoluted tubule of the nephron.
B. The Na$^+$/Glucose transporter is malfunctioning in the nephrons of all diabetic patients.
C. This transport occurs at the collecting duct of the nephron.
D. This is active transport.

14. In which section of the nephron is water NOT reabsorbed?

A. Proximal convoluted tubule
B. Descending loop of Henle
C. Ascending loop of Henle
D. Collecting duct

STARLING FORCES

A patient with kidney disease has extensive damage to the glomerular capillaries. These capillaries have become permeable to plasma proteins. What other symptoms will this patient have as a result of this kidney damage?

1) Determine the effect of glomerular capillaries that are permeable to proteins.

Glomerular capillaries do not normally allow the passage of plasma proteins or red blood cells. If the capillaries are damaged so that plasma proteins enter the renal tubule, these proteins will be lost because they cannot be reabsorbed along the tubule.

2) Examine the forces at work on capillaries.

The relationship of the different forces at work in the capillaries is explained by Starling forces as follows. Capillary hydrostatic pressure (P_c) is blood pressure, and it is the major force in capillary filtration. Osmotic pressure is the major force that keeps fluid from leaving the capillaries and is considered the oncotic pressure (π_c) of the plasma proteins. The interstitial fluid also has hydrostatic pressure (P_i), which opposes filtration out of the capillary. The proteins of the interstitial fluid exert oncotic pressure (π_i) and tend to favor filtration out of the capillary. To recap in simpler terms, the blood pressure in the capillary tries to force fluid out the capillary, whereas the pressure of the fluid in the interstitial space tries to hold the fluid in the capillary. The proteins in the interstitial space try to "suck" fluid out of the capillary, whereas the proteins in the blood try to hold the fluid in the capillary.

When blood enters the arterial end of a capillary, the P_c pressure acts to force fluids to leave the capillary and enter the interstitial space. This loss of fluid along the capillary increases the concentration of the solute, or proteins, in the blood. This increase in oncotic pressure "pulls" fluid back into the capillary at the venous end. Any fluid that is not returned to the capillary is generally picked up by the lymphatic system.

3) Determine the effect when proteins are lost from the blood.

The loss of plasma proteins will cause a drop in oncotic pressure in the blood. As a result, water that leaves the arteriole end of the capillary will not be reabsorbed at the venule end. Fluid in large quantities cannot be picked up by the lymphatic system, so this fluid will remain in the interstitial space and back up in the extremities, a condition known as edema. The failure of fluid to be reabsorbed from the interstitial space also leads to a large drop in blood volume and therefore blood pressure.

SIMILAR QUESTIONS

1) What factors increase the loss of fluid to the interstitial space at the arterial end of a capillary?

2) What physiological conditions can increase capillary oncotic pressure?

3) What symptoms will patients with inadequate lymphatic function have?

CHAPTER 11

ENDOCRINE SYSTEM

The endocrine system acts as a means of internal communication, coordinating the activities of the organ systems. **Endocrine glands** (see Figure 11.1) synthesize and secrete chemical substances called **hormones** directly into the circulatory system. (In contrast, **exocrine glands,** such as the gall bladder, secrete substances that are transported by ducts.) Hormones regulate the function of **target organs** or tissues.

TEACHER TIP

KEY POINT: Unlike the other organ systems we have discussed thus far, the basis of the endocrine system is ACTION AT A DISTANCE. Each organ has a local effect that is then passed though the bloodstream to affect the entire organism.

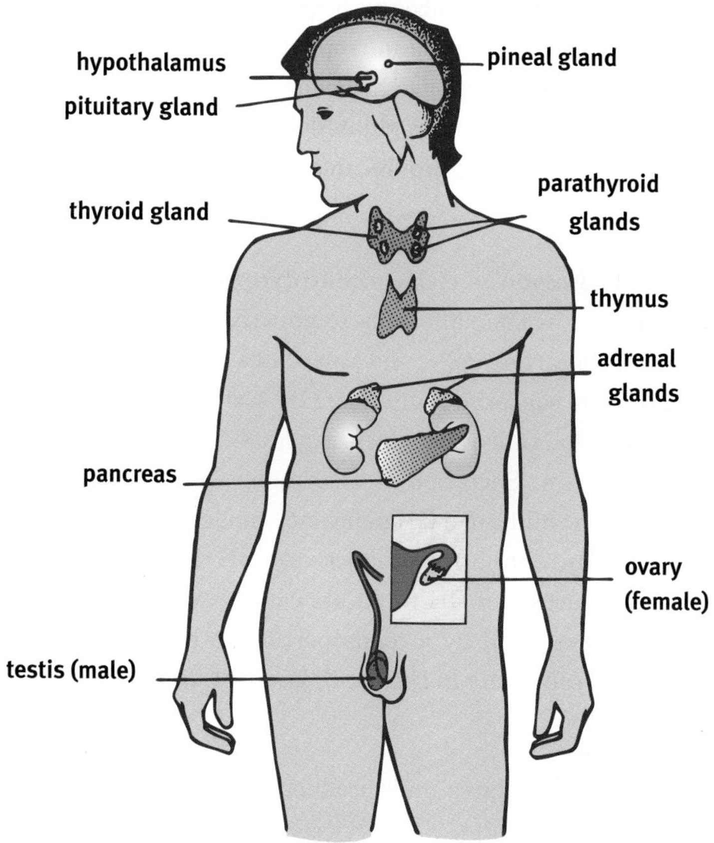

hypothalamus

pituitary gland

pineal gland

thyroid gland

parathyroid glands

thymus

adrenal glands

pancreas

ovary (female)

testis (male)

Figure 11.1. Human Endocrine System

ENDOCRINE GLANDS

Glands that synthesize and/or secrete hormones include the **pituitary, hypothalamus, thyroid, parathyroids, adrenals, pancreas, testes, ovaries, pineal, kidneys, gastrointestinal glands, heart,** and **thymus.** Some hormones regulate a single type of cell or organ, while others have more widespread actions. The specificity of hormonal action is determined by the presence of specific receptors on or in the target cells.

A. PITUITARY GLAND

The pituitary (**hypophysis**) is a small, trilobed gland lying at the base of the brain. The two main lobes, **anterior** and **posterior,** are functionally distinct. (In humans, the third lobe, the intermediate lobe, is rudimentary.)

1. Anterior Pituitary

The anterior pituitary synthesizes both direct hormones, which directly stimulate their target organs, and tropic hormones, which stimulate other endocrine glands to release hormones. The hormonal secretions of the anterior pituitary are regulated by hypothalamic secretions called **releasing/inhibiting hormones** or factors.

a. Direct hormones
- **Growth hormone (GH, somatotropin)**
  GH promotes bone and muscle growth, inhibits the uptake of glucose by certain cells, and stimulates the breakdown of **fatty acid,** thus conserving glucose. GH secretion is stimulated by the hypothalamic releasing hormone **GHRH** and inhibited by somatostatin. Secretion is also under neural and metabolic control. In children, a GH deficiency can lead to stunted growth (**dwarfism**), while overproduction of GH results in **gigantism.** Overproduction of GH in adults causes **acromegaly,** a disorder characterized by a disproportionate overgrowth of bone, localized especially in the skull, jaw, feet, and hands.

- **Prolactin**
  Prolactin stimulates milk production and secretion in female **mammary glands.**

b. Tropic hormones
- **Adrenocorticotropic hormone (ACTH)**
  ACTH stimulates the adrenal cortex to synthesize and secrete glucocorticoids and is regulated by the releasing hormone **corticotropin releasing factor (CRF).**

TEACHER TIP

While it seems like the pituitary has all the power, the anterior pituitary is being controlled by the hypothalamus directly above it. This makes the hypothalamus the "master control gland."

TEACHER TIP

Flashback to enzymes: remember that enzymes were often regulated via feedback inhibition. The endocrine system is exactly the same. As levels of the final effector molecule rise, the feedback to the hypothalamus and pituitary decrease their actions.

- **Thyroid-stimulating hormone (TSH)**

  TSH stimulates the thyroid gland to absorb iodine and then synthesize and release thyroid hormone. TSH is regulated by the releasing hormone **TRH.**

- **Luteinizing hormone (LH)**

  In females, LH stimulates ovulation and formation of the corpus luteum. In males, LH stimulates the interstitial cells of the testes to synthesize **testosterone.** LH is regulated by **estrogen, progesterone,** and **gonadotropin releasing hormone (GnRH).**

- **Follicle-stimulating hormone (FSH)**

  In females, FSH causes maturation of ovarian follicles; in males, FSH stimulates maturation of the seminiferous tubules and sperm production. FSH is regulated by estrogen and by GnRH.

2. Posterior Pituitary

The posterior pituitary does not synthesize hormones; it stores and releases the hormones **oxytocin** and **ADH,** which are produced by the neurosecretory cells of the hypothalamus. Hormone secretion is stimulated by action potentials descending from the hypothalamus.

a. Oxytocin

Oxytocin, which is secreted during childbirth, increases the strength and frequency of uterine muscle contractions. Oxytocin secretion is also induced by suckling; oxytocin stimulates milk secretion in the mammary glands.

b. Antidiuretic hormone (ADH, vasopressin)

ADH increases the permeability of the nephron's collecting duct to water, thereby promoting water reabsorption and increasing blood volume (see chapter 10). ADH is secreted when plasma osmolarity increases, as sensed by **osmoreceptors** in the hypothalamus, or when blood volume decreases, as sensed by **baroreceptors** in the circulatory system.

B. HYPOTHALAMUS

The hypothalamus is part of the forebrain and is located directly above the pituitary gland. The hypothalamus receives neural transmissions from other parts of the brain and from peripheral nerves that trigger specific responses from its neurosecretory cells. The neurosecretory cells regulate pituitary gland secretions via negative feedback mechanisms and through the actions of inhibiting and releasing hormones.

EXCLUSIVE

To remember the six hormones of the anterior pituitary, think FLAT PiG:

FSH
LH
ACTH
TSH

Prolactin
i(gnore)
GH

TEACHER TIP

The posterior pituitary is controlled differently than the anterior. The posterior pituitary serves simply as a jumping off point for the hormones ADH and oxytocin (made in the hypothalamus) and does not make any hormones of its own.

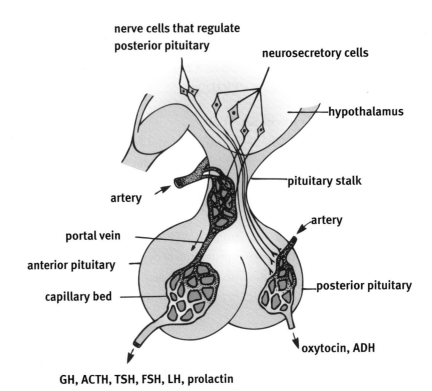

nerve cells that regulate
posterior pituitary

neurosecretory cells

hypothalamus

pituitary stalk

artery

artery

portal vein

anterior pituitary

posterior pituitary

capillary bed

oxytocin, ADH

GH, ACTH, TSH, FSH, LH, prolactin

Figure 11.2. Hypothalamus and Pituitary Gland

1. Interactions with Anterior Pituitary

Hypothalamic releasing hormones are hormones that stimulate or inhibit the secretions of the anterior pituitary. For example, GnRH stimulates the anterior pituitary to secrete FSH and LH. Releasing hormones are secreted into the **hypothalamic–hypophyseal portal system** (see Figure 11.2). In this circulatory pathway, blood from the capillary bed in the hypothalamus flows through a portal vein into the anterior pituitary, where it diverges into a second capillary network. In this way, releasing hormones can immediately reach the anterior pituitary.

Oversecretion of hormones is potentially harmful to an organism and so a preventive mechanism, called **negative feedback,** has evolved (see chapter 2). A high hormone level inhibits further production of that hormone. For example, when plasma levels of adrenal cortical hormones reach a critical level, the hormones themselves exert an inhibitory effect on the pituitary and on the hypothalamus, inhibiting CRF and ACTH release. In the absence of CRF, the anterior pituitary stops ACTH secretion, and the adrenal cortex stops secreting adrenal cortical hormones. When adrenal hormone levels are too low, the hypothalamus is stimulated to release CRF. This stimulates the anterior pituitary to secrete

TEACHER TIP

While most of the hormones in the anterior pituitary require a factor from the hypothalamus to be released (e.g., GnRH for FSH and LH), prolactin is actually the opposite. As long as the hypothalamus secretes prolactin inhibitory factor (PIF, dopamine), no prolactin will be released. It is the *absence* of PIF that allows for prolactin release. This fact is worth knowing for Test Day.

ACTH, which, in turn, stimulates the adrenal cortex to release adrenal cortical hormones (see Figure 11.3).

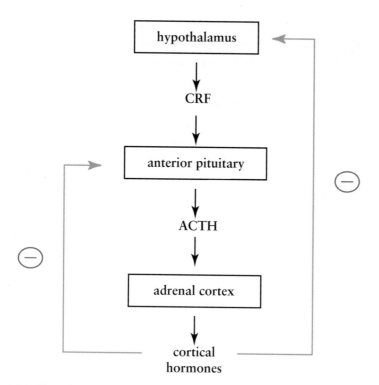

Figure 11.3. Negative Feedback Mechanism

2. Interactions with Posterior Pituitary

Neurosecretory cells in the hypothalamus synthesize both oxytocin and ADH and transport them via their axons into the posterior pituitary for storage and secretion.

C. THYROID GLAND

The thyroid gland is a bilobed structure located on the ventral surface of the trachea. It produces and secretes **thyroxine, triiodothyronine (the thyroid hormones),** and **calcitonin.**

1. Thyroid Hormones (Thyroxine and Triiodothyronine)

Thyroxine (T_4) and triiodothyronine (T_3) are derived from the iodination of the amino acid tyrosine. Thyroid hormones are necessary for growth and neurological development in children. They increase the rate of cellular respiration and the rate of protein and fatty acid synthesis and degradation in many tissues. High plasma levels of thyroid hormones inhibit TRH and TSH secretion, thereby returning plasma levels to normal.

TEACHER TIP

Iodine is absolutely required for the thyroid to carry out its function. In the Western world, shortage of iodine is very rare, as most salt is now iodized.

Inflammation of the thyroid or iodine deficiency causes **hypothyroidism,** in which thyroid hormones are undersecreted or not secreted at all. Common symptoms of hypothyroidism include a slowed heart rate and respiratory rate, fatigue, cold intolerance, and weight gain. Hypothyroidism in newborn infants, called **cretinism,** is characterized by mental retardation and short stature. In **hyperthyroidism,** the thyroid is overstimulated, resulting in the oversecretion of thyroid hormones. Symptoms often include increased metabolic rate, feelings of excessive warmth, profuse sweating, palpitations, weight loss, and protruding eyes. In both disorders, the thyroid often enlarges, forming a bulge in the neck called a **goiter.**

2. Calcitonin

Calcitonin decreases plasma Ca^{2+} concentration by inhibiting the release of Ca^{2+} from bone. Calcitonin secretion is regulated by plasma Ca^{2+} levels.

D. PARATHYROID GLANDS

The parathyroid glands are four small pea-shaped structures embedded in the posterior surface of the thyroid. These glands synthesize and secrete **parathyroid hormone (PTH),** which, together with calcitonin and vitamin D, regulates plasma Ca^{2+} concentration. In turn, the plasma Ca^{2+} concentration regulates PTH secretion by means of a negative feedback mechanism. PTH raises the Ca^{2+} concentration in the blood by stimulating Ca^{2+} release from bone and decreasing Ca^{2+} excretion in the kidneys. In addition, PTH converts vitamin D into its active form, which stimulates intestinal calcium absorption.

E. ADRENAL GLANDS

The adrenal glands are situated on top of the kidneys and consist of the **adrenal cortex** and the **adrenal medulla.**

1. Adrenal Cortex

In response to stress, ACTH stimulates the adrenal cortex to synthesize and secrete the steroid hormones, which are collectively known as **corticosteroids.** The corticosteroids, derived from cholesterol, include **glucocorticoids, mineralocorticoids,** and **cortical sex hormones.**

a. Glucocorticoids

Glucocorticoids, such as **cortisol** and **cortisone,** are involved in glucose regulation and protein metabolism. Glucocorticoids raise blood glucose levels by promoting gluconeogenesis and decrease protein synthesis. They also reduce the body's immunological and inflammatory responses. Cortisol secretion is governed by a negative feedback mechanism.

b. Mineralocorticoids

Mineralocorticoids, particularly **aldosterone,** regulate plasma levels of sodium and potassium and, consequently, the total extracellular water volume. Aldosterone causes active reabsorption of sodium and passive reabsorption of water in the nephron (see chapter 10). This results in a rise in both blood volume and blood pressure. Aldosterone also stimulates the secretion of potassium ion and hydrogen ion into the nephron and their subsequent excretion in urine.

Aldosterone secretion is regulated by the **renin-angiotensin** system. When blood volume falls, the juxtaglomerular cells of the kidney produce **renin**—an enzyme that converts the plasma protein **angiotensinogen** to **angiotensin I.** Angiotensin I is converted to **angiotensin II,** which stimulates the adrenal cortex to secrete aldosterone. Aldosterone helps to restore blood volume by increasing sodium reabsorption at the kidney, leading to an increase in water reabsorption. This removes the initial stimulus for renin production.

c. Cortical sex hormones

The adrenal cortex secretes small quantities of **androgens** (male sex hormones) in both males and females. Because, in males, most of the androgens are produced by the testes, the physiologic effect of the adrenal androgens is quite small. In females, however, overproduction of the adrenal androgens may have masculinizing effects, such as excessive facial hair.

2. Adrenal Medulla

The secretory cells of the adrenal medulla can be viewed as specialized sympathetic nerve cells that secrete hormones into the circulatory system. The adrenal medulla produces **epinephrine (adrenaline)** and **norepinephrine (noradrenaline),** both of which belong to a class of amino acid-derived compounds called **catecholamines.** Epinephrine increases the conversion of glycogen to glucose in liver and muscle tissue, causing a rise in blood glucose levels and an increase in the basal metabolic rate. Both epinephrine and norepinephrine increase the rate and strength of the heartbeat and dilate and constrict blood vessels in such a way as to increase the blood supply to skeletal muscle,

TEACHER TIP

Too much volume in the vasculature results in high blood pressure (hypertension). One way to relieve this is to decrease the volume of fluid by preventing the kidneys from reabsorbing as much fluid. Certain drugs known as ACE-inhibitors do this by preventing the conversion of angiotensin I to angiotensin II. This prevents aldosterone from being released and salt and water are not reabsorbed, thereby decreasing fluid volume.

FLASHBACK

The secretions of the exocrine pancreas (see chapter 7) are components of the pancreatic juice that enters into the duodenum:

- Amylase (carbohydrate digestion)
- Lipase (lipid digestion)
- Trypsin, chymotrypsin and carboxypeptidase (protein digestion)

the heart, and the brain, while decreasing the blood supply to the kidneys, skin, and digestive tract. These effects are known as the **"fight or flight response,"** and are elicited by sympathetic nervous stimulation in response to stress. Both of these hormones are also neurotransmitters (see chapter 12).

F. PANCREAS

The pancreas is both an exocrine organ and an endocrine organ. The exocrine function is performed by the cells that secrete digestive enzymes into the small intestine via a series of ducts. The endocrine function is performed by small glandular structures called the **islets of Langerhans,** which are composed of **alpha, beta,** and **delta cells.** Alpha cells produce and secrete **glucagon;** beta cells produce and secrete **insulin;** delta cells produce and secrete **somatostatin.**

1. Glucagon

Glucagon stimulates protein and fat degradation, the conversion of glycogen to glucose, and gluconeogenesis, all of which serve to increase blood glucose levels. Glucagon secretion is stimulated by a decrease in blood glucose and by gastrointestinal hormones (e.g., CCK and gastrin) and is inhibited by high plasma glucose levels. Glucagon's actions are largely antagonistic to those of insulin.

2. Insulin

Insulin is a protein hormone secreted in response to a high blood glucose concentration. It stimulates the uptake of glucose by muscle and adipose cells and the storage of glucose as glycogen in muscle and liver cells, thus lowering blood glucose levels (see Figure 11.4). It also stimulates the synthesis of fats from glucose and the uptake of amino acids. Insulin's actions are antagonistic to those of glucagon and the glucocorticoids. Insulin secretion is regulated by blood glucose levels. Overproduction of insulin causes **hypoglycemia** (low blood glucose levels). Underproduction of insulin, or an insensitivity to insulin, leads to **diabetes mellitus,** which is characterized by **hyperglycemia** (high blood glucose levels). High blood glucose levels lead to excretion of glucose and water loss. In addition, diabetes is associated with weakness and fatigue, and may lead to **ketoacidosis,** which is a dangerous lowering of blood pH due to excess keto acids and fatty acids in the plasma.

MCAT SYNOPSIS

Insulin decreases plasma glucose. Glucagon increases plasma glucose.

Don't forget that growth hormone, the glucocorticoids, and epinephrine are also capable of increasing plasma glucose.

TEACHER TIP

There are two types of diabetes. One is due to auto-immune destruction of the beta cells of the pancreas (type I) while the other is due to the body resisting the effects of insulin (type II).

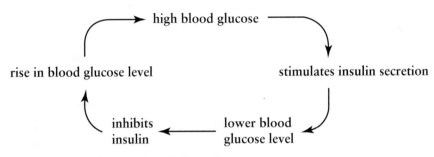

Figure 11.4. Regulation of Insulin Secretion

NOTE

Somatostatin is always inhibitory, regardless of where it acts.

3. Somatostatin

Pancreatic somatostatin secretion is increased by high blood glucose or high amino acid levels, leading to both decreased insulin and glucagon secretion. Somatostatin is also regulated by CCK and GH levels.

G. TESTES

The interstitial cells of the testes produce and secrete androgens, e.g., testosterone (see chapter 4). Testosterone induces embryonic sexual differentiation and male sexual development at puberty and maintains secondary sex characteristics. Testosterone secretion is controlled by a negative feedback mechanism involving FSH and LH. Insensitivity to testosterone results in a syndrome called **testicular feminization,** in which a genetic male (XY) has female secondary sexual characteristics.

H. OVARIES

The ovaries synthesize and secrete estrogens and progesterone. The secretion of both estrogens and progesterone is regulated by LH and FSH, which, in turn, are regulated by GnRH.

1. Hormones

a. Estrogens

Estrogens are steroid hormones necessary for normal female maturation. They stimulate the development of the female reproductive tract and contribute to the development of secondary sexual characteristics and sex drive. Estrogens are also responsible for the thickening of the **endometrium** (uterine wall). Estrogens are secreted by the ovarian follicles and the **corpus luteum.**

b. Progesterone

Progesterone is a steroid hormone secreted by the corpus luteum during the luteal phase of the menstrual cycle. Progesterone stimulates

TEACHER TIP

The MCAT likes to test your ability to identify FSH, LH, estrogen, and progesterone throughout the menstrual cycle. Be sure to know when each peaks.

the development and maintenance of the endometrial walls in preparation for implantation.

2. The Menstrual Cycle

The hormonal secretions of the ovaries, the hypothalamus, and the pituitary play important roles in the female reproductive cycle. From **puberty** through **menopause,** interactions between these hormones result in a monthly cyclical pattern known as the **menstrual cycle.** The menstrual cycle may be divided into the **follicular phase, ovulation,** the **luteal phase,** and **menstruation** (see Figure 11.5).

a. Follicular phase

The follicular phase begins with the cessation of the **menstrual flow** from the previous cycle. During this phase, FSH and LH act together to promote the development of several ovarian follicles, which grow and begin secreting estrogen. Rising levels of estrogen in the latter half of this phase stimulate GnRH secretion, which in turn further stimulates LH secretion.

b. Ovulation

Midway through the cycle **ovulation** occurs—a mature ovarian follicle bursts and releases an **ovum.** Ovulation is caused by a surge in LH which is preceded by and, in part, caused by a peak in estrogen levels.

c. Luteal phase

Following ovulation, LH induces the ruptured follicle to develop into the corpus luteum, which secretes estrogen and progesterone. Progesterone causes the glands of the endometrium to mature and produce secretions that prepare it for the implantation of an embryo. Progesterone and estrogen are essential for the maintenance of the endometrium. Progesterone and estrogen together inhibit secretion of GnRH, thereby inhibiting LH and FSH secretion. This prevents the maturation of additional follicles during the remainder of the cycle.

d. Menstruation

If the ovum is not fertilized, the corpus luteum atrophies. The resulting drop in progesterone and estrogen levels causes the endometrium (with its superficial blood vessels) to slough off, giving rise to the menstrual flow **(menses).** Progesterone and estrogen levels decline and GnRH is no longer inhibited. GnRH restimulates LH and FSH secretion, and so the cycle begins anew. However, if the ovum is fertilized, menstruation ceases for the duration of the pregnancy.

MCAT Synopsis

- Follicles mature during the follicular phase (FSH, LH).
- The LH surge at midcycle triggers ovulation.
- A ruptured follicle becomes corpus luteum and secretes estrogen and progesterone to build up uterine lining in preparation for implantation; LH and FSH inhibited.
- If fertilization doesn't occur, corpus luteum atrophies, progesterone and estrogen levels decrease, menses occurs, and LH and FSH levels begin to rise again.

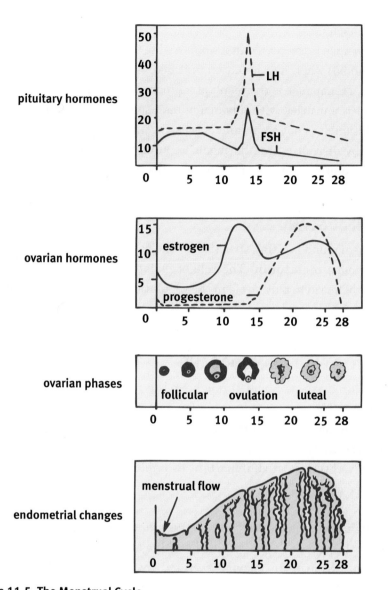

Figure 11.5. The Menstrual Cycle

3. Pregnancy

During the first trimester of pregnancy, the corpus luteum is preserved by **human chorionic gonadotropin (HCG),** a hormone produced by the blastocyst and the developing placenta. Hence, progesterone and estrogen secretion by the corpus luteum is maintained during the first trimester. During the second trimester, HCG levels decline, but progesterone and estrogen levels rise, since they are now secreted by the placenta itself. High levels of progesterone and estrogen inhibit GnRH secretion, thus preventing FSH and LH secretion and the onset of a new menstrual cycle.

4. Menopause

Menopause is the period in a woman's life (usually between the ages of 45 and 55) when menstruation first becomes irregular and eventually stops. Menopause is the result of a progressive decline in the functioning of the ovaries with advancing age; some follicles fail to rupture, ovulation does not occur, and less estrogen is produced by the ovaries, thereby disrupting the hormonal regulation of other glands. Women undergoing menopause may experience symptoms such as bloating, hot flashes, and headaches.

I. PINEAL GLAND

The pineal gland is a tiny structure at the base of the brain that secretes the hormone **melatonin.** The role of melatonin in humans is unclear, but it is believed to play a role in the regulation of **circadian rhythms**—physiological cycles lasting 24 hours. Melatonin secretion is regulated by light and dark cycles in the environment.

J. OTHER ENDOCRINE ORGANS

Glandular tissue is found throughout the mucosa of the stomach and intestines. The primary stimulus for gastrointestinal hormone release is the presence of food in the gut, though neural input and exposure to other hormones also affect their release. Over 20 gastrointestinal peptides have been isolated; important examples are gastrin, secretin, and CCK (see chapter 7).

Although the primary function of the kidneys is urine formation (see chapter 10), special cells within the kidneys have important endocrine functions. **Renin,** an enzyme secreted by the kidney, is involved in the regulation of aldosterone secretion. **Erythropoietin** is secreted by the kidney in response to decreased renal oxygen levels and stimulates bone marrow to produce red blood cells.

It has also been discovered that the heart and brain are endocrine organs; they release **atrial natriuretic hormone (ANH) and brain natriuretic peptide (BNP),** respectively. ANH and BNP are involved in the regulation of salt and water balance.

The thymus gland is located in the front neck region and secretes hormones such as **thymosin** during childhood. Thymosin stimulates T lymphocyte development and differentiation (see chapter 9). The thymus atrophies by adulthood, after the immune system has fully developed. See Table 11.1 for a listing of the principal hormones.

CLINICAL CORRELATE

Patients with chronic kidney disease can become anemic due to impaired erythropoietin production, causing inadequate red cell production from the bone marrow. Recently, genetically engineered erythropoietin has been employed to stimulate the bone marrow to produce more red blood cells in such patients.

Table 11.1. Principal Hormones in Humans

Hormone	Source	Action
Growth hormone	Anterior pituitary	Stimulates bone and muscle growth
Prolactin	Anterior pituitary	Stimulates milk production and secretion
Adrenocorticotropic hormone (ACTH)	Anterior pituitary	Stimulates the adrenal cortex to synthesize and secrete glucocorticoids
Thyroid-stimulating hormone (TSH)	Anterior pituitary	Stimulates the thyroid to produce thyroid hormones
Luteinizing hormone (LH)	Anterior pituitary	Stimulates ovulation in females; testosterone synthesis in males
Follicle-stimulating hormone (FSH)	Anterior pituitary	Stimulates follicle maturation in females; spermatogenesis in males
Oxytocin	Hypothalamus; stored in posterior pituitary	Stimulates uterine contractions during labor, and milk secretion during lactation
Vasopressin (ADH)	Hypothalamus; stored in posterior pituitary	Stimulates water reabsorption in kidneys
Thyroid hormone	Thyroid	Stimulates metabolic activity
Calcitonin	Thyroid	Decreases the blood calcium level
Parathyroid hormone	Parathyroid	Increases the blood calcium level
Glucocorticoids	Adrenal cortex	Increase blood glucose level and decreases protein synthesis
Mineralocorticoids	Adrenal cortex	Increase water reabsorption in the kidneys
Epinephrine and Norepinephrine	Adrenal medulla	Increase blood glucose level and heart rate
Glucagon	Pancreas	Stimulates conversion of glycogen to glucose in the liver; increases blood glucose
Insulin	Pancreas	Lowers blood glucose and increases storage of glycogen
Somatostatin	Pancreas	Suppresses secretion of glucagon and insulin
Testosterone	Testis	Maintains male secondary sexual characteristics
Estrogen	Ovary/placenta	Maintains female secondary sexual characteristics
Progesterone	Ovary/placenta	Promotes growth/maintenance of endometrium
Melatonin	Pineal	Unclear in humans
Atrial natriuretic hormone	Heart	Involved in osmoregulation
Thymosin	Thymus	Stimulates T lymphocyte development

MECHANISMS OF HORMONE ACTION

Hormones are classified on the basis of their chemical structure into three major groups: **peptide hormones, steroid hormones,** and **amino acid-derived hormones.** There are two ways in which hormones affect the activities of their target cells: via extracellular receptors or intracellular receptors.

A. PEPTIDES: SECONDARY MESSENGER

Peptide hormones range from simple short peptides (amino acid chains) such as ADH, to complex polypeptides such as insulin. Synthesis of peptide hormones begins with the synthesis of a large polypeptide (see chapter 14). The polypeptide is then cleaved into smaller protein units and transported to the Golgi apparatus, where it is further modified into the active hormone. The hormone is packaged into secretory vesicles and stored until it is released by the cell via exocytosis.

Peptide hormones act as **first messengers.** Their binding to specific receptors on the surface of their target cells triggers a series of enzymatic reactions within each cell, the first of which may be the conversion of ATP to **cyclic adenosine monophosphate (cAMP)**; this reaction is catalyzed by the membrane-bound enzyme **adenylate cyclase.** Cyclic AMP acts as a **second messenger,** relaying messages from the extracellular peptide hormone to cytoplasmic enzymes and initiating a series of successive reactions in the cell. This is an example of a **cascade effect**; with each step, the hormone's effects are amplified. Cyclic AMP activity is inactivated by the cytoplasmic enzyme **phosphodiesterase.**

B. STEROIDS: PRIMARY MESSENGER

Steroid hormones, such as estrogen and aldosterone, belong to a class of lipid-derived molecules with a characteristic ring structure. They are produced by the testes, ovaries, placenta, and adrenal cortex. In the synthesis of steroid molecules, precursors already present in the cell (such as cholesterol) undergo enzymatic reactions that convert them into active hormones. Steroid hormones pass through the cell membrane with ease because they are lipid-soluble. Steroid hormones are not stored, but are secreted at a rate determined by their rate of synthesis.

Steroid hormones enter their target cells directly and bind to specific receptor proteins in the cytoplasm. This receptor-hormone complex enters the nucleus and directly activates the expression of specific genes by

MCAT SYNOPSIS

Peptide hormones:

- Surface receptors
- Generally act as first messengers

Steroid hormones:

- Intracellular receptors
- Hormone/receptor binding to DNA promotes transcription of specific genes

TEACHER TIP

Flashback to the cell: Membrane trafficking is an MCAT favorite. The differences in the precursor molecules for steroid and peptide hormones governs their ability to cross membranes, which in turn controls where their receptors exist, which in turn affects what type of effects they will have on the cell.

binding to receptors on the chromatin. This induces a change in mRNA transcription and protein synthesis.

C. AMINO ACID DERIVATIVES

Amino acid derivatives are hormones composed of one or two modified amino acids. They are synthesized in the cytoplasm of glandular cells. Some are further modified and stored in granules until the cell is stimulated to release them, while others are initially synthesized as component parts of larger molecules and stored.

Some amino acid–derived hormones, such as epinephrine, activate their target cells as peptide hormones do; i.e., via second messengers. Others, such as thyroxine, act in the same manner as steroid hormones, entering the nucleus of their target cells and regulating gene expression.

PRACTICE QUESTIONS

Questions 1 and 2 refer to the paragraph below.

Antidiuretic hormone (ADH) is a peptide hormone produced in the hypothalamus and released by the posterior pituitary in response to an increase in serum osmolarity. Diabetes insipidus is a disease characterized by a physical or functional lack of antidiuretic hormone and production of dilute urine.

1. One would expect which of the following derangements in a patient with diabetes insipidus?

   A. Increase in urine osmolarity
   B. Decrease in serum osmolarity
   C. Increase in serum glucose
   D. Decrease in urine osmolarity

2. Given the symptoms of diabetes insipidus, one would expect ADH to act on

   A. Na/K/Cl channels in the Loop of Henle.
   B. NaCl channels in the distal collecting tubule.
   C. H_2O channels in the distal collecting tubule and collecting duct.
   D. Na/H channels in the proximal tubule.

3. Which of the following hormonal abnormalities most likely accounts for an elevated heart rate?

   A. Elevated estrogen
   B. Elevated growth hormone
   C. Decreased aldosterone
   D. Increased T_3

4. Thyroid hormone exerts its effects by

   A. direct elevation of cyclic AMP.
   B. direct augmentation of gene transcription.
   C. indirect elevation of cyclic AMP.
   D. indirect depression of phosphodiesterase.

5. Exogenous administration of T_4 is as efficacious as T_3 in treating hypothyroidism because of

   A. adequate iodine intake.
   B. adequate levels of deiodinase.
   C. adequate levels of thyroperoxidase.
   D. circulating levels of thyroglobulin.

6. Which of the following observations would be expected in the thyroid gland if serum calcium levels were to rise?

   A. Increased activation of the second messenger pathway leading to an increase in calcitonin secretion
   B. Decreased activation of the second messenger pathway leading to a decrease in calcitonin secretion
   C. Reduced calcium influx into the cell leading stimulation of calcitonin release
   D. Decreased transmembrane potentials across C cells of the thyroid leading to stimulation of calcitonin release

7. $GLUT_4$ is the main transporter of glucose into cells following the administration of insulin. Given that $GLUT_4$ is thought to be a glucose/sodium symporter, which of the following changes in extracellular concentrations would you expect after the administration of insulin and glucose?

	Sodium	Potassium	Glucose
A.	Increase	Increase	Increase
B.	Increase	Increase	Decrease
C.	Increase	Decrease	Increase
D.	Decrease	Increase	Increase
E.	Decrease	Decrease	Increase

8. The secretory endometrium is maintained by the change of hormone levels in which of the following patterns?

	Estrogen	Progesterone	FSH
A.	Decrease	No change	No change
B.	No change	Decrease	No change
C.	No change	No change	Increase
D.	Increase	Increase	No change
E.	Increase	Increase	Decrease

9. Administration of steroids exacerbates hyperglycemia secondary to type II diabetes by which of the following mechanisms?

   A. Inhibition of white blood cell migration to the source of injury
   B. Induction of pancreatic beta cell destruction
   C. Induction of lipolysis and glycogenolysis in the liver
   D. Augmentation of muscle mass leading to increased demand for glucose

10. Stimulation of glucose metabolism is a direct effect of which of the following hormones?

	Thyroid Hormone	Growth Hormone	Estrogen
A.	+	−	−
B.	−	+	−
C.	−	−	+
D.	+	+	−
E.	+	+	+

11. Radioactive iodine (I_{131}) would be likely to destroy cells in which of the following organs?

   A. Kidney
   B. Lung
   C. Thyroid
   D. Liver

12. Whereas norepinephrine is synthesized in many parts of the body to mediate the fight-or-flight response in animals, it is made into epinephrine in the

   A. hypothalamus.
   B. anterior pituitary.
   C. posterior pituitary.
   D. adrenal medulla.

13. Menstruation generally does not occur once a pregnancy has been established because of the inhibitory effects of

   A. testosterone secretion from the placenta.
   B. estrogen and progesterone secretion from the corpus luteum.
   C. beta-HCG secretion from the corpus luteum.
   D. estrogen secretion from the uterine lining.

14. Drugs with dopaminergic antagonist activity are commonly used to treat the symptoms of many psychotic diseases. Which of the following side effects is most commonly seen with use of these drugs?

A. Parkinsonism
B. Impaired lactogenesis
C. Uterine contractions
D. Increased blood pressure

15. Primary aldosteronism, a condition in which unusually high levels of aldosterone are produced from the adrenal cortex, would likely cause which of the following electrolyte abnormalities?

A. Low sodium (hyponatremia)
B. Low potassium (hypokalemia)
C. Low blood pressure (hypotension)
D. High levels of angiotensin II

16. The following lab results reflect which of the following conditions?

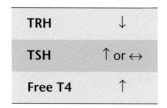

TRH	↓
TSH	↑ or ↔
Free T4	↑

A. Primary hyperthyroidism
B. Secondary hyperthyroidism
C. Tertiary hyperthyroidism
D. Primary hypothyroidism

17. Prepubertal exposure to estrogen would cause which of the following?

A. Early onset of regular menses
B. Axillary hair eruption
C. Breast development
D. Uterine contraction

18. Administration of progesterone daily prevents pregnancy primarily by which of the following mechanisms?

A. Thickening the endometrial lining
B. Inhibiting cholesterol synthesis in the ovary
C. Contracting the uterus to prevent implantation
D. Impairing sperm motility through the uterus and fallopian tubes

19. PTH secretion causes a rise in serum calcium by which of the following mechanisms?

A. Increased cardiac muscle activity
B. Release of protein bound calcium in the blood
C. Release of stored calcium from GI mucosal cells
D. Increased osteoclastic activity in the bone

MENSTRUAL CYCLE

During the follicular phase of the menstrual cycle, a dominant follicle is produced that secretes estrogen. If this follicle produces normal amounts of estrogen during the early days of its maturity but declines in estrogen production by day 10 of the menstrual cycle, what would be the result?

1) Visualize the menstrual cycle, focusing on the follicular phase.

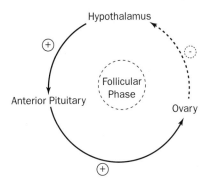

In the follicular phase, the hypothalamus secretes GnRH, which acts on the anterior pituitary to promote the release of FSH. FSH acts on the ovary and promotes the development of several ovarian follicles. The mature follicle begins secreting estrogen.

2) Determine the normal role of estrogen up until day 10.

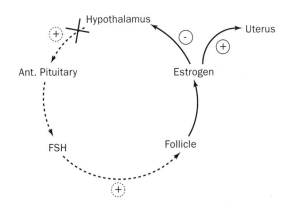

Estrogen has both positive and negative feedback effects in the menstrual cycle. Early in the follicular phase, the estrogen acts on the uterus, causing vascularization of the uterine wall. It also acts in a negative feedback loop to

KEY CONCEPTS

Menstrual cycle

FSH

LH

Estrogen

Progesterone

Positive/negative feedback

TAKEAWAYS

It is important to have a good understanding of the normal way that systems such as the menstrual cycle function. Using that knowledge, different variables, such as disease or dysfunction, can be applied to the system and the results of that dysfunction can be found in a methodical way.

THINGS TO WATCH OUT FOR

Estrogen has both negative and positive feedback effects on FSH and LH at different times in the menstrual cycle. Remember that estrogen levels fall dramatically after the LH surge but rise again during the luteal phase. During this phase, however, both estrogen and progesterone are now produced by the corpus luteum, and both have a negative feedback effect.

SIMILAR QUESTIONS

1) At what point in the follicular phase is FSH inhibited?

2) What are the actions of estrogen in the follicular phase of the menstrual cycle?

3) How can ovulation during the menstrual cycle be prevented?

inhibit the release of FSH from the anterior pituitary in order to prevent the development of multiple eggs. Because the question stem states that early levels of estrogen are normal, vascularization of the uterus and inhibition of FSH will both occur normally.

---

3) Determine the normal role of estrogen after day 10.

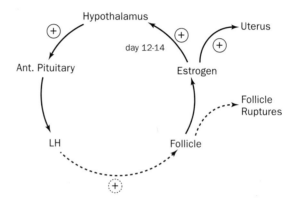

The question also states that estrogen levels decline after day 10. Now focus on the role of estrogen after day 10. Estrogen levels increase rapidly around day 12 of the cycle, and this burst of estrogen has a positive feedback effect on the secretion of FSH and LH. This results in the LH surge. The LH surge is responsible for ovulation, or the release of an egg.

---

4) Examine the consequence a decrease in estrogen after day 10.

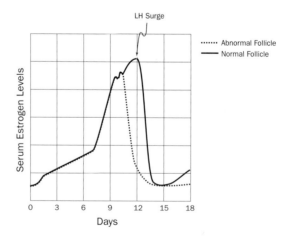

Therefore, if estrogen levels decrease after day 10 rather than increase as they normally should, then there will be no ovulation.

CHAPTER 12

NERVOUS SYSTEM

The nervous system enables organisms to receive and respond to **stimuli** from their external and internal environments. **Neurons** are the functional units of the nervous system. A neuron converts stimuli into electrochemical signals that are conducted through the nervous system.

NEURONS

A. STRUCTURE

The neuron is an elongated cell consisting of **dendrites,** a **cell body,** and an **axon.** Dendrites are cytoplasmic extensions that receive information and transmit it toward the cell body. The cell body **(soma)** contains the nucleus and controls the metabolic activity of the neuron. The **axon hillock** connects the cell body to the axon (nerve fiber), which is a long cellular process that transmits impulses away from the cell body. Most mammalian axons are ensheathed by an insulating substance known as **myelin,** which allows axons to conduct impulses faster. Myelin is produced by cells known as **glial cells. (Oligodendrocytes** produce myelin in the central nervous system, and **Schwann cells** produce myelin in the peripheral nervous system.) The gaps between segments of myelin are called **nodes of Ranvier.** Ultimately, the axons end as swellings known as **synaptic terminals** (sometimes also called synaptic boutons or knobs) (see Figure 12.1). Neurotransmitters are released from these terminals into the **synapse** (or **synaptic cleft**), which is the gap between the axon terminals of one cell and the dendrites of the next cell.

B. FUNCTION

Neurons are specialized to receive signals from sensory receptors or from other neurons in the body and transfer this information along the length of the axon. Impulses, known as **action potentials,** travel the length of the axon and invade the nerve terminal, thereby causing the release of neurotransmitter into the synapse. When a neuron is at rest, the potential difference between the extracellular space and the intracellular space is called the **resting potential.**

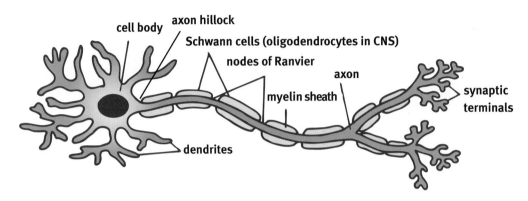

Figure 12.1. Peripheral Nerve

1. Resting Potential

Even at rest, a neuron is polarized. This potential difference is the result of an unequal distribution of ions between the inside and outside of the cell. A typical resting membrane potential is –70 millivolts (mV), which means that the inside of the neuron is more negative than the outside. This difference is due to selective ionic permeability of the neuronal cell membrane and is maintained by the **Na⁺/K⁺ pump** (also called the Na⁺/K⁺ ATPase).

The concentration of K^+ is higher inside the neuron than outside; the concentration of Na^+ is higher outside than inside. Additionally, negatively charged proteins are trapped inside of the cell. The resting potential is created because the neuron is selectively permeable to K^+, so K^+ diffuses down its concentration gradient, leaving a net negative charge inside. (Neurons do not allow much Na^+ to enter the cell under resting conditions, so the cell remains polarized.)

Because the transmission of action potentials leads to the disruption of the ionic gradients (see next section), the gradients must be restored by the Na^+/K^+ pump. This pump, using ATP energy, transports 3 Na^+ out for every 2 K^+ it transports into the cell (see Figure 12.2).

2. Action Potential

The nerve cell body receives both excitatory and inhibitory impulses from other cells. If the cell becomes sufficiently excited or **depolarized** (i.e., the inside of the cell becomes less negative), an action potential is generated. The minimum **threshold membrane potential** (usually around –50 mV) is the level at which an action potential is initiated.

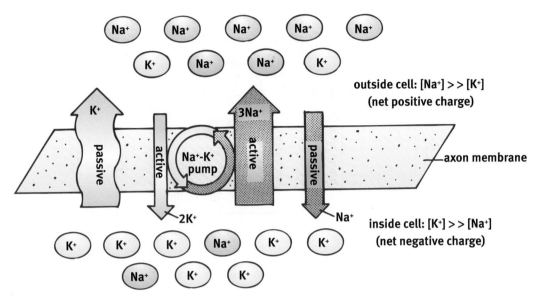

Figure 12.2. Resting Potential of a Neuron

Ion channels located in the nerve cell membrane open in response to these changes in voltage and are therefore called **voltage-gated ion channels.** An action potential begins when **voltage-gated Na+ channels** open in response to depolarization, allowing Na+ to rush down its **electrochemical gradient** into the cell, causing a rapid depolarization of that segment of the cell. The voltage-gated Na+ channels then close, and **voltage-gated K+ channels** open, allowing K+ to rush out down its electrochemical gradient. This returns the cell to a more negative potential, a process known as **repolarization.** In fact, the neuron may shoot past the resting potential and become even more negative inside than normal; this is called **hyperpolarization** (see Figure 12.3). Immediately following an action potential, it may be very difficult or impossible to initiate another action potential; this period of time is called the **refractory period.**

The action potential is often described as an **all-or-none response.** This means that whenever the threshold membrane potential is reached, an action potential with a consistent size and duration is produced. Neuronal information is coded by the frequency and number of action potentials rather than the size of the action potential. (In other words, the harder you hit your thumb with a hammer, the more action potentials will travel up your pain fibers, but the size and duration of each individual action potential will remain the same.)

TEACHER TIP

Flashback to the musculoskeletal system: As we saw in muscles, each fiber twitches in an all-or-nothing fashion. We see now (and remember) that this is due to how they are innervated. Because each muscle fiber has only one neuron innervating it, when the neuron fires, the muscle contracts. Because neurons fire in an all-or-nothing fashion, so too must the muscle fiber.

CLINICAL CORRELATE

Local anesthetics work by blocking the voltage-gated Na+ channels. These drugs work particularly well on sensory neurons, and therefore block the transmission of pain. They work so well on pain neurons because these neurons have small axonal diameters and have little or no myelin. This makes it easier to prevent action potential propagation.

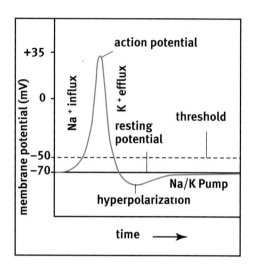

Figure 12.3. Action Potential

3. Impulse Propagation

If there is an adequate stimulus, the action potential will first be initiated at the axon hillock. Na^+ rushes into the neuron and diffuses to adjacent parts of the axon, causing nearby voltage-gated Na^+ channels to open. This occurs as previous segments are repolarizing. This chain of events (depolarization followed by a subsequent repolarization) continues along the length of the axon (see Figure 12.4). Although axons can theoretically propagate action potentials bidirectionally, information transfer will occur only in one direction: from dendrite to synaptic terminal. (This is because synapses operate only in one direction and because refractory periods make the backward travel of action potentials impossible.) Different axons can propagate action potentials at different speeds. The greater the diameter of the axon and the more heavily it is myelinated, the faster the impulses will travel. Myelin increases the conduction velocity by insulating segments of the axon, so that the membrane is permeable to ions only in the nodes of Ranvier. In this way, the action potential "jumps" from node to node; this process is called **saltatory conduction.**

SYNAPSE

The synapse is the gap between the axon terminal of one neuron (called the **presynaptic neuron** because it is before the synapse) and the dendrites of another neuron (**postsynaptic neuron**). Neurons may also communicate with postsynaptic cells other than neurons, such as cells in muscles or glands; these are called **effector cells.** The vast majority of synapses in the human are **chemical synapses.** In chemical synapses,

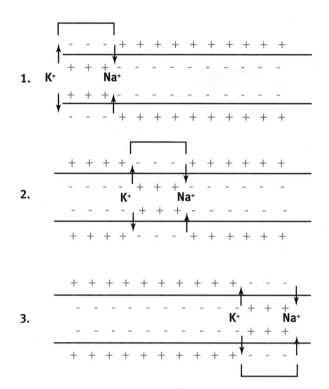

Figure 12.4. Propagation of an Action Potential

the nerve terminal contains thousands of membrane-bound vesicles full of chemical messengers known as **neurotransmitters.** When the action potential arrives at the nerve terminal and depolarizes it, the synaptic vesicles fuse with the presynaptic membrane and release neurotransmitter into the synapse via a calcium-dependent process of exocytosis. The neurotransmitter diffuses across the synapse and acts on receptor proteins embedded in the postsynaptic membrane (see Figure 12.5). Depending on the nature of the receptor, the neurotransmitter may have an excitatory or an inhibitory effect on the postsynaptic cell. Neurotransmitter is removed from the synapse in a variety of ways: it may be taken back up into the nerve terminal (via a protein known as an **uptake carrier**) where it may be reused or degraded; it may be degraded by enzymes located in the synapse (e.g., **acetylcholinesterase** inactivates the neurotransmitter acetylcholine); it may simply diffuse out of the synapse.

ORGANIZATION OF THE VERTEBRATE NERVOUS SYSTEM

There are many different kinds of neurons in the vertebrate nervous system. Neurons that carry information about the external or internal environment to the brain or spinal cord are called **afferent neurons.**

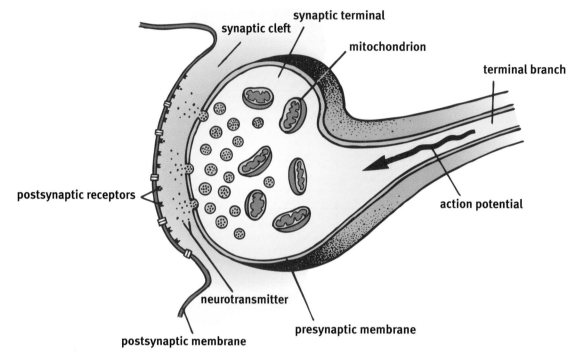

synaptic terminal

synaptic cleft

mitochondrion

terminal branch

postsynaptic receptors

action potential

neurotransmitter

presynaptic membrane

postsynaptic membrane

Figure 12.5. The Synapse

Neurons that carry commands from the brain or spinal cord to various parts of the body (e.g., muscles or glands) are called **efferent neurons.** Some neurons **(interneurons)** participate only in local circuits; their cell bodies and their nerve terminals are in the same location.

Nerves are essentially bundles of axons covered with connective tissue. A nerve may carry only sensory fibers (a **sensory nerve**), only motor fibers (a **motor nerve**), or a mixture of the two (a **mixed nerve**). Neuronal cell bodies often cluster together; such clusters are called **ganglia** in the periphery; in the central nervous system, they are called **nuclei.** The nervous system itself is divided into two major systems, the **central nervous system** and the **peripheral nervous system** (see Figure 12.6).

TEACHER TIP

While it may seem complex to separate the nervous system into these two divisions, it is actually quite simple. The CNS is the brain and spinal cord. Everything else falls under the purview of the PNS.

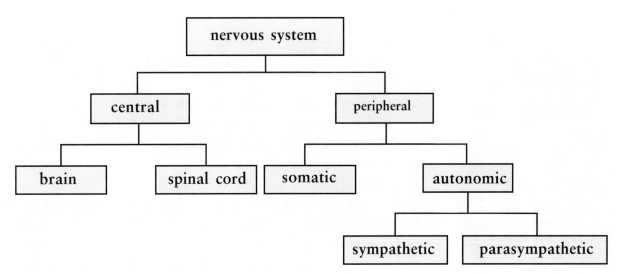

Figure 12.6. Organization of the Vertebrate Nervous System

A. CENTRAL NERVOUS SYSTEM

The central nervous system (CNS) consists of the **brain** and the **spinal cord.**

1. Brain

The brain is a jellylike mass of neurons that resides in the skull. Its functions include interpreting sensory information, forming motor plans, and cognitive function (thinking). The brain consists of **gray matter** (cell bodies) and **white matter** (myelinated axons). The brain can be divided into the **forebrain, midbrain,** and **hindbrain.**

a. Forebrain

The forebrain consists of the **telencephalon** and the **diencephalon.** The telencephalon consists of right and left hemispheres; each hemisphere can be divided into four different lobes: **frontal, parietal, temporal,** and **occipital.** A major component of the telencephalon is the **cerebral cortex,** which is the highly convoluted gray matter that can be seen on the surface of the brain. The cortex processes and integrates sensory input and motor responses and is important for memory and creative thought. Right and left cerebral cortices communicate with each other through the **corpus callosum.**

The diencephalon contains the **thalamus** and **hypothalamus.** The thalamus is a relay and integration center for the spinal cord and cerebral cortex. The hypothalamus controls visceral functions such as hunger, thirst, sex drive, water balance, blood pressure, and temperature regulation. It also plays an important role in the control of the endocrine system (see chapter 11).

> **TEACHER TIP**
>
> As much as the digestive system has infoldings to increase the effective surface area, so too does the brain. The increased folds (gyri) in the human cerebral cortex allow for higher-level cognitive functions to be carried out.

b. Midbrain

The midbrain is a relay center for visual and auditory impulses. It also plays an important role in motor control.

c. Hindbrain

The hindbrain is the posterior part of the brain and consists of the **cerebellum,** the **pons,** and the **medulla.** The cerebellum helps to modulate motor impulses initiated by the motor cortex and is important in the maintenance of balance, hand-eye coordination, and the timing of rapid movements. One function of the pons is to act as a relay center to allow the cortex to communicate with the cerebellum. The medulla (also called the medulla oblongata) controls many vital functions such as breathing, heart rate, and gastrointestinal activity. Together, the midbrain, pons, and medulla constitute the **brainstem.**

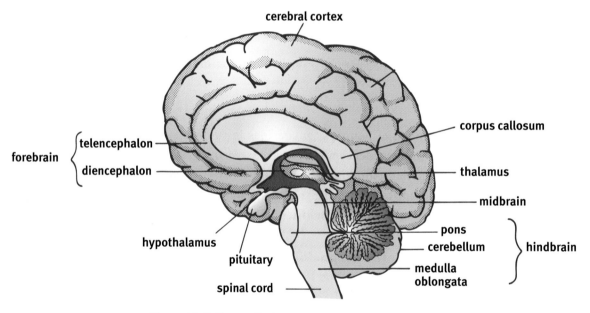

Figure 12.7. Human Brain

2. Spinal Cord

The spinal cord is an elongated structure, continuous with the brainstem, that extends down the dorsal side of vertebrates. Nearly all nerves that innervate the viscera or muscles below the head pass through the spinal cord, and nearly all sensory information from below the head passes through the spinal cord on the way to the brain. The spinal cord can also integrate simple motor responses (e.g., reflexes) by itself. A cross-section of the spinal cord reveals an outer white matter area containing motor and sensory axons and an inner gray matter area containing nerve cell bodies. Sensory information enters the spinal cord dorsally; the cell bodies of these sensory neurons are located in the **dorsal root ganglia.** All motor information exits the spinal cord ventrally. Nerve branches entering and leaving the cord are called **roots** (see Figure 12.8). The spinal cord is divided into four regions (going in order from the brainstem to the tail): **cervical, thoracic, lumbar,** and **sacral.**

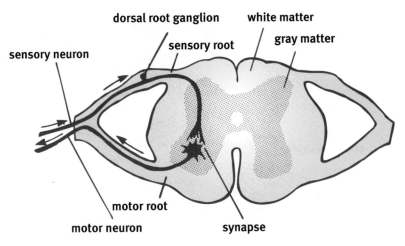

Figure 12.8. Spinal Cord

B. PERIPHERAL NERVOUS SYSTEM

The peripheral nervous system (PNS) consists of 12 pairs of cranial nerves, which primarily innervate the head and shoulders, and 31 pairs of spinal nerves, which innervate the rest of the body. Cranial nerves exit from the brainstem and spinal nerves exit from the spinal cord. The PNS has two primary divisions: the somatic and the autonomic nervous systems, each of which has both motor and sensory components.

1. Somatic Nervous System

The somatic nervous system (SNS) innervates skeletal muscles and is responsible for voluntary movement. Motor neurons release the neurotransmitter acetylcholine (ACh) onto ACh receptors located on skeletal muscle. This causes depolarization of the skeletal muscle, leading to muscle contraction. In addition to voluntary movement, the somatic nervous system is also important for reflex action. There are both **monosynaptic** and **polysynaptic** reflexes.

- Monosynaptic reflex pathways have only one synapse between the sensory neuron and the motor neuron. The classic example is the **knee-jerk reflex.** When the tendon covering the patella (kneecap) is hit, stretch receptors sense this and action potentials are sent up the sensory neuron and into the spinal cord. The sensory neuron synapses with a motor neuron in the spinal cord, which in turn, stimulates the quadriceps muscle to contract, causing the lower leg to kick forward (see Figures 12.8 and 12.9).

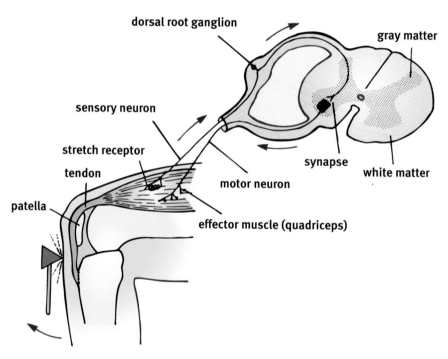

Figure 12.9. Reflex Arc for Knee-Jerk

- In polysynaptic reflexes, sensory neurons synapse with more than one neuron. A classic example of this is the **withdrawal reflex.** When a person steps on a nail, the injured leg withdraws in pain, while the other leg extends to retain balance.

2. Autonomic Nervous System

The autonomic nervous system **(ANS)** is sometimes also called the involuntary nervous system because it regulates the body's internal environment without the aid of conscious control. Whereas the somatic nervous system innervates skeletal muscle, the ANS innervates cardiac and smooth muscle. Smooth muscle is located in areas such as blood vessels, the digestive tract, the bladder, and bronchi, so it isn't surprising that the ANS is important in blood pressure control, gastrointestinal motility, excretory processes, respiration, and reproductive processes. ANS pathways are characterized by a two-neuron system. The first neuron (preganglionic neuron) has a cell body located within the CNS and its axon synapses in peripheral ganglia. The second neuron (postganglionic neuron) has its cell body in the ganglia and then synapses on cardiac or smooth muscle. The ANS is comprised of two subdivisions, the **sympathetic** and the **parasympathetic nervous systems,** which generally act in opposition to one another.

a. Sympathetic nervous system

The sympathetic division is responsible for the "flight or fight" responses that ready the body for action. It basically does everything you would want it to do in an emergency situation. It increases blood pressure and heart rate; it increases blood flow to skeletal muscles and it decreases gut motility. The preganglionic neurons emerge from the thoracic and lumbar regions of the spinal cord and use acetylcholine as their neurotransmitter; the postganglionic neurons typically release norepinephrine. The action of preganglionic sympathetic neurons also causes the adrenal medulla to release adrenaline (epinephrine) into the bloodstream.

b. Parasympathetic nervous system

The parasympathetic division acts to conserve energy and restore the body to resting activity levels following exertion ("rest and digest"). It acts to lower heart rate and to increase gut motility. One very important parasympathetic nerve that innervates many of the thoracic and abdominal viscera is called the **vagus nerve.** Parasympathetic neurons originate in the brainstem (cranial nerves) and the sacral part of the spinal cord. Both the preganglionic and postganglionic neurons release acetycholine.

SPECIAL SENSES

The body has three types of sensory receptors to monitor its internal and external environment: **interoceptors, proprioceptors,** and **exteroceptors.** Interoceptors monitor aspects of the internal environment such as blood pressure, the partial pressure of CO_2 in the blood, and blood pH. Proprioceptors transmit information regarding the position of the body in space. These receptors are located in muscles and tendons to tell the brain where the limbs are in space and are also located in the inner ear to tell the brain where the head is in space. Exteroceptors sense things in the external environment such as light, sound, taste, pain, touch, and temperature.

MCAT SYNOPSIS

The first neuron in the autonomic nervous system is called the preganglionic neuron and the second is the postganglionic neuron.

MCAT SYNOPSIS

To help you remember the effects of the sympathetic nervous system ("fight or flight"), imagine that you are being chased by a bear. What would you expect or want to happen?

- Increased heart rate and breathing rate
- Blood directed away from skin and toward big muscles (want blood flow to muscle to facilitate running away)
- Decreased digestion
- Pupil dilation

TEACHER TIP

KEY POINT: Be sure to know which neurotransmitters are released pre- and postsynaptically at sympathetic and parasympathetic neurons. This is a classic case for an MCAT discrete question.

BRIDGE

The lens in the eye is a converging (convex) lens. A convex lens with a smaller radius of curvature (i.e., thicker) has more refractive power and a shorter focal length (good for near vision). A lens with a larger radius of curvature (i.e., flatter) has less refractive power and a longer focal length (good for far vision). A convex lens forms an inverted and reversed image on the focal plane (i.e., the retina); it is up to the brain to sort that out.

1. The Eye

The eye detects light energy (as photons) and transmits information about intensity, color, and shape to the brain. The eyeball is covered by a thick, opaque layer known as the **sclera,** which is also known as the white of the eye. Beneath the sclera is the **choroid** layer, which helps to supply the retina with blood. The innermost layer of the eye is the **retina,** which contains the photoreceptors that sense the light. The transparent **cornea** at the front of the eye bends and focuses light rays. The rays then travel through an opening called the **pupil,** whose diameter is controlled by the pigmented, muscular **iris.** The iris responds to the intensity of light in the surroundings (light makes the pupil constrict). The light continues through the lens, which is suspended behind the pupil. The lens, the shape of which is controlled by the **ciliary muscles,** focuses the image onto the retina. In the retina are photoreceptors that **transduce** light into action potentials. There are two main types of photoreceptors: **cones** and **rods.** Cones respond to high-intensity illumination and are sensitive to color, while rods detect low-intensity illumination and are important in night vision. The cones and rods contain various pigments that absorb specific wavelengths of light. The cones contain three different pigments that absorb red, green, and blue wavelengths; the rod pigment, **rhodopsin,** absorbs one wavelength. The photoreceptor cells synapse onto **bipolar cells,** which in turn synapse onto **ganglion cells.** Axons of the ganglion cells bundle to form the right and left **optic nerves,** which conduct visual information to the brain. The point at which the optic nerve exits the eye is called the **blind spot** because photoreceptors are not present there. There is also a small area of the retina called the **fovea,** which is densely packed with cones and is important for high acuity vision (see Figure 12.10).

The eye also has its own circulation system. Near the base of the iris, the eye secretes aqueous humor, which travels to the anterior chamber of the eye from which it exits and eventually joins venous blood.

2. The Ear

The ear transduces sound energy (pressure waves) into impulses perceived by the brain as sound. The ear is also responsible for maintaining equilibrium (balance) in the body.

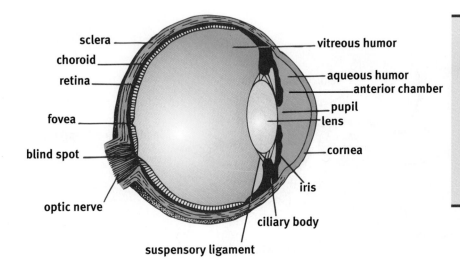

Figure 12.10. Human Eye

Sound waves pass through three regions as they enter the ear. First, they enter the **outer ear,** which consists of the **auricle** (pinna) and the **auditory canal.** At the end of the auditory canal is the **tympanic membrane (eardrum)** of the **middle ear,** which vibrates at the same frequency as the incoming sound. Next, the three bones, or **ossicles (malleus, incus,** and **stapes),** amplify the stimulus and transmit it through the **oval window,** which leads to the fluid-filled **inner ear.** The inner ear consists of the **cochlea** and the **semicircular canals.** The cochlea contains the **organ of Corti,** which has specialized sensory cells called hair cells. Vibration of the ossicles exerts pressure on the fluid in the cochlea, stimulating the hair cells to transduce the pressure into action potentials, which travel via the **auditory (cochlear) nerve** to the brain for processing (see Figure 12.11).

The three semicircular canals are each perpendicular to the other two and filled with a fluid called **endolymph**. At the base of each canal is a chamber with sensory hair cells; rotation of the head displaces endolymph in one of the canals, putting pressure on the hair cells in it. This changes the nature of impulses sent by the vestibular nerve to the brain. The brain interprets this information to determine the position of the head.

3. The Chemical Senses

The chemical senses are taste and smell. These senses transduce chemical changes in the environment, specifically in the mouth and nose, into **gustatory** and **olfactory** sensory impulses, which are interpreted by the nervous system.

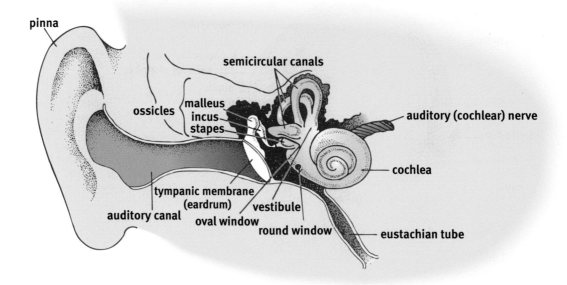

Figure 12.11. Human Ear

a. Taste

Taste receptors, or **taste buds,** are located on the tongue, the soft palate, and the epiglottis. Taste buds are composed of approximately 40 epithelial cells. The outer surface of a taste bud contains a **taste pore,** from which microvilli, or **taste hairs,** protrude. The receptor surfaces for taste are on the taste hairs. Interwoven around the taste buds is a network of nerve fibers that are stimulated by the taste buds. These neurons transmit gustatory information to the brainstem via three cranial nerves. There are four kinds of taste sensations: sour, salty, sweet, and bitter. Although most taste buds will respond to all four stimuli, they respond preferentially; i.e., at a lower threshold, to one or two of them.

b. Smell

Olfactory receptors are found in the olfactory membrane, which lies in the upper part of the nostrils over a total area of about 5 cm². The receptors are specialized neurons from which **olfactory hairs,** or **cilia,** project. These cilia form a dense mat in the nasal mucosa. When odorous substances enter the nasal cavity, they bind to receptors in the cilia, depolarizing the olfactory receptors. Axons from the olfactory receptors join to form the **olfactory nerves.** The olfactory nerves project directly to the **olfactory bulbs** in the base of the brain.

TEACHER TIP

Have you ever gone into a room with a very strong smell, which, after a while was hardly noticeable? Olfactory receptors can be overpowered and after constant stimulation, will desensitize to a given stimulus. This desensitization is a hallmark of much of the nervous system.

PRACTICE QUESTIONS

1. Myelin sheaths do NOT serve which of the following functions?

   A. Saltatory conduction
   B. Protection of axons
   C. Prevention of leakage of current
   D. Increase in speed of signal transmission

2. The Nernst equation shown below determines the membrane potential of a neuron for only one ion. "Out" denotes the extracellular concentration whereas "in" denotes in the intracellular concentration. Assuming sodium ions are the major determinant of resting potential (E) and that (RT)/F > 0, which of the following about resting potential is true?

$$E = \frac{RT}{F} \ln \frac{[Na^+]_{out}}{[Na^+]_{in}}$$

   A. E > 0
   B. E < 0
   C. E = 0
   D. E is indeterminable.

3. A postsynaptic potential stimulates the cell body of a neuron directly. The potential is strong enough to overcome threshold and cause action potential propagation at the axon hillock of a postsynaptic neuron. Which of the following is the main reason why the postsynaptic potential does not progress back down from the cell body toward the dendrites?

   A. The membrane of the neuron does not have a requisite amount of ion channels.
   B. No myelin sheath is around the neuron.
   C. The above statement is not true. The postsynaptic potential does in fact progress down toward the dendrites.
   D. None of the above is true.

4. During a flight-or-fight response, which of the following is NOT expected to occur?

   A. Inhibition of sexual arousal
   B. Acetylcholine release at synaptic clefts
   C. Pupil constriction
   D. Increase in heart rate

5. In a sympathetic response, which of the following is activated?

   A. Gastrointestinal activity
   B. Redirection of blood from digestive tract to muscles
   C. Cardiac contractility decreases
   D. Constriction of blood circulation in muscles

6. Which of the following statements of the parasympathetic nervous system is true?

   I. It is subject to control by the brain stem.
   II. Signals are transmitted mainly by interneurons
   III. It causes a decrease in heart rate.

   A. I
   B. II
   C. III
   D. I and III

7. The following is a graph of an action potential. At the top of the peak at 20 ms, which of the following best characterizes what is occurring?

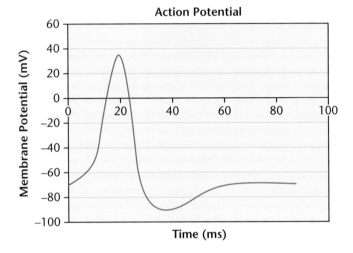

Action Potential

A. Some sodium channels have inactivated and some potassium channels have begun to open.
B. All sodium channels are open and all potassium channels are closed.
C. Sodium channels are beginning to open and some potassium channels have inactivated.
D. Both sodium and potassium channels are closed.

8. The following is a diagram of a rod cell. When there is an absence of light, the sodium channels of the rod cell are open. When there is light detected by the pigments found in the top section of the diagram, the sodium channels close. Which of the following is NOT a reasonable conclusion based on this information?

A. Depolarization of the cell occurs when the external environment is dark.
B. The neurotransmitter (shown at the bottom of the diagram) released by this cell transmits a signal that there is light detected by the pigments of the rod cell.
C. The diagram shown depicts a situation when the external environment is dark.
D. Hyperpolarization, not depolarization, signals when the external environment is lit.

9. The following is a picture of a typical nerve synapse. Which of the following is true without being readily observed in the diagram?

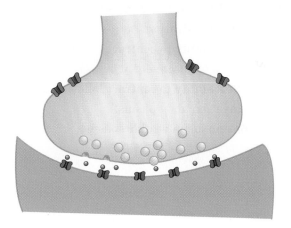

A. Vesicles contain neurotransmitters, which do not determine whether there is an excitatory or inhibitory response.
B. Voltage-gated calcium channels are independent of the formation of neurotransmitter-containing vesicles.
C. The degree of postsynaptic response is independent of the amount of neurotransmitter release into the synapse.
D. None of the above

10. Which of the following gives eyes their color (blue, green, brown, or red)?

A. Cornea
B. Pupil
C. Iris
D. Lens

11. A patient has suffered physical trauma to her right eye and has found that her vision is impaired mainly in the center of her field of view. She has great deficit in reading and color recognition in that eye. What is the most likely area of the injury to the right eye?

A. Any part of the retina
B. Optic nerve
C. Fovea
D. Blind spot

12. The following is a graph of a cardiac action potential. Skeletal muscle action potentials, by contrast, have a more gradual increase in potential and decrease more drastically without a pronounced plateau. Which of the following is true of cardiac muscle action potentials?

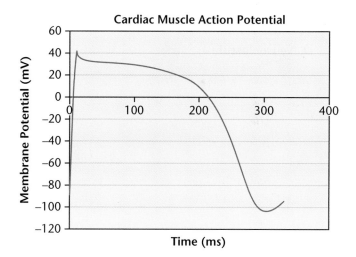

A. Sodium channels and potassium channels open faster in cardiac muscle than they do in skeletal muscle.
B. Sodium channels open faster in cardiac muscle but potassium channels open more slowly.
C. Sodium channels and potassium channels open more slowly in cardiac muscle.
D. Sodium channels open more slowly in cardiac muscle but potassium channels open faster.

13. Multiple sclerosis is a disease where the central nervous system is sporadically demyelinated and is believed to be autoimmune in nature. Which of the following is the most likely immunological target?

A. Schwann cells

B. Astrocytes

C. Lymphocytes

D. Leukocytes

14. A clinical researcher discovers a developmental defect in the retina. Based on experimental data, it seems that the disorders stem from a mutation that affects fetal development in the first trimester. Which of the following is the most likely fetal site affected?

A. Endoderm

B. Mesoderm

C. Ectoderm

D. Neuroblastula

15. Tetrapropylammonium ion (TPA) is a known inhibitor of the Na^+/K^+ pump. When administered to motor neurons, there will be a(n)

A. inability to contract muscles immediately on administration.

B. initial ability to contract but inability to contract subsequently.

C. initial ability to contract followed by quick relaxation and spasms.

D. continuous muscular spasms.

ACTION POTENTIAL

A nerve action potential is depicted below. If, during the action potential, a stimulus were to be applied as indicated by the arrow, what would result?

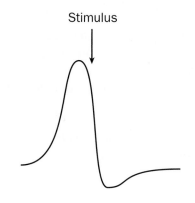

1) Visualize the graph of the action potential.

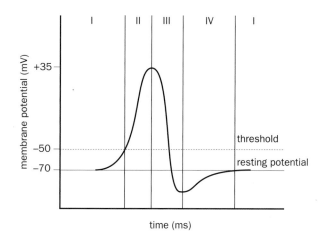

Region I—The cell is at rest and all gates are closed.

Region II—Depolarization: sodium gates are open and sodium flows into the cell, moving the membrane towards the sodium equilibrium potential.

Region III—Repolarization: sodium gates close and potassium gates open, moving the cell closer to the potassium equilibrium potential.

Region IV—Hyperpolarization: all gates are closed and the cell is ready to undergo another action potential, but the distance to the threshold is farther so it is harder to stimulate the cell. This is known as the relative refractory period.

SIMILAR QUESTIONS

1) At what point in the action potential is sodium closest to its electrochemical equilibrium?

2) What forces can increase the speed of an action potential?

3) How can an action potential be inhibited?

2) Review the characteristics of the action potential.

Action potentials propagate by the spread of currents to adjacent membranes; they are considered "all or nothing" because once threshold is reached, an action potential will continue. During an action potential (regions II and III) no other action potential can be elicited, no matter how large the stimulus. This is known as the absolute refractory period.

3) Evaluate the region in which the new stimulus is being applied.

The new stimulus being applied to the action potential occurs during repolarization. This is also during the absolute refractory period, a time during which no new action potentials can be elicited. Therefore, the new stimulus will not produce a new action potential.

Remember: *Action potentials are all or nothing. Once one begins it will continue, and a new action potential cannot be stimulated until after the absolute refractory period.*

CHAPTER 13

GENETICS

Genetics is the study of how traits are inherited from one generation to the next. The basic unit of heredity is the **gene.** Genes are composed of DNA and are located on chromosomes. When a gene exists in more than one form, the alternate forms are called **alleles.** The genetic makeup of an individual is the individual's **genotype**; the physical manifestation of the genetic makeup is the individual's **phenotype.** Some phenotypes correspond to a single genotype, while other phenotypes correspond to several different genotypes.

> **TEACHER TIP**
>
> Know the difference between genotype and phenotype. If you are given the genotype of an organism, you should be able to predict the phenotype. However, if you are given the phenotype, you cannot always predict the genotype because dominant and recessive alleles are present.

MENDELIAN GENETICS

In the 1860s, Gregor Mendel developed the basic principles of genetics through his experiments with the garden pea. Mendel studied the inheritance of individual pea traits by performing genetic crosses: He took **true-breeding** individuals (which, if self-crossed, produce progeny only with the parental phenotype) with different traits, mated them, and statistically analyzed the inheritance of the traits in the progeny.

A. MENDEL'S FIRST LAW: LAW OF SEGREGATION

Mendel postulated four principles of inheritance:

- Genes exist in alternate forms (now referred to as alleles).

- An organism has two alleles for each inherited trait, one inherited from each parent.

- The two alleles segregate during meiosis, resulting in gametes that carry only one allele for any given inherited trait.

- If two alleles in an individual organism are different, only one will be fully expressed and the other will be silent. The expressed allele is said to be **dominant,** the silent allele, **recessive.** In genetics problems, dominant alleles are typically assigned capital letters, and recessive alleles are assigned lower case letters. Organisms that contain two copies of the same allele are **homozygous** for that trait; organisms that carry two different alleles are **heterozygous.**

1. Monohybrid Cross

The principles of Mendelian inheritance can be illustrated in a cross between two true-breeding pea plants, one with purple flowers and the other with white flowers. Since only one trait is being studied in this particular mating, it is referred to as a **monohybrid cross.** The individuals being crossed are the **Parental or P generation**; the progeny generations are the **Filial** or **F generations,** with each generation numbered sequentially (e.g., F_1, F_2, etc.).

The purple flower parent has the genotype PP (i.e., it has two P alleles) and is homozygous dominant. The white flower parent has the genotype pp and is homozygous recessive. When these individuals are crossed, they produce F_1 plants that are 100 percent heterozygous (genotype = Pp). Because purple is dominant to white, all the F_1 progeny have the purple flower phenotype.

2. Punnett Square

One way of predicting the genotypes expected from a cross is by drawing a **Punnett square** diagram. The parental genotypes are arranged around a grid, as shown in Figure 13.1. Because the genotype of each progeny will be the sum of the alleles donated by the parental gametes, their genotypes can be determined by looking at the intersections on the grid. A Punnett square indicates all the potential progeny genotypes, and the relative frequencies of the different genotypes and phenotypes can be easily calculated (see Figure 13.1).

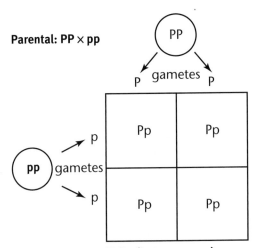

Figure 13.1. Monohybrid Cross

When the F_1 generation from our monohybrid cross is **self-crossed,** i.e., Pp × Pp, the F_2 progeny are more genotypically and phenotypically diverse than their parents. Because the F_1 plants are heterozygous, they will donate a P allele to half of their descendants and a p allele to the other half. One-fourth of the F_2 plants will have the genotype PP; 50 percent will have the genotype Pp; and 25 percent will have the genotype pp. Because the homozygous dominant and heterozygous genotypes both produce the dominant phenotype, purple flowers, 75 percent of the F_2 plants will have purple flowers, and 25 percent will have white flowers (see Figure 13.2).

This is a standard pattern of Mendelian inheritance. Its hallmarks are the disappearance of the silent (recessive) phenotype in the F_1 generation and its subsequent reappearance in 25 percent of the individuals in the F_2 generation.

> **TEACHER TIP**
> This common pattern of inheritance for a cross (disappearance of the silent allele in the F_1 with its reappearance in F_2) is worth memorizing. You should also learn the distribution for a dihybrid cross.

F_1: Pp × Pp

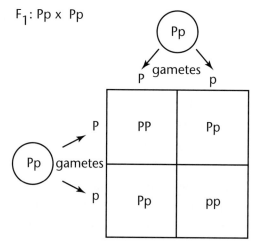

F_2 genotypes: 1:2:1; 1PP: 2Pp:1pp

F_2 phenotypes: 3:1; 3 purple:1 white

Figure 13.2. Self-Cross of F_1 Generation

3. Testcross

Only with a recessive phenotype can genotype be predicted with 100 percent accuracy. If the dominant phenotype is expressed, the genotype can be either homozygous dominant or heterozygous. Thus, homozygous recessive organisms always breed true. This fact can be used to determine the unknown genotype of an organism with a dominant phenotype. In a procedure known as a **testcross** or **backcross,** an organism with a dominant phenotype of unknown genotype (Ax) is crossed with a phenotypically recessive organism (genotype aa). Because

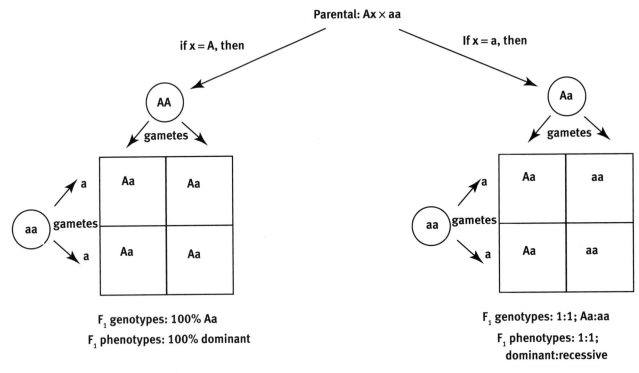

Figure 13.3. Testcross

the recessive parent is homozygous, it can donate only the recessive allele, a, to the progeny. If the dominant parent's genotype is AA, all of its gametes will carry an A, and thus all of the progeny will have genotype Aa. If the dominant parent's genotype is Aa, half of the progeny will be Aa and express the dominant phenotype, and half will be aa and express the recessive phenotype. In a testcross, the appearance of the recessive phenotype in the progeny indicates that the phenotypically dominant parent is genotypically heterozygous (see Figure 13.3).

B. MENDEL'S SECOND LAW: LAW OF INDEPENDENT ASSORTMENT

1. Dihybrid Cross

The principles of the monohybrid cross can be extended to a dihybrid cross in which the parents differ in two traits, as long as each trait assorts independently; i.e., the alleles of unlinked genes assort independently during meiosis. This is known as Mendel's **law of independent assortment.**

In the following example, a purple-flowered tall pea plant is crossed with a white-flowered dwarf pea plant; both plants are doubly homozygous (tall is dominant to dwarf, T = tall allele, t = dwarf allele;

purple is dominant to white, P = purple allele, p = white allele). The purple parent's genotype is TTPP, and it thus produces only TP gametes; the white parent's genotype is ttpp and produces only tp gametes. The F_1 progeny will all have the genotype TtPp and will be phenotypically dominant for both traits.

When the F_1 generation is self-crossed (TtPp × TtPp), it produces four different phenotypes: tall purple, tall white, dwarf purple, and dwarf white, in the ratio 9:3:3:1, respectively. This is the typical pattern for Mendelian inheritance in a dihybrid cross between heterozygotes with independently assorting traits (see Figure 13.4).

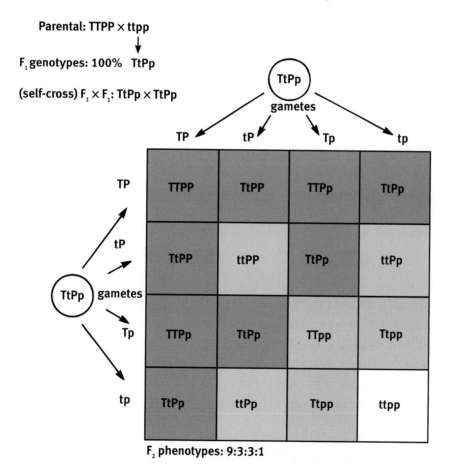

Parental: TTPP × ttpp

F_1 genotypes: 100% TtPp

(self-cross) $F_1 × F_1$: TtPp × TtPp

F_2 phenotypes: 9:3:3:1

9 tall purple:3 tall white:3 dwarf purple:1 dwarf white

Figure 13.4. Dihybrid Cross

2. Statistical Calculations

Each F_1 parent in the dihybrid cross can produce four possible gametes: TP, Tp, tP, and tp. The probability of a particular genotype appearing in the F_2 progeny can be determined by calculating the number of different gamete combinations that will produce this genotype. For example, the genotype TTPP can be produced in only one way, by the fusion of two TP gametes. Because ¼ of each parent's gametes will be TP, ¼ of the other parent's gametes will also be TP, ¼ × ¼ or $\frac{1}{16}$ of the total progeny will be TTPP. In statistical terms, the probability that one parent will donate a particular gamete (¼ in this case) is independent of the probability that the other parent will donate a particular gamete (also ¼). Consequently, the probability of producing a genotype that requires the occurrence of both these independent events is equal to the *product* of the individual probabilities that these events will occur ($\frac{1}{16}$).

In contrast, the genotype TtPp can be produced by four different gamete combinations, TP + tp; Tp + tP; tP + Tp; and tp + TP. The probability of any one of these combinations is ¼ × ¼ or $\frac{1}{16}$ (e.g., ¼ of one parent's gametes will be TP, and ¼ of the other parent's gametes will be TP; the probability of these gametes fusing is the product of the individual probabilities). Because there are four ways to produce a TtPp genotype, the frequency of the TtPp genotype in the F_2 generation is $\frac{1}{16} + \frac{1}{16} + \frac{1}{16} + \frac{1}{16} = \frac{4}{16} = \frac{1}{4}$. In statistical terms, the probability of producing a genotype that can be the result of more than one event is equal to the *sum* of the individual probabilities that these events will occur. (Note that statistical calculations are most accurate with a large sample size.)

3. Problem Solving

In solving problems involving two independently assorted traits, it generally helps to consider each trait individually. For example, consider the cross between a purple tall plant of unknown genotype and a white tall plant, also of unknown genotype. The F_1 generation consists of 62 tall plants with purple flowers, 59 tall plants with white flowers, 20 dwarf plants with purple flowers, and 21 dwarf plants with white flowers. What are the genotypes of the parental generation?

Because both parents are tall, but the F_1 generation contains dwarf plants, both parents must be heterozygous for tallness and hence of genotype Tt. If so, then tall plants should outnumber dwarf plants in the F_1 generation by a ratio of 3 to 1. In fact, the ratio of tall plants (62 + 59 = 121) to dwarf plants (20 + 21 = 41) is 121:41 or approximately 3:1.

In addition, one parent is white; it must therefore be homozygous pp. But Because the F_1 generation contained white-flowered plants, the purple parent must also have the allele for white flowers. If we now look at the segregation of purple and white alone, we find that the ratio of purple (62 + 20 = 82) to white (59 + 21 = 80) is almost 1:1. This is the ratio expected in a cross between a heterozygous dominant individual (Pp) and a homozygous recessive (pp). Thus, the genotype of the purple tall parent must be TtPp, and the genotype of the white tall parent must be Ttpp.

THE CHROMOSOMAL THEORY OF INHERITANCE

The principles of Mendelian genetics reflect the linear arrangement of genes on chromosomes. **Diploid** species have chromosome pairs **(homologues).** In diploids, the alleles for a given trait are segregated; one allele is located on one chromosome, and the other allele is found on its homologue.

A. SEGREGATION AND INDEPENDENT ASSORTMENT

Mendelian segregation and independent assortment are the consequences of chromosomal behavior during meiosis. Prior to meiosis, each chromosome is replicated, but the daughter copy remains attached to the parental chromosome via the centromere, forming sister chromatids. The sister chromatids pair with their homologues and align at the equatorial plate during metaphase I. During the first meiotic division, the homologous pairs separate, and following cytokinesis, the number of chromosomes per cell is reduced from 2N to N. This is the step in meiosis during which segregation and independent assortment occur. In the second meiotic division, the sister chromatids separate. Each gamete receives the haploid (N) complement of chromosomes; i.e., one sister chromatid from every homologous pair. The fusion of two gametes during fertilization restores the diploid number, 2N.

B. NONINDEPENDENT ASSORTMENT: GENETIC LINKAGE

Not all traits assort independently in a dihybrid cross. In the sweet pea plant, the allele for purple-colored pollen (A) is dominant to the allele for red pollen (a); the allele for long pollen (B) is dominant to the allele for round pollen (b). In a cross between two purple long dihybrids (AaBb × AaBb), if the two traits assort independently, then the expected phenotypic ratio is 9 purple long:3 purple round:3 red long:1 red round. The purple long F_1 progeny have the **parental phenotype**, purple long; the other phenotypes are **recombinant phenotypes**, Because they recombine the parental traits. However, in this dihybrid cross, the F_1 genotypic ratio is 4 AABB:8 AaBb:4 aabb, or 1:2:1. The F_1 phenotypic ratio

---

FLASHBACK

Now may be an opportune time to review meiosis. See chapter 4.

TEACHER TIP

What is the value of segregation and independent assortment? It allows for greater genetic diversity in the offspring.

TEACHER TIP

KEY POINT: The 3:1 and 9:3:3:1 distribution we learned for monohybrid and dihybrid crosses, respectively, only works if the genes are inherited independently (i.e., not linked). If they are linked, then the numbers aren't valid. Don't worry about this too much, though. It's far more likely you'll be asked IF genes are linked than if you can calculate the exact statistical numbers.

is 12 purple long:4 red round, or 3:1; the parental phenotype is overly represented in the progeny. In fact, the segregation pattern for these two traits in a dihybrid cross is like that of a single trait in a monohybrid cross. This is because genes A and B are **linked**; they are located on the same chromosome and are usually inherited together. This means that the parent AaBb does not produce four different types of gametes (AB, Ab, aB, ab). Instead, only two different gametes are produced; in this case, AB and ab. (If the two types of gametes were Ab and aB, then the genotypic ratio would have been 1 AAbb:2 AaBb:1 aaBB.)

Genetic linkage is a direct result of the organization of genes along chromosomes: linked genes are located on the same chromosome. Recall that during meiosis I, homologous chromosomes segregate into different cells. If two genes are located on the same chromosome, they tend to segregate together. The degree of genetic linkage can be tight and complete, with no recombinant phenotypes. Linkage can also be weak, as when the number of recombinants in the F_1 progeny approaches the number expected from independent assortment. Tightly linked genes recombine at a frequency close to 0 percent; weakly linked genes recombine at frequencies approaching 50 percent.

C. RECOMBINATION FREQUENCIES: GENETIC MAPPING

Linked genes can recombine at frequencies between 0 and 50 percent to produce recombinants. The recombinant chromosomes arise through the physical exchange of DNA between homologous chromosomes paired during meiosis. This process is called **crossing over** or **genetic recombination** (see chapter 4). Crossing over can unlink linked genes (see Figure 13.5).

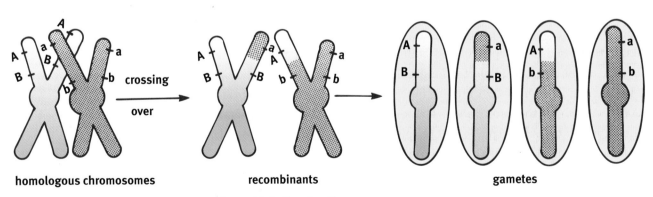

homologous chromosomes   recombinants   gametes

Figure 13.5. Crossing Over

The degree of genetic linkage is a measure of how far apart two genes are on the same chromosome. The probability of a crossover and exchange occurring between two points is generally directly proportional to the distance between the points. For example, pairs of genes that are far apart from each other on a chromosome have a higher probability of being separated during crossing over than pairs of genes that are located close to each other. Thus, the frequency of genetic recombination between two genes is related to the distance between them.

Recombination frequencies can be used to construct a **genetic map.** One **map unit** is defined as a 1 percent **recombinant frequency.** Recombination frequencies are roughly additive. If genes are found on a map in the order XYZ, then the recombination frequency between X and Y plus the recombination frequency between Y and Z will be roughly equal to the recombination frequency between X and Z. Likewise, if you are given the recombinant frequencies for X and Y, X and Z, and Y and Z (which can be determined by dividing the number of recombinant offspring by the total number of offspring), then you can determine the relative positions of these genes on the chromosome. In Figure 13.6, we are given that X and Y have a recombination frequency of 8 percent; i.e., they are 8 map units apart. If X and Z recombine 12 percent of the time, then they are 12 map units apart. Depending on where you draw Z in relation to X on your map, Y and Z are either 20 map units apart, or 4 map units apart. Since we are also given that Y and Z recombine with a frequency of 4 percent, the genes are in the order XYZ (or ZYX) on the chromosome.

TEACHER TIP

KEY POINT: Crossing over allows for increased genetic diversity and hopefully greater reproductive fitness of the offspring. While this is a simple point and has been repeated many times already, it should indicate to you how important a concept it will be on the MCAT.

FLASHBACK

Recall in chapter 4 that crossing over occurs when the homologous chromosomes pair up into tetrads during prophase I.

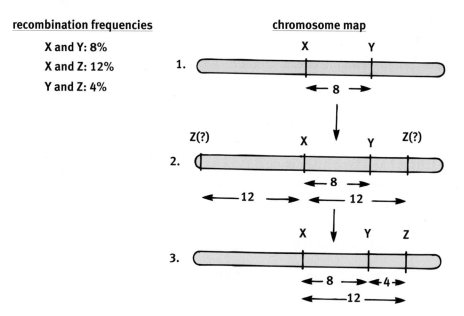

Figure 13.6. Chromosome Mapping

VARIATIONS ON MENDELIAN GENETICS

In real life, inheritance patterns are often more complicated than Mendel would have hoped. One major source of complication is in the relationship between phenotype and genotype. In theory, 100 percent of individuals with the recessive phenotype have a homozygous recessive genotype, and 100 percent of individuals with the dominant phenotype have either homozygous or heterozygous genotypes. Such clean concordance between genotype and phenotype is not always the case.

A. INCOMPLETE DOMINANCE

Some progeny phenotypes are apparently blends of the parental phenotypes. The classic example is flower color in snapdragons: homozygous dominant red snapdragons when crossed with homozygous recessive white snapdragons produce 100 percent pink progeny in the F_1 generation. When F_1 progeny are self-crossed, they produce red, pink, and white progeny in the ratio of 1:2:1, respectively (see Figure 13.7). The pink color is the result of the combined effects of the red and white genes in heterozygotes. An allele is **incompletely dominant** if the phenotype of the heterozygote is an intermediate of the phenotypes of the homozygotes.

B. CODOMINANCE

Codominance occurs when multiple alleles exist for a given gene and more than one of them is dominant. Each dominant allele is fully dominant when combined with a recessive allele, but when two dominant alleles are present, the phenotype is the result of the expression of both dominant alleles simultaneously.

The classic example of codominance and multiple alleles is the inheritance of ABO blood groups in humans. Blood type is determined by three different alleles, I^A, I^B, and i. Only two alleles are present in any single individual, but the population contains all three alleles. I^A and I^B are both dominant to i. Individuals who are homozygous I^A or heterozygous I^Ai have blood type A; individuals who are homozygous I^B or heterozygous I^Bi have blood type B; and individuals who are homozygous ii have blood type O. However, I^A and I^B are codominant; individuals who are heterozygous I^AI^B have a distinct blood type, AB, which combines characteristics of both the A and B blood groups.

C. PENETRANCE AND EXPRESSIVITY

A dominant allele is not necessarily expressed to the same degree in all individuals who carry it; phenotype is a combination of genetics and

snapdragons
R = allele for red flowers
r = allele for white flowers
Parental: RR × rr (red × white)

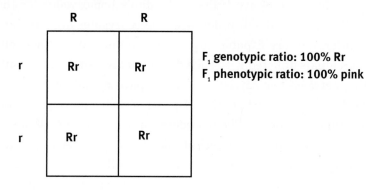

F₁ genotypic ratio: 100% Rr
F₁ phenotypic ratio: 100% pink

F₁: Rr × Rr (pink × pink)

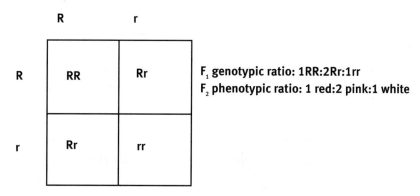

F₁ genotypic ratio: 1RR:2Rr:1rr
F₂ phenotypic ratio: 1 red:2 pink:1 white

Figure 13.7. Incomplete Dominance

environment. The **penetrance** of a genotype is the percentage of individuals in the population carrying the allele who actually express the phenotype associated with it. The **expressivity** of a genotype is the degree to which the phenotype associated with the genotype is expressed in individuals who carry the allele. Both penetrance and expressivity can be affected by environment; e.g., in the fruitfly *Drosophila melanogaster*, the dominant gene curly (C^Y) gives rise to adult flies with abnormal wings that curl up if the pupae are kept at 25°C, but remain uncurled if the pupae are kept at 19°C. At 25°C, C^Y is 100 percent penetrant, whereas at 19°C, C^Y is 0 percent penetrant. The expressivity is the degree of curliness of the wings.

D. INHERITED DISORDERS

1. Recessive

Recessively inherited disorders are caused by recessive alleles that are inherited as simple recessive traits. Individuals homozygous for the recessive allele exhibit the disorder, while heterozygotes are **carriers** of the disorder, and are capable of passing the allele on to their offspring. Individuals afflicted with such disorders are usually the result of a mating between two carriers. As in a typical dominant/recessive monohybrid cross, one-fourth of the offspring of such a mating are predicted to have the disorder. The disorders can be mild, like albinism, a lack of skin pigmentation; or **lethal,** like Tay-Sachs disease, which results from a malfunctioning enzyme that causes lipids to accumulate in the brain, causing death in early childhood. Since these alleles are recessive and do not typically affect carriers, the allele remains in the gene pool, "hidden" in carriers who are not selected against by natural selection. Most lethal genes are **early acting,** i.e., they program an early death for homozygotes, typically during embryonic development. Sometimes, lethal genes impart an advantage to heterozygous individuals, as in the case of sickle-cell anemia. Heterozygous individuals are resistant to malaria, while homozygous individuals have abnormal hemoglobin, which causes the painful and often fatal anemia.

2. Dominant

Lethal alleles can also be dominant. These are **late-acting** genes; the classic example is the gene for Huntington's chorea in humans. Huntington's chorea is 100 percent penetrant and fully dominant; all individuals carrying the allele succumb to the disease. Since the Huntington's chorea gene isn't expressed until middle age, most of its victims have already had children by the time of diagnosis; assuming the other parent is normal, 50 percent of the children are predicted to inherit the Huntington's chorea gene.

E. SEX DETERMINATION

Different species vary in their systems of sex determination. In sexually differentiated species, most chromosomes exist as pairs of homologues called **autosomes** but sex is determined by a pair of **sex chromosomes.** All humans have 22 pairs of autosomes; additionally, females have a pair of homologous **X chromosomes,** and males have a pair of heterologous chromosomes, an **X** and a **Y** chromosome. The sex chromosomes pair during meiosis and segregate during the first meiotic division. Because females can produce only gametes containing the X chromosome, the

---

TEACHER TIP

Keep this early-versus late-acting idea in mind. You may be asked if a condition is likely to be recessive or dominant based on a phenotypic model.

MCAT SYNOPSIS

The odds of a child being a boy or a girl are 50 percent. That means that regardless of how many sons or daughters a couple might have, the odds of having a boy or girl the next time around remains 50 percent. Each fertilization is an independent event!

gender of a zygote is determined by the genetic contribution of the male gamete. If the sperm carries a Y chromosome, the zygote will be male; if it carries an X chromosome, the zygote will be female. For every mating there is a 50 percent chance that the zygote will be male and a 50 percent chance that it will be female.

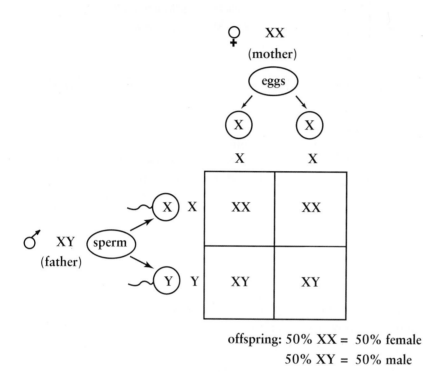

offspring: 50% XX = 50% female
50% XY = 50% male

Figure 13.8. Sex Determination in Humans

Genes that are located on the X or Y chromosome are called **sex-linked.** In humans, most sex-linked genes are located on the X chromosome, though some Y-linked traits have been found (e.g., hair on the outer ears).

F. SEX LINKAGE

In humans, females have two X chromosomes, and males have only one. As a result, recessive genes that are carried on the X chromosome will produce the recessive phenotypes whenever they occur in males, since no dominant allele is present to mask them. The recessive phenotype will thus be much more frequently found in males. Examples of sex-linked recessives in humans are the genes for hemophilia and for color blindness.

The pattern of inheritance for a sex-linked recessive is somewhat complicated. Because the gene is carried on the X chromosome, and males pass the X chromosome only to their daughters, affected males *cannot* pass

a. Cross between a carrier female (X^hX) and a normal male (XY):

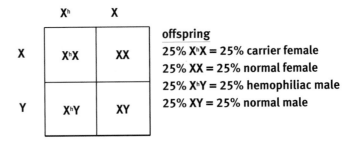

offspring
25% X^hX = 25% carrier female
25% XX = 25% normal female
25% X^hY = 25% hemophiliac male
25% XY = 25% normal male

b. Cross between a carrier female ($X^h X$) and a hemophiliac male (X^hY)

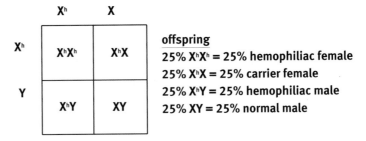

offspring
25% X^hX^h = 25% hemophiliac female
25% X^hX = 25% carrier female
25% X^hY = 25% hemophiliac male
25% XY = 25% normal male

Figure 13.9. Inheritance of Hemophilia Gene

the trait to their male offspring. Affected males will pass the gene to *all* of their daughters. However, unless the daughter also receives the gene from her mother, she will be a phenotypically normal carrier of the trait. Because all of the daughter's male children will receive their only X chromosome from her, half of her sons will receive the recessive sex-linked allele (see Figure 13.9). Thus, sex-linked recessives generally affect only males; they cannot be passed from father to son, but can be passed from father to grandson via a daughter who is a carrier, thereby skipping a generation.

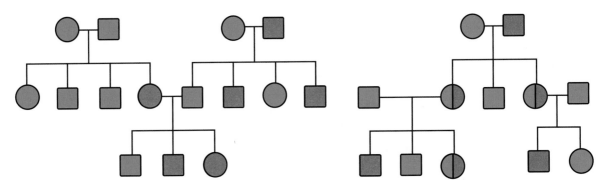

Figure 13.10a. Autosomal Recessive

Figure 13.10b. Sex-linked Recessive

PEDIGREE ANALYSIS

Ethical constraints forbid geneticists from performing testcrosses on human populations. Instead, they must rely on examining matings that have already occurred. A **pedigree** is a family tree depicting the inheritance of a particular genetic trait over several generations. By convention, males are indicated by squares and females by circles. Matings are indicated by horizontal lines, and descendants are listed below. Individuals affected by the trait are generally shaded, and unaffected individuals are unshaded. When carriers of sex-linked traits have been identified (typically, female heterozygotes), they are usually half shaded in family trees.

A human pedigree for a recessive autosomal trait, such as albinism, is shown in Figure 13.10a (an affected child born to parents that are normal) and, for a sex-linked trait, such as hemophilia, in Figure 13.10b (the key here is more affected males than females). In analyzing pedigrees, look for individuals with the recessive phenotype. Such individuals have only one possible genotype: homozygous recessive. Matings between them and the dominant phenotype behave as testcrosses; the ratio of phenotypes among the offspring allows deduction of the dominant genotype.

CHROMOSOMAL ABERRATIONS

Chromosome number and structure can be altered by abnormal cell division during meiosis or by mutagenic agents.

A. NONDISJUNCTION

Nondisjunction is either the failure of homologous chromosomes to separate properly during meiosis I, or the failure of sister chromatids to separate properly during meiosis II (usually in a secondary spermatocyte or secondary oocyte). In the case of a secondary spermatocyte, it results in one gamete with two copies of the chromosome (polyploid), two normal haploid gametes, and one gamete with no copies of the chromosome (aneuploid). The resulting zygote may have either three copies of that chromosome, called **trisomy** (somatic cells will have $2N + 1$ chromosomes) or a single copy of that chromosome, called **monosomy** (somatic cells will have $2N - 1$ chromosomes). A classic case of trisomy is the birth defect **Down's syndrome,** which is caused by trisomy of **chromosome 21.** Victims of Down's syndrome are of short stature, have characteristic facial features, and are mentally retarded. They are also usually sexually underdeveloped and have shorter-than-normal lifespans.

TEACHER TIP
The human body deals with extra sex chromosomes better than it does with extra autosomal chromosomes. In fact, the only autosomal aberration compatible with long-term life is trisomy-21.

Most monosomies and trisomies are lethal, causing the embryo to spontaneously abort early in the pregnancy.

Nondisjunction of the sex chromosomes may also occur, resulting in individuals with extra or missing copies of the X and/or Y chromosomes. **XXY** individuals are afflicted with **Klinefelter's syndrome**; they are sterile males with abnormally small testes. **XO** females have only one sex chromosome and suffer from **Turner's syndrome**; they fail to develop secondary sexual characteristics and are sterile and of short stature. **XXX** females are referred to as **metafemales** and are usually mentally retarded and sometimes infertile. **XYY** males are normal males, though they tend to be taller than average and, according to some studies, may be more violent.

B. CHROMOSOMAL BREAKAGE

Chromosomal breakage may occur spontaneously or be induced by environmental factors, such as mutagenic agents and X rays. The chromosome that loses a fragment is said to have a deficiency. The fragment may join with its homologous chromosome, resulting in a **duplication,** or it may join with a nonhomologous chromosome, an event termed a **translocation.** The fragment may also rejoin its original chromosome but in the reverse position; this is known as an **inversion.** For example, Down's syndrome can also be caused by the translocation of a chromosome 21 fragment.

PRACTICE QUESTIONS

1. A 46-year-old man had a brother who died at the age of three from infantile Tay-Sachs disease, which is always fatal by age six. What is the probability that this man is a carrier of a disease gene?

   A. 100%
   B. 25%
   C. 50%
   D. Cannot be determined from the information given

2. During which phase of the meiotic division is crossing-over expected to occur?

   A. Anaphase I
   B. Prophase I
   C. Anaphase II
   D. Telophase I

3. A scientist interested in preparing a genetic map would expect a higher probability of a crossing-over to occur when

   A. the genes are located farther apart on the chromosome.
   B. there are fewer genes on the chromosome.
   C. there are more genes on the chromosome.
   D. the genes are located close to each other on the chromosome.

4. A mother with blood type I (O) has two children, one with blood type II (A) and another from the same father with blood type III (B). It can be concluded that the father's blood type is

   A. type III (B).
   B. type II (A).
   C. type IV (AB).
   D. Cannot be determined without further information

5. The ABO blood system is encoded by a single gene located on chromosome 9. How many primary alleles does this gene have?

   A. 1
   B. 2
   C. 3
   D. 4

6. Before the blood type system was discovered, the fatal transfusion of blood type III (B) to an individual with blood type II (A) would result in an agglutination (clumping) reaction between

   A. anti-A antibodies of the receiver and antigens A of the donor's blood.
   B. anti-A and anti-B antibodies of the donor's blood with antigens A of the receiver.
   C. anti-B antibodies of the donor's blood with antigens B of the receiver.
   D. anti-B antibodies of the receiver with antigens B of the donor's blood.

7. A couple has two sons. What is the probability that their next child is a boy?

   A. 50%
   B. 25%
   C. 12.5%
   D. 6.25%

8. A customer is interested in buying a purebred dog (homozygous dominant) in which black coat color is dominant. To make sure that the black dog he is offered is a purebred and not a heterozygote, which of the following would be the best mating to test the genotype?

A. Mating with a purebred (homozygous dominant)

B. Mating with a heterozygous dog

C. Mating with a homozygous recessive dog

D. Either A or B

9. Albinism is an autosomal recessive disease that disrupts the metabolic pathway normally leading to the production of the pigment melanin. If a man and a woman who are both carriers of a disease allele have a child, what is the probability of a phenotypically healthy child

A. 100%

B. 75%

C. 50%

D. 25%

10. Retinoblastoma, a disorder causing a malignant eye tumor, is an autosomal dominant disease with about 90 percent penetrance. This most likely means

A. 90 percent of people carrying the disease allele develop the disease.

B. 90 percent of people carrying the disease allele don't develop the disease.

C. 10 percent of people carrying the disease allele develop the disease.

D. 90 percent of people homozygous for the disease allele develop the disease.

11. Marfan syndrome is an autosomal dominant disorder affecting the cardiovascular system, the skeleton and the eye. This is an example of

A. full penetrance.

B. codominance.

C. imprinting.

D. pleiotropy.

12. Down syndrome is caused by trisomy 21. This is most likely the result of which of the following?

A. Nondisjunction

B. Insertion

C. Deletion

D. Inversion

13. A man who has phenylketonuria, an autosomal recessive disorder, marries a woman who is a carrier of the recessive allele of this gene. They have four sons. What is the probability that all children are affected?

A. $\frac{1}{2}$

B. $\frac{1}{4}$

C. $\frac{1}{8}$

D. $\frac{1}{16}$

14. Duchenne muscular dystrophy is a recessive X-linked disorder. If both sons in a family are affected, it can be inferred that the mother's genotype is which of the following?

I. Homozygous recessive

II. Homozygous dominant

III. Heterozygous

A. Only I

B. II or III

C. I or III

D. I, II, or III

15. From the pedigree of family X shown below, what is the most likely mode of inheritance?

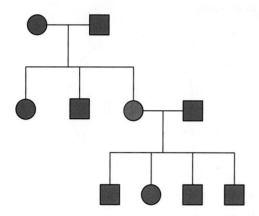

    A. X-linked recessive
    B. Autosomal recessive
    C. Autosomal dominant
    D. Mitochondrial inheritance

16. The pedigree below is for adult polycystic kidney disease, an autosomal dominant disorder. What is the risk that the offspring in generation III will develop the disorder?

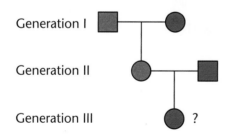

    A. 100%
    B. 75%
    C. 50%
    D. Cannot be determined without further information

17. The pedigree below is for Leber's hereditary optic neuropathy. This disorder has a mitochondrial mode of inheritance. All offspring of affected females have the disorder. This is most likely due to which of the following?

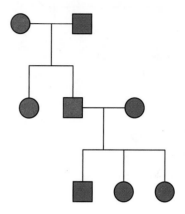

    I. Males don't pass mitochondria to offspring.

    II. The condition is X-linked.

    III. Mitochondria are located in the cytoplasm.

    A. I only
    B. I and II
    C. I and III
    D. I, II, and III

18. Based on the pedigree below, which of the following can be concluded?

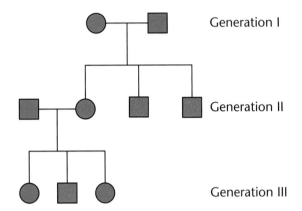

Generation I

Generation II

Generation III

A. The disorder is X-linked dominant.
B. The father in generation II is a carrier of the disease.
C. This is an autosomal recessive disorder.
D. The mother in generation I is a carrier of the disease.

19. Having an extra chromosome 18, as shown on the drawing, leads to Edwards syndrome and is an example of

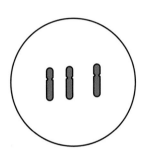

A. polyploidy.
B. triploidy.
C. monosomy.
D. aneuploidy.

20. A genetic disorder affects 1 in 10,000 members of the population. Determine the frequency of the normal allele of the gene in this population.

A. 0.01
B. 9999
C. 0.99
D. 0.0001

CLASSICAL GENETICS—PROBABILITY & PENETRANCE

KEY CONCEPTS

Penetrance

Genotype

Phenotype

Probability

Dystonia is a syndrome of involuntary spasms and sustained contractions of the muscles. One form of the disease is childhood dystonia, in which dystonia begins in the leg or foot and eventually spreads to involve the entire body. If one parent has this type of dystonia, while the other parent has no alleles for the disease, a child of those parents has a 50 percent chance of having the genotype for the disease. Given that the gene's penetrance is 40 percent, if a man with the disease (his mother was homozygous recessive) and a woman with no alleles for the disease have two children, what is the probability that both children will be healthy?

1) Identify the inheritance pattern.

No generation is skipped, and gender does not matter; thus, dystonia is an autosomal, dominant trait.

Whether it is presented in a pedigree diagram or indirectly given in the question stem, the inheritance pattern should be identified quickly. In the question stem above, we are told that if just one parent has the disease, there is at least a 50 percent chance she will pass it on to a child; thus, the trait must be dominant. The probabilities cited in the question stem are independent of the gender of the parent or the child; thus, sex-linked inheritance is ruled out.

2) Identify the relevant genotypes to set up the Punnet square.

Because the man is afflicted with the disease, and we have determined that the disease is autosomal dominant, he must be homozygous (DD) for the trait or heterozygous (Dd). Because his mother was homozygous recessive (dd), he must be heterozygous for the disease, as he received one recessive allele from his mother. The woman has no alleles for the disease and thus must be homozygous recessive (dd).

	D	d
d	Dd	dd
d	Dd	dd

The relevant genotypes may vary depending on the question. In this question, the relevant genotypes are those of the parents because we are interested in the probability of conceiving a healthy child.

TAKEAWAYS

After identifying the pattern of inheritance for the gene and the genotypes of the parental generation, set up the Punnet square to aid in the calculations of the probability questions posed. Unless otherwise stated, it is safe to assume that the penetrance of a gene in a given question is 100 percent.

247

Beware of tricky probability questions. One typical trap was on your diagnostic: a disease is expressed in individuals who are homozygous recessive for the gene. Given parents who are both heterozygotes, what is the probability that a healthy child will be homozygous dominant? The Punnet square indicates 25 percent, but the trick is that we know the child is healthy; thus, there are only three possible outcomes—not four. Therefore, the probability is ⅓ instead of ¼.

3) Use the Punnet square to calculate the probability for each event.
The probability that the couple will bear two healthy children is $(80\%)^2 = 64\%$.

There is a 50 percent chance that a child will be homozygous recessive (healthy) and a 50 percent chance that the child will inherit the genotype for the disease. However, because penetrance is only 40 percent, there is only a 20 percent ($50\% \times 40\%$) chance of the child actually expressing the disease. Therefore, there is an 80 percent chance that the child will be healthy.

Recall that penetrance is the dependence of an organism's phenotype on the genotype. One hundred percent penetrance signifies no environmental effects, whereas 0 percent penetrance signifies no genetic influence of a particular gene on a physical trait. Here, we have 40 percent penetrance, which means that only 40 percent of the heterozygotes will actually suffer from childhood dystonia.

Remember: To find the probabilities of both events occurring, multiply the probabilities of each event.

SIMILAR QUESTIONS

1) The phenotype of an individual is known, but her genotype is not. Given a pedigree, could you determine the probability that she is homozygous dominant for this trait?

2) If normal parents have a colorblind son, what is the probability that he inherited the gene for colorblindness from his mother? What is the probability that he inherited the gene from his father?

3) A woman with blood genotype B marries a man with blood genotype A. What is the chance that their first child will have blood type B? What is the chance that their first and second children will have blood type B?

CHAPTER 14

MOLECULAR GENETICS

Genes are composed of **DNA (deoxyribonucleic acid),** which contains information coded in the sequence of its base pairs, providing the cell with a blueprint for protein synthesis. Furthermore, DNA has the ability to self-replicate, which is crucial for cell division, and hence for organismal reproduction. DNA is the basis of heredity; self-replication ensures that its coded sequence will be passed on to successive generations. This is the central dogma of molecular genetics and it is summarized in Figure 14.1.

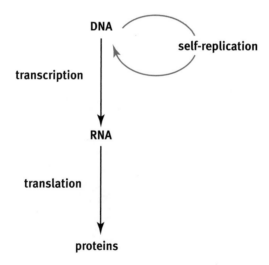

Figure 14.1. Central Dogma of Molecular Genetics

> **TEACHER TIP**
>
> The MCAT has become increasingly focused on molecular genetics, of which this theory forms the core. Also important to know is that some viruses (retroviruses, including HIV) use RNA as their genetic material, which is then turned back into DNA in a process called reverse transcription.

DNA

A. STRUCTURE

The basic unit of DNA is the **nucleotide,** which is composed of **deoxyribose** (a sugar) bonded to both a **phosphate group** and a **nitrogenous base.** There are two types of bases: the double-ringed **purines** and the single-ringed **pyrimidines.** The purines in DNA are **adenine (A)** and **guanine (G),** and the pyrimidines are **cytosine (C)** and **thymine (T)** (see Figure 14.2).

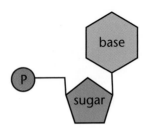

Figure 14.2. Nucleotide

Nucleotides bond together to form polynucleotides. The 3′ hydroxyl group of the sugar on one nucleotide is joined to the 5′ hydroxyl group of the adjacent sugar by a phosphodiester bond. The phosphate and sugar form a chain with the bases arranged as side groups off the chain.

A DNA molecule is a **double-stranded helix** with the sugar-phosphate chains on the outside of the helix and the bases on the inside. T always forms **two** hydrogen bonds with A; G always forms **three** hydrogen bonds with C. This **base-pairing** forms "rungs" on the interior of the double helix that link the two polynucleotide chains together (see Figure 14.3).

MCAT Synopsis

Due to complementary base pairing in DNA, the amount of A will equal the amount of T and G will equal C. Also, because G is triple bonded to C, the higher the G/C content of DNA, the more tightly bound the two strands will be.

Teacher Tip

If A-T forms two hydrogen bonds and C-G forms three, what does this mean about the relative stability of DNA strands that are A/T-rich versus those that are C/G-rich? Because H-bonds are INTER-molecular interactions, you can use heat to melt the two strands of DNA apart. This is the basis of the polymerase chain reaction. This A/T versus C/G ratio tells us how high the temperature needs to be, with more C/G requiring a higher temperature.

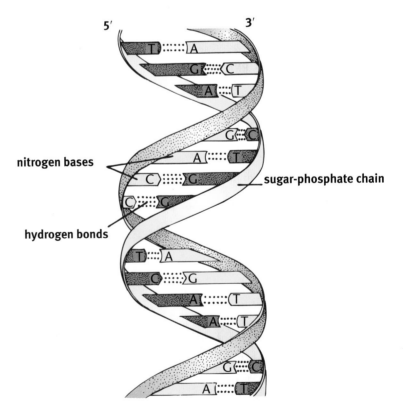

Figure 14.3. DNA Molecule

The strands are positioned **antiparallel** to each other, i.e., one strand has a **5′ → 3′ polarity,** and its complementary strand has a **3′ → 5′ polarity.** The 5′ end is designated as the end with a free hydroxyl group (or phosphate group) bonded to the 5′ carbon of the terminal sugar; the 3′ end is designated as the one with a free hydroxyl group attached to the 3′ carbon of the terminal sugar. This is known as the **Watson-Crick** model of DNA (see Figure 14.4).

MCAT SYNOPSIS

1) Watson-Crick double helix
2) Antiparallel
3) 5′ → 3′ polarity
4) Adenine bonds to thymine with 2-hydrogen bonds
5) Cytosine bonds to guanine with 3-hydrogen bonds

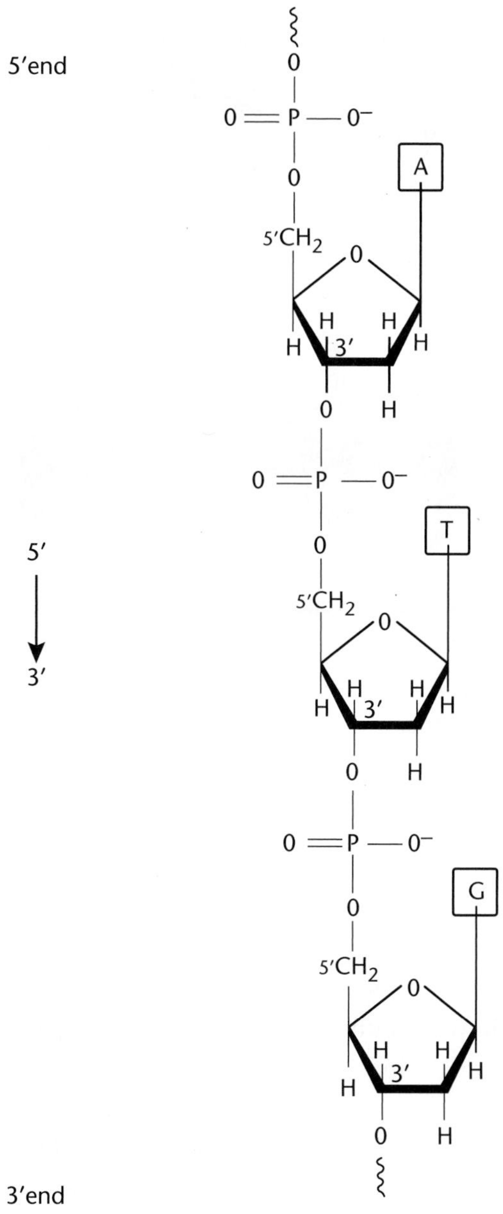

Figure 14.4. Single-Stranded DNA

TEACHER TIP

One of the most common MCAT topics is the 5′ → 3′ nature of DNA. This may be in the form of a discrete or passage-based question. It may be on transcription, translation, or general base pairing. The bottom line is that DNA and RNA work in a 5′ → 3′ direction.

TEACHER TIP

Previous MCAT administrations have asked how you can tell the new strand from the old immediately following replication. The answer is methylation. As DNA ages, methyl groups may be added to it for a variety of reasons. When the new complimentary strand is synthesized, these methyl groups aren't immediately present, so you can tell the old strand from the new simply by looking for methylation!

B. DNA REPLICATION (EUKARYOTIC)

1. Semiconservative Replication

During replication, the helix unwinds and each strand acts as a template for complementary base-pairing in the synthesis of two new daughter helices. Each new daughter helix contains an intact strand from the parent helix and a newly synthesized strand; thus DNA replication is **semiconservative.** The daughter DNA helices are identical in composition to each other and to the parent DNA (see Figure 14.5).

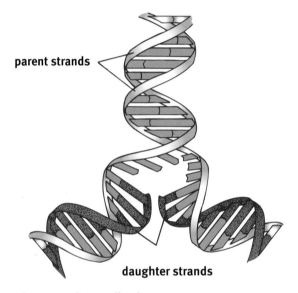

parent strands

daughter strands

Figure 14.5. Semiconservative Replication

2. Origin of Replication

As the helix unwinds, both strands are simultaneously copied with the aid of more than a dozen enzymes, at the rate of about 50 nucleotide additions per second (in mammals). Replication begins at specific sites along the DNA called **origins of replication** and proceeds in both directions simultaneously. As replication proceeds in a given direction, a **replication fork** forms (see Figure 14.6).

3. Unwinding and Initiation

The enzyme **helicase** unwinds the helix, while **single-strand binding** protein (SSB) binds to the single strands and stabilizes them, preventing them from recoiling and reforming a double helix. **DNA gyrase** is a type of *topoisomerase* that enhances the action of helicase by the introduction of negative supercoils into the DNA molecule.

A **primer** chain, usually several nucleotides long and composed of RNA, is necessary for the initiation of DNA synthesis. An RNA polymerase, **primase,** synthesizes the primer, which binds to a segment of DNA to

TEACHER TIP

Bacteria have topoisomerases as well. Some of our antibiotics poison these as their mechanism of actions. Because the topoisomerases of bacteria are somewhat different from ours, the human isn't hurt. We also use topoisomerase poisons in cancer treatment. In that case, we want to stop cell division so we prevent DNA replication (required for cell division) by keeping it from unwinding.

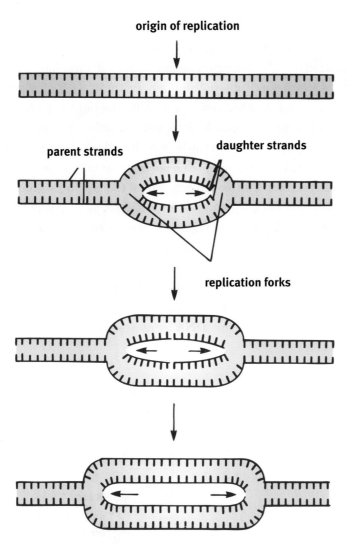

origin of replication

parent strands

daughter strands

replication forks

Figure 14.6. Origin of Replication

which it is complementary and serves as the site for nucleotide addition. The first nucleotide binds to the 3′ end of the primer chain.

4. Synthesis

DNA synthesis proceeds in the 5′ → 3′ direction and is catalyzed by a group of enzymes collectively known as **DNA polymerases.** The double-stranded DNA ahead of the DNA polymerase is unwound by a helicase, and SSB again keeps the unwound DNA in a single-stranded form so that both strands can serve as templates. DNA gyrase concurrently introduces negative supercoils to relieve the tension created during unwinding. As the helix unwinds, free nucleotides (attached to pyrophosphate groups [PPi]) are aligned opposite the parent strands. The nucleotides form phosphodiester linkages, releasing the pyrophosphate, and the bases form H-bonds with their complements.

One daughter strand is the **leading strand** and the other daughter strand is the **lagging strand.** The leading strand is continuously synthesized by DNA polymerase in the 5′ → 3′ direction. The lagging strand is synthesized discontinuously in the 5′ → 3′ direction (since DNA polymerase synthesizes only in that direction) as a series of short segments known as **Okazaki fragments**; however, overall growth of the lagging strand occurs in the 3′ → 5′ direction (see Figure 14.7). The lagging strand loops through DNA polymerase in the same direction as the leading strand. The looped segment of the lagging strand is primed with RNA, and DNA polymerase adds a short sequence of nucleotides (approximately 1,000). The lagging strand is released and a new loop is formed. Primase again synthesizes a short stretch of primer to initiate the formation of another Okazaki fragment. The RNA primers are removed and replaced by DNA. The gaps between the Okazaki fragments are also filled in with DNA. Finally, the fragments are covalently linked by the enzyme **DNA ligase** (see Figure 14.7).

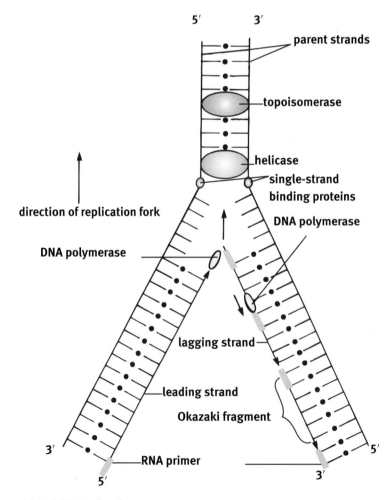

Figure 14.7. DNA Replication

RNA

RNA, ribonucleic acid, is a polynucleotide structurally similar to DNA except that its sugar is ribose, it contains uracil (U) instead of thymine, and it is usually **single-stranded.** RNA can be found in both the nucleus and the cytoplasm. There are several types of RNA, all of which are involved in some aspect of protein synthesis: **mRNA, tRNA, rRNA,** and **hnRNA.**

A. MESSENGER RNA (mRNA)

mRNA carries the complement of a DNA sequence and transports it from the nucleus to the ribosomes, where protein synthesis occurs. mRNA is **monocistronic**; i.e., one mRNA strand codes for one polypeptide.

B. TRANSFER RNA (tRNA)

tRNA is found in the cytoplasm and aids in the translation of mRNA's nucleotide code into a sequence of amino acids. tRNA brings amino acids to the ribosomes during protein synthesis. There is at least one type of tRNA for each amino acid, and approximately 40 known types of tRNA.

C. RIBOSOMAL RNA (rRNA)

rRNA is a structural component of ribosomes and is the most abundant of all RNA types. rRNA is synthesized in the nucleolus.

D. HETEROGENEOUS NUCLEAR RNA (hnRNA)

hnRNA is a large ribonucleoprotein complex that is the precursor of mRNA.

PROTEIN SYNTHESIS (EUKARYOTIC)

A. TRANSCRIPTION

Transcription is the process whereby information coded in the base sequence of DNA is transcribed into a strand of mRNA. The strand of mRNA is synthesized from a DNA template in a process similar to DNA replication. The DNA helix unwinds at the point of transcription, and synthesis occurs in the $5' \rightarrow 3'$ direction, using only one DNA strand (the **antisense strand**) as a template. The base-pairing rules are the same as for DNA, with U replacing T (G bonds with C; A bonds with U). mRNA is synthesized by the enzyme **RNA polymerase,** which must bind to sites on the DNA called **promoters** to begin RNA synthesis. Synthesis continues until the polymerase encounters a **termination sequence,** which signals RNA polymerase to stop transcription, thus allowing the DNA helix to reform. The mRNA strand is then processed and leaves the nucleus through nuclear pores.

MCAT SYNOPSIS

DNA:
- Double-stranded
- Sugar = deoxyribose
- Base pairing: A/T, G/C
- Found in nucleus only

RNA:
- Single-stranded
- Sugar = ribose
- Base pairing: A/U, G/C
- Found in nucleus and cytoplasm

TEACHER TIP

mRNA is the messenger. The DNA codes for proteins but can't carry out any of the enzymatic reactions itself. Proteins can carry out the reactions but need to know how to build themselves in order to do the right chemistry. mRNA takes the work orders from the DNA to the ribosomes to create the proteins, which allow for reactions necessary for life to occur.

KAPLAN EXCLUSIVE

INtrons are cut **OUT!**
Exons are **ex**pressed.

B. POST-TRANSCRIPTIONAL RNA PROCESSING

Most eukaryotic DNA does not code for proteins; noncoding or "garbage" sequences are found between coding sequences. A typical gene consists of several coding sequences, **exons,** interrupted by noncoding sequences, **introns.** The RNA initially transcribed is a precursor molecule, hnRNA, which contains both introns and exons. During hnRNA processing, the introns are cleaved and removed, while the exons are spliced to form a mRNA molecule coding for a single polypeptide. Processing occurs within the nucleus, and is also necessary for tRNA and rRNA production (see Figure 14.8).

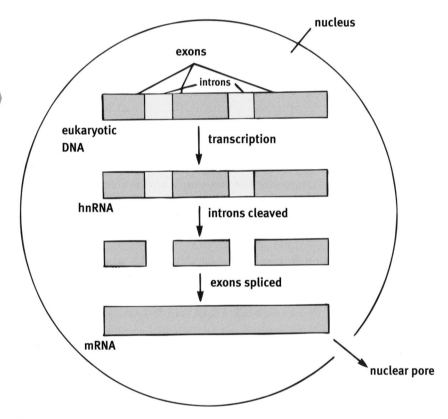

Figure 14.8. mRNA Processing

C. THE GENETIC CODE

The language of DNA consists of four "letters": A, T, C, and G. The language of proteins consists of 20 "words": the 20 amino acids. The DNA language must be translated by mRNA in such a way as to produce the 20 words in the amino acid language; hence, the **triplet code.** (A 2-letter [doublet] code would not suffice; with only four letters in the DNA alphabet, there would be only $4^2 = 16$ words possible—not enough to code for all 20 amino acids.) The base sequence of mRNA is translated as a series of triplets, otherwise known as **codons.** A sequence of three consecutive bases codes for a particular amino acid; e.g., the codon GGC specifies glycine, and the codon GUG specifies valine. The genetic code is universal for almost all organisms. (The exceptions are found in single-celled eukaryotes called ciliated protozoa, in mycoplasma, and in the mitochondria of several species.)

Given that there are 4^3, or 64, different codons possible based on the triplet code, and there are only 20 amino acids that need to be coded, the code must contain synonyms. Most amino acids have more than one codon specifying them. This property is referred to as the **degeneracy** or **redundancy** of the genetic code (see Table 14.1).

Table 14.1. The Genetic Code

		Second Base			
		U	C	A	G	
First Base (5')	U	UUU UUC } Phe UUA UUG } Leu	UCU UCC UCA UCG } Ser	UAU UAC } Tyr UAA UAG } Stop	UGU UGC } Cys UGA } Stop UGG } Trp	U C A G
	C	CUU CUC CUA CUG } Leu	CCU CCC CCA CCG } Pro	CAU CAC } His CAA CAG } Gln	CGU CGC CGA CGG } Arg	U C A G
	A	AUU AUC AUA } Ile AUG } Start or Met	ACU ACC ACA ACG } Thr	AAU AAC } Asn AAA AAG } Lys	AGU AGC } Ser AGA AGG } Arg	U C A G
	G	GUU GUC GUA GUG } Val	GGU GGC GGA GGG } Ala	GAU GAC } Asp GAA GAG } Glu	GGU GGC GGA GGG } Gly	U C A G

Third Base (3')

D. TRANSLATION

Translation is the process whereby mRNA codons are translated into a sequence of amino acids. Translation occurs in the cytoplasm and involves tRNA, ribosomes, mRNA, amino acids, enzymes, and other proteins.

1. tRNA

tRNA brings amino acids to the ribosomes in the correct sequence for polypeptide synthesis; tRNA "recognizes" both the amino acid and the mRNA codon. This dual function is reflected in its three-dimensional structure: one end contains a three-nucleotide sequence, the **anticodon,** which is complementary to one of the mRNA codons; the other end is the site of amino acid attachment and consists of a CCA sequence for all tRNA. Each amino acid has its own **aminoacyl-tRNA synthetase,** which has an active site that binds to both the amino acid and its corresponding tRNA, catalyzing their attachment to form an **aminoacyl-tRNA complex.** (This is an energy-requiring process.)

2. Ribosomes

Ribosomes are composed of two subunits (consisting of proteins and rRNA), one large and one small, that bind together only during protein synthesis. Ribosomes have three binding sites: one for mRNA, and two for tRNA: the **P site** (peptidyl-tRNA binding site) and the **A site** (aminoacyl-tRNA complex binding site). The P site binds to the tRNA attached to the growing polypeptide chain, while the A site binds to the incoming aminoacyl-tRNA complex.

3. Polypeptide Synthesis

Polypeptide synthesis can be divided into three distinct stages: **initiation, elongation,** and **termination.** All three stages are energy-requiring and are mediated by enzymes.

a. Initiation

Synthesis begins when the small ribosomal subunit binds to the mRNA near its 5′ end in the presence of proteins called **initiation factors.** The ribosome scans the mRNA until it binds to a start codon (AUG). The initiator aminoacyl-tRNA complex, **methionine-tRNA** (with the anticodon 3′-UAC-5′), base pairs with the start codon. The large ribosomal unit then binds to the small one, creating a complete ribosome with the met-tRNA complex sitting in the P site.

b. Elongation

Hydrogen bonds form between the mRNA codon in the A site and its complementary anticodon on the incoming aminoacyl-tRNA complex. The enzyme **peptidyl transferase** catalyzes the formation of a peptide bond between the amino acid attached to the tRNA in the A site and the met attached to the tRNA in the P site. Following peptide bond formation, a ribosome carries uncharged tRNA in the P site and peptidyl-tRNA in the A site. The cycle is completed by **translocation,** in which the ribosome advances three nucleotides along the mRNA in the 5′ → 3′ direction. In a concurrent action, the uncharged tRNA from the P site is expelled and the peptidyl-tRNA from the A site moves into the P site. The ribosome then has an empty A site ready for entry of the aminoacyl-tRNA corresponding to the next codon (see Figure 14.9).

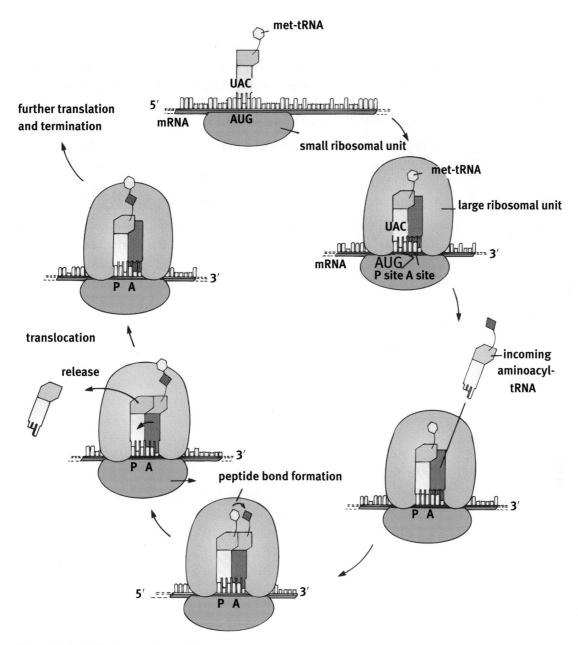

Figure 14.9. Initiation and Elongation

c. Termination

Polypeptide synthesis terminates when one of three special mRNA **termination codons** (UAA, UAG, or UGA) arrives in the A site. These codons signal the ribosome to terminate translation; they do not code for amino acids. Instead of another aminoacyl-tRNA complex coming into the A site and binding to the codon, a protein called **release factor** binds to the termination codon, causing a water molecule to be added to the polypeptide chain. This reaction

---

MCAT FAVORITE

Point mutations do not result in a change of the length of the genome or gene, even if it is a nonsense mutation and results in a truncated protein. This is because point mutations are always substitutions.

precipitates the release of the polypeptide chain from the tRNA and the ribosome itself; the ribosome then dissociates into its two subunits. Frequently, many ribosomes simultaneously translate a single mRNA molecule, forming a structure known as a **polyribosome.**

E. POST-TRANSLATIONAL MODIFICATIONS

During and after its release, the polypeptide assumes the characteristic conformation determined by the primary sequence of amino acids. Disulfide bonds can form within or between polypeptide chains. There are often other post-translational modifications made to the polypeptide before it becomes a functional protein. For example, there might be cleavages and/or additions at the terminal ends of the chain; certain amino acids within the chain might be phosphorylated, carboxylated, methylated, or glycosylated.

F. MUTATIONS

A mutation is a change in the base sequence of DNA that may be inherited by offspring. The common types of mutations are **base-pair substitutions, base-pair insertions,** and **base-pair deletions.**

1. Types of Mutations

a. Point mutations

A point mutation occurs when a single nucleotide base is substituted by another. If the substitution occurs in a noncoding region, or if the substitution is transcribed into a codon that codes for the same amino acid, there will be no change in the amino acid sequence (a "silent" mutation). If the substitution changes the sequence, the result can range from insignificant to lethal, depending on the effect the substitution has on the protein. Sickle-cell anemia most commonly results from a single base-pair substitution; sickle-cell hemoglobin has a valine (codon GUG) where normal hemoglobin has a glutamic acid (codon GAG).

b. Frame shift mutations

Base-pair insertions and deletions involve the addition or loss of nucleotides, respectively. Such mutations usually have more serious effects on the coded protein, because nucleotides are read as a series of triplets. The addition or loss of a nucleotide(s) (except in multiples of three) will change the **reading frame** of the mRNA and is known as a **frameshift mutation.** The protein, if synthesized at all, will most likely be nonfunctional.

TEACHER TIP

PTM are a great way for a peptide to know where it is targeted. Cells have many different compartmentalized structures and functions to carry out. PTM often are the way in which proteins are correctly sorted within the cell.

MCAT SYNOPSIS

A nonsense mutation is a mutation that produces a premature termination of the polypeptide chain by changing one of the codons to a stop codon. Nonsense mutation can have disastrous effects. Thalassemia is a genetic disease in which erythrocytes are produced with little or no functional hemoglobin leading to severe anemia. Thalassemia can be caused by a variety of different mutations: point mutations can change a codon into a stop codon; frame-shift mutations (insertions and deletions) can introduce a stop codon in the altered reading frame.

TEACHER TIP

Recall from the previous page that silent mutations result from the degeneracy of the genetic code. It makes sense that those amino acids that are used most commonly are redundant. That way, if the third position gets changed, no effect will be seen in the organism.

---

2. Mutagenesis

Mutagenesis is the creation of mutations; it can be caused by internal genetic "mistakes" or by external cancer-causing agents called **mutagens.** Internal mistakes can occur during DNA replication, resulting in gene mutations and dysfunctional proteins. Physical mutagens, such as X rays and ultraviolet radiation, and chemical mutagens, such as base analogs, all result in mutations. Furthermore, DNA itself can act as a mutagen; mobile pieces of DNA called **transposons** can insert themselves in genes and cause mutation.

> **MCAT FAVORITE**
>
> Remember, a mutation will only be inherited if it occurs in the germ (sex) cell line. Mutations limited to somatic cells will not be passed on to the next generation. They may, however, play an important role in the development of tumors.

VIRAL GENETICS

The viral genome contains anywhere from several to several hundred genes and has either double-stranded **or** single-stranded DNA **or** RNA. Viruses are highly specific with respect to host selection and can be generally grouped into plant viruses, animal viruses, and bacteriophages (DNA viruses that infect bacteria).

A. INFECTION OF HOST CELL

A virus can only infect a host cell that has a surface receptor for the virus' capsid (protein coat). Viruses enter their host cells by a variety of mechanisms. Some viruses introduce only their nucleic acid into the host cell's cytoplasm, while others enter the host cell entirely (their nucleic acid is liberated from its capsid intracellularly).

B. GENOME REPLICATION AND TRANSCRIPTION

1. DNA-Containing Viruses

Viral DNA is replicated and viral mRNA is transcribed inside the host cell's nucleus (or nuclear region), using the host's DNA polymerases, RNA polymerases, and nucleotide pool. A few DNA viruses replicate and transcribe in the cytoplasm; these viruses must bring their own DNA and RNA polymerases with them.

2. RNA-Containing Viruses

Viral RNA is replicated and is transcribed in the host cell's cytoplasm. An enzyme called **RNA replicase** transcribes new RNA from an RNA template. Some viruses bring RNA replicase with them into the host; otherwise a portion of viral RNA functions as mRNA, which is translated to RNA replicase immediately after entering the host cell. **Retroviruses** are a special group of RNA viruses that use their genome as a template for DNA synthesis rather than for RNA synthesis.

DNA is synthesized by the enzyme **reverse transcriptase.** The retroviral DNA becomes integrated into the host DNA. When viral DNA becomes integrated into host DNA it is called a **provirus** (animal viruses) or **prophage** (bacteriophages). The proviral DNA is later transcribed into mRNA that is needed for prophage assembly.

C. TRANSLATION AND PROGENY ASSEMBLY

The mRNA transcribed from viral nucleic acid is translated into the polypeptide chains that compose the viral protein coats with the aid of the host cell's tRNA, amino acids, ribosomes, and enzymes. Viral progeny self-assemble; the protein-nucleic acid configuration forms either spontaneously or with the aid of viral enzymes. A single virus is capable of producing hundreds of progeny.

D. PROGENY RELEASE

Once assembled, viral progeny may be released either by lysis of the host cell or by **extrusion,** a process similar to budding. In extrusion, the progeny are enclosed in vesicles derived from the host cell membrane; this permits viral replication without killing the host cell. The process of viral replication and extrusion in animal viruses is called a **productive cycle** (see Figure 14.10).

host cell membrane

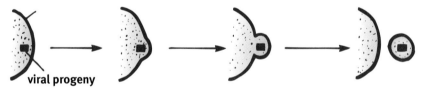

viral progeny

Figure 14.10. Extrusion

E. BACTERIOPHAGE

A bacteriophage infects its host bacterium by attaching to it, boring a hole through the bacterial cell wall, and injecting its DNA, while its protein coat remains attached to the cell wall. Once inside its host, the bacteriophage enters either a **lytic cycle** or a **lysogenic cycle.**

1. Lytic Cycle

The phage DNA takes control of the bacterium's genetic machinery and manufactures numerous progeny. The bacterial cell then bursts (lyses), releasing new virions, each capable of infecting other bacteria. Bacteriophages that replicate by the lytic cycle, killing their host cells, are called **virulent.**

2. Lysogenic Cycle

If the bacteriophage does not lyse its host cell, it becomes integrated into the bacterial genome in a harmless form (prophage or probacteriophage), lying dormant for one or more generations. The virus may stay integrated indefinitely, replicating along with the bacterial genome. However, either spontaneously or as a result of environmental circumstances (e.g., radiation, ultraviolet light, or chemicals), the prophage can reemerge and enter a lytic cycle (see Figure 14.11). Bacteria containing prophages are normally resistant to further infection ("superinfection") by similar phages.

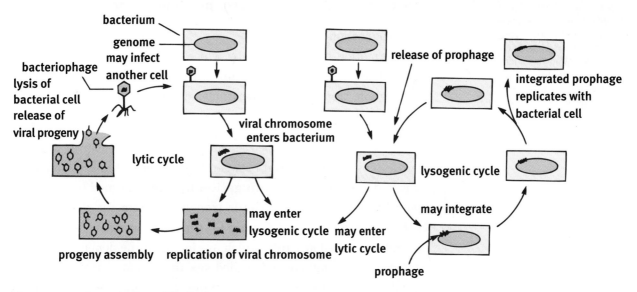

Figure 14.11. Bacteriophage Life Cycle

BACTERIAL GENETICS

A. BACTERIAL GENOME

The bacterial genome consists of a single circular chromosome located in the nucleoid region of the cell (see chapter 1). Many bacteria also contain smaller circular rings of DNA called **plasmids,** which contain accessory genes. **Episomes** are plasmids that are capable of integration into the bacterial genome. Because the bacterial chromosome is not separated from the cytoplasm by a nuclear membrane, transcription and translation occur almost simultaneously. As soon as a small portion of newly synthesized mRNA separates from its DNA template, translation begins. A strand of prokaryotic mRNA may be **polycistronic,** i.e., coding for more than one polypeptide (usually a group of related proteins).

B. REPLICATION

Replication of the bacterial chromosome begins at a unique origin of replication and proceeds in both directions simultaneously. DNA is synthesized in the $5' \rightarrow 3'$ direction. Replication occurs at the rate of approximately 500 nucleotide additions per second.

C. GENETIC VARIANCE

Bacterial cells reproduce by binary fission and proliferate very rapidly under favorable conditions. Although binary fission is an asexual process, bacteria have three mechanisms for increasing the genetic variance of a population: **transformation, conjugation,** and **transduction.**

1. Transformation

Transformation is the process by which a foreign chromosome fragment (plasmid) is incorporated into the bacterial chromosome via recombination, creating new inheritable genetic combinations.

2. Conjugation

Conjugation can be described as sexual mating in bacteria; it is the transfer of genetic material between two bacteria that are temporarily joined. A cytoplasmic **conjugation bridge** is formed between the two cells and genetic material is transferred from the **donor male (+) type** to the **recipient female (–) type.** The bridge is formed from appendages called **sex pili,** which are found on the donor male. Only bacteria containing plasmids called **sex factors** are capable of forming pili and conjugating. The best studied sex factor is the **F factor** in *Escherichia coli*. Bacteria possessing this plasmid are termed **F⁺ cells,** those without it are called **F⁻ cells.** During conjugation between an F⁺ and an F⁻ cell, the F⁺ cell replicates its F factor and donates the copy to the recipient, converting it to an F⁺ cell (see Figure 14.12). Plasmids that do not induce pili formation may transfer into the recipient cell along with the sex factor.

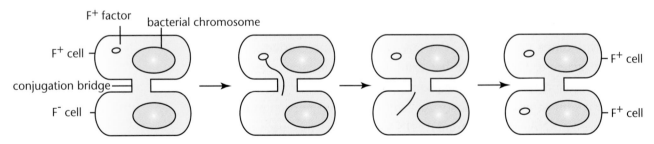

Figure 14.12. Conjugation

Sometimes the sex factor becomes integrated into the bacterial genome. During conjugation the entire bacterial chromosome replicates and begins to move from the donor cell into the recipient cell. The conjugation bridge usually breaks before the entire chromosome is transferred, but the bacterial genes that enter the recipient cell can easily recombine with the bacterial genes already present to form novel genetic combinations. These bacteria are called **Hfr cells,** meaning that they have a high frequency of recombination.

3. Transduction

Transduction is when fragments of the bacterial chromosome accidentally become packaged into viral progeny produced during a viral infection. These virions may infect other bacteria and introduce new genetic arrangements through recombination with the new host cell's DNA (see Figure 14.13). This process is similar to conjugation and may reflect an evolutionary relationship between viruses and plasmids.

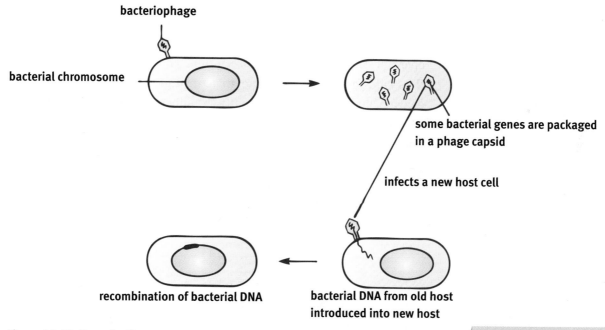

Figure 14.13. Transduction

D. GENE REGULATION

The regulation of gene expression (transcription) enables prokaryotes to control their metabolism. Regulation of transcription is based on the accessibility of RNA polymerase to the genes being transcribed and is directed by an **operon,** which consists of **structural genes,** an **operator gene,** and a **promoter gene.** Structural genes contain sequences

TEACHER TIP

Although bacteria are much simpler and their genomes are quite different (smaller, circular, no introns), they are still subject to levels of control. Gene regulation is critical to all organisms' survival; cancer (simply defined as unregulated cell division), for instance, is due to a loss of genetic regulation of cell division.

of DNA that code for proteins. The operator gene is the sequence of non-transcribable DNA that is the repressor binding site. The promoter gene is the noncoding sequence of DNA that serves as the initial binding site for RNA polymerase. There is also a **regulator gene,** which codes for the synthesis of a repressor molecule that binds to the operator and blocks RNA polymerase from transcribing the structural genes.

Regulation may be via **inducible systems** or **repressible systems.** Inducible systems are those that require the presence of a substance, called an **inducer,** for transcription to occur. Repressible systems are in a constant state of transcription unless a **corepressor** is present to inhibit transcription.

1. Inducible Systems

In an inducible system, the repressor binds to the operator, forming a barrier that prevents RNA polymerase from transcribing the structural genes. The repressor is active until it binds to the inducer. For transcription to occur, an inducer must bind to the repressor, forming an **inducer-repressor complex.** This complex cannot bind to the operator, thus permitting transcription. The proteins synthesized are thus said to be inducible. The structural genes typically code for an enzyme, and the inducer is usually the substrate, or a derivative of the substrate, upon which the enzyme normally acts. When the substrate (inducer) is present, enzymes are synthesized; when it is absent, enzyme synthesis is negligible. In this manner, enzymes are transcribed only when they are actually needed. An example of an inducible system is the *lac* **operon** (see Figure 14.14).

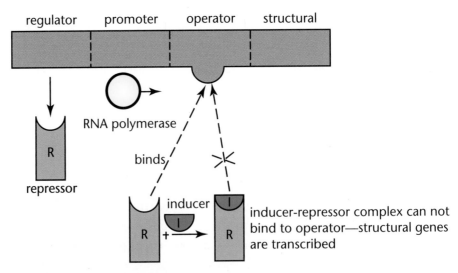

Figure 14.14. Inducible System

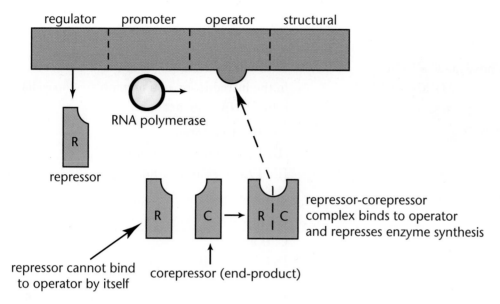

Figure 14.15. Repressible System

2. Repressible Systems

In a repressible system, the repressor is inactive until it combines with the corepressor. The repressor can bind to the operator and prevent transcription only when it has formed a **repressor-corepressor complex.** Corepressors are often the end-products of the biosynthetic pathways they control. The proteins produced (usually enzymes) are said to be repressible since they are normally being synthesized; transcription and translation occur until the corepressor is synthesized. An example of a repressible system is the ***trp* operon** (see Figure 14.15)

TEACHER TIP

Much as we want to be able to turn genes on as needed, we'd also like to be able to turn them off. Repressible systems allow us to do this.

PRACTICE QUESTIONS

1. In the laboratory you have made a DNA primer with the sequence 5'-AGCGCTAT-3'. Which of the following sequences will the primer most likely recognize?

   A. 5'-TCGCGATA-3'
   B. 5'-ATAGCGCT-3'
   C. 5'-AGCGCTAT-3'
   D. 5'-CGCATATG-3'

2. In the laboratory you are working on a silencing RNA project, where small strands of RNA are introduced into cells to bind DNA and activate a DNA lysis pathway. If the DNA sequence you want to recognize is 5'-TAGATCC-3', which of the following RNA sequences would be most appropriate to use?

   A. 5'-GGATCTA-3'
   B. 5'-AUCUAGG-3'
   C. 5'-ATCTAGG-3'
   D. 5'-GGAUGUA-3'

3. A new disease is discovered. It is the result of a point mutation in the area of a gene coding for an intron interfering with post-transcriptional RNA processing. Where in the cell does this process occur?

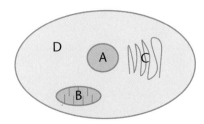

   A. Nucleus
   B. Mitochnodria
   C. Endoplasmic reticulum
   D. Cytoplasm

4. Which of the following mutations can result in the introduction of a premature stop codon into a DNA sequence?

   I. Point mutation
   II. Frame-shift insertion
   III. Frame-shift deletion

   A. I
   B. III
   C. II and III
   D. I, II, and III

5. Varicella virus, the DNA virus responsible for chicken pox, replicates in the cytoplasm of its host cell. Which of the following is most likely true about varicella virus replication?

   A. It is reverse trancriptase-dependent.
   B. It utilizes the host DNA polymerase.
   C. It requires the encoding for DNA polymerase in its viral genome.
   D. It requires co-infection with another virus to provide the necessary DNA polymerase.

6. Which of the following comparisons between eukaryotic and prokaryotic DNA polymerase enzymes is correct?

   A. Eukaryotic DNA polymerases always have 3'→5' polymerase activity.
   B. Prokaryotic DNA polymerases always have 3'→5' polymerase activity.
   C. Prokaryotic DNA polymerases never have 5'→3' polymerase activity.
   D. Eukaryotic DNA polymerases never have 5'→3' exonuclease activity.

7. Which of the following is true of eukaryotic DNA synthesis on the lagging strand of a DNA replication fork?

   I. It occurs in the 5′→3′ direction.
   II. It connects the 5′ phosphate group to the 3′ hydroxyl group.
   III. It requires a primer.

A. I and II
B. I and III
C. II and III
D. All of the above

8. Which of the following correctly depicts a eukaryotic peptide?

   A. NH_3 —— Met —— Val —— COOH

   B. NH_3 —— Arg —— Met —— COOH

   C. NH_3 —— Arg —— Met —— NH_3

   D. COOH —— Met —— Val —— NH_3

9. Which of the following statements appropriately identifies the role of the helicase and topoisomerase enzymes in DNA replication?

A. Helicase unwinds the DNA strands while topoisomerase winds them.
B. Helicase winds the DNA strands while topoisomerase unwinds them.
C. Helicase unwinds the DNA strands while topoisomerase relieves the resulting tension.
D. Topoisomerase unwinds the DNA strands while helicase relieves the resulting tension.

10. The addition of CAG repeats into the Huntingtin gene correlates with the risk of developing Huntington's disease. How would you categorize this type of mutation?

A. Nonsense
B. Insertion
C. Frame-shift
D. Silent

11. After spending a day in the sun without wearing any sun protection, Dr. X is worried about possible sun damage. What are the likely effects of his exposure?

	Epithelial Cell Damage	DNA Damage Repair	Germ Cell Mutation
A.	Yes	No	No
B.	Yes	Yes	Yes
C.	No	No	Yes
D.	Yes	Yes	No

12. The most common types of point mutations involve the substitution of a purine for a purine or a pyramidine for a pyramidine. Which of the following substitutions fits one of these patterns?

A. Adenine to thymine
B. Adenine to cytosine
C. Guanine to thymine
D. Cytosine to thymine

13. Macrolide antibiotics act by binding the large ribosomal subunit in bacteria, inhibiting ribosomal translocation. Which of the following translation steps would be directly affected by a macrolide?

A. Peptide elongation
B. Binding of the small ribosomal subunit to RNA
C. Binding of the small and large ribosomal subunits
D. Aminoacylation of the tRNA

DNA TRANSCRIPTION

An RNA strand with the sequence 5′-GACTGAUCAGACTA-3′ was erroneously created when a mutant RNA polymerase substituted a thymine for the second cysteine when it encountered a GG in the reading frame of the DNA. What is the antisense strand of the DNA from which this RNA was transcribed? (Assume that "GA" is not in the antisense strand.)

1) Determine the correct primary structure of RNA.

We can substitute CC for CT in the fragment in order to produce the correct sequence of RNA: 5′-GACCGAUCAGACCA-3′.

In this case, when C precedes T, we know that it is due to the mutant polymerase. The first G in the DNA sequence GG will correctly have been transcribed as C, but the second G will have been incorrectly transcribed as T, yielding CT instead of CC.

2) Determine the sense strand.

We can simply replace the uracils with thymines to get the following sense strand: 5′-GACCGATCAGACCA-3′.

Transcription always proceeds in the 5′ to 3′ direction starting at the 3′ end of the anti-sense strand. The RNA corresponds to the sense strand (minus any introns that were spliced out—in this problem we will assume there were no introns).

We are working backwards, going from RNA to DNA. The RNA produced represents the sense strand with the thymines replaced by uracil.

3) Determine the antisense strand.

5′-GACCGATCAGACCA-3′ → sense strand
3′-CTGGCTAGTCTGGT-5′ → anti-sense strand

The antisense strand of DNA is the complement of the sense strand of DNA. We can determine the sense strand by remembering that G pairs with C, that T pairs with A, and that the antisense strand is antiparallel to the sense strand (meaning that the 3′ end of the sense strand will line up with the 5′ end of the antisense strand and vice versa).

SIMILAR QUESTIONS

1) What is the base sequence of the mRNA produced from the following sense strand of DNA: 3′-TAGGGTACGTACCTA-5′?

2) What are the possible primary structures of mRNA produced from the antisense strand 3′-GAATACCAGTAGTATTTGCCGATGACTAGTTAGCCGTTAGC-5′ after splicing by a splisosome that makes blunt end cuts between GG in the sequence 5′-CGGC-3′?

DNA REPLICATION

The following molecule of DNA is replicated using two cycles of PCR in the presence of N^{15} labeled guanine. What percentage of the DNA strands will contain the labeled guanine in both strands (sense and antisense strands)?

5'-CATACTGATCATCTAGCGTATGCGT-3'
3'-GTATGACTAGTAGATCGCATACGCA-5'

1) Determine what happens after the first round of replication.

DNA replication is semiconservative, which means that for every strand of original DNA, one new strand of DNA is synthesized as its new complement.

Our templates for this first round of replication are:

5'-CATACTGATCATCTAGCGTATGCGT-3'
3'-GTATGACTAGTAGATCGCATACGCA-5'

Neither of these original strands contains the labeled guanine. So the first round of replication gives us:

5'-CATACTGATCATCTAGCGTATGCGT-3'
3'-GTATGACTAGTAGATCGCATACGCA-5'*

and

5'-CATACTGATCATCTAGCGTATGCGT-3'*
3'-GTATGACTAGTAGATCGCATACGCA-5'

where the * marks strands containing the labeled guanine.

The original strand with the 5' to 3' polarity at the site of replication will be the lagging strand because nucleotides can only be added in the 5' to 3' direction. Primase lays down a new primer to which DNA polymerase can bind in intervals of about 500 nucleotides, so that its new complementary strand can be created in short fragments called Okazaki fragments. The primer for these Okazaki fragments is RNA and is replaced with DNA before ligase joins the short fragments together. This process eliminates the need to create the replicate strand in the 3' to 5' direction.

2) Determine what happens after the second round of replication.

Our templates for the second round of replication are:

5'-CATACTGATCATCTAGCGTATGCGT-3'
3'-GTATGACTAGTAGATCGCATACGCA-5'*

KEY CONCEPTS

Semiconservative replication

DNA

TAKEAWAYS

DNA replication is semiconservative. The newly synthesized strand of DNA will be identical to the old complementary strand, provided that there are no mutations.

THINGS TO WATCH OUT FOR

Be careful in noting the polarity of the strands. Remember that DNA is always synthesized in the 5' to 3' direction.

and

5'-CATACTGATCATCTAGCGTATGCGT-3'
3'-GTATGACTAGTAGATCGCATACGCA-5'*

So this second round of replication gives us:

5'-CATACTGATCATCTAGCGTATGCGT-3'
3'-GTATGACTAGTAGATCGCATACGCA-5'*

and

5'-CATACTGATCATCTAGCGTATGCGT-3'*
3'-GTATGACTAGTAGATCGCATACGCA-5'*

and

5'-CATACTGATCATCTAGCGTATGCGT-3'*
3'-GTATGACTAGTAGATCGCATACGCA-5'*

and

5'-CATACTGATCATCTAGCGTATGCGT-3' *
3'-GTATGACTAGTAGATCGCATACGCA-5'

with the asterisks again indicating strands containing labeled guanine.

In the second round of replicati on, the new strands from the first round of replication are used as templates to create newer strands.

SIMILAR QUESTIONS

1) What is the product after 5'-ACGAGCTATGCTACTATATG-3' goes through two rounds of replication?

2) A molecule of DNA is replicated using three cycles of PCR in the presence of N^{15} labeled nuclei acids. What percentage of the newly formed DNA will contain an unlabeled strand?

3) Determine the percentage of DNA molecules that only have "new" strands.
fifty percent of the double stranded DNA molecules will have both strands with the labeled N^{15} guanine.

After two rounds of replication, the middle two double-stranded DNA molecules have both strands labeled with the N^{15} guanine, whereas the outer two double strands of DNA still maintain one original strand.

CHAPTER 15

EVOLUTION

Evolution is a process of change and adaptation leading to the development of new life forms and genetic diversity.

THEORIES OF EVOLUTION

A. LAMARCK

Jean Baptiste Lamarck was an early evolution theorist. He formulated the concept of **use and disuse**: organs that are used extensively develop, while organs that are not used atrophy. Lamark theorized that newer, more complex species arise from older and simpler species through the accumulation and modification of **acquired characteristics.** Although it is now known that characteristics are inherited rather than acquired through use, Lamarck's work was the first systematic approach to understanding evolutionary processes.

B. DARWIN

Charles Darwin developed a theory of evolution in *The Origin of Species,* published in 1859. In it, Darwin outlined a number of basic agents leading to evolutionary change:

1. Organisms produce offspring, very few of which survive to reproductive maturity.

2. There are chance variations between individuals in any given population, some of which are inheritable. Variations that give the organism a slight advantage in the struggle for existence are called favorable variations.

3. Individuals who have inherited favorable variations are likely to live longer and produce more offspring than others; thus favorable variations become more common from generation to generation. This process is known as **natural selection.** Gradually, natural selection leads to variations that differentiate organisms into groups and ultimately into distinct species. **Fitness** is measured in terms of reproductive success and the relative genetic contribution of an

PAVLOV'S DOG

If you see any hint of the buzz phrases "use and disuse" or "inheritance of acquired characteristics," think Lamarck. And don't forget—Lamarck was wrong!

TEACHER TIP

Natural selection is not equivalent to evolution. It is simply a *mechanism* for evolution. Natural selection is equivalent to "survival of the fittest." Know this for the exam.

individual to the future of the population. Natural selection is the driving force of evolution.

C. NEO-DARWINISM (THE MODERN SYNTHESIS)

Most of Darwin's ideas persist in the current view of evolution, termed neo-Darwinism, or the modern synthesis. The science of genetics revealed that the ultimate source of hereditary variation lies in the processes of mutation and genetic recombination. Some gene combinations increase chances for survival and reproduction, while others decrease them. This leads to **differential reproduction**; i.e., individuals with favorable genes produce more offspring. As a result, after many generations, these favorable genes will have become pervasive in the **gene pool**; the gene pool consists of all of the genes in all individuals in a population at a given time.

D. PUNCTUATED EQUILIBRIUM

One remarkable aspect of the fossil record is that many organisms do not demonstrate gradual changes; instead there seem to be short periods of rapid change with long static periods between them. To explain this phenomenon, Eldredge and Gould (1972) proposed the model of **punctuated** equilibrium. They contend that evolution is characterized by long periods of stasis "punctuated" by evolutionary changes occurring in spurts. This is in contrast to Darwin's model, which proposes that evolutionary changes accumulate gradually and evenly over time.

EVIDENCE OF EVOLUTION

Evidence supporting modern evolutionary theory is drawn from many disciplines, including **paleontology, biogeography, comparative anatomy, comparative embryology,** and **molecular biology.**

A. PALEONTOLOGY

Paleontology, which is the study of the fossil record, is of particular significance to the study of evolution. With the use of radioactive dating techniques, paleontologists are able to determine the age of fossils, thus allowing them to determine the chronological succession of species in the fossil record.

B. BIOGEOGRAPHY

Biogeography refers to the distribution of life forms throughout the globe. Darwin observed that many species found on one of the Galapagos Islands seemed more closely related to species inhabiting the neighboring

---

MCAT SYNOPSIS

Natural Selection:

- Chance variations occur thanks to mutation and recombination.
- If the variation is "selected for" by the environment, that individual will be more "fit" and more likely to survive to reproductive age.
- Survival of the fittest leads to an increase of those favorable genes in the gene pool.

TEACHER TIP

Evolution is a theory, not a fact. The kinds of passages that are likely to include the topic of evolution are persuasive argument types. Be sure to consider how the passage information you are given would fit within a given mechanism or concept, e.g., punctuated equilibrium.

mainland than to species inhabiting the other Galapagos Islands. The biogeography of the Galapagos suggests that species migrated from the mainland to neighboring islands, where they adapted to the different island environments in isolation from each other.

C. COMPARATIVE ANATOMY

Homologous structures are similar in structure and share a common evolutionary origin. A classic example of homologous structures is found in the forelimbs of mammals: bat wings, whale flippers, horse forelegs, and human arms are all modifications of a common anatomical theme. In contrast, **analogous structures** share a functional similarity but arose from different evolutionary origins. The wings of insects and birds are both adaptations for flight but evolved from separate lines of descent. **Vestigial structures** are remnants of organs that have lost their ancestral functions, and thus are evidence of evolutionary forces at work. Examples include vestiges of limb bones in the adult python and the appendix and vestiges of the tail bone (coccyx) in man.

D. COMPARATIVE EMBRYOLOGY

The stages of embryonic development in closely related organisms resemble each other, indicating common evolutionary origins. The earliest stages tend to be the most similar. For example, all chordates exhibit certain features as embryos, such as gills.

E. MOLECULAR BIOLOGY

Through comparative DNA studies, biologists have been able to detect similarities in the DNA composition of related species. Taxonomically close species have a greater percentage of similar DNA than taxonomically distant species.

GENETIC BASIS OF EVOLUTION

Genetic variation functions as the raw material for natural selection. Sources of genetic variation include inheritable mutations and recombination. Mutations are random changes in the nucleotide sequence of DNA. Recombination refers to novel genetic combinations resulting from sexual reproduction and crossing over.

FLASHBACK

If you didn't get it the first time out, it's time to revisit the concepts of recombination and mutation. See chapters 4 and 14.

A. THE HARDY-WEINBERG EQUILIBRIUM

Evolution can be viewed as a result of changing **gene frequencies** within a population. Gene frequency is the relative frequency of a particular allele. When the gene frequencies of a population are not changing, the gene pool is stable, and the population is not evolving. However, this is true only in ideal situations in which the following conditions are met:

1. The population is very large.
2. There are no mutations that affect the gene pool.
3. Mating between individuals in the population is random.
4. There is no net migration of individuals into or out of the population.
5. The genes in the population are all equally successful at reproducing.

Under these idealized conditions, a certain equilibrium will exist between all of the genes in a gene pool, which is described by the **Hardy-Weinberg equation.**

For a gene locus with only two alleles, T and t, p = the frequency of allele T and q = the frequency of allele t. By definition, for a given gene locus, p + q = 1, because the combined frequencies of the alleles must total 100 percent. Thus $(p + q)^2 = (1)^2$ and

$$p^2 + 2pq + q^2 = 1$$

where p^2 = frequency of TT (dominant homozygotes)
$2pq$ = frequency of Tt (heterozygotes)
q^2 = frequency of tt (recessive homozygotes)

The Hardy-Weinberg equation may be used to determine gene frequencies in a large population in the absence of microevolutionary change (defined by the five conditions given above). For example, individuals from a non-evolving population can be randomly crossed to demonstrate that the gene frequencies remain constant from generation to generation. Assume that in the original gene pool the gene frequency of the dominant gene for tallness, T, is .80, and the gene frequency of the recessive gene for shortness, t, is .20. Thus, p = .80 and q = .20. In a cross between two heterozygotes, the resulting F1 genotype frequencies are: 64 percent TT, 16 percent + 16 percent = 32 percent Tt, and 4 percent tt (see the following Punnett square).

	$p = .80$ (T)	$q = .20$ (t)
$p = .80$ (T)	($p^2 = .64$) TT = 64%	($pq = .16$) Tt = 16%
$q = .20$ (t)	($pq = .16$) Tt = 16%	($q^2 = .04$) tt = 4%

The gene frequencies of the F_1 generation can be calculated as follows:

64% TT = 64% T allele + 0% t allele

32% Tt = 16% T allele + 16% t allele

4% tt = 0% T allele + 4% t allele

Gene frequencies = 80% T allele + 20% t allele

Thus, $p = .80$ and $q = .20$. These frequencies are the same as those in the parent generation, thus demonstrating Hardy-Weinberg equilibrium in a nonevolving population.

B. MICROEVOLUTION

No population can be represented indefinitely by the Hardy-Weinberg equilibrium because such idealized conditions do not exist in nature. Real populations have unstable gene pools and migrating populations. The agents of microevolutionary change—**natural selection, mutation, assortive mating, genetic drift,** and **gene flow**—are all deviations from the five conditions of a Hardy-Weinberg population.

1. Natural Selection
Genotypes with favorable variations are selected through natural selection, and the frequency of favorable genes increases within the gene pool.

2. Mutation
Gene mutations change allele frequencies in a population, shifting gene equilibria.

3. Assortive Mating
If mates are not randomly chosen, but rather selected according to criteria such as phenotype and proximity, the relative genotype ratios will be affected, and will depart from the predictions of the Hardy-Weinberg equilibrium. On the average, the allele frequencies in the gene pool remain unchanged.

TEACHER TIP

Hardy-Weinberg equilibrium equations allow you to find two pieces of information: the relative frequency of genes in a population and the frequency of a given phenotype in the population. Remember, there will be twice as many genes as individuals in a population—because each individual has two autosomal copies of each gene.

TEACHER TIP

These five points simply reinforce what we already learned. For Hardy-Weinberg equilibrium to exist, we need a stable (nonevolving) gene pool. These points are basically all exceptions to one of the rules for Hardy-Weinberg equilibrium to exist. For example, the equilibrium requires no migrations, but points 4 and 5 (genetic drift and gene flow) are both exceptions to this.

4. Genetic Drift

Genetic drift refers to changes in the composition of the gene pool due to chance. Genetic drift tends to be more pronounced in small populations, where it is sometimes called the **founder effect.**

5. Gene Flow

Migration of individuals between populations will result in a loss or gain of genes, and thus change the composition of a population's gene pool.

MODES OF NATURAL SELECTION

Natural selection is the only evolutionary process that assembles and maintains particular gene combinations over extended periods of time. Three different modes of natural selection are discussed below: **stabilizing selection, directional selection,** and **disruptive selection** (see Figure 15.1).

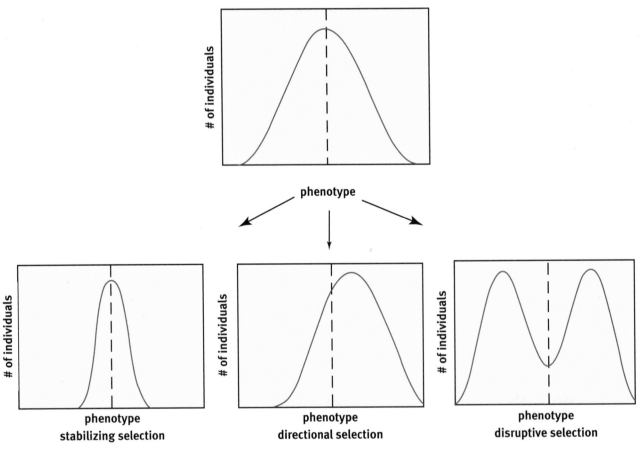

Figure 15.1. Modes of Natural Selection

A. STABILIZING SELECTION

Stabilizing selection maintains a well-adapted uniform character in a population by eliminating deviations from the norm. This process reduces the frequency of extreme phenotypes, thereby reducing variation. For example, stabilizing selection maintains human birth weights within a very narrow range.

B. DIRECTIONAL SELECTION

Directional selection produces an adaptive change over time, with an increase in the proportion of individuals with an extreme phenotype. Directional selection occurs when organisms must adapt to a changing environment. A familiar example of directional selection is the emergence of the DDT-resistant mosquito. The introduction of DDT produced a selectional advantage for those mosquitoes possessing the mutant gene for DDT resistance. After a period of time, the population of mosquitoes all possessed the gene for DDT resistance.

C. DISRUPTIVE SELECTION

Disruptive selection favors variants of both phenotypic extremes over the intermediates, leading to the existence of two or more phenotypic forms within a population (**polymorphism**).

ALTRUISTIC BEHAVIOR

Altruistic behavior is behavior that benefits one individual at the expense of another. An example is bee societies in which worker bees are sterile but labor for the benefit of the hive. Explaining the existence of such behavior in terms of natural selection has been a challenge to Darwinian theory. **Group selection** is the now-discredited hypothesis that certain individuals in a population inherit a gene for not reproducing, thus controlling population size at an advantageous level. This hypothesis is flawed because such a gene could not be passed on by its nonreproducing carriers. However, it led to the development of **kin selection** theory, which holds that natural selection can lead to behavior that does not improve the survival of an individual but does improve the survival of his near kin. Since increasing the survival and reproductive success of near kin, who share alleles, will often increase the survival of the individual's alleles, such behavior is consistent with neo-Darwinism. Since worker bees are the genetic sisters of the queen bee, their labor ensures the survival of their own alleles. **Inclusive fitness** describes fitness as the number of an individual's alleles that are inherited by the next generation.

> **TEACHER TIP**
>
> Again, natural selection is a theory. Each of these forms of selection would be pressured by a different environment. For the MCAT, consider why a particular situation might engender stabilizing selection rather than disruptive selection.

> **TEACHER TIP**
>
> Like all theories, evolution also has detractors and problems in its completeness. These challenges may seem to make the answers less clear on Test Day, but remember that the MCAT is written in a one-right/three-wrong format. If an answer isn't completely RIGHT, it is completely WRONG. Keep your basic facts in mind for Test Day success.

ADAPTIVE RADIATION

Adaptive radiation is the emergence of a number of lineages from a single ancestral species. A single species may diverge into a number of distinct species; the differences between them are those adaptive to a distinct lifestyle, or **niche.** A classic example is Darwin's finches of the Galapagos Island chain. Over a comparatively short period of time, a single species of finch underwent adaptive radiation, resulting in 13 separate species of finches, some of them on the same island. Such adaptations minimized the competition among the birds, enabling each emerging species to become firmly established in its own environmental niche.

PATTERNS OF EVOLUTION

When examining apparent similarities in form or function between two species, it is important to determine whether the similarities are the result of a close evolutionary relationship or the result of similar adaptations to similar environments. Patterns of evolution are described in terms of **convergent evolution, divergent evolution,** and **parallel evolution** (see Figure 15.2).

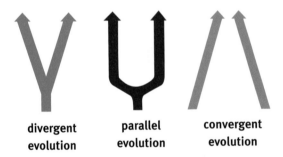

divergent evolution   parallel evolution   convergent evolution

Figure 15.2. Evolutionary Patterns

A. CONVERGENT EVOLUTION

Convergent evolution refers to the independent development of similar characteristics in two or more lineages **not** sharing a recent common ancestor. For example, fish and dolphins have come to resemble one another physically, although they belong to different classes of vertebrates. They evolved certain similar features in adapting to the conditions of aquatic life.

B. DIVERGENT EVOLUTION

Divergent evolution refers to the independent development of dissimilar characteristics in two or more lineages sharing common ancestry.

For example, seals and cats are both mammals belonging to the order Carnivora, yet differ markedly in general appearance. These two species live in very different environments, and adapted to different selection pressures while evolving.

C. PARALLEL EVOLUTION

Parallel evolution refers to the process whereby related species evolve in similar ways for a long period of time in response to analogous environmental selection pressures.

TEACHER TIP
What sorts of pressures or environments might push a species to pursue divergent or convergent evolution?

ORIGIN OF LIFE

The earliest evidence of primitive prokaryotic life is found in stromatolites, which are fossilized bands of sediment that contain microorganisms approximately 3.5 billion years old. It is not clear how life on Earth originated, but a hypothesis has been developed based on a theory proposed independently by both Oparin and Haldane in the 1920s and tested for the first time in the 1950s by Stanley Miller.

A. FORMATION OF ORGANIC MOLECULES

Oparin and Haldane proposed that conditions during the early years of Earth's existence favored the abiotic synthesis of organic molecules. Carbon, hydrogen, nitrogen, and small amounts of oxygen present in the atmosphere and seas bonded together in various ways and accumulated, forming a **"primordial soup"** of organic precursor molecules. The energy for the formation of these bonds was supplied by a number of sources, including the sun, lightning, radioactive decay, and volcanic activity. Miller tested this hypothesis in a laboratory by simulating the conditions believed to have existed on primitive Earth. A mixture of gases was circulated past a source of electrical discharge (simulating lightning), and after one week, the reaction apparatus was found to contain a variety of organic compounds, including simple amino acids. During numerous modified replications of this experiment, all twenty amino acids, many lipids, and the five nitrogenous bases of DNA and RNA have all been generated. It is postulated that organic monomers were abiotically synthesized in a similar way on primitive Earth, and as they accumulated, were brought into close proximity, allowing them to react and form polymers.

B. FORMATION OF PROTOBIONTS

In laboratory experiments, abiotically produced polymers in an aqueous solution can spontaneously assemble into tiny proteinaceous droplets called **microspheres.** These microspheres have a selectively permeable membrane that separates them from their surroundings and maintains an independent internal chemical environment. Colloidal droplets called **coacervates** had been formed in Oparin's laboratory from a solution of polypeptides, nucleic acids, and polysaccharides. These coacervates are capable of carrying out enzymatic activity within their membrane if enzymes and substrate are present. Although microspheres and coacervates have some properties characteristic of life, they are not living cells. The molecular aggregates of organic polymers that are believed to have been the primitive ancestors of living cells are called **protobionts.**

C. FORMATION OF GENETIC MATERIAL

These hypothetical protobionts had the ability to grow in size and divide, but did not have a way of transmitting information to their next generation. The evolution of genetic material is difficult to map out, but it is believed that short strands of RNA were the first molecules capable of self-replication and of storing and transmitting information from one generation to the next. Experiments in the laboratory have shown that free bases can align with their complementary bases on a pre-existing short RNA sequence and bind together, creating a new short RNA chain. Natural selection may have favored RNA sequences whose three-dimensional conformations were more stable and could replicate faster. The next evolutionary step might have involved the association of specific amino acids with specific RNA bases. Thus, an RNA sequence could bring a number of amino acids together in a particular sequence and facilitate their bonding together to form a particular peptide. Natural selection could have selected for the synthesis of those peptides that enhanced the replication and/or the further activity of the RNA. Once this hereditary mechanism developed, protobionts would have been able to grow, split, and transmit important genetic information to their progeny. Self-replicating molecules eventually evolved to code for many of the molecules needed by primitive cells. Evolutionary trends led to the eventual establishment of DNA, which is a more stable molecule than RNA, as the primary warehouse of genetic information.

PRACTICE QUESTIONS

1. Lamark and Darwin are both known for their theories regarding the origin and descent of present day species. Upon which of the following statements would Darwin and Lamark have disagreed?

   A. Chronologically later organisms have a reproductive advantage over their predecessors.
   B. The evolution of new traits is fueled by chance.
   C. Present day animals are descendants of past animals.
   D. Traits become vestigial because they confer little or no reproductive advantage.

2. The fossil record of species A suggests that its evolutionary history was marked by periods of rapid change interspersed with periods of little or no change. This is an example of

   A. Eldredge and Gould's theory of punctuated equilibrium.
   B. Darwin's theory of evolution and natural selection.
   C. Lamark's theory of acquired characteristics.
   D. neo-Darwinian belief in differential reproduction.

3. Paleontologists discovered a bird fossil that stratigraphic analysis dates to around 200,000 B.C. Subsequent radioactive dating revealed that the prehistoric bird fossil contained 10 percent carbon-14. Scientists hypothesize that this fossil is related to a dinosaur fossil that contains 20 percent carbon-14. This data

   A. supports the theory that the prehistoric bird is an evolutionary descendant of the dinosaur.
   B. conflicts with the theory that the prehistoric bird is an evolutionary descendant of the dinosaur.
   C. is invalid because carbon-14 has a half-life of roughly 5,700 years, and is reliable only for dating objects up to 60,000 years old.
   D. does not support or conflict with the theory that prehistoric bird is an evolutionary descendant of the dinosaur.

4. On Tree Island off the coast of Juvialand, researchers discover a small population of swallows with brightly colored red feathers and long pointy beaks. Juvialand also has a larger population of swallows, though they have black feathers and short flat beaks. This is most likely a result of

   A. founder effect.
   B. sexual selection for red feathers over black feathers.
   C. natural selection for red feathers over black feathers,
   D. codominance between the red feather phenotype and the black feather phenotype.

5. The Bottleneck effect refers to an evolutionary event that causes a large proportion of a population to be killed off or isolated from the rest. Which of the following statements is true?

A. The Founder effect is a specific instance of the Bottleneck effect.

B. The Bottleneck effect is a specific instance of the Founder effect.

C. The Founder effect is not related to the Bottleneck effect.

D. Both the Bottleneck and Founder effects are examples of genetic drift.

6. The red bird is a descendant of the blue bird, and the orange bird is a descendant of the black bird. The blue bird and the black bird do not have a common ancestor. Which of the following statements is NOT true?

A. The blue bird's wings are analogous structures to the orange bird's wings.

B. The red bird's wings are analogous structures to the orange bird's wings.

C. The red bird's wings are analogous structures to the black bird's wings.

D. The red bird's wings are analogous structures to the blue bird's wings.

7. Given the diagram below, species Z and B are

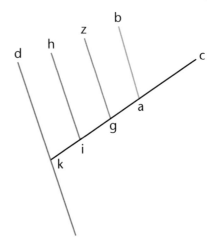

A. paraphyletic.

B. monophyletic.

C. parsimonious.

D. polyphyletic.

8. A population of gophers lives in an area with a large number of predatory squirrels. Their main means of defense is hiding in small crevices or intimidating the squirrels with their size. What evolutionary force would you expect is at play on the gophers' population?

A. Stabilizing selection

B. Directional selection

C. Disruptive selection

D. Hardy-Weinberg equilibrium

9. If p represents the frequency of allele A, and q represents the frequency of allele B in a population of hummingbirds, then assuming a state of Hardy-Weinberg equilibrium,

A. $p + q = 100$.

B. $p + q = 1$.

C. $p^2 + q^2 = 1$.

D. $p^2 + q^2 = 100$.

10. Hardy-Weinberg equilibrium refers to a population in which gene frequencies are not changing and the gene pool remains in a stable state. Which of the following conditions is necessary for this to occur?

A. Small populations, because there are fewer individuals and thus, less genetic diversity

B. Genes in a population that all confer roughly the same reproductive advantage

C. Large amount of migration between several populations, ensuring that selection remains random

D. Individuals with certain traits who mate more, thus keeping these traits in equilibrium

11. Given the following information, what do we know is true?

I. Species A and species B belong in a monophyletic group.

II. Species A and species B both have beaks.

A. Species A's beaks and species B's beaks are homologous structures.

B. Species A's beaks and species B's beaks are analogous structures.

C. Species A and species B share a common ancestor.

D. Both A and C

12. If the following conditions are true, which of the following phylogenetic trees is possible?

Condition 1: Species A, B, and E are paraphyletic.
Condition 2: Species D and C are polyphyletic.
Condition 3: Species I, E, B, Z, and A are monophyletic.

A.
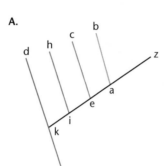

B.
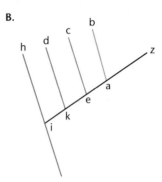

C.
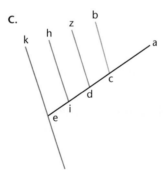

D.
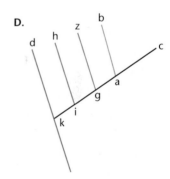

13. Given the diagram below, which of the following statements is NOT correct?

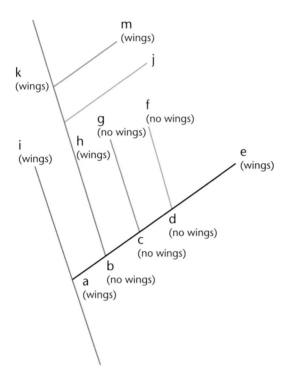

A. Species A and species M have an analogous wings trait.

B. Species A and species I have a homologous wings trait.

C. Species A and species H have a homologous wings trait.

D. Species D and species G have a homologous wings trait.

14. The founder effect is most likely a catalyst of which of the following?

A. Convergent evolution

B. Parallel evolution

C. Divergent evolution

D. Extinction

15. If a population of dogs undergoes adaptive radiation, one would expect that the environment in which the dogs lived was:

A. diverse, with a wide array of different niches.

B. homogenous, with very few different niches.

C. extremely crowded.

D. very sparsely populated.

16. Assortative mating is an evolutionary

A. phenomenon in which individuals attempt to mate with as many different genetic phenotypes as possible in order to improve genetic variation in their offspring.

B. phenomenon in which mates are not randomly chosen but rather selected according to expression of genetic phenotypes similar to their own.

C. force exerted on individuals to sacrifice personal reproductive success for the overall advantage of the group, by preventing overpopulation and overcompetition.

D. phenomenon in which individuals mate with multiple partners to maximize their chances for reproductive success.

17. A population bottleneck event is best depicted in which of the following graphs?

A.
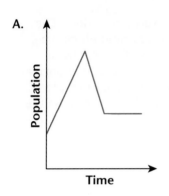

B.
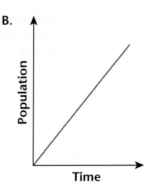

C.
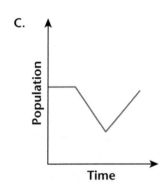

D.
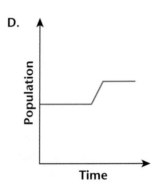

18. In honeybee populations, worker bees are born sterile and only the queen bee produces offspring. Honeybees are considered eusocial insects, a category of organisms in which not every individual reproduces. Which of the following statements is NOT true?

A. Honeybee reproduction is an instance of inclusive fitness.

B. Honeybee reproduction is an instance of altruism.

C. Honeybee reproduction is an instance of group selection.

D. Honeybee reproduction is an instance of kin selection.

19. If the frequency of allele A in a population is 80 percent and the frequency of allele B in a population is 20 percent, and that population is at Hardy-Weinberg equilibrium, what are the respective frequencies of recessive homozygotes and dominant heterozygotes in the population? Assume that allele A is dominant over allele B.

A. 4 percent recessive homozygotes, 36 percent dominant heterozygotes

B. 40 percent recessive homozygotes, 32 percent dominant heterozygotes

C. 4 percent recessive homozygotes, 32 percent dominant heterozygotes

D. 20 percent recessive homozytoes, 0 percent dominant heterozygotes

HARDY-WEINBERG

The gene for gigantism is known to be on a recessive allele. The dominant allele for the same gene codes for a normal phenotype. In North Carolina, nine people out of a sample of 10,000 were found to have gigantism phenotypes, whereas the rest had normal phenotypes. Assuming Hardy-Weinberg equilibrium, calculate the frequency of the recessive and dominant alleles as well as the number of heterozygotes in the population.

1) **Solve for the frequency of the recessive allele.**
gigantism = homozgygous recessive = gg = q^2
$q^2 = 9/10{,}000 = .0009$
$q = .03$
Recessive allele frequency = 3%

Refer back to the Hardy-Weinberg equation:

☞ $p^2 + 2pq + q^2 = 1$

Because gigantism will only emerge with a recessive genotype, it will be represented as gg. From the Hardy-Weinberg equation, the recessive genotype is depicted as q^2. By taking the square root of q^2 we get the frequency of the recessive gigantism allele or .03.

2) **Solve for the frequency of the dominant allele.**
$p + q = 1$
$p = 1 - q$
$1 - .03 = .97$
Dominant allele frequency = 97%

The frequency of the dominant allele plus the recessive allele equals 1. To solve for the frequency of the dominant allele, you subtract the recessive allele frequency from 1.

3) Solve for the heterozygous population.

$2pq$ = frequency of heterozygotes

Gg = 2 (.97) × (.03)

Gg = .058 or 6%

.058 × 10,000 = 580 people

To find the heterozygous population, we need to use the heterozygous portion of the Hardy-Weinberg equation. Plugging in $2pq$ gives us the frequency of the heterozygous genotype.

THINGS TO WATCH OUT FOR

There are five circumstances in which the Hardy-Weinberg law may fail to apply. These five are: mutation, gene migration, genetic drift, nonrandom mating, and natural selection.

SIMILAR QUESTIONS

1) Suppose a similar survey was done in New York. However, this time they found 90 people with gigantism out of a survey of 200,000 people. Calculate the same parameters with the new survey.

2) An allele x occurs with a frequency of 0.8 in a wolf pack population. Give the frequencies of the genotypes XX, Xx, and xx.

3) If the homozygous recessive frequency of a certain allele is 16 percent, determine the percentage of phonetically normal individuals.

PART II
PRACTICE SECTIONS

INSTRUCTIONS FOR TAKING THE PRACTICE SECTIONS

Before taking each Practice Section, find a quiet place where you can work uninterrupted. Take a maximum of 70 minutes per section (52 questions) to get accustomed to the length and scope.

Keep in mind that the actual MCAT will not feature a section made up of Biology questions alone, but rather a Biological Sciences section made up of both Biology and Organic Chemistry questions. Use the following three sections to hone your Biology skills.

Good luck!

PRACTICE SECTION 1

Time—70 minutes

QUESTIONS 1–52

Directions: Most of the questions in the following Biology Practice Section are organized into groups, with a descriptive passage preceding each group of questions. Study the passage, then select the single best answer to the question in each group. Some of the questions are not based on a descriptive passage; you must also select the best answer to these questions. In you are unsure of the best answer, eliminate the choices that you know are incorrect, then select an answer from the choices that remain.

PASSAGE I (QUESTIONS 1–7)

Certain species of hermit crabs inhabit gastropod shells for protection from predators and the environment. Studies have shown that crabs have the ability to take advantage of chemical cues emitted by gastropod flesh, not only informing them that the original shell occupant is dead, but also guiding and orienting the crab to the shell's location at a great range (Diaz et al. 1995). Factors influencing shell choice include size (Blackstone 1985), structural integrity (Rotjan et al. 2004), and material. A 1995 study by Humberto Diaz et al. showed that at closer distances, crabs also rely heavily on visual cues to locate a shell and gauge its quality. They showed specifically that crabs employ visual assessment of shell shape, in delicate combination with shell color and chemical cues, in choosing a shell. Crabs presented with a choice of silhouettes favored horizontal rectangle shapes, exhibiting distaste for vertical diamond shapes. Furthermore, crabs presented with single silhouettes had difficulty orienting to suboptimal shell shapes such as triangles, but easily oriented to optimal shell shapes, such as horizontal diamonds, (Diaz et al. 1995).

An experiment was designed by behavioral ecology students to examine the effect of color on hermit crab shell choice. They hypothesized that hermit crabs would prefer shells that offer a camouflage advantage and design an experiment to test the hypothesis that hermit crab shell choice is influenced by color.

In the first control experiment, 50 hermit crabs were presented with a choice between shells with a clear coat of paint or no paint. The shells were set on a background of natural black rocks. In the second experiment, 50 hermit crabs were presented with a choice between shells with a pink coat of paint or a clear coat of paint, set on a background of pink colored rocks. In the third experiment, 50 hermit crabs were presented with a choice between shells with a pink coat of paint and a clear coat of paint, set on a background of natural black rock.

Crabs were deshelled two hours in advance and placed in heated tanks prior to the experiment. The shells were painted immediately before use and allowed to dry for roughly 10 minutes before the experiment began.

The following morning, the shell choice of each crab was recorded. A crab was recorded as choosing a particular shell only if it was physically inside of it at the time of observation.

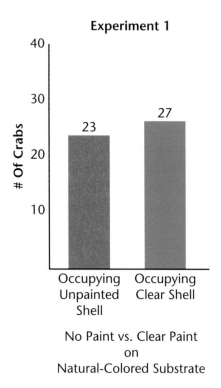

Experiment 1

No Paint vs. Clear Paint
on
Natural-Colored Substrate

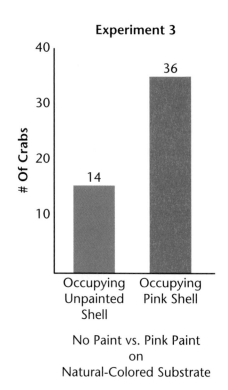

Experiment 2

No Paint vs. Pink Paint
on
Pink-Colored Substrate

Experiment 3

No Paint vs. Pink Paint
on
Natural-Colored Substrate

1. Which of the following would be a reasonable null hypothesis for this experiment?

A. Hermit crabs do not show preference for shells based on color.

B. Hermit crabs prefer shells most similar in color to their environment.

C. Hermit crabs prefer shells different in color to their environment.

D. Hermit crabs always prefer darker-colored shells.

2. Which of the following is not a legitimate concern over the experiment set-up?

A. Shell sizes were not identical.

B. Shells were not identical distances away from the subject crabs.

C. The black paint released olfactory signals.

D. The black paint became a dark gray after drying.

3. Based on the data, which of the following conclusions is most likely to be true?

  A. Hermit crabs show a preference for color.
  B. Hermit crabs always prefer black shells.
  C. Hermit crabs always prefer white shells.
  D. Hermit crabs prefer black shells because their natural environment is black sand.

4. Which of the following statements is least likely to explain the data?

  A. Hermit crabs communicate to one another visually.
  B. Hermit crabs' natural environment is light-colored.
  C. Hermit crabs' natural predators are all color-blind.
  D. Natural selection favors hermit crabs that stand out in their environment.

5. Based on the data, what evolutionary forces could be at play on these hermit crabs in an environment with many areas of pure pink rocks and many areas of pure black rocks?

  A. Disruptive selection
  B. Directional selection
  C. Both A and B
  D. Neither A nor B because null hypothesis is true

6. A hypothetical population of 89 black-shelled hermit crabs was discovered in the red sands of Jordan's Wadi Rum desert. Hermit crabs are not native to this region and experts believe they were introduced to the environment by South American tourists. Scientists began tracking this unique population of crabs in 1992. By 2007, only four crabs remained. These findings

  A. strongly call into question the hypothesis that shell color affects hermit crab shell choice.
  B. do not call into question the validity of the hypothesis that shell color affects hermit crab shell choice.
  C. strongly support the hypothesis that shell color affects hermit crab shell choice.
  D. are invalid because the hermit crabs are not native to Jordan.

7. The species of hermit crab used in the experiment and a second species of hermit crab are monophyletic. This second species is color-blind. Which of the following scenarios is most likely?

  A. These two species of hermit crabs do not share a common ancestor.
  B. Color-blindness is an analogous trait between the two species.
  C. This second species of hermit crab was influenced by evolutionary pressures of the founder effect.
  D. Color-blindness is a homologous trait between these two species.

PASSAGE II (QUESTIONS 8–17)

Cystic fibrosis is a serious genetic disorder causing fibrotic lesions of the pancreas, obstruction of the lungs with thick mucus, and reproductive and intestinal problems. With respiratory obstruction, some patients have mild difficulty while others experience serious problems that sharply decrease their life span. The most common form of the disease results from the loss of three nucleotides coding for the amino acid phenylalanine. The pedigree of an affected family is presented below:

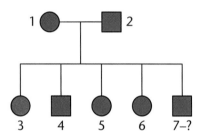

A researcher interested in identifying genotypes of each family member assayed polymorphisms revealed through the variation in length of restriction fragments containing the locus for cystic fibrosis. DNA of each family member was obtained from blood samples. Then, under specific conditions, DNA was digested by restriction enzymes, which recognize specific DNA sequences. The lengths of the DNA fragments were compared through gel electrophoresis. The fragments migrate down the gel and are separated based on their sizes. Smaller fragments move faster through the gel of specific density. The gel is shown below, with the DNA fragments moving from the top toward the bottom of the page:

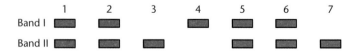

8. According to the pedigree, the disease alleles of the gene are most likely

A. codominant.
B. X-linked.
C. recessive.
D. dominant.

9. If male 7 from the pedigree marries a female carrier, the probability of their having a healthy noncarrier child is

A. 0 percent.
B. 25 percent.
C. 50 percent.
D. 75 percent.

10. According to the passage, what can be concluded about the expressivity of the disease?

A. The expressivity is homogeneous in the population.
B. Expressivity varies.
C. Expressivity approaches 90 percent.
D. There is not enough information to make a decision.

11. It can be inferred from the passage that a mutation leading to the most common form of cystic fibrosis can be classified as a (n)

A. deletion.
B. nondisjunction.
C. inversion.
D. insertion.

12. Based on the polymorphisms of DNA fragments, family member 7 is most likely

  I. heterozygous.
  II. homozygous recessive.
  III. homozygous dominant.

A. I only
B. II only
C. I or II
D. I or III

13. Which family member is not carrying the disease allele?

    A. 1
    B. 4
    C. 6
    D. 7

14. According to the passage, when compared to the fragment with the normal allele, the speed of movement through the gel of DNA fragment containing the disease allele would be

    A. slower, as the disease allele fragment is larger.
    B. slower, as the disease allele fragment is shorter.
    C. faster, as the disease allele fragment is larger.
    D. faster, as the disease allele fragment is shorter.

15. According to its functional significance, cystic fibrosis mutation can be referred to as

    A. missense.
    B. nonsense.
    C. silent.
    D. None of the above

16. The researcher later used the restriction fragment length polymorphism method described to assay 100 members of the U.S. population for cystic fibrosis. One person had the disorder. Identify the observed frequency of the disease allele.

    A. 0.01
    B. 0.1
    C. 1
    D. 0.9

17. Family member 5 marries a carrier of the cystic fibrosis allele. On average, what proportion of their children will be affected?

    A. ¼
    B. ¾
    C. ½
    D. 0

QUESTIONS 18 THROUGH 21 ARE NOT BASED ON A DESCRIPTIVE PASSAGE.

18. Young patients after an untreated throat infection with streptococci bacteria can develop rheumatic heart disease later in life. Studies have shown that the heart disease affects primarily the mitral valve whose surface cells have proteins similar to a surface protein common to many strains of streptococcal bacteria.

    Based solely on the information above, what class of disease best describes rheumatic heart disease?

    A. Congenital endocrine abnormality such as type I diabetes
    B. Hypersensitivity reaction such as an autoimmune disease
    C. Allergic reaction such as a bee sting
    D. Congenital structural abnormality of the heart such as a patent foramen ovale

19. The activation of phosphofructokinase-1 by glucagon-mediated increase in PKA activity is an example of what type of modulation of protein activity?

    A. Competitive antagonism
    B. Synergism
    C. Noncompetitive antagonism
    D. Allosteric activation

20. What is the purpose of hexokinase?

A. Phosphorylate Glucose-6-phosphate to Glucose-1, 6-bisphosphate

B. Phosphorylate Glucose-6-phosphate to Fructose-1, 6-bisphosphate

C. Isomerize Glucose-6-phosphate to Fructose-6-phosphate

D. Phosphorylate Glucose to Glucose-6-phosphate

21. Both oxalacetate and acetyl-CoA can be generated from pyruvate. Which of the following ratios, if greater than one, would favor the production of pyruvate from oxalacetate and acetyl-CoA, rather than the usual 'forward' reaction?

A. Carbon dioxide/Oxygen

B. FAD/FADH2

C. Glycogen/Glucose

D. Glucose/Fructose-1, 6-bisphosphate

PASSAGE III (QUESTIONS 22–28)

The electron transport chain (ETC) is the site of the final process in glucose catabolism where most of the ATP is produced. The ETC is comprised of a series of carrier proteins that pass electrons along the inner membrane of mitochondria. The carrier proteins are embedded in the inner membrane. Each carrier is first reduced when it accepts electrons, and then oxidized as it passes electrons along to the next carrier. In the figure below, steps 1 through 6 show ETC carriers starting with NAD^+ (nicotinamide adenine dinucleotide) and ending with molecular oxygen.

The passage of electrons along the ETC does not in itself explain ATP production. The chemiosmotic hypothesis is used to tie electron transport with phosphorylation. According to this theory, as electrons are passed from carrier to carrier in the chain, protons (H^+) are pumped across the impermeable inner mitochondrial membrane into the intermembrane space, building up the electrical and pH gradients. The energy of the gradient is responsible for ATP production. When a specific gradient is reached, accumulated protons pass through the transmembrane enzyme complex ATP-synthase from intermembrane space back into the mitochondrial matrix dissipating the gradient and making ATP.

The fact that the highly specific order of the carriers and their oxidation is tied with phosphorylation makes the final ATP synthesis fully susceptible to any interruptions along the chain. Some of the currently identified blockers and their sites of action are listed in the table below:

Inhibitors	Site blocked
Rotenone	Step 2 of ETC
Antimycin A	Step 4 of ETC
Sodium azide	Step 6 of ETC
Cyanide	Step 6 of ETC
Carbon monoxide	Step 6 of ETC
Oligomycin	Inhibits ATP synthase
2, 4-dinitrophenol	↑ Permeability of inner mitochondrial membrane

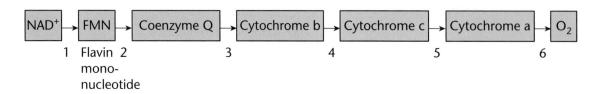

NAD⁺ → FMN → Coenzyme Q → Cytochrome b → Cytochrome c → Cytochrome a → O₂

1   Flavin   2   3   4   5   6
    mono-
    nucleotide

22. According to the chemiosmotic hypothesis described in the passage, the electrical and pH gradients developed across the inner mitochondrial membrane can be described as having

   A. more positive charge and higher pH in the intermembrane space than in the matrix.
   B. more negative charge and lower pH in the intermembrane space than in the matrix.
   C. more negative charge and higher pH in the intermembrane space than in the matrix.
   D. more positive charge and lower pH in the intermembrane space than in the matrix.

23. Applying the information from the previous table, in cells treated with antimycin A, all of the following can be expected EXCEPT

   A. oxygen remains the final acceptor of electrons.
   B. the proton gradient is decreased.
   C. ATP synthesis is decreased.
   D. cytochrome b is fully reduced.

24. While testing an unknown electron transport chain inhibitor, a researcher measured a high proton gradient while no ATP synthesis could be detected. Using the information in the previous table, what could be the unknown inhibitor?

   A. 2,4-dinitrophenol
   B. Antimycin A
   C. Rotenone
   D. Oligomycin

25. Application of which of the following inhibitors will prevent electrons from reaching oxygen?

   I. Oligomycin
   II. Rotenone and antimycin A
   III. Cyanide and carbon monoxide

   A. I only
   B. II and III only
   C. II only
   D. I, II, and III

26. It can be inferred from the passage that the higher permeability of inner mitochondrial membrane due to 2,4-dinitrophenol most likely results in

   A. more protons accumulated in the intermembrane space, increasing the electric gradient.
   B. protons escaping the intermembrane space, decreasing the electric gradient.
   C. more ATP produced by ATP synthase.
   D. oxygen leaving the mitochondria.

27. It can be inferred from the passage that the mitochondrial matrix has

   A. ATP synthase.
   B. ADPs.
   C. phosphates.
   D. ADPs and phosphates.

28. A researcher is interested in isolating fully reduced cytochrome a. All of the following inhibitors can be used for this purpose EXCEPT

   A. cyanide.
   B. sodium azide.
   C. rotenone.
   D. carbon monoxide.

PASSAGE IV (QUESTIONS 29–32)

The pathophysiology of asthma involves the inflammatory cascade and constriction of bronchiole airways. Treatment of asthma requires the use of several medications in combination. Traditional treatment of asthma involves use of a beta agonist to decrease the amount of bronchiole constriction that decreases the size of the airway. Additional treatments include corticosteroids to reduce inflammation, and anticholinergic medication to decrease the amount of parasympathetic stimulation to the respiratory system. Newer medications block the leukotriene pathway that contributes to the inflammatory cascade. Other medications block IgE mediated histamine release that can trigger an asthma attack.

Many of the medications used to treat asthma are delivered directly to the lungs by inhalers. The effectiveness of the medication is directly related to the amount of medication that is present in the lung. If the inhaler is used incorrectly, more of the medication will end up in the back of the throat instead of within the lung tissue.

In any effort to determine the best inhaler for treating asthma, a scientist used three different drug delivery devices to deliver a radiolabeled bronchodilator directly to the lung. Patients were then imaged with a PET scanner to determine how much of the radiolabeled medication had been delivered directly to the lung. This technique of radiolabeling a medication for delivery is analogous to radiolabeling a monoclonal antibody that is being used for cancer treatment. The monoclonal antibody will hone to the cancer cells and block receptors crucial to the functioning of the tumor mass, while the radioactivity that is delivered will caused apoptosis and necrosis of the cancer mass. The direct use of radiolabelling, for drug delivery or treatment, has become very popular because imaging technology is sophisticated enough to detect where radioactivity is present.

The scientist delivered a set amount of radiolabeled bronchodilator to 11 asthma patients using three different inhalers. The amount of radioactivity (in Bq/unit of lung tissue) detected was as follows:

	Inhaler A	Inhaler B	Inhaler C
Subject 1	6	9	15
Subject 2	10	7	0
Subject 3	18	3	3
Subject 4	6	11	0
Subject 5	6	4	5
Subject 6	9	7	8
Subject 7	3	9	2
Subject 8	0	2	5
Subject 9	7	1	12
Subject 10	4	0	8
Subject 11	9	0	7

29. What additional variable could have affected the results?

A. Presence of pre-existing lung disease beyond asthma
B. Tidal volume
C. Sex
D. Zero order kinetics of bronchodilators

30. IgE is traditionally associated with which of the following immunocytes?

A. Neutrophil
B. Basophil
C. T-lymphocyte
D. Mast cells

31. Anticholinergic medication during an asthma attack is appropriate because

A. the parasympathetic response encourages exercise.

B. there is reduced blood flow to the lungs during exercise.

C. sympathetic drive encourages bronchodilation.

D. parasympathetic drive encourages bronchoconstriction.

32. Which inhaler, on average, was most effective in delivering bronchodilator to the lungs?

A. A

B. B

C. C

D. They were all equally effective.

QUESTIONS 33–35 ARE NOT BASED ON A DESCRIPTIVE PASSAGE.

33. Those with abetalipoproteinemia exhibit, among other things, low levels of chlyomicrons in their bloodstream. Which of the following symptoms is likely caused by this metabolic disorder?

A. Diarrhea or excessive watery stool

B. Steatorrhea or excessive fat in the stool

C. Hyperlipidemia or excessive fat in the blood stream

D. Hypertriglyceridemia or elevated levels of triglycerides in the blood stream

34. Which of the following DNA replication errors would be expected to have the LEAST severe consequence?

A. $A \rightarrow T$

B. $A \rightarrow G$

C. $A \rightarrow C$

D. $A \rightarrow U$

35. The discovery of which of the following enzymes challenged the central dogma of molecular biology and why?

A. Reverse transcriptase, because transcription was thought to be unidirectional only from DNA to RNA.

B. Reverse transcriptase, because transcription was thought to be unidirectional only from 5′ to 3′ and never 3′ to 5′.

C. Integrase, because the central dogma did not account for movement of DNA within the chromosome.

D. Integrase, because the central dogma did not account for the existence of DNA outside of the nucleus.

PASSAGE V (QUESTIONS 36–41)

Sheryl Williams, a 45-year-old real estate agent comes to your office. She is a new patient. She states up front that she's extremely busy and that she is pressed for time. Her only reason for being there is for health insurance purposes; she claims there is nothing wrong with her. With that in mind, you proceed with your history taking and physical exam. You have only just started when the patient grimaces and clutches her stomach. She asks you how much longer the exam would be.

You realize this is not typical behavior, and begin to question the patient further. She states that the pain will gradually subside within the next few hours. She says she's been having these episodes for the past few months, and thinks they must be hunger pains. Because food can worsen the pain, she has cut back on her caloric intake. As a result, she has lost weight, which she considers a good thing. You ask about other symptoms she may have, and after some consideration, she tells you that she feels bloated a lot. She mentions in passing that she has been having frequent diarrhea, and she noticed that her feces have started to look a bit oily. She wonders if she should cut back on eating fatty foods.

You sense that these are more than just hunger pains and inform Sheryl of your concerns. She agrees to further testing. You order a serum gastrin level test, secretin stimulation test, endoscopy, and abdominal CT. The test results come back indicating highly elevated serum gastrin levels. Endoscopy shows multiple small ulcers in the distal duodenum, and CT shows a small mass on the head of the pancreas.

36. The mass is determined to be a gastrinoma (a gastrin secreting tumor). The patient undergoes surgery and the tumor is removed. How does gastrin affect H^+ secretion?

A. Activates the cholecystokinin-B (CCK_B) receptor

B. Activates H2 receptors

C. Activates the muscarinic (M3) receptor

D. Activates somatostatin

37. The patient noted that her feces appeared "oily." When there is fat in the stool, this condition is called steatorrhea. This could be an indication of malabsorption of dietary lipids. How does the patient's condition affect her ability to absorb lipids?

A. Inhibition of the liver to produce bile salts

B. Inactivation of pancreatic enzymes

C. Autoimmune reaction to gluten

D. Facilitating intestinal colonization by flagellated bacterium

38. Which of the following substances does not stimulate H^+ secretion by gastric parietal cells?

A. GIP

B. Ach

C. Histamine

D. Gastrin

39. Gastrin is secreted from G cells located in the antrum of the stomach. One function of gastrin is to

A. promote fat digestion and absorption.

B. inhibit gastric emptying.

C. promote secretion of pancreatic and biliary HCO_3^-.

D. stimulate gastric mucosa growth.

40. The patient stated that she had been experiencing frequent diarrhea, and that the feces appeared to be oily. Why would someone with Zollinger-Ellison syndrome have frequent episodes of diarrhea?

A. Decreased ability of the large intestine to absorb water and compact feces

B. Increased parasympathetic stimulation

C. Overproduction of motilin by M cells of the small intestine in conjunction with oversecretion of gastrin by G cells

D. Malabsorption due to villi blunting

41. In Zollinger-Ellison syndrome, proper regulation over gastrin production and H^+ secretion is lost. Normally, what type of physiologic control is exhibited once the proper gastric pH is reached?

A. Baroreceptor (pressure-regulated)

B. Positive feedback control

C. Negative feedback regulated

D. Pulsatile regulation

PASSAGE VI (QUESTIONS 42–46)

Estrogen is a hormone that is very important in the female (and to a lesser extent, male) reproductive cycle and for other body structures, particularly promoting healthy bone and muscle. However, estrogen has also been implicated with many types of gynecological cancers, particularly breast cancer. Scientists have found that an ideal way to target this cancer is through targeting the enzyme-catalyzed production of estrogen. Aromatase is an enzyme in the cytochrome 450 family that catalyzes the conversion of testosterone to estrogen. This enzyme is found primarily in the brain, gonads, and adipose (fat) tissue. The first figure shows a generalized reaction coordinate under standard conditions.

Reaction Coordinate for Estrogen Production

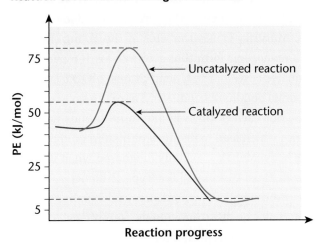

The next figure shows the Michaelis-Menten model for aromatase in the adipose (breast tissue) of a healthy woman under standard conditions.[1]

Michaelis-Menten Model of Aromatase

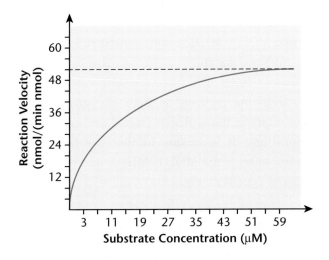

42. What is the overall change in the free energy (ΔG) of the *catalyzed* reaction?

A. 70 kJ/mol
B. 45 kJ/mol
C. 35 kJ/mol
D. 0 kJ/mol

43. By approximately what percentage does aromatase lower the activation energy of the reaction?

A. 0%
B. 33%
C. 66%
D. 100%

44. Studies have found that aromatase activity is high in obese individuals, yet in animal models, those lacking aromatase are obese. What is the best explanation for this?

A. At high concentrations of fat tissue, the aromatase reaction rate increases past the V_{max} in a nonobese individual.
B. The reaction's product serves to inhibit aromatase when it is present at high levels.
C. The enzyme requires a higher activation energy to successfully complete the reaction in the obese individual.
D. The enzyme structure changes in obese individuals, and the wrong substrate is being catalyzed by the reaction.

[1]Kagawa N., H. Hori, M.R. Waterman, and S. Yoshioka, "Characterization of Stable Human Aromatase Expressed in *E. coli*," *Steroids* 69, no. 4 (2004): 235–43.

The table below shows several types of aromatase inhibitors used in the treatment of breast cancer:[2]

Prescription Aromatase Inhibitors

Drug	Mechanism	Notes
Formestane	Suicidal	Injection only
Exemestane	Suicidal	Androgen steroid; similar affect to competitive inhibitors
Letrozole	Competitive	Approved in US
Fadrozole	Competitive	Approved in Japan only; less weight gain
Anastrozole	Competitive	Approved in US

45. What type of regulation mechanism does exemestane use?

    A. Allosteric inhibition

    B. Allosteric activation

    C. Feedback inhibition

    D. None of the above

46. 'Male menopause' is characterized by unusually low androgen levels. How can androgen levels be increased in an affected man?

    A. Aromatase activation

    B. Aromatase inhibition

    C. Artificial injection of aromatase from female cells

    D. None—aromatase has no effect in men

PASSAGE VII (QUESTIONS 47–52)

Diabetes mellitus (DM) is a metabolic disease affecting blood sugar that results from defects in insulin secretion. It is relatively common, affecting 23.6 million people in the United States, 8 percent of the U.S. population.[3] Type I, or juvenile diabetes, occurs when the body does not produce any insulin at all. Type II, often called 'adult-onset' diabetes (though children can be affected as well), occurs when the body is resistant to normal levels of insulin that are produced, and is often diagnosed in adulthood.

While diabetes does have some genetic influence, its incidence is often combined with other risk factors such as age and obesity. However, there are two rare forms of diabetes that are entirely due to genetics. Maturity-Onset Diabetes of the Young (MODY) is a monogenic form that accounts for 1–5 percent of diabetes cases in the United States. MODY is an autosomal dominant condition. There are several varieties, but each of them is due to mutations in single genes which lead to insufficient insulin production in the body. MODY is usually diagnosed when patients are in their twenties. Like Type II diabetes, MODY can be controlled without artificial insulin, and for otherwise healthy individuals, symptoms may not become apparent until later in life.

Another rare genetic form of Type II diabetes is Maternally Inherited Diabetes and Deafness (MIDD), which accounts for ~1 percent of diabetes cases. Like MODY, MIDD is usually diagnosed at a younger age than Type II diabetes, and is not associated with obesity or other typical risk factors. Unlike MODY, MIDD requires artificial insulin to control blood sugar.

The following pedigree is from an isolated rural community in the southern United States over four generations. It is unique in that the family has presented with the MODY, MIDD, and traditional forms of Type II diabetes.[4]

---

[2]Buzdar, A.U. "Endocrine Therapy for Breast Cancer." In *Breast Cancer*, by K.K. Hunt and J. Mendelsohn, eds. *MD Anderson Cancer Series*. Houston, TX: University of Texas Press, 2001.

[3]American Diabetes Association. Total Prevalence of Diabetes & Pre-Diabetes. http://www.diabetes.org/diabetes-statistics/prevalence.jsp

[4]Derived from C. Cervin et al., "Cosegregation of MIDD and MODY in a Pedigree: Functional and Clinical Consequences." *Diabetes* 53 (2004): 1894–1899.

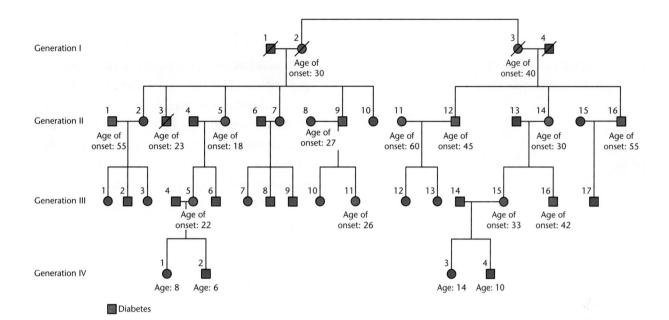

Generation I

Generation II

Generation III

Generation IV

☐ Diabetes

47. The two sisters in generation I of this pedigree both have diabetes. What are their genotypes? (capital letter = dominant allele, lowercase letter = recessive allele)

A. MM, MM
B. Mm, Mm
C. Mm, mm
D. None of the above

48. Based on the available information, what forms of diabetes could individual II-1 present with?

  I. Type I Diabetes

 II. Type II Diabetes

III. MODY

IV. MIDD

A. I or III only
B. II or IV only
C. III or IV only
D. I, II, III, or IV

49. What is the likelihood that individual IV-2 (the six-year-old boy) will develop diabetes before age 40?

A. 0%
B. 25%
C. 50%
D. 100%

50. What is the likelihood that individuals III-12 and III-13 will both develop diabetes before age 40?

A. 0%
B. 12.5%
C. 25%
D. 50%

51. If the penetrance of the MODY allele is 85 percent, what is the likelihood that all of the nondiabetic children of individuals I-1 and I-2 are heterozygous carriers?

A. 03%

B. 2.25%

C. 15%

D. 85%

52. A form of MODY, called atypical diabetes mellitus (ADM), which has been identified only in African-American and some Asian populations, is characterized by initial need for insulin that eventually gives way to Type II diabetic symptoms. If individual III-17 was to marry a heterozygote for ADM, what is the likelihood that their child would inherit a permanently insulin-dependent form of diabetes?

A. 0%

B. 25%

C. 50%

D. 100%

Time—70 minutes

QUESTIONS 1–52

Directions: Most of the questions in the following Biology Practice Section are organized into groups, with a descriptive passage preceding each group of questions. Study the passage, then select the single best answer to the question in each group. Some of the questions are not based on a descriptive passage; you must also select the best answer to these questions. If you are unsure of the best answer, eliminate the choices that you know are incorrect, then select an answer from the choices that remain.

PASSAGE I (QUESTIONS 1–7)

Human immune deficiency virus (HIV) is responsible for over 2 million deaths annually worldwide and 40,000 thousand new infections each year in the United States. The current approach to treatment for HIV infections consists of highly active antiretroviral therapy, combination-based medical therapy. Some early therapeutics focused on the inhibition of reverse transcription and consisted of two drug classes: nucleotide/nucleoside reverse-transcriptase inhibitors (NRTIs) and nonnucleoside reverse transcriptase inhibitors (nNRTIs). NRTIs generally mimic nucleic acids and terminate chain elongation. nNRTIs generally bind to a nonactive site on reverse transcriptase to cause a conformational change that interferes with transcription.

As a student interested in the molecular genetics of infectious diseases, you decide to set up an experiment examining three antiretroviral drugs (drugs A, B, and C) that target the reverse transcriptase enzyme. You culture recombinant CD4+ T cells (one of the major targets of HIV) and infect them with HIV. You then either expose them to plain cell culture media or one of three antiretroviral drugs. After 24 hours, you process cells and measure the levels of viral RNA and reverse transcriptase activity. Your results (as compared to the control group) are shown below:

	Viral RNA Concentration	Reverse Transcriptase Activity
Drug A	↓	↔
Drug B	↓	↔
Drug C	↓	↓
Drug D	↔	↔

1. The purpose of this experiment was most likely to

   A. test the efficacy of four new antiretroviral drugs.
   B. contrast the different mechanisms of antiretroviral drugs.
   C. test a new line of recombinant T cells as models for human infection.
   D. test the reliability over time of new assays.

2. If the mechanism of drug A was related to its ability to mimic the nucleotide adenine and terminate the addition of further nucleotides to the nascent DNA strand, with which parent strand base would it pair with in reverse transcription?

   A. Thymine
   B. Guanine
   C. Uracil
   D. Cytosine

3. Given the results of the experiment, what is a possible mechanism for drug C?

   A. Binding and inhibition of viral elongation factor activity
   B. Binding and inhibition of reverse transcriptase activity
   C. Inhibition of viral entry into host cells
   D. Early DNA chain termination during reverse transcription

4. The experiment described in the passage was performed on drug D, a drug recently approved by the FDA to treat HIV. The results of the experiment show no change in viral RNA products or the reverse transcriptase activity. Which of the following best explains these results?

   A. Poor sample quality of drug D
   B. Drug D's mode of action is not related to reverse transcription
   C. Drug D is quickly metabolized to an inactive form by the host cell
   D. Drug D has no effect on the virus

5. As described in the above passage, the action of non-nucleotide reverse transcriptase inhibitors is most similar to which of the following?

   I. Competitive inhibitor
   II. Noncompetitive inhibitor

   A. I
   B. II
   C. I and II
   D. Neither I nor II

6. Based on the information in the passage, which of the following is true of nucleotide/nucleoside reverse transcriptase inhibitors?

   A. They cause early termination of translation.
   B. They are noncompetitive inhibitors of reverse transcriptase.
   C. They cannot be removed after incorporation into the virus DNA.
   D. They bind a site separate from the active enzymatic site on reverse transcriptase.

7. After cell entry and reverse transcription, HIV can become a latent provirus, inserting itself into the host genome. During this stage, where in the cell is viral DNA normally found?

   A. Lysosome
   B. Cytoplasm
   C. Nucleus
   D. Storage vesicles

PASSAGE II (QUESTIONS 8–17)

Teratology is the branch of science that focuses on the causes, mechanisms, and patterns associated with abnormal embryological development. Until the 1940s, it was believed that human embryos were protected from environmental agents such as drugs and viruses. It was thought that barriers such as the fetal membranes and the mother's abdominal and uterine walls provided sufficient protection for the developing fetus.

Then, in the 1940s, well-documented cases were being reported about certain drugs and viruses that were producing severe anatomic deformities and even fetal death. For simplicity sake, the causes of congenital anatomic anomalies are divided into genetic factors and environmental factors. But experience has shown that many of the common congenital anomalies are caused by multifactorial inheritance.

The causes of human congenital anomalies or birth defects break down into the following categories:

   50–60% unknown etiology
   20–25% multifactorial inheritance
   7–10% environmental agents
   7–8% mutant genes
   6–7% chromosomal abnormalities

8. Thalidomide was popularly prescribed and ingested during the 1960s. The main targeted consumers were pregnant women suffering from morning sickness and difficulty sleeping. Because of inadequate testing, many infants were born with severe birth defects. In general, what is considered to be the most critical stage of fetal development?

   A. Third trimester
   B. Embryonic stage
   C. Fertilization
   D. Fetal stage

9. Sometimes the separation of chromosome DNA does not go accordingly, and nondisjunction occurs. This can result in gametes containing either more or less of the standard amount of genetic material. Which of the following disorders is due to nondisjunction?

   A. Cystic fibrosis
   B. Sickle cell disease
   C. Down syndrome
   D. Polycythemia vera

10. A newborn is presented to you with a huge mass located at the anal region. You recognize it as a sacrococcygeal teratoma. You know it is the persistence of the primitive streak, formed from the

   A. hypoblast.
   B. prochordal plate.
   C. epiblast.
   D. exocoelomic membrane.

11. A four year-old girl presents with five days of total blindness. There was no history of trauma, and intracranial pressure is normal. An MRI is taken and reveals a large suprasellar mass compressing upon the lateral ventricles and pituitary fossa. Urgent surgery is performed and her eyesight is eventually recovered. This tumor was most likely which of the following?

A. Medulloblastoma
B. Craniopharyngioma
C. Glioblastoma multiforme
D. Optic nerve glioma

12. Which abdominal wall defect does not involve the umbilical cord?

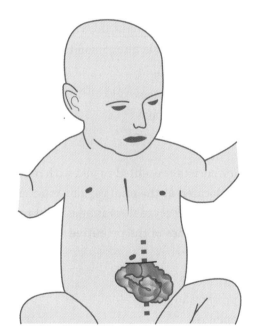

A. Myeloschisis
B. Omphalocele
C. Meckel diverticulum
D. Gastroschisis

13. A young couple comes to your office with concerns about miscarriage. They have heard stories about how a person can suddenly lose her pregnancy, and they want to know as much as they can about the subject. They mention something about extra chromosomes and want to know what that means. You explain that triploidy is which of the following?

A. 47 XXX
B. 48 XXX
C. 69 XXX
D. 92 XXXX

14. An often-seen complication of pregnancy is that of a fertilized ovum implanting itself upon tissue other than the uterine wall. There are multiple sites in which this may occur, but the most common site for an ectopic pregnancy is

A. isthmic.
B. cornual.
C. ampullary.
D. abdominal.

15. You meet with a young couple that has been trying to get pregnant for the past year without success. During your initial workup, the woman states that she has a history of PID (Pelvic Inflammatory Disorder) and wants to know if that could be the reason. What is the most common cause of PID?

A. Syphillis
B. Human papilloma virus
C. Chlamydia
D. Herpes

16. The physician is worried that the fetus may be suffering from fetal erythroblastosis, a disease caused by

    A. rubella.

    B. point mutation of the beta-globin chain of haemoglobin.

    C. CFTR gene mutation.

    D. anti-Rh antibodies.

17. The usual result of an oocyte fertilized by two sperms is

    A. dizygotic twins.

    B. partial mole.

    C. normal pregnancy.

    D. fetal gigantism.

QUESTIONS 18 THROUGH 21 ARE NOT BASED ON A DESCRIPTIVE PASSAGE.

18. Recent studies have shown that viruses can make many DNA and/or RNA transcripts from the same genomic strand of either DNA or RNA, each of which has different frames. Which of the following organisms uses a process in translation that is MOST similar to this?

    A. Eukaryote

    B. Prokaryote

    C. Both of the above

    D. Neither of the above

19. Although many classes of bacteria exhibit antibiotic resistance, researchers have noted that more classes of Gram-negative bacteria have antibiotic resistance than gram positive. What is the unique structural feature of Gram-negative bacteria which MOST LIKELY contributes to this phenomenon?

    A. Capsid

    B. Membrane-bound organelles

    C. Inner cell wall

    D. Outer cell wall

20. The lumen of the nuclear membrane is continuous with what organelle?

    A. Nucleolus

    B. Endoplasmic reticulum

    C. Golgi apparatus

    D. Ribosome

21. Which type of cell releases glucagon?

    A. Beta cell

    B. Alpha cell

    C. Plasma cell

    D. Delta cell

PASSAGE III (QUESTIONS 22–31)

The female menstrual cycle is a synchronized set of events that results in the ovulation of a solitary follicle and ensures that the uterus is prepared to receive an embryo. The cycle is controlled by gonadotropin releasing hormones (GnRH) released by the hypothalamus. The pituitary gonadotropins secrete luteinizing hormones (LH) and follicle stimulating hormones (FSH) that dictate menstruation.

The cycle is divided into three main phases. The beginning of phase 1 is typically taken to be the first day of menses. In this phase, the failure to achieve fertilization after ovulation causes the uterine lining to be discharged. Simultaneously, new tertiary follicles begin to develop. In phase 2, the follicles continue to grow. As they enlarge, they secrete increasing amounts of estradiol, which stimulates endometrial growth in preparation of implantation. Moderately high estradiol levels inhibit GnRH secretion by the hypothalamus, while very high levels of estradiol stimulate GnRH secretion. When estradiol levels reach a certain threshold, positive feedback causes LH secretion to surge. The LH surge causes meiosis to resume in the oocyte of the largest follicle, and ultimately results in ovulation at the beginning of phase 3. The corpus luteum is also formed in this phase, which secretes estradiol and progesterone. The combination of these two hormones in high concentration maintains the uterine wall, and serves as a negative feedback loop in LH production. If fertilization does not occur, the ovum begins to disintegrate, typically 24 hours after ovulation but occasionally as late as 72 hours after ovulation. In contrast, male sperm can typically survive inside a woman's reproductive tract for 72 to 96 hours.

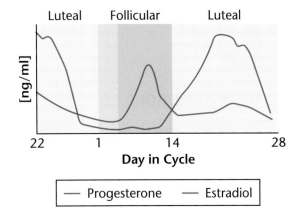

22. Which of the following is not a phase of menstruation?

A. Destructive
B. Secretory
C. Gestational
D. Proliferative

23. Below is an image of Mary's menstrual cycle. How many ova does she produce per year?

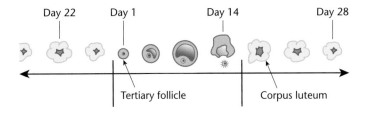

A. 11
B. 12
C. 13
D. 14

24. The corpus luteum is

A. the disintegrated ovum, when fertilization fails to occur.
B. the product of ovum and sperm fertilization.
C. the follicle before ovulation occurs.
D. the follicle following ovulation.

25. Which of the following conditions would NOT contribute to infertility?

A. Extremely low levels of body fat
B. Abnormally high levels of progesterone
C. Abnormally low levels of estrogen
D. Abnormally short luteal cycles coupled with long follicular cycles

26. The combination pill affects a woman's menstrual flow by

A. making it lighter, in that it mimics the circulating levels of progesterone and estradiol during pregnancy.
B. making it lighter, in that it mimics the surge of FSH and LH right before ovulation. This tricks your body into believing it is about to ovulate, preventing the proliferative uterine phase.
C. making it heavier, in that it mimics the circulating levels of progesterone and estradiol during pregnancy. This tricks your body into believing it is pregnant, stimulating the proliferative uterine phase.
D. making it heavier, in that it mimics the surge of FSH and LH right before ovulation. This tricks your body into believing it is about to ovulate, stimulating the proliferative uterine phase.

27. Which of the following is not contained in menstrual discharge?

   A. Blood
   B. Cells previously lining the vagina
   C. Stratum functionalis
   D. Zygote

28. At the beginning of the follicular phase, circulating estradiol levels are low. However, by midfollicular phase, estradiol has reached moderately high circulating levels. Which of the following is true of the follicular phase?

   A. FSH levels are lower just before the midpoint of the follicular phase than at the beginning.
   B. FSH levels are lower at the midpoint of the follicular phase than at the end.
   C. FSH levels see a decline at about the midpoint of the follicular phase.
   D. FSH levels are held constant throughout the menstrual cycle via a complex mechanism of positive and negative feedback loops.

29. Which of the following graphs accurately depicts the relationship between FSH and estradiol?

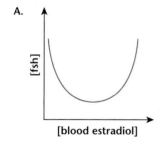

A.

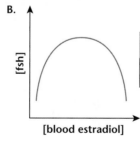

B.

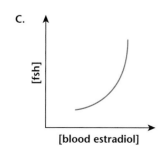

C.

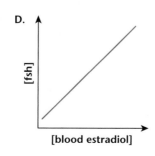

D.

30. Studies have shown that a combination of estradiol and progesterone causes release of FSH and LH before ovulation, yet a combination of estradiol and progesterone inhibits release of FSH and LH after ovulation. Which of the following is true?

   A. Very high estradiol and very high progesterone levels cause the FSH and LH surges that lead to ovulation.
   B. Very high estradiol and very low progesterone levels suppress FSH and LH production after ovulation.
   C. Very high estradiol and very low progesterone levels cause the FSH and LH surges that lead to ovulation. The opposite conditions contribute to FSH and LH suppression after ovulation.
   D. Both A and B

31. There is a 0.3 to 0.5° Celsius rise in basal body temperature immediately after ovulation during a woman's menstrual cycle. If a couple wanted to use the basal body temperature method as a form of birth control, which of the following minimum considerations should they follow? Assume a cycle of 28 days according to the following chart.

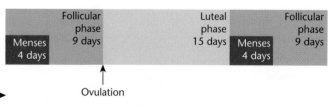

   A. Limit sexual intercourse to three days after temperature rise, for 21 days.
   B. Limit sexual intercourse to three days after temperature rise, for 12 days.
   C. Limit sexual intercourse to 14 days after temperature rise, for 21 days.
   D. Limit sexual intercourse to 14 days after temperature rise, for 12 days.

PASSAGE IV (QUESTIONS 32–38)

Mitochondrial inheritance disorders are a particular family of diseases that are inherited from mother to child. All are related to a group of underlying mutations affecting mitochondrial functioning. Because mitochondria are found in all human cells, these mitochondrial defects can affect any tissue in the body. Disease presentations include muscle weakness, strokes, epilepsy, or heart failure.

Mitochondria are the only cellular organelles, aside from the nucleus, that contain their own DNA, known as mitochondrial DNA (or mtDNA). mtDNA is inherited through the mother. Mutations in mtDNA can affect energy production within cells and therefore lead to disease. Tissues that consume the most energy are maximally affected by defective mitochondria.

As part of a laboratory experiment you isolate the mtDNA of several families who have known mitochondrial inheritance disorders. From each family you isolate gene X, a commonly mutated mitochondrial gene involved in oxidative phosphorylation. You then analyze the genes via gel electrophoresis, including a negative control of gene X from a healthy individual.

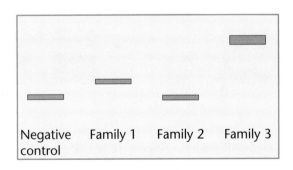

Negative control   Family 1   Family 2   Family 3

32. Given the results regarding the control gene and the gene from family 2, which of the following explains the presence of a mitochondrial inheritance disorder in family 2?

  I. Mutation of another vital mitochondrial gene in family 2

  II. Point mutation in gene X of family 2

 III. No genetic mutations in family 2

  A. I
  B. II
  C. III
  D. I and II

33. On further investigation, it is found that gene X produces a transmembrane protein. Taking this into account, along with the information in the passage, what is the most likely location of this protein in the cell?

  A. Outer mitochondrial membrane
  B. Nuclear membrane
  C. Inner mitochondrial membrane
  D. Nonmembrane bound protein in the mitochondrial matrix

34. If we assume that a specific mitochondrial inheritance disorder affects the ability of the electron transport chain to donate electrons to oxygen, the most likely compound to increase in someone with this disorder is

  A. lactic acid.
  B. phospholipids.
  C. alanine.
  D. carbon dioxide.

35. According to the passage, mitochondrial inheritance disorders have

A. multiple genotypes and multiple phenotypes.

B. one genotype with multiple phenotypes.

C. multiple genotypes with one phenotype.

D. one genotype with one phenotype.

36. Consider a scenario where scientists have just discovered a mitochondrial inheritance disorder that does not obey the traditional maternal inheritance pattern. It is found to be due to a mutation in the nuclear DNA of the cell. Which of the following explains how a mutation in nuclear DNA could cause a disease with similar presentation to a mitochondrial inheritance disorder?

A. Mitochondrial DNA can recombine with nuclear DNA.

B. All the genes needed for mitochondrial function are located in nuclear DNA.

C. Certain nuclear DNA products are transported to the mitochondria where they play a vital role in mitochondrial function.

D. All the genes needed for mitochondrial function are located in the mitochondrial DNA.

37. The family tree below depicts the inheritance of MELAS (mitochondrial encephalomyopathy, lactic acidosis, and stroke-like episodes), a mitochondrial inheritance disorder.

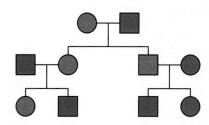

Which of the following contributes to this inheritance pattern?

I. Maternal inheritance pattern of mitochondria

II. Mitochondria possess their own separate genome

III. Sperm cell mitochondria contribute to ova during fertilization

A. I

B. II

C. I and II

D. I, II, and III

38. Which of the following statements is true of mitochondrial DNA and eukaryotic nuclear DNA?

A. Mitochondria and nuclear DNA each encode for their own ribosomes.

B. Mitochondrial DNA and nuclear DNA are always circular.

C. Mitochondrial DNA and nuclear DNA have the same pattern of inheritance.

D. Mitochondrial DNA and nuclear DNA often recombine during cell division.

QUESTIONS 39 THROUGH 41 ARE NOT BASED ON A DESCRIPTIVE PASSAGE.

39. Which of the following enzymes decomposes polysaccharides into maltose?

A. Amylase

B. Lipase

C. Trypsinogen

D. Pepsin

40. Which of the following mutations in an RNA codon would be expected to produce the least severe result?

A. AAA → AGA

B. AAA → AAG

C. AAA → GAA

D. AAA → AAT

41. What is the genetic basis for the statement, "Males drive evolution"?

A. Genes from males are dominant to those expressed by females.

B. Genes from males have been exposed to more positive selection than those of females.

C. Gametogenesis in the male produces four unique sperm cells whereas in the female it produces only one ovum.

D. Males can procreate for a longer time than females and thus a male has a larger contribution to the next generation's genes than a female.

PASSAGE V (QUESTIONS 42–48)

Epilepsy affects approximately 100 million people living in the world and afflicts all nationalities indiscriminately. Seizures are the symptoms of this disease and may vary greatly in type and degree. These seizures result from sudden excessive electrical discharges of neurons in any number of areas in the brain, manifesting in different ways such as disturbances of movement, loss of vision, loss of hearing, and abrupt changes in mood. Although epilepsy is one of the oldest conditions known to man, much is still unknown about the disorder. In the elderly, epilepsy is more likely caused by an underlying brain disease or may be the result of brain trauma. Still, there are many people, especially adolescents and infants, for whom the cause of epilepsy is unknown. In these cases the most commonly accepted theory is that there is an imbalance of neurotransmitters, which causes a lower threshold for convulsions. The following are two controversial proposed mechanisms—not mutually exclusive of each other—for how epilepsy develops from a normal, healthy brain.

The kindling model is one proposed mechanism by which epileptogenesis may occur. In the kindling model, seizures begin to occur spontaneously after repeated subconvulsive stimuli. Typically, the model is used in research to induce epilepsy in various research animals. This is done through very low, usually electrical stimulation of the brain. After a prolonged period of such stimulation, the animals would start to convulse due to voltage sensitization. This sensitization may last for as long as 12 weeks after discontinuation of stimuli.

Excitotoxicity is another proposed mechanism by which epileptogenesis may occur. The process revolves around the actions of certain endogenous excitotoxins, including glutamate, a prominent excitatory neurotransmitter. Glutamate is known to cause apoptosis when left in the synaptic cleft in elevated concentrations via overactivation of NMDA receptors. Brain trauma may actually initiate this mechanism by causing ischemia, which is defined as a restriction in blood supply to particular areas, which then through a cascade of events causes an elevated accumulation of glutamate at the synapse.

42. Based on the passage, which of the two mechanisms would be supported by a finding that carbamazepine, an anticonvulsive medication commonly used to treat epilepsy, was found to stabilize the inactivated state of the voltage-gated sodium channels responsible for action potential propagation?

    A. Excitotoxicity
    B. Kindling model
    C. Both of the mechanisms can be supported.
    D. Neither of the mechanisms can possibly be supported.

43. Which of the following accurately describes the differences between the above two models of epileptogenesis?

    A. The kindling model, unlike the excitotoxicity model, concerns primarily processes at the synapse.
    B. The kindling model, unlike the excitotoxicity model, does not involve the use of chemical stimulation.
    C. Excitotoxicity is concerned with a possible chemical process by which epileptogenesis occurs, whereas the kindling model is mainly concerned with a possible electrical process by which epileptogenesis occurs.
    D. Both models are essentially the same.

44. Assuming you accept the excitotoxicity view of epileptogenesis, which of the following methods would best treat acute seizure activity in a patient with extremely elevated concentration of glutamate?

    A. Extracellular administration of an enzyme, which degrades glutamate
    B. Increasing vesicle release into the synaptic clefts in the brain
    C. Lowering the threshold stimulus for action potentials to occur in the brain
    D. A and C

45. Glutamate is known to be the major excitatory neurotransmitter in mammals. Glutamate does NOT

    A. depend on its receptors in whether it will be excitatory or inhibitory.
    B. become released into the synaptic cleft by vesicles.
    C. mediate epileptogenesis via its receptors.
    D. All of the above

46. Based on the given information, which of the following is a plausible mechanism by which trauma to the brain results in epilepsy?

    A. Ischemia depletes metabolic nutrients necessary for production of uptake carriers.
    B. Trauma agitates the synaptic cleft, which increases the movement and activity of neurotransmitters.
    C. Trauma causes increased action potentials.
    D. A and C

47. Which of the following phenomena could plausibly explain the kindling model?

    A. The phenomenon that an action potential may not occur if the threshold stimulus is reached very slowly
    B. The existence of a time period after an action potential has been initiated in which no stimulus could possibly create another action potential
    C. The existence of a time period after action potential initiation during which only an abnormally large stimulus could create another action potential
    D. None of the above is plausible.

48. Which of the following could possibly explain an abrupt loss of balance in someone with elevated levels of glutamate in his brain?

A. Trauma to the cerebellum
B. Trauma to the thalamus
C. Trauma to the hypothalamus
D. Trauma to the brainstem

PASSAGE VI (QUESTIONS 49–52)

The human body is made up of approximately 60 percent water, with the percentage varying based on the fat content of the individual. In general, lean muscle contains about 75 percent water, while adipose tissue contains only 14 percent water. Therefore, athletes, who have very low concentrations of body fat, have particularly high water content and need to be adequately hydrated. However, for athletes in high-endurance events, such as marathon runners, excessive water concentration can actually be harmful, and sometimes fatal, as evidenced by the death of a 28-year-old female runner in the Boston Marathon in 2002 from hyponatremic encephalopathy.

Figure 1 shows sodium and potassium concentrations in a normal cell and serum. The normal sodium concentration in the blood is ~140 mEq/L.[5] Hyponatremia is a disorder caused by abnormally low sodium concentration in the blood (below 130 mEq/L). For high-endurance athletes, sodium concentration can be rapidly diluted by drinking excess water. When this occurs in brain cells, it causes brain swelling, sometimes leading to coma or death.

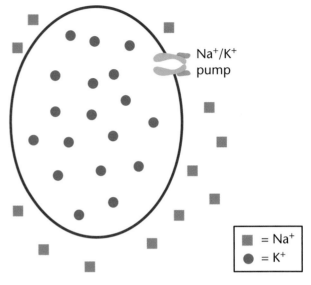

Figure 1

49. Given the information in figure 1, what is the standard H_2O concentration within and outside the cell, respectively?

A. 50%/50%
B. 60%/40%
C. 75%/25%
D. None of the above

50. What molecule is required to control the balance of sodium and water within a cell?

A. NaCl
B. Glucose
C. ATP
D. Urea

[5] http://www.ncbi.nlm.nih.gov/bookshelf/br.fcgi?book=cm&part=A5466

51. Hyponatremic encephalopathy has particularly severe consequences for women, as evidenced by the sole death in the Boston Marathon. What is the most likely explanation for this?

A. Women consume more water during strenuous exercise than men.

B. Women have a smaller brain mass than men do, so the same amount of cell deaths yields a higher proportion of lost brain capacity.

C. Sex hormones impair brain cell adaptation to excess water levels.

D. Vasopressin is present at high levels in affected women.

52. While intravenous sodium is necessary to reverse the effects of hyponatremia, doing so too rapidly can cause a serious problem in the myelin sheath. What part of the brain cell does myelin represent?

A. Nucleus

B. Cell wall

C. Cell membrane

D. Cytoplasm

PRACTICE SECTION 3

Time—70 minutes

QUESTIONS 1–52

Directions: Most of the questions in the following Biology Practice Section are organized into groups, with a descriptive passage preceding each group of questions. Study the passage, then select the single best answer to the question in each group. Some of the questions are not based on a descriptive passage; you must also select the best answer to these questions. If you are unsure of the best answer, eliminate the choices that you know are incorrect, then select an answer from the choices that remain.

PASSAGE I (QUESTIONS 1–8)

Many enzymes require certain ranges of physical conditions to be met for their proper functioning. One such enzyme, tyrosinase (also known as catechol oxidase), is responsible for coloration in the skin and hair of several animal species. There are several metabolic pathways involved in coloration that are mediated by this enzyme. For example, tyrosinase converts the amino acid tyrosine into melanin in pigment producing cells but in other cells, oxidizes catechol to become the yellow benzoquinone.

Tyrosinase is responsible for coloration in Himalayan rabbits. To understand its functioning within certain temperature ranges, an experiment was performed on the rabbits at varying temperatures. Three groups of rabbits were raised at three different temperatures. The results in the following table show the percentage of individuals of each group exhibiting a type of fur coloration:

	% Dark	% Medium	% Light
32°C Group	1	7	92
28°C Group	6	85	9
10°C Group	90	8	2

The study concluded that tyrosinase is thermoliable, meaning that it functions best at certain temperatures.

However, in humans, skin coloration, long thought to be due to tyrosinase activity, has been shown to act independent of temperature variations. While melanin synthesis pathways are mediated by tyrosinase at several stages, the extent of its role in determining skin pigmentation is unclear. Results from several studies with human epidermal cell cultures show a high correlation between melanin concentration and tyrosinase activity. This would indicate that tyrosinase levels determine skin coloration.

Other data contradict this finding. Results from several immunotitration experiments and Western immunoblots show no statistical differences between the actual numbers of tyrosinase molecules among tissue sample groups and different levels of melanin concentrations.

Thus, two alternate, opposing hypotheses are currently accepted:

- Hypothesis 1: Tyrosinase levels determine skin color because of a high correlation between the melanin concentration and tyrosinase activity.
- Hypothesis 2: Tyrosinase levels do not determine skin color because of findings from immunotitration experiments and Western immunoblots.

1. What further data would best support hypothesis 2 without refuting the results of hypothesis 1?

   A. Post-translational alterations in tyrosinase to change its activity levels differ with varying melanin levels.
   B. Genetic alterations in tyrosinase to change its activity levels differ with varying melanin levels.
   C. Tyrosinase activity varies with temperature in most animal species but not in humans.
   D. Melanin concentration and skin coloration are not positively correlated with each other.

2. From the passage, one could logically infer that the metabolic activity of tyrosinase in Himalayan rabbits is

   A. least active in cooler climates.
   B. independent of body temperature.
   C. inactive at or below cooler, arctic temperatures.
   D. more active at cooler body temperatures.

3. Based on the data presented in the passage, which region of the rabbit is likely to be dark in color at 25°C?

   A. Chest
   B. Dorsal
   C. Limb
   D. Ventral

4. Which portion of tyrosinase is most important in terms of its overall functioning?

   A. Active site
   B. Allosteric site
   C. Substrate site
   D. Enzyme-substrate complex

5. What level of structural organization of tyrosinase is first and most importantly affected by temperature changes?

   A. 0°
   B. 1°
   C. 2°
   D. 3°

[Source: Journal of Investigative Dermatology (1993) 100, 806–811; doi:10.1111/1747.ep12476630. Role of Tyrosinase as the Determinant of Pigmentation in Cultured Human Melanocytes. Ken Iozumi, George E Hoganson, Raffaele Pennella, Mark A Everett and Bryan B Fuller].

6. If a future study were conducted on chemical activity in melanin-producing cells, which finding would best support hypothesis 2 while accepting the results of hypothesis 1?

A. Gene epistasis in melanin-producing cells
B. Allosteric interactions with tyrosinase
C. Transcriptional variations within melanin producing cells
D. Elevated pH changes within cell organelles

7. Based on findings from the passage, what is true about the thermoliability of tyrosinase between 10°C and 35°C?

A. Its active site is completely denatured at 10°C.
B. Its active site is partially denatured at 10°C.
C. Its allosteric site is completely denatured at 25°C.
D. Its allosteric site is completely denatured at 35°C.

8. What other physical factors might likely determine tyrosinase activity?

A. pH
B. Pressure
C. Both of the above
D. Neither of the above

PASSAGE II (QUESTIONS 9–16)

Renal clearance (C) is given by the equation:

$$C = (U \times V)/P$$

U is the concentration of the solute in the urine, and V is the urine flow rate. P is the concentration of the solute in the blood.

The general definition for filtration fraction (FF) is defined as the percentage of blood plasma that filters through the glomerulus. Filtration fraction is given by the equation:

$$FF = GFR/RPF$$

GFR is the glomerular filtration rate and RPF is the renal plasma flow. The glomerular filtration rate is equal to the clearance of inulin, a polysaccharide that is neither secreted nor reabsorbed. RPF is approximately equal to the clearance of p-aminohippuric acid (PAH).

In standard clinical practice, plasma creatinine concentration (P_{cr}) is used to measure glomerular function. Creatinine is an inert product of creatine metabolism and is produced at a constant rate by muscle tissue. Creatinine is almost exclusively excreted by the kidney and enters the kidney via filtration through the glomerulus. The production rate of creatinine (Cr_{Prod}) is given by the equation:

$$P_{cr} \times GFR = Cr_{Prod}$$

Rearranged, the same equation gives us the plasma creatinine concentration, which is:

$$P_{cr} = Cr_{Prod}/GFR$$

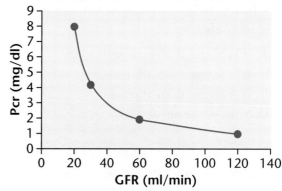

Plasma Creatinine as an Index for GFR

9. Which of the following cannot be true when GFR = C?

   A. The solute is neither secreted nor reabsorbed.
   B. The solute is inulin.
   C. Glucose is reabsorbed from the proximal convoluted tubules.
   D. All of the above

10. Which of the following is true when C < GFR?

    A. Reabsorption of the solute has occurred
    B. Secretion of the solute has occurred.
    C. Both of the above
    D. None of the above

11. Which of the following must be assumed when using inulin to measure glomerular filtration rate?

    A. The filtered concentration of inulin is exactly the same as the plasma concentration.
    B. Inulin increases the rate of filtration.
    C. Inulin lowers renal plasma flow.
    D. Inulin lowers renal blood flow.

12. Which of the following statements of inulin is most likely true?

    A. It is bigger than an erythrocyte.
    B. It is bigger than albumin.
    C. It is bigger than glucose.
    D. None of the above

13. No known solute is completely filtered from the blood after a single pass through the glomerular apparatus. PAH is most likely

    A. bigger than an erythrocyte.
    B. bigger than albumin.
    C. both filtered and secreted by the kidney.
    D. None of the above

14. Which of the following is true when C > GFR?

    A. The solute is being secreted into the tubules of the nephron.
    B. There is more filtration than clearance occurring.
    C. The solute is being resabsorbed from the tubules of the nephron.
    D. None of the above

15. A patient has a plasma creatinine concentration of 4 mg/dL. Her clearance of PAH is 550 mL/min. Approximately what percent of plasma is filtered by the patient's kidneys per min?

    A. 5.5%
    B. 7.5%
    C. 10%
    D. 14.5%

16. Is renal blood flow typically greater or less than the PAH clearance?

    A. Greater
    B. Less
    C. Equal
    D. Indeterminable

PASSAGE III (QUESTIONS 17–23)

Interferons are molecules produced by leukocytes and fibroblasts in response to viral infections. When a virus enters a cell and begins replication, it also stimulates transcription of antiviral genes in the infected cell, which are translated and released. These antiviral genes are responsible for the protective effect of interferons in widespread viral infections. This is thought to occur by prevention of viral RNA translation thereby blocking viral protein synthesis. A set of interferons secreted by T cells, gamma-interferons, also potentiate phagocytosis towards virally infected cells of the body.

17. The following are the results of an experiment to test interferon production in response to various pathogens.

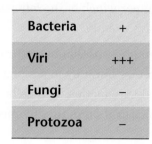

Bacteria	+
Viri	+++
Fungi	–
Protozoa	–

What is the most likely explanation for these findings?

A. Fungi and protozoa are generally extracellular pathogens.

B. Variation in the structure of bacterial cell walls.

C. Differences between prokaryotic and eukaryotic life cycles.

D. Locomotive properties of bacteria and protozoa.

18. The following are the results of an experiment where interferon was added to plates of virally infected cells two hours after initial inoculation with (high titers of a) virus. The control represents a plate of virally infected cells before and two hours after addition of culture medium. Which of the following patterns of growth would be expected in the control group, assuming the virus is cytolytic?

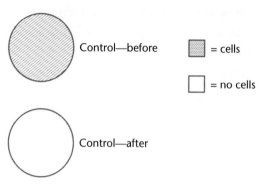

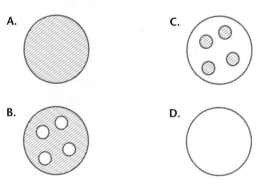

19. Which of the following findings on microscopy would provide proof that interferons inhibited viral RNA synthesis?

  A. Lack of a viral envelope
  B. Lack of the viral cytopathic effect
  C. Lack of viral penetration into the nucleus
  D. Lack of viral capsid protein

20. Gamma interferon, synthesized by T lymphocytes, stimulates the humoral immune system to fight viral infections. Which of the following findings would provide evidence that the humoral immune system has been recruited?

  A. Increased phagocytosis of virally infected cells
  B. Increased inflammation at the site of viral entry
  C. Increased concentration of B lymphocytes at the site of viral entry
  D. Increased concentration of immunoglobulins at the site of viral entry

21. Cytotoxic T cells are capable of killing virally infected cells via a number of ways. Interferon production by cytotoxic T cells leads to which of the following?

  A. Involvement of immunoglobulins
  B. Release of cytolytic enzymes
  C. Use of intracellular machinery to break down infectious particles
  D. Recruitment of macrophages to the site of infection

22. People born without a thymus would have which of the following laboratory derangements?

  A. Low lymphocyte count
  B. Low immunoglobulin titer
  C. High immunoglobulin titer
  D. High interferon concentrations

23. Certain diseases affecting tissue perfusion can have a profound effect on the efficiency of the immune system. Poor oxygen delivery would hamper which of the following immunoprotective events?

  A. Antigen presentation by natural killer cells
  B. Respiratory burst by macrophages
  C. Antibody production by B cells
  D. T cell maturation in the thymus

QUESTIONS 24 THOUGH 29 ARE NOT BASED ON A DESCRIPTIVE PASSAGE.

24. Which of the following describes the central reaction of a Western blot?

  A. Insertional mutagenesis
  B. Nucleotide template-directed polymerization
  C. Plasmid-driven transcription
  D. Nucleotide hybridization

25. Which of the following is an assumption of the Hardy-Weinberg model?

  A. Mating between species occurs at a set rate.
  B. Mutation occurs at a set frequency.
  C. Positive selection for certain genotypes occurs but does not eliminate any genes.
  D. The population being studied is large and stable.

26. Angiotensin DIRECTLY causes the release of which of the following from the adrenal cortex?

  A. Renin
  B. Aldosterone
  C. Calcitonin
  D. Thyroxine

27. Cystic fibrosis is a genetic disorder inherited through an autosomal recessive gene.

If a male heterozygous carrier and a female heterozygous carrier have a female child who is homozygous for the diseased trait, what is the chance that a second child will develop cystic fibrosis?

A. 0%
B. 12.5%
C. 25%
D. 75%

28. Given the principle of independent assortment, how many unique gametes could be produced from the genotype AaBbCc?

A. 4
B. 6
C. 8
D. 12

29. Some types of mammals have especially long loops of Henle that maintain a steep osmotic gradient. This adaptation enables the organism to

A. excrete urine that is more hypertonic.
B. excrete less sodium across the membrane.
C. produce urine that is isotonic to body fluids.
D. reabsorb more blood proteins such as albumin.

QUESTIONS 30–36 ARE NOT BASED ON A DESCRIPTIVE PASSAGE.

30. Mice are administered a drug that inhibits endocytosis. Then, they are intravenously infused with a substance that is found to accumulate rapidly inside cells. This substance is most likely a

A. steroid hormone.
B. polypeptide.
C. second messenger.
D. glucose analog.

31. The lung is a more common site for primary tuberculosis than the duodenum because

A. the mycobacterium that causes tuberculosis cannot survive in organs other than the lungs.
B. the lung has a more readily available supply of oxygen than does the alimentary canal.
C. the bile salts present in the small intestine destroy the tubercle bacilli.
D. the low pH of the digestive secretions in the stomach kills mycobacteria before they enter the duodenum.

32. An MRI scan of a child's brain reveals a tumor growing on her posterior pituitary gland. Which of the following symptoms might have predicted this finding?

A. Hypertension
B. Increased plasma calcium levels
C. Decreased plasma calcium levels
D. Precocious puberty

33. A researcher investigates the cells involved in bone formation and reabsorption. From which of the following types of cells are osteoclasts most likely to be differentiated?

A. Red blood cells
B. Fibroblasts
C. Plasma cells
D. Macrophages

34. Many runners find that smoking cigarettes decreases their speed and endurance. This finding is due to all of the following effects of nicotine EXCEPT

A. constriction of the terminal bronchioles of the lungs.
B. increase in surfactant secretion by type II alveolar epithelial cells.
C. swelling of the epithelial linings.
D. paralysis of the cilia on the surfaces of respiratory epithelial cells.

35. Which of the following structures is found in bacterial cells?

A. Ribosome

B. Mitochondrion

C. Golgi apparatus

D. Nuclear membrane

36. One type of DNA mutation that can occur as a result of environmental toxin exposure is a deletion, in which one or more nucleotides are deleted during the replication of the cell's genome. However, in mutations in which three base pairs are deleted, the mutated gene often codes for a relatively normal protein. This is likely due to

A. most DNA mutations have no effect on cellular function.

B. codons ability to expand in size to fill the gaps creates by base-pair deletions.

C. retention of the original reading frame.

D. occurrence of a back-mutation.

PASSAGE IV (QUESTIONS 37–46)

Erythropoietin (EPO) is a hormone synthesized in the kidney that is responsible for stimulating red blood cell production. Therapeutically, it is used to treat severe anemia as seen in kidney disease and cancer. However recently, it has gained notoriety as a performance-enhancing drug capable of providing the user with additional oxygen carrying capacity. Because intense aerobic training stimulates endogenous production of EPO, absolute levels are not helpful in determining whether or not an athlete has used it for doping. Current methods of detecting exogenous EPO administration extort the aberrant glycosylation of the recombinant form of EPO.

Although erythropoeisis can be stimulated by EPO, production of effective red blood cells is dependent on the availability of iron in the body. Iron is an ion integrated into the heme molecule. Formed heme molecules negatively feedback on the rate-limiting step of heme synthesis.

Endogenous EPO production is regulated by oxygen levels sensed by the kidneys. Adequate oxygen levels allow for hydroxylation and thus inactivation of hypoxia-inducible factor (HIF), a transcription factor of EPO found in kidney cells.

37. In the healthy human adult, erythropoeisis occurs in which of the following locations

I. Liver

II. Spleen

III. Skull

A. I only

B. II only

C. III only

D. I and III

38. The kidney is also involved in the processing of which of the following substances?

A. Folic acid

B. Vitamin D

C. Vitamin K

D. Riboflavin

39. Which of the following laboratory findings would you expect in a patient with chronic kidney disease who is unable to produce adequate EPO levels?

A. Larger than normal (macrocytic) red blood cells

B. Smaller than normal (microcytic) red blood cells

C. Normal sized (normocytic) red blood cells

D. Fragments of red blood cells (shistocytes)

40. Which of the following laboratory techniques would be most useful for distinguishing exogenous from endogenous EPO?

    A. Northern blot
    B. Peripheral smear
    C. Spectrophotometry
    D. Enzyme-linked immunoabsorbant assay (ELISA)

41. The following data were obtained in a mouse population exposed to varying levels of oxygen. Biologically active HIF was measured by ELISA. Red blood cell percentage by volume was measured by centrifuging a blood sample and comparing the volume of sediment to the total volume of the sample.

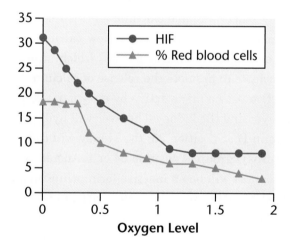

Oxygen Level

The most likely explanation for the shape of the curve at low oxygen levels in the graph above is

A. insensitivity of ELISA to high levels of HIF.
B. exhaustion of iron stores in chronic low oxygen states.
C. impairment of HIF transcription secondary to chronic low oxygen states.
D. red blood cell clumping.

42. Genetic mutations resulting in insuppressable HIF would express

    A. abnormally high numbers of red blood cells.
    B. abnormally low numbers of red blood cells.
    C. abnormally high levels of EPO at elevated oxygen concentrations.
    D. abnormally low levels of EPO at elevated oxygen concentrations.

43. Which of the following properties of the red blood cell allows it to complete its course through the circulation?

    A. Lack of a nucleus
    B. Lack of protein production
    C. Lack of a structural protein network
    D. Lack of cholesterol in the cell membrane

44. According to the passage, HIF acts at which of the following steps?

Hypoxia $\xrightarrow{A}$ EPO $\xrightarrow{B}$ Erythropoiesis $\xrightarrow{D}$ RBC

Heme precurors $\xrightarrow{C}$ Heme↑

A. Hypoxia → EPO
B. EPO → Erythropoiesis
C. Heme precursors → Heme↑
D. Erythropoiesis → RBC

45. Epinephrine works systemically to shunt blood to the skeletal muscles, brain, and heart away from nonessential organs such as the stomach, intestines, and kidneys. One would expect which of the following responses to a prolonged administration of epinephrine?

    A. Increase in EPO production
    B. Accelerated gastric emptying
    C. Decrease in renin secretion
    D. Increased endogenous catecholamine production

46. In order to bind oxygen, the iron contained in heme needs to be retained in the Fe^{2+} state. Which of the following enzymes is likely responsible for returning Fe^{3+} to its most efficient oxygen-binding state?

    A. Catalase
    B. Enolase
    C. Reductase
    D. Oxidase

PASSAGE V (QUESTIONS 47–52)

Bones break when subjected to forces greater than their mechanical strength to bear force. Whether a bone will fracture under a given load depends on both the inherent strength of the bone and the magnitude of the force. Materials, such as bone, whose mechanical properties are dependent on the loading rate of an applied force are said to be viscoelastic. The viscoelasticity of bone is important clinically because when force is applied at low speeds, bone is weak, and when force is applied at higher speeds, bone is stronger.

Fractures of bone are a common occurrence. They are important to note and treat not only because they are painful and debilitating, but also because they may reflect underlying medical disease such as an endocrine disorder or cancer.

Bone healing is divided into primary and secondary processes. Primary healing requires precise reapproximation of the fracture ends, and rarely occurs naturally. It requires rigid immobilization of the fracture and compression of the cortices of the bone together. Primary bone healing is simply the deposition of new bone across the fracture by osteoblasts. This new bone integrates into the two opposing sides through tunnels created by osteoclasts called cutting cones. There will be local bone resorption and eventual recreation of normal bone structure. In secondary bone healing the body first produces a mass of cartilage scar that is subsequently transformed to bone by matrix deposition and calcification.

In addition to serving as the framework of the body, bone is the main storage depot for calcium and phosphorus. A full 99 percent of calcium in the body is stored as hydroxyapatite in the bone. In a typical 24-hour period, 500 mg of calcium is released by the bone and 500 mg is replaced by osteoblast formation of new bone. Like calcium, phosphorus is stored in the body primarily in the bone, although nearly 100 g is present in the extracellular fluid, approximately 10 times the amount of extra-skeletal calcium. The primary circulating factors that affect calcium balance are PTH, vitamin D, calcitonin, and calcium. PTH is released by the parathyroid in response to low calcium levels and acts directly on osteoblasts, which stimulate osteoclasts to promote the release of calcium. Vitamin D must be made active by enzymatic steps in the liver and the kidney. The liver will hydroxylate vitamin D at position 25; the kidney will they add a hydroxyl group at position 24 or 1. An addition to position 24 will be an inactive form, while an addition at 1 will be an active form of vitamin D to work on calcium reabsorption in the body. Vitamin D will act at the kidney to promote reabsorption of calcium from glomerular filtrate and at the intestine to promote absorption directly from the gut.

47. Why might bone development be hampered in cloudy climates?

    A. Poor development of the periosteum
    B. Less sunlight to produce vitamin C from endogenous precursors
    C. Barometric pressure changes increase the likelihood of a break
    D. Less sunlight to produce vitamin D from endogenous precursors

48. Bone loss would result from overactivity of which of the following cells?

A. Osteoblasts
B. Osteoclasts
C. T lymphocytes
D. B lymphocytes

49. It can be inferred from the passage that the majority of bone healing occurs by

A. endochondral ossification.
B. membranous ossification.
C. primary healing.
D. secondary healing.

50. A patient who has had her thyroid removed complains of nausea, tetany, numbness, and tingling around her lips. Excess of what mineral most likely contributes to these symptoms?

A. PTH
B. Calcitonin
C. Phosphorus
D. Calcium

51. Vitamin D is stored in which of the following?

A. Interstitial fluid
B. Fat
C. Muscle
D. Liver

52. T and B cells are both developed in the bone, but T cells mature in which of the following?

A. Liver
B. Spleen
C. Thymus
D. Thyroid

ANSWERS AND EXPLANATIONS

CHAPTER 1: THE CELL

1. A

Estrogen is a steroid hormone that can freely pass through the cell and nuclear membranes to bind estrogen receptors, found in the nucleus. Therefore, antibodies against estrogen receptors will be found in the nucleus. Protein hormone receptors are often found on the cell membrane, where they mediate signaling cascades within the cytoplasm when activated (C).

2. A

Microtubules are composed of tubulin and provide cellular structure and organelle movement. Eukaryotic cilia and flagella are also made up of microtubules; therefore, any antibody against microtubules will tag spermatozoa flagella in addition to cell structure elements. Actin filaments are composed on actin, a type of microfilament and other structural element within the cell. Prokaryotic cilia evolved separately from eukaryotic cilia and are not composed of microtubules.

3. C

This patient has been exposed to a toxin that is metabolized by the liver. One of the major functions of smooth endoplasmic reticulum is poison/chemical detoxification. Other functions include steroid synthesis and cellular transport packaging. Rough endoplasmic reticulum is responsible for protein synthesis (A). Hyperplasia with irregularities would signify increased cell division associated with cancer-like growth (B). While toxins may cause liver cell death, human cells do not possess cell walls (D).

4. B

Colchicine blocks polymerization of microtubules. Of the mechanisms listed, the only one which would result in blocked polymerization would be if colchicines bound the tubulin polymerization site. Stabilization of centrioles, which are made of tubulin, would enhance polymerization as taxane drugs do (A). The prompt states that colchicine acts without destroying tubulin, therefore it is unlikely that has hydrolase activity (C). Increasing tubulin production would not affect tubulin polymerization (D)

5. C

Protein folding after protein synthesis occurs in both the cytoplasm (for most soluble proteins) and the endoplasmic reticulum (for most membrane-bound and compartmentalized proteins). The nucleus and Golgi apparatus do not play a role in protein folding after synthesis (A, D)

6. A

Lactose is an osmotically active molecule that creates a diffusion gradient, drawing water into the lumen of the GI tract. As suggested by the passage, without the enzyme required to break down lactose (lactase), lactose cannot be absorbed out of the GI tract. In secretory diarrhea, the pumping of chloride ions into the GI lumen pulls sodium ions into the GI lumen as well, creating a hypertonic solution and drawing water into the GI lumen.

7. D

Antidiuretic hormone is released by the posterior pituitary when the body is dehydrated (low blood pressure/increased osmotic pressure). Its main function is to help conserve water. It does this by binding in the collecting duct of the nephron, which activates the fusion of aquaporin receptors to the cell membrane. These allow water to travel down its diffusion gradient, concentrating the urine.

8. C

Membrane carrier proteins transport molecules across cellular membranes. While small nonpolar molecules are often able to diffuse through the cellular membrane, and small polar molecules through channels, larger molecules often require carrier proteins. Steroids are able to diffuse across the membrane.

9. D

This question tests your understanding of the movement of sodium and potassium via the Na/K pump, which pumps sodium out and potassium into the cell. If cAMP were depleted, the pump would not be running, causing sodium to leak in and potassium to leak into the cell via various permeability channels. This would cause an elevated level of sodium and decreased level of potassium. Once cAMP was replenished, the Na/K pump would begin running again, pumping out sodium and pumping in potassium, reversing the previous effect.

10. D

Antiporters allow one molecular to move down its diffusion gradient in exchange for harnessing that energy to move another molecule up its diffusion gradient. Active transport such as the Na/K pump requires ATP, whereas secondary active transport does not directly require ATP (A, C). One molecule must move down the diffusion gradient in order for another molecule to move against its diffusion gradient (B)

11. B

This question is testing your knowledge of tissue types. All of the structures listed are made from connective tissues, except for epidermis, which is an example of epithelial tissue.

12. A

Enzymes are manufactured in cells (gene transcribed, translated into a protein) before being secreted into the extracellular space (in this case, the tear drops/mucus) by exocytosis (the fusing of a vesicle to the cell membrane to release its contents). Endocytosis involves cell membrane invagination to engulf extracellular medium (C).

13. D

Transport of molecules against their diffusion gradient is done by active transport. Simple diffusion is the movement of particles down their diffusion gradient (A). Facilitated diffusion is the movement of particles down their diffusion gradient with the help of carrier particles (B). Exocytosis involves the fusion of a vesicle to the cell membrane to release its contents into the extracellular space (C).

14. B

Prokaryotes have cell walls and lack nuclei. Eukaryotes have nuclei, and only fungi and plants have cell walls. Identification of the presence of a nucleus and a cell wall would be important in determining if the organism was a prokaryote or eukaryote. Ribosomal subunit size cannot be determined via light microscopy (C, D).

15. C

Glycosylation occurs in the Golgi bodies via a series of glycosylation pathways. Golgi bodies are also responsible for the production of secretory vesicles. Storage of glycogen occurs in storage vacuoles (A). Aerobic respiration occurs in the mitochondrion

(B). Protein synthesis occurs in the cytoplasm and associated with the endoplasmic reticulum (D).

CHAPTER 2: ENZYMES

1. A

(A) is correct because it represents the amount of activation energy reduced by the addition of an enzyme. The other answer choices fail to address the lowered activation energy mathematically.

2. D

(D) is correct because by limiting enzyme 1 activity, the rest of the mechanism is slowed, which is the definition of negative feedback. (A) is wrong because there is no competition for the active site with allosteric interactions. There is not enough information for (B) to be correct because we aren't given whether the inhibition is reversible or not. Generally, allosteric interactions are temporary, making this distractor wrong. (C) is wrong as it is the opposite of what is happening when the enzyme 1 is reduced in activity.

3. D

(D) is correct because it competitively reduces the rate of substrate C production. (A) and (B) fail to act competitively on the active site by definition because they are allosteric in nature. (C) is competitive but occurs after substrate C is produced in the chain, thereby not affecting the production of C but only substrate D.

4. A

(A) is correct by definition of an enzyme, whereby it remains unchanged after the reaction it catalyzes. (B) is irrelevant because it is a substrate. (C) is not true, as the enzyme would decrease the rate of a reaction; (D) is wrong because it is a substrate, which has no relevance for increasing or decreasing activation energy.

5. C

(C) is correct because, by definition, enzymes lower activation energy required for a reaction to take place. (A) and (B) are wrong because G is not altered by the enzyme. (D) is wrong because enzyme energy levels are not affected by the enzymes but by the overall kinetic energy surrounding the reaction.

6. A

(A) is correct because enzymes are proteins in nature and macromolecules, and so the other choices do not fit to bonds found in macromolecules and/or proteins in particular. (B) is a type of polysaccharide bonding, and (C) and (D) aren't found between amino acids. (D) is a possibility that may form from secondary or tertiary structures but it's not a certain choice like (A).

7. C

(C) is correct because it is the only organelle that contains hydrolytic enzymes capable of intracellular destruction if it were to leak out.

8. C

(C) is correct because glycerol is a product of lipid breakdown and it should speed up in its formation due to the enzyme lipase's activity. The other choices are all true of the enzyme's influence on a rate of a reaction.

9. A

(A) is correct because there is a limit to the amount of an enzyme's activity above a certain concentration—the enzymes' active sites are already occupied and cannot increase in their rates of processing the substrate, no matter how much more substrate is produced. The other choices make no sense as they are not addressing the slowing rate of the reaction.

10. C

(C) is correct because the quaternary structure of hemoglobin often requires the complexity of an active site to span several polypeptides. Choices A and B would produce too simplistic an active site. (D) does not make sense because relegating active site structure only to small functional groups would not befit a large macromolecule such as an enzyme.

11. C

(C) is correct because the delta G for any reaction remains unchanged. The distracter choices all point to a change in delta G making them wrong.

12. D

(D) is the only correct choice because allosteric interactions always change the shape of the enzyme. Allosteric interactions can be inhibitory or excitatory to a metabolic pathway thus making all of the distracters wrong.

CHAPTER 3: CELLULAR METABOLISM

1. D

Glycolysis is the process of primary importance in glucose catabolism in RBC as it occurs in cytoplasm. All other answer choices require mitochondria to be present.

2. B

Electron transport chain requires oxygen as a final acceptor for electrons. ETC also produces the highest amount of ATP (36 ATPs per molecule of glucose). Answer choices (A), (C), and (D) produce less ATP and don't account for the major oxygen consumption.

3. D

Pyruvate is converted to ethanol in yeast in the absence of oxygen. Other answer choices are not produced in yeast when oxygen is not present.

4. C

Conversion of pyruvate to acetyl CoA by enzyme occurs in the mitochondrial matrix before the beginning of Krebs cycle. Theoretically, the fluorescence should be expected there. Other locations are not relevant for this question.

5. A

β-ketoacids result from fat breakdown. Before fat can be converted to acetyl CoA, it goes through cycles of β-oxidation, during which β-ketoacids are produced and can be detected in the patient's urine. Other answer choices are not characterized by this product.

6. C

ATP is structurally similar to nucleic acids that also contain ribose or deoxyribose, a phosphate, and a thymine, adenine, cytosine, or a guanine base. Other answer choices have a different structure.

7. D

Before entering the citric acid cycle, amino acids need to undergo the process of transamination to detach an amino group. As a result, an α-ketoacid would be formed that then could be converted to acetyl CoA. Thus, only the amino group of the amino acid needs to be detached before the citric acid cycle can proceed, making other answer choices wrong.

8. B

Anaerobic glycolysis is of special importance when oxygen supply is limited as in the example of intense exercise and since oxygen is needed for oxidative phosphorylation choice I is correct. When tissues have few or no mitochondria, glycolysis is the main process that provides energy from glucose breakdown, as the Krebs cycle and the electron transport chain occur in the mitochondria; therefore, III is correct. Limited glucose supply does not explain the special importance of glycolysis. On the contrary, if there is less glucose present, it is even more important to break it down fully via oxidative phosphorylation to provide more energy. (A), (C), and (D) are incomplete or include wrong statements.

9. A

The question requires you to understand that the production of lactic acid involves an alternative (anaerobic) pathway to the Krebs cycle and oxidative phosphorylation (aerobic) pathway. Oxidative phosphorylation may not be happening because pyruvate is being converted to lactic acid instead of being transformed into acetyl CoA and entering the Krebs cycle (B). Production of lactic acid requires conversion of pyruvate to lactate and is the result of anaerobic glycolysis ((B) and (D) are indeed happening). As lactic acid gets accumulated, the intracellular (inside the cell) pH decreases as a general response to acid addition ((C) is occurring as well).

10. B

Competitive inhibition occurs when an inhibitor binds to an active site, preventing substrate from binding. (A) defines noncompetitive inhibition.

11. B

Negative feedback is observed when the product of the reaction inhibits further reaction as in the situation described in the question. Positive feedback (C) would further promote the reaction. There is no mention that hormones or the nervous system affect hexokinase activity, so (A) and (D) are wrong as well.

12. D

Each molecule of glucose is converted to two molecules of pyruvate during glycolysis. In anaerobic glycolysis, each molecule of pyruvate then gets transformed into a molecule of lactic acid. Thus each molecule of glucose produces two molecules of lactic acid. Other answer choices are wrong.

13. B

Acetyl CoA enters the tricarboxylic acid cycle. After glycolysis, pyruvate needs to get converted into acetyl CoA in order for the TCA cycle to proceed. In a answer (A): glucose enters glycolysis. In a answer (C): NAD^+ gets reduced during TCA cycle. In a answer (D): malate is one of the intermediate products in TCA cycle.

14. B

NADH produces about three ATPs when it passes it electrons along the electron transport chain. (A) $FADH_2$ produces two ATPs as it enters ETC further in the carrier chain. (C) GTP produces 1 ATP. (D) cytochrome a is one of the ETC carriers and is not a high-energy molecule responsible for ATP production directly.

15. C

You're asked to use the information provided to calculate the amount of ATP produced per 1 glucose molecule. First, calculate the total amount of ATP produced per 1 acetyl CoA : 3×3 (from NADH) + 2 ($FADH_2$) + 1(GTP) = 12. Then, as each glucose produces 2 Acetyl CoA, multiply the answer by 2: $2 \times 12 = 24$. The final answer is 24, (C).

16. A

CO_2 is produced during the tricarboxylic acid cycle when pyruvate molecules are modified and cleaved. Electron transport chain and phosphorylation deal with electrons and do not produce CO_2—(B) and (C) are wrong. Glycolysis breaks down glucose (6 carbons) into two 3-carbon pyruvates without releasing CO_2—(D) is wrong.

CHAPTER 4: REPRODUCTION

1. B

N represents the haploid number of an organism, or a single set of chromosomes. Eukaryotic orgaisms have haploid germ cells and diploid somatic cells. Each chromosome is made up of two sister chromatids. If a germ cell passes on N chromosomes, then it passes on 2N chromatids.

2. D

Binary fission is a process in which a cell is reproduced asexually by equal division into two parts. Parthogenesis is a form of asexual reproduction that occurs in females in which the embryo develops without fertilization by a male germ cell. Unequal cytokinesis is found in yeast reproductive cycle.

3. D

Crossing over is a form of genetic recombination in which homologous chromosomes pair up and exchange pieces of their genetic material. Crossing over occurs in prohpase I of meiosis, and is often referred to as synapsis. However, crossing over occurs between homologous chromosomes, and not between the sister chromatids of an individual chromosome. Sister chromatids are the identical pieces of DNA joined at the centromere to make up one chromosome.

4. A

DNA is amplified by a process know as PCR or the polymerase chain reaction. This process requires the use of two primers, which should bracket the region of DNA you wish to amplify. DNA polymerase is used and it synthesize new DNA in the $5'$ to $3'$ direction, so the primers must be complementary to the DNA regions at the $3'$ to $5'$ ends. Therefore, for the top strand, you need a primer complementary from the $3'$ end towards the $5'$ end, In answer choice (A), this is primer 2. For the bottom strand (which is not shown), you need a primer complementary from the $3'$ end towards the $5'$ end as well. Conveniently, the genetic code of this complementary primer would be identical to the upper strand, which is a complement of the bottom strand. In answer choice (B), this is represented by primer 1.

5. A

To complete this question, we must first determine which strand is the DNA template strand and which strand is the DNA coding strand. The DNA template strand is read $3'$ to $5'$ by RNA polymerase to synthesize mRNA $5'$ to $3'$. This mRNA therefore is identical to other DNA strand (aside from using U instead of T), also known as the coding DNA strand. mRNA is then translated $5'$ to $3'$ by tRNAs into amino acids.

The question states that the above genetic code is taken from the *middle* of a protein. Therefore, the mRNA must not code for any stop codons—the stop codon must be taken from outside this region. Because the mRNA is identical to the coding strand, and it is read from $5'$ to $3'$, the coding strand must be the strand when read from $5'$ to $3'$ without any stop codons. Based on this information we can determine which strand is the template strand and which strand is the coding strand.

According to the genetic code table, we see that the stop codons are TGA, TAA, TAG. We see that if the top strand is the coding strand, the mRNA would have a stop codon in it.

$5'$ TCU AGC CTG AAC **TAA** TGC $3'$

The bottom strand does not. Therefore it must be the coding strand. Therefore the amino acid sequence that is produced must be:

$5'$ GCA TTA GTT CAG GCT AGA $3'$
Aminno Ala Leu Val Gln Ala Ser Carboxy

6. C

Running the SSR on the gel reveals that at least four distinct phenotypes exist for this marker, which has been separated on the gel by size. Individuals A and D can be the children of B and C because the alleles they have for this marker are present in at least one of their parents, from whom they must have inherited the allele. For the same reason, individuals B and C could the children of A and D.

7. B

Semiconservative replication refers to the fact that when DNA is replicated, one strand of the newly synthesized DNA is a complement, and the other strand is identical to the original DNA. This occurs because during replication, the two strands of DNA split in two. Each strand serves as the template for creating a new complement strand. The original template and the new complement together form a new DNA helix. Conservative replication theory suggests that one of the replicated helixes is an exact math of the original DNA, while the other replicated helix is composed of strands that are both complements of the original DNA. Semiconservative replication has been proved through the use of nitrogen isotopes to track the original strands.

Semiconservative Replication Visual

8. D

The LH surge is the catalyst for ovulation in the female menstrual cycle. It begins right at the start of ovulation and ends immediately following the start of ovulation.

9. B

This question assumes basic knowledge of embryonic development, specifically the fact that embryos develop female external genitalia as a default. In male embryos, male sex hormones turn on and turn off specific genes that cause development of male external genitalia instead. Knowing this, we can discount option (A). Without the male sexual hormones, female genitalia should develop by default. We can also discount option (C), because development would not be prevented, it would follow the default course—female development. Option (D) can also be discounted because without male sexual hormones, the genes that are required in development of male genitalia are never turned on.

10. A

Sertoli cells are found in the male reproductive system. If these cells inhibit Mullerian hormone from being release, then this hormone must not play a role in the development of the male reproductive system. Moreover, Mullerian ducts that from through the effects of Mullerian hormone must not be present in males, thus male sex accessory ducts could not develop from them. Based on the information provided, options b, c, and d are all possible. In regards to option B, if Sertoli cells must secrete Mullerian inhibiting substance, this suggests that production of Mullerian hormone and that Mullerian ducts are the default condition. For option (C), if Mullerian ducts do not develop into male sexual organs, than they likely function in the development of the female reproductive system, while Wolffian ducts likely develop into the male reproductive system.

11. C

You can see from the chart that one spermatogonium results in four sperm. This process involves one meiotic division and one nonreductive division. Therefore the ploidy of the sperm will be N.

It is important to note that spermiogenesis is not an additional step in the number of sperm produced—it is a term describing the cytoplasmic maturation that results in activation of spermatids to sperm.

12. C

Disruption of mitosis will only affect the chromosomes of the daughter cells and subsequent daughter cells of those cells. Disruption of meiosis will result in germ cells with trisomy 21 and affect all cells. A duplication even involving chromosome 21, like options (A) and (B), is isolated to one event and will not affect all cells.

13. C

If the urethra is blocked, no fluids can be secreted. This would be readily apparent. Blockage of the seminiferous tubules, bulbourethral gland, or vas deferens would cause components of seminal fluid from being secreted. However, you would be unable to detect this without testing, because the other components would still be released, and fluid would be secreted.

14. C

Options (A), (B), and (D) would all result in sibling who has a higher degree of relatedness than normal siblings, who develop from two distinct ova and two distinct sperm.

15. C

Fallopian tubes are another name for oviducts. These ducts lead from the ovaries into the uterus. Urination and menstruation would not be affected by the blockage of this pathway. Likewise, ovulation could still occur, though the produced ovum would be unable to implant into the uterus. Fertilization would be less likely because scarring will increase the difficulty of sperm reaching the egg. Male sperm swim up the uterus and through the fallopian tubes. Fertilization typically occurs in the outer ⅓ of the female fallopian tubes.

16. D

Vas deferens is the tube that carries sperm from epididymis and testes to the penis. The seminiferous tubules are tubules found in the testes that produce spermatozoa. Sertoli cells are also known as nurse cells. They are found in the seminiferous tubule walls, and aid in the development of spermatozoa. The epididymis is a tubular organ connected to the testicles. Sperm travel through them as they mature and are stored here after maturation.

17. A

Two homozygous guinea pigs would result in all offspring displaying the dominant phenotype. Two heterozygous guinea pigs would result in three offspring displaying the dominant trait and one offspring displaying the recessive trait. Only in the case of one homozygous and one heterozygous guinea pig would the offspring ratio be two dominant phenotypes to two recessive phenotypes.

18. D

An estrogen analog would compete with estrogen for the receptors. An estradiol analog would also compete with estrogen for the receptors. Increasing the concentration of estradiol would also increase competition for the estrogen receptors, especially because we know that the receptors have a greater affinity for estradiol. Thus, the answer is (D). Increasing the concentration of estrogen would help increase its ability to bind to the estrogen receptors because the ratio of estrogen to estradiol would become higher.

HIGH-YIELD SIMILAR QUESTIONS

Fetal Circulation

1. If the ductus arteriosus does not close at birth blood will continue to be shunted away from the lungs. This will lead to a decrease in oxygenated blood being sent to the body which causes

cyanosis, giving the baby a bluish appearance. The heart will increase its rate in order to pump more blood to the body and breathing rate will also increase.

2. The foramen ovale shunts some blood from the right atrium to the left atrium in order to by-pass the lungs. However, blood will still move into the right ventricle and to the lungs. There-fore at rest the baby will have no symptoms since the oxygenation should be adequate. During times of strain, such as crying or feed-ing, the body will have higher oxygen demands and the baby will show signs of cyanosis (will turn blue).

3. Major changes occur at birth, including the clo-sure of the umbilical vein and artery and the functioning of the lungs for gas exchange. When air fills the lungs pulmonary vascular resist-ance decreases dramatically. This decrease in pulmonary vascular resistance coupled with the changes in pressure due to closure of the um-bilical cord raises the pressure in the left atria above the pressure in the right atria.

CHAPTER 5: EMBRYOLOGY

1. D

During prophase, chromosomes condense, nuclear envelope breaks down, and spindle formation oc-curs. Metaphase (C) is when the homologous pairs line up at the cell's equator. Anaphase (A) is the stage where the pairs separate and begin migrat-ing to opposite poles of the cell. For (B), during mei-osis in telophase I, microtublues are still present, and two daughter cells have been formed and are awaiting meiosis II to begin. During telophase II, microtubules of the spindle network disappear, nu-clear envelopes form, and four daughter cells each with a haploid set of chromosomes are created.

2. D

Primary oocytes begin the first meiotic division be-fore birth but enter a prolonged period of dormancy during prophase I, choice (D). This dormancy lasts until puberty, shortly before ovulation due to an LH surge. (A) Shortly before ovulation, the pri-mary oocyte completes the first meiotic division, giving rise to a secondary oocyte and a polar body. Upon ovulation, the secondary oocyte (B) and (C) begins the second meiotic division and pauses at metaphase II.

3. D

Mitochondrial DNA in all adult cells originates from (D) maternal DNA. Once the sperm enters the cytoplasm of the oocyte, the male pronucleus is formed and the sperm tail degenerates. The sperm's mitochondrial DNA is located on the sperm's tail and therefore degenerates along with the tail.

4. C

Gonadotropin-releasing hormone (GnRH) is pro-duced in the hypothalamus and is carried to the anterior pituitary gland by the hypophysial por-tal system, stimulating the release of FSH and LH. Both FSH and LH are key components in the ovarian cycle, from follicular development to ovulation and to corpus luteum formation. (A) Ovaries are important sources of estrogen and progesterone, hormones essential for the develop-ment of secondary sex characteristics and pregnancy regulation. (B) The adrenal gland is comprised of the adrenal cortex and adrenal medulla. The adrenal medulla s are the body's main source of epinephrine, norepinephrine, and dopamine. The adrenal cortex produces cortisol, aldosterone, and androgens. (D) The posterior pituitary produces oxytocin and vasopressin.

5. B

At birth, the female has about two million primary oocytes. By puberty, the number of oocytes has dropped to about 40,000. (B) Primary oocytes remain in a prolonged state of dormancy in prophase I of meiosis. Prior to ovulation, the primary oocyte completes meiosis I and a secondary oocyte is formed while the (A) first polar body is formed and degenerates. The (D) secondary oocyte remains in metaphase II of meiosis II. After ovulation and with successful fertilization, the secondary oocyte completes meiosis II to form a mature oocyte and a (C) second polar body.

6. C

Lyonization (aka X-inactivation) occurs when one of two copies of the X-chromosome in female mammals is inactivated. This is so that the female does not have twice as many X-chromosome gen products as the male (who only have one X-chromosome copy). The choice of which X-chromosome is inactivated in random. (A) Attenuation is the reduction in amplitude and intensity of a signal. (B) Attrition refers to the loss of participants such as in a study or class. (D) Hybridization in biology refers to the mating of individuals from different species or subspecies.

7. D

The corpus luteum remains functionally active through-out the first 20 weeks of pregnancy. For the first eight weeks, it is progesterone produced by the corpus luteum that maintains pregnancy. By week eight, the placenta takes over progesterone production.

8. D

Dizygotic (fraternal) twins are (D) not genetically alike. They are due to the fertilization of two separate secondary oocytes by two different sperms. Two blastocysts are implanted seperately in the uterus. Dizygotic twins have two placentas, two amniotic sacs, and two chorions. Monozygotic (identical) twins are (B) genetically identical. They are the result of (A) one secondary oocyte being fertilized by one sperm. The blastocyst was (C) split into two, and about 66 percent of the time, the twins have (E) one placenta, one chorion, and two amniotic sacs.

9. C

No human structures develop from the fifth (V) arch; it exists only transiently during embryonic development. Some notable derivatives of the other arches are:

Arch III: Glossopharyngeal nerve (CN IX); common carotid/internal carotid artery

Arch IV: Thyroid cartilage; epiglottic cartilage

Arch VI: Vagus nerve (CN X); recurrent laryngeal nerve

10. C

The cells from the three germ layers will go through countless divisions, migrations, and aggregations in order to form the various organs and tissues. The heart (C) is derived from mesoderm cells. The central nervous system and pituitary gland arise from the ectoderm, while the thyroid and parathyroid glands arise from endoderm cells.

11. D

The umbilical cord contains three major vessels, (D) two umbilical arteries and one umbilical vein. Highly oxygenated blood is delivered to the fetus via the left umbilical vein. This blood reached the inferior vena cava via the (B) ductus venosus. Passing through the inferior vena cava, blood reaches the right atrium and enters the left atrium through the (C) foramen ovale, bypassing the right ventricle. From the left atrium, blood leaves through the left ventricle, is pumped out of the aorta, and delivered throughout the body. A small amount of the blood does enter the right ventricle instead of passing through the foramen ovale, where upon this portion enters the pulmonary trunk, bypasses the fetal lungs via the (A) ductus arteriosus, and is diverted into the aortic arch.

12. C

One of the first signs of gastrulation is the formation of the primitive streak. This process leads to the formation of the three distinctive embryonic germ layers (ectoderm, mesoderm, and endoderm), with completion around day 20. The primitive streak forms a visible longitudinal axis down the midline of the embryonic disk and consists of the primitive groove, primitive knot, and primitive pit. The notochord (A) is formed of mesoderm and is located in the midline of the trilaminar embryonic disk; it is involved in the differentiation of ectoderm into neuroectoderm, (D) which later becomes the neural tube, upon which the brain and spinal cord arise. The process of formation of the tertiary chorionic villi (B) does not involve gastrulation. The chorionic villi are derived from extraembryonic mesoderm and trophoblast cells.

13. A

Somites are derived from paraxial mesoderm. Thirty-five pairs of somites are eventually formed, from which the sclerotome, myotome, and dermatome are derived. The lateral mesoderm (B) is the portion of the mesoderm on the lateral sides of the embryo, as the name states. Both the intraembryonic somatic (C) and visceral mesoderms (D) are derived from the lateral mesoderm.

14. B

By the fourth week of development, the intraembryonic coelom had been divided into three well-defined body cavities: pericardial cavity, peritoneal cavity, and two pericardioperitoneal canals. Kidneys and gonads are formed from intermediate mesoderm. Cartilage and bone are formed from sclerotome, derivatives of the paraxial mesoderm. Nucleus pulposus is formed from the notochord.

15. B

The cardiovascular system is the first organ system to reach a functional state. During the third week of development, paired endocardial heart tubes develop and fuse to form a primitive heart tube. The tube later joins with embryonic blood vessels, chorion, and umbilical vesicle to develop into the primordial cardiovascular system. At the end of the third week, the heart begins to beat and blood is circulating. Neurulation (A), the formation of the neural plate and neural tube does not begin until about 21 days into development. The respiratory system (C) does not begin development until 28 days after conception, when the larygotracheal groove starts to develop from the ventral wall of the primordial pharynx. Mesodermal cells (D) give rise to mesenchyme, from which both bone and cartilage develop. Bones appear first as mesenchymal cell condensations which form into bone models, and cartilage first appears during the fifth week of development.

16. C

All the extrinsic muscles of the tongue are supplied by the hypoglossal nerve (CN XII), except for the palatoglossus muscle (C), which is supplied from the pharyngeal branch of the vagus nerve (CN X). As for the other answer choices, most of the tongue muscles are derived from myoblasts which migrate from the occipital myotomes during fetal development. The hypoglossal nerve accompanies the myoblasts during migration and innervates the tongue muscles as they develop.

17. B

Hematopoiesis first begins around week 3 of development, within the extraembryonic visceral mesoderm surrounding the yolk sac. By week 5, certain embryonic organs take over this duty. The organ sequence is (B) liver, spleen, thymus, and bone marrow.

18. D

Upon fertilization, the genotype of the embryo (46, XX or 46, XY) is established. During weeks 1–6, the embryo is still sexually undifferentiated phenotypically. By week 7, phenotypic sexual differentiation begins. Week 12 is when the external genitalia can first be recognized.

CHAPTER 6: MUSCULOSKELETAL SYSTEM

1. A

Bone has much more innervation and capillary blood flow as compared to cartilage. Hence, they would be expected to heal faster than cartilage, i.e. ruptured tendons.

2. B

Mesoderm gives rise to the skeletal system. Mesoderm also gives rise to the musculature.

3. D

When discussing the muscle, the answer is very likely to be calcium, regardless of the question. Calcium is the most important conductor of the neuronal stimulus to the muscle. Acetylcholine diffuses across the neuromuscular junction and activates nicotinic acetylcholine receptors on the motor end plate. This causes sodium to flood the muscle fiber. The action potential spreads through the T tubule network, causing the sarcoplasmic reticulum to release calcium that binds the troponin C and initiates a muscle contraction. Iron and magnesium do not play a significant role in this process, and phosphate is not an element.

4. A

The bone marrow houses lymphocytes (T and B cells) as well as the precursors for other immunocytes, platelets, and red blood cells. The other cells are not derived from the bone marrow.

5. A

Anaerobic metabolism does not utilize oxygen to create ATP. As such, the only ATPs produced from the Krebs cycle in an anaerobic condition will be produced during glycolysis in the cytoplasm. This process yield 2 ATP. The complete cycle will result in a total of 38 ATPs being produced per unit of oxidized glucose. It is easiest to remember this by recalling that glycolysis yields 2 ATP. The game is over for the anaerobic state after this; there is no oxygen to act as the electron transport carriers, so no more ATP can be made.

6. B

Osteoporosis. Recall that PTH kicks in when calcium is low. Calcium is drawn from the bone into the blood. An inappropriate elevation in PTH will cause increased resorption of bone.

7. A

Rigor mortis is the term used to define the musculoskeletal system after someone dies. The processes of relaxation and contraction both require ATP, hence, the lack of ATP will result in rigid muscles that cannot be contracted or relaxed.

8. C

Vitamin D is ingested or developed in the skin in an inactive form. It must be hydroxylated at two positions before it becomes active in the kidney and the intestine. The kidney is responsible for hydoxylation at the 1 site, and the liver is responsible for hydroxylation at 25.

9. A

The important distinction here is 'what moves on its own, and what requires initiative to do?' Smooth muscle lines, for example, the GI tract. You don't have to think about its action—it is autonomic, or AUTOMATIC. In contrast, striated muscle required voluntary movement, and is known as somatic nervous system. The autonomic nervous system is composed of both the parasympathetic and sympathetic nervous systems; hence, answer choices (C) and (D) are wrong.

10. C

The appropriate term for the enlargement of skeletal muscles in response to exercise is hypertrophy. In this process, the number of contractile units per muscle fiber is increased, but there is not cell division. The number of cells remains the same; each cell is just larger due to the stimulus to increase the contractile force in the muscle to match the applied load. Hypertension is a term related to blood pressure and has nothing to do with muscle growth. Hyperplasia is a term meaning an increased number of cells in response to a stimulus. This is the term that will trip you up if you do not understand the fundamental basis skeletal muscle growth. Hyperextension refers to the movement of a joint beyond its normal range of motion. This can cause injury, not growth in muscle size.

11. D

This is an easy question if you understand the fundamental unit of skeletal muscle. The sarcomere is arranged between Z lines; there is no Z band. The Z line at each end is considered the boundary of an individual sarcomere. The I band is the area of sarcomere that is only thin actin monomers. The H band is the center portion of a sarcomere that is only myosin monomers. The A band is the region in which the actin and myosin fibers will overlap.

When the actin and myosin engage to cause a contraction, the I and H regions shorten. The area of overlaps, the A band, will remain of the same length.

12. B

In menopause, there is a decrease of estrogen. Hence, there will be decreased stimulation of the osteoblasts. Because the osteoblasts and osteoclasts are always in constant opposition (bone remodeling theory, discuss in Kaplan Biology Homes study notes), decreaed stimulation of the osteoblasts will result in an INCREASED ration of osteoclast to osteoblast activity.

13. B

This question relies on an understanding of the feedback mechanisms of the parathyroid and the bones. In the case of bone loss, we may be suspicious of an increase in the amount of parathyroid hormone (PTH) circulating in the blood. An elevated PTH in the context of an underlying disturbance would be considered a secondary hyperparathyroidism. For example, if a patient had chronic kidney failure, they may not be absorbing calcium appropriately, and they are unable to convert vitamin D to its active form. The calcium will be low because of kidney dysfunction, and the PTH will be elevated in an effort to leech calcium from the bone to keep the serum levels normal. Primary hyperthyroidism would not be related to calcium status or loss of bone mass. Pseudo hypoparathyroidism occurs when there is a relative insensitivity of the osteoblast-osteocyte system to PTH. The PTH may be elevated, but the calcium remains low in the blood. The presence of bone loss in this patient suggests that PTH does work on the bones, in this case, to excess.

CHAPTER 7: DIGESTION

1. C

Opsonization is the coating of microbes (i.e., bacterium) with complement components, such as C3b. (A) propulsion allows for ingested food to be moved towards the rectum. (B) secretions of electrolytes and enzymes aid in (D) digestion, which allows for nutrients to reach the bloodstream.

2. D

The correct linear arrangement of the gastrointestinal tract is: (D) mouth, esophagus, stomach, duodenum, jejunum, ileum, large intestine, and anus. The trachea or windpipe is part of the respiratory system. During swallowing, the epiglottis (a lid-like flap of elastic cartilaginous tissue covered by a mucous membrane) that is attached to the root of the tongue, will prevent food from entering the trachea.

3. A

Both the vagus nerve (CN X) and the pelvic nerve are considered to be part of the parasympathetic system of the gastrointestinal tract (B), (C), and (D). The vagus nerve innervates the upper GI tract (striated muscle of the upper third of the esophagus, stomach wall, small intestine (duodenum, jejunum, ileum), and ascending colon). The pelvic nerve supplies the lower GI tract (striated muscle of the external anal canal, transverse colon, descending colon, and sigmoid colon) (A).

4. D

(A) mucosal layer is subdivided into the epithelial cells layer, lamina propria, and muscularis mucosae. The specialized epithelial cells are capable of absorption and secretion. (C) lamina propria contains some blood and lymph vessels, but it is comprised primarily of connective tissue. (B) muscularis mucosae, as the name indicates, consists of smooth muscle cells. (D) submucosal layer is considered to be the layer that contains the main blood vessels of the gastrointestinal tract.

5. C

The most frequently affected region is the ileum. The next most frequently affected region is the duodenum. The atretic ileum would probably appear as a narrow segment connecting the proximal and distal small bowel segments. Ileal atresia most likely occurred because of a prenatal interruption of the blood supply to the ileum.

6. B

Cholecystokin (CCK) is secreted by I cells, located in the mucosa of the duodenum and jejunum. Cholecystokinin is essential for fat digestion and absorption. (A) CCK stimulates gallbladder contraction, which leads to bile release into the lumen of the small intestine. Bile is required for the emulsificiation of dietary lipids. (C) CCK increases the secretion of bicarbonate from the pancreas, enhancing the effects of secretin. The process of fat digestion and absorption takes a long time in the stomach. CCK inhibits/slows down gastric emptying and increases gastric emptying time (D). Gastric inhibitory peptide (GIP) is secreted by the mucosa cells of the duodenum and jejunum. It inhibits gastric H^+ secretion (B).

7. C

When food is ingested, both gastrin and the Vagus nerve stimulates the release of pepsinogen and HCl. Pepsinogen is secreted by the chief cells of the stomach, while HCl is secreted by the stomach's parietal cells. This causes an acidic environment within the stomach, between pH 1 and 2. This causes pepsingoen to unfold and undergo an autocatalytic process, leading to active pepsin. Pepsin will then proceed with protein digestion and also convert more pepsinogen into pepsin.

8. C

The proximal, dilated megacolon has the normal number of ganglion cells, but distal to it, the section that lacks innervations is unable to relax, thereby preventing movement of intestinal contents. Constipation is a very common and typical presentation. Absorption primarily takes place in the small intestine. Only a small portion of the digestive process takes place in the large intestine (B). Instead, the large intestine primarily absorbs water and compacts feces.

9. D

During embryonic development, structures within the abdominal cavity will shift positions before reaching their final positions. During the stomach development, the stomach will undergo its first 90° rotation along the embryonic axis; therefore, posterior structures are moved to the left of the stomach. Later, a second rotation occurs—this time along the frontal plane—causing structures on the left side of the stomach to shift inferiorly. Structures that start out posterior to the stomach, then, would find their final positions to be inferior to the stomach.

10. B

In order for bile salts to be formed from cholesterol, multiple processes need to take place beforehand. Hepatocytes utilize cholesterol in order to synthesize two types of primary bile acids: cholic acid and chenodeoxycholic acid. These primary bile acids are secreted into the intestinal lumen. There, intestinal bacteria will dehydroxylate the primary bile acids, producing secondary bile acids: deoxycholic acid and lithocholic acid (B).

11. C

The liver conjugates secondary bile acids with either glycine or taurine to form bile salts. Arginine (A) is the immediate precursor of nitric oxide (NO), urea, and is necessary for the synthesis of creatine.

Carnitine (B) is required for lipid transport within the cell, transporting long-chain fatty acid acyl groups into the mitochondrial matrix. Phenylalanine (D) is converted into tyrosine, which is required for the production of dopamine, norepinephrine, and epinephrine. A lack of phenylanine hydroxylase (PAH) in one's system will lead to a buildup of phenylalanine, a genetic disorder known as phenylketonuria (PKU). If left untreated, this condition can lead to severe mental retardation and seizures.

12. C

There are four primary bile acid functions. The majority of secreted bile salts are extracted by the liver and reused (A). About 600 mg/day of bile salts are lost through fecal excretion out of the body's total bile salt pool of 2.5 g. Although the amount appears minimal, this is the only significant mechanism with which the body has to eliminate excess cholesterol. In order to prevent cholesterol from precipitating in the gallbladder, bile acids and phospholipids solubilize cholesterol in the bile (B). In order for solubilization to work, dietary lipids need to be emulsified first (D). The negatively charged bile acids surrounds the lipds, creating small lipid droplets within the intestinal lumen. The negative charges on the bile salts will repel other bile salts, tearing apart the lipid droplets. This increases the surface area, allowing for more digestive enzymes to work. Bile acids facilitate the absorption of fat-soluble vitamins (K, A, D, E)(C). Vitamins B_1, B_2, B_6, B_{12}, and C are water-soluble vitamins. These water-soluble vitamins are usually absorbed via Na^+-dependent cotransporters in the small intestine.

13. C

α-amylase found in saliva begins the process of starch and lipid digestion. Amylase is also found in pancreatic juice. Pepsinogen (A) is secreted by the chief cells of the stomach, while HCl is secreted by the stomach's parietal cells. This causes an acidic environment within the stomach, between pH 1 and 2. This causes pepsingoen to unfold and undergo an autocatalytic process, leading to active pepsin. Pepsin will then proceed with protein digestion and also convert more pepsinogen into pepsin. Trypsin (D) in produced by the pancreas, in the inactive form of trypsinogen. Trypsinogen in secreted into the small intestine and the enzyme, enteropeptidase, converts trypsingoen in the active form, trypsin. Chymotrypsin (B) is synthesized in the pancreas, in the inactive form of chymotrypsinogen. It is converted to its active form through cleavage by trypsin.

14. A

Aldosterone is produced in the adrenal cortex and increases blood volume by reabsorption of sodium in the kidneys. Somatostatin (B) is produced by the delta cells of the pancreatic islets of Langerhans. Somatostatin has the ability to inhibit insulin release from pancreatic beta cells and inhibit glucagon release from pancreatic alpha cells. Vasopressin (C) (Antidiuretic Hormone) is produced in the posterior pituitary and increases the retention of water in the kidneys. Cholecystokinin (D) is secreted into the duodenum, whose function is to stimulate the process of fat and protein digestion.

15. C

CCK stimulates the release of hepatic bile and pancreatic lipase to digest fat. CCK stimulates chymotrypsin, which is required for the digestion of protein. Somatostatin (C) is an inhibitory hormone. One of its function is the inhibition of Cholecystokinin.

16. C

The digestion of starch starts in the mouth by salivary amylase. The pancreas also produces amylase to further assist in the breakdown of starch. Protein digestion begins in the stomach (A) and continues in the small intestine. The duodenum (B) is essential in the breakdown of food. The duodenum helps regulate the rate of emptying of the stomach. The liver and gall bladder release bile, and the pancreas releases bicarbonate and digestive enzymes ie trypsin, amylase, and lipase into the duodenum to aid in food breakdown. The jejunum (D), located between the duodenum and ileum, functions mainly in absorption of digested material.

17. B

Carbohydrate digestion starts in the mouth. Final disaccharide digestion and absorption takes place in the microvilli (brush border) of the small intestine, The large intestine (colon) is primarily responsible for water reuptake.

18. C

Three major vessels supply blood to the abdomen and abdominal organs. Superior mesenteric artery (SMA) (A) supplies the distal duodenum, jejunum, ileum, and colon to the splenic flexure. Inferior mesenteric artery (IMA) (B) supplies the descending colon, sigmoid colon, and rectum. Celiac trunk (D) supplies the esophagus, stomach, proximal duodenum, liver, gallbladder, pancreas, and spleen. The answer is the common iliac, which supplies blood to the lower limbs and the pelvis, ending the abdominal aorta.

HIGH-YIELD SIMILAR QUESTIONS

Digestive System

1. A large dose of antacid would increase the pH of the stomach and therefore inactivate pepsin. The optimum pH for pepsin is between 1 and 3; pepsin is denatured and therefore inactivated at a pH greater than 5.

2. If the pancreas could not secrete bicarbonate the acidic chyme that moves into the duodenum would not be neutralized and pancreatic lipases would not be able to function. This will result in the malabsorption of lipids and steatorrhea.

3. Inadequate amounts on lipase enzymes will lead to steatorrhea. If lipids are not broken down by lipases they cannot be absorbed by the small intestine.

Osmosis

1. Decrease

2. Interstitial fluid is hypertonic to filtrate; filtrate is hypotonic/hypoosmotic to interstitial fluid

3. Hypotonic

CHAPTER 8: RESPIRATION

1. C

The electron transport chain will work fine since it is not inhibited. As a result, the NADH will transfer electrons and oxidize to NAD^+. Hence, the cell will become depleted of the NADH, but will not reap the benefits of ATP production from lack of generation of the proton gradient.

2. A

Minute ventilation is the product of tidal volume multiplied by respiratory rate. The man in this case has a minute ventilation of 6L, while the son has a minute ventilation of 2.4 L.

3. B

Inadequate intercostal muscle function will greatly compromise respiratory function. These muscles, known as accessory muscles of breathing, act to expand the chest cavity and increase the negative pressure required for respiration. Cardiac muscle is not extensive damaged in muscular dystrophy; the histology of cardiac muscle is distinct from the skeletal muscle primarily affected in muscular

dystrophy. A narrowed trachea is not a hallmark of MS; the trachea is made of collagen, epithelium, and connective tissue that are not involved in the fundamental defects of skeletal muscle in muscular dystrophy. Lung tissue compliance is not a function of skeletal muscle integrity.

4. A

The surface tension is more markedly decreased with artificial surfactant A because there is a greater degree of hydrophobic molecules in the compound. These hydrophobic lipids will disrupt the loose bonds of polar molecules that are responsible for surface tension on the alveoli. The greater amount of hydrophobic molecules, the more disrupted the lattice responsible for surface tension. Sample B is less hydrophobic than A, and will integrate with the polar molecules, rather than cause a disruption of the polar lattice that promote alveolar collapse. The presence of protein in sample A does not contribute nearly as effectively to hydrophobicity as the elevated lipid in sample A. While some of the protein may be hydrophobic, much will be charged and engaged with the polar molecules. It is the increased lipid, not the presence of protein that allows A to decrease surface tension more effectively than B. The rate of respiration of subjects will have no bearing on surface tension.

5. B

At higher altitudes, there is lower oxygen concentrations, as compared to sea level. Thus, a person will feel subjectively shirt of breath and need to increase the respiratory rate to obtain more oxygen in a given amount of time.

6. B

Increased minute ventilation will result in the air in the lungs containing more carbon dioxide than they would in the case of a normal ventilation rate. As such, the carbon dioxide remaining in the lungs will diffuse into the blood and be buffered by the bicarbonate system. The result of the CO_2/H_2O buffer will be the production of bicarbonate and hydrogen ions. Hydrogen ions will decrease the pH of the system per the equation $pH = -\log [H^+]$.

7. C

The oxygen saturation curve is a graphical representation of the propensity of hemoglobin to 'give up' its oxygen under certain conditions. Consider what occurs during exercise. Temperature is increased in the body, oxygen is used more rapidly, and lactic acid is produced. The body becomes hot, deoxygenated, and acidic. 2, 3 DPG is produced by the red blood cells to facilitate offloading of oxygen. Delivery of oxygen to these tissues will allow the body to regain equilibrium towards homeostasis. A shift to the right off this curve signals that at identical partial pressures of oxygen, hemoglobin saturation will be lower, indicating that more oxygen is shifted off of hemoglobin and into the tissue. Under normal conditions, less than a quarter of the oxygen on hemoglobin is used by the tissues. The system is built to unload more oxygen at time of stress. You will never forget this curve shift if you just recall that exercise is the 'right' thing for the body—the curve shifts to the right. Answer (D) suggests there is no synergy, or increased uptake of oxygen at lower partial pressure, but this is not true. The relationship is not linear; it accelerates variably at different partial pressures of oxygen, as indicated by considering the answers in terms of rate of change. The sinusoidal change of correct answer (C) reflects this, while the rate of change in (D) is 0.

8. D

The replacement of the compliant lung tissue with fibrous tissue will make the lung less compliant. As a result it will "stretch" less. This will lead to low lung volumes. Destruction of the alveoli will decrease the lung's ability to effectuate gas exchange, leading to hypoxia. Patients ill then become subjectively short of breath.

9. B

Iron is the element required for proper functioning of hemoglobin. Decreased levels of iron in the blood, known as iron-deficiency anemia, will result in small red blood cells that are widely varying in their size and shape. Copper, manganese, and selenium all play important roles in the body as micronutrients, but are not important for proper functioning of hemoglobin.

10. C

The brainstem is home to the autonomic function that causes us to breath without thinking about it. The forebrain is involved with higher level thinking and executive judgment. The midbrain is responsible for sensory integration and other higher level tasks. The cerebellum is important in balance, coordination, and memory.

11. B

The most important thing to remember about respiratory mechanics is that the thoracic cavity is essentially a negative pressure system that draws air into the chest. The diaphragm plays a crucial role in this system. Upon inspiration, the diaphragm falls, increasing the size of the thoracic cavity. Recall that pressure and volume are inversely related per Charles' law. The larger the volume, the lower the pressure. The pressure in the airways becomes increasing negative relative to the ambient pressure of air outside the system. Air will be forced to fill the vacuum—in this case, the chest. This system is driven by a functioning diaphragm. Injury to neck can cause problems with respiratory because the phrenic nerve innervating the diaphragm, emerges from the spinal cord at C 3, 4, and 5. Without the phrenic nerve and a functioning diaphragm, this negative pressure system is compromised, and breathing becomes more difficult.

12. A

This question is strictly anatomy. Unoxygenated blood is sent to the lungs from the heart via the pulmonary artery. This can be tricky because it is an artery carrying deoxygenated blood, while arteries usually carry oxygenated blood. Pulmonary veins return oxygenated blood to the heart. The aorta is the major artery to the rest of the body from the left ventricle. Foramen ovale is a small hole between the atria of the heart.

13. A

Acetyl CoA is not involved in the transport of carbon dioxide in the blood. In physiologic terms, acetate is an organic molecule that is produced as the result of fatty chain oxidation. Acetyl CoA is then fed into the oxidative phosphorylation pathway and used to create ATP. (B), (C), and (D) are all used to carry carbon dioxide, with bicarb being the most heavily relied upon way of CO_2 to be transported in the blood.

14. A

Blood in the pulmonary vein is returning from the lungs, where it has been oxygenated. Oxyhemoglobin is the appropriate term for hemoglobin equipped with oxygen. Lactic acid would not be present in excess in blood in the pumolnary veins under normal conditions. Chyme is a term for food passing into the digestive system. Blood in pulmonary veins will be no more or less enriched with hemoglobin than any other blood. The key concept to remember here is that pulmonary veins equals richly oxygenated hemoglobin.

HIGH-YIELD SIMILAR QUESTIONS

Respiratory System

1. If respiration is occurring normally but there is no blood flow to the left lung then there is no gas exchange occurring in the left lung. If no oxygen is being diffused from the air into the blood and no CO_2 is being released then the Po_2 of the alveoli will equal the Po_2 of inspired air.

2. If there is an airway obstruction but blood flow to the lung is normal there is no gas exchange. The blood that flows into the lung will have the same value of Po_2 and Pco_2 as venous blood. Since no gas exchange occurs this value will remain the same for blood as it exits the lung.

3. When the Po_2 of inspired air equals the Po_2 of capillary blood then diffusion will stop.

CHAPTER 9: CIRCULATION

1. A

The relative lack of smooth muscle in the vein walls allows it to stretch in order to store a majority of the blood in the body. Valves in the veins allow for one-way flow of blood towards the heart. Both arteries and veins are close to lymphatic vessels and that has no bearing on the difference in volume. Both arteries and veins have a thin endothelial lining.

2. C

Carbon dioxide is a byproduct of metabolism in cells, which later combines with water to form bicarbonate. Food and fluid absorption of buffer are not significant sources.

3. A

Eosinophils are the body's protection against parasitic infections, such as tapeworm and the various species of malaria. Parasites, by definition, are organisms that invade and live in a host, using nutrients provided by the host and often causing damage to the host. Sickle cell anemia (B) is an inherited blood disorder. Hepatitis B (C) and influenza (D) are caused by viruses.

4. A

Allergic reactions to pollen, ragweed, pet dander, and so on. are mediated by histamine release from granules in basophils. Red blood cells and lymphocytes have nothing to do with allergic reactions. Granules of neutrophils contain enzymes aimed at damaging bacteria.

5. A

Systolic blood pressure is the pressure of blood during systole, when blood is being pumped out of the ventricles and into circulation. This would be the time at which the aortic and pulmonic valves are open, allowing blood out of the ventricles to circulate to the extremities and the lungs. The mitral valve opens during diastole to allow ventricular filling. Atrial and ventricular pressure become equal also during diastole.

6. C

Diastolic blood pressure is the pressure in the arterial system when the heart is at rest. This occurs during ventricular filling, when the ventricular pressure is less than the atrial pressure, allowing blood to fill the ventricle. Arterial pressure does not normally equal venous pressure, nor does pressure normally equalize over both sides of the heart.

7. B

The parasympathetic nervous system mediates the cardiovascular system the majority of the time because we do not often require acute augmentation of stroke volume and/or heart rate. Thus, if adrenergic input is blocked (epinephrine and norepinephrine from the sympathetic nervous system), little to no difference would be evident in our cardiovascular status. If acetylcholine receptors were

blocked, the effects of the sympathetic nervous system would be amplified.

8. C

The fact that the couple's first child is Rh positive implies that during birth, the mother could potentially have been exposed to the Rh-positive blood, stimulating antibody production against Rh. Rh-immune globin administration would have no effect at this point. The red blood cells of the first child are not in the maternal circulation. The father's Rh factor will determine the Rh status of the second child. The fetus does not generate any of its own antibodies until after birth.

9. D

Insoluble fibrin conveys the most strength to a clot. Thrombin, once activated, converts fibrinogen to fibrin. Fibrin then becomes cross-linked with the help of factor XIII to assume its insoluble state.

10. D

The liver lies *in series with*, as opposed to *in parallel*, with blood coming from the upper and lower extremities after oxygen has been extracted in the capillary beds. This allows blood to be filtered for waste products before returning back to the heart to be reoxygenated.

11. C

The half-life of epinephrine is short; oftentimes, the sympathetic nervous system needs an acute augmentation of cardiac output and thus a short-lived molecule would be ideal to mediate these effects. The half-life is the amount of time required for the level of a drug to decrease by half of its original concentration. By the graph, the substance was injected at t = 10 seconds and falls to half of its original concentration approximately 120 seconds later.

12. B

The graph shows antibody levels as if the body were exposed to a new antigen. It takes time for rearrangement of heavy and light chains specific to the antigen to be formed by the B lymphocyte, and thus a lag is created between the time at which the body is exposed to an antigen and the time at which it is capable of mounting an antibody mediated defense. Passive immunization is the direct administration of preformed antibodies to a given antigen.

13. A

When an antigen is encountered, B cells are stimulated to proliferate in order to manufacture specific antibodies to the antigen. The manufacturing process requires rearrangement of the heavy and light chains so that the variable regions of the immunoglobulins bind only the antigen. Once it does, phagocytosis is triggered by the binding of the specific antibody to the antigen.

14. B

Phagocytosis plays an important role in both the non specific and humoral response to foreign pathogens. At the level of the skin, macrophages dwell in the connective tissue surrounding the organs of the body. Neutrophils are recruited to the site of entry and become part of the non specific response to invading bacteria, working in combination with monocytes and macrophages to completely decompose bacteria. The cell-mediated branch of the immune system does not result in pus formation.

15. D

The coronary arteries are the first branch off of the aorta, and would thus receive normal blood flow. Beyond the first branch, a heartbeat with a diminished stroke volume is less likely to perfuse the brain or extremities. With time, the body preferentially will protect perfusion to the brain by vasoconstricting the coronary arteries in order to improve cerebral oxygenation, but that occurs later.

HIGH-YIELD SIMILAR QUESTIONS

Circulation

1. In mitral valve stenosis the valve between the left atrium and the left ventricle narrows and restricts blood flow into the left ventricle. This increases blood pressure in the left atrium.

2. Left ventricle

3. Pulmonary arteries

Normal Oxygen Dissociation Curve

1. At P = 50 mm Hg, venous blood has about 60% hemoglobin saturation. Arterial blood, on the other hand, has greater hemoglobin saturation (approximately 90%).

2. Fetal hemoglobin has a greater affinity for O_2 than adult hemoglobin, so the curve is shifted to the left.

3. PO_2 is reduced, but over time, hemoglobin "learns" to bind oxygen at this lower pressure (shifting the curve left).

Abnormal Oxygen Dissociation Curve

1. Exercise will lead to an increase in body temperature as well as in increase in CO_2 production, and thereby a decrease in pH, by tissues. Increases in Pco_2, decreases in pH and increases in temperature all shift the oxygen dissociation curve to the right.

2. High levels of Pco_2 lead to an increase in ventilation rate in order to blow off the excess CO_2.

3. In metabolic alkalosis blood pH will be increased due to the loss of H^+ ions. Increased pH leads to a left shift in the oxygen dissociation curve.

Lymphatic System

1. If a patient's lymphatic channels are obstructed then fluid that filters into the interstitial space from capillaries cannot be returned to circulation by lymph vessels. This fluid will build up in the interstitial space and edema will result.

2. Blocked lymphatic channels, excess proteins in the interstial fluid, loss of proteins from the plasma (as can happen in kidney or liver disease)

3. Distortion of lymphatic vessels by the movement of skeletal muscles allows proteins and interstitial fluid to enter the lymphatic system. This lymph is carried through lymphatic vessels, which have valves to prevent backflow, and eventually dumped back into blood circulation at the thoracic duct or subclavian vein.

CHAPTER 10: HOMEOSTASIS

1. C

The glomerulus will allow glucose to pass through into the filtrate when functioning properly. Glucose will usually not be present in the filtrate, however, because it undergoes reabsorption in the proximal convoluted tubule, which is located adjacent to the glomerulus. (A), (B), and (D) are wrong because all three are too large to pass through the glomerulus, and only upon malfunction of the glomerulus would any of the three be present in the filtrate.

2. C

Urine will not have a high concentration of Na$^+$ due to reabsorption of Na$^+$ caused by aldosterone stimulation. (A), (B), and (D) are wrong because aldosterone stimulates reabsorption of Na$^+$, which increases the blood pressure and also lowers the concentration of Na$^+$ that will be passed in the urine.

3. B

Ingesting a large quantity of water will effect a low solute concentration in the blood. The low concentration will inhibit ADH (vasopressin) secretion such that more water will remain in the filtrate and eventually the urine. Therefore, (A) is wrong. (C) is wrong as well because an increase in water will inevitably result in a rise in blood volume, which would decrease the amount of aldosterone release from the adrenal cortex.

4. A

(B) and (C) are wrong because the glomerulus is a capillary bed and thus does not ever house the filtrate. It is across this capillary bed into the Bowman's capsule where filtrate makes its first appearance. (C) and (D) are wrong because of wrong ordering.

5. B

Although the liver will produce some amino acids by interconversion, essential amino acids cannot be synthesized by the body.

6. A

Sweat glands are in the dermis layer. The sweat pore, however, is located in the epidermis. (B) and (C) are wrong because the keratinized epidermal cells protect against harmful bacteria and excess water loss. (D) is wrong because melanocytes, which are located in the epidermis, protect against UV radiation via production of melanin.

7. C

The kidneys only regulate osmolarity of the blood and filtrate/urine. The excreted urine is no cooler or warmer than the blood in the kidneys. (A) and (B) are wrong because the thyroid gland and skin do regulate temperature. (D) is wrong because (C) is correct.

8. B

Nearly all glucose (and all other solutes) is reabsorbed from the proximal convoluted tubule. Therefore, (A), (C), and (D) are wrong.

9. A

Even though the osmolarity inside the collecting duct is smaller relative to the outside due to aldosterone release, because water will only be able to slowly passively diffuse to the outside of the duct, much more water will be staying inside the duct. Therefore, water will not be able to be reabsorbed so the blood pressure will be the same as before aldosterone release. (B) is wrong because more water will be excreted in the urine due to the blocking of vasopressin release. (C) and (D) are wrong because aldosterone will still directly cause an increase in Na^+ reabsorption and decrease in K^+ reabsorption regardless of the block on vasopressin.

10. D

A patient who has overactive sweat glands would feel cooler than normal due to more evaporation of sweat, which is mostly water. Remember, water has a relatively high heat of vaporization. (B) is wrong because hyperthyroidism would boost the basal metabolic rate of the patient, and thus, she would be warmer than normal. (A) and (C) are also wrong because both would also result in a warmer than usual patient.

11. D

In a diabetic patient, which we can assume given the patient's family history, the glucose transport across the proximal convoluted tubules cannot cope with a higher influx of glucose into the filtrate. (A) is not correct because glucose reabsorption does not stop. (B) is not correct because glucose is only reabsorbed in the proximal convoluted tubule. (C) is not correct because glucose is not secreted into the tubule.

12. C

One of the functions of the liver is the interconversion of carbohydrates and fats (as well as proteins). Higher concentrations of glucose produced from glycogenolysis may be interconverted into fat and vice-versa. (A) is wrong because the process occurs in the liver, not the kidney. (B) is wrong because low levels stimulates glycogenolysis. (D) is wrong because the reaction is also under nervous control.

13. D

This transport process requires ATP. (A) and (C) are wrong because this transport occurs at the proximal convoluted tubule. (B) is wrong because these transporters in diabetic patients are not malfunctioning, but rather the nephrons are overtaxed with a greater influx of glucose than is seen in normal patients.

14. C

Water is normally reabsorbed from the proximal convoluted tubule and descending loop of Henle. Water is also reabsorbed from the collecting duct upon vasopressin stimulation.

HIGH-YIELD SIMILAR QUESTIONS

Starting Forces

1. Factors that increase filtration out of the capillaries are: increased arterial or venous pressure (remember P_c is blood pressure), a decrease in the hydrostatic pressure of the interstitial fluid (P_i), decreased protein in the blood which lowers the π_c, or an increase in proteins in the interstitial fluid (π_i).

2. Capillary oncotic pressure will be increased by any factor that increases the protein concentration in the blood. For example, loss of fluid, as in dehydration, will increase capillary oncotic pressure.

3. Fluids and protein that are filtered from the capillary into the interstitial space are normally returned to circulation via the lymphatic system. Inadequate lymphatic function will

increase π_i which will favor filtration of fluids out of the capillaries and prevent fluid reabsorption at the venule end leading to edema.

CHAPTER 11: ENDOCRINE SYSTEM

1. D

Lack of or unresponsiveness to ADH causes an inability to concentrate urine. This would cause a dilution in urine, and a subsequent increase in serum osmolarity. An increase in serum glucose would be more evident of diabetes mellitus. Oxytocin is a hormone also released from the posterior pituitary responsible for the onset of labor as well as milk letdown.

2. C

ADH acts by concentrating urine by encouraging reabsorption of water in the distal collecting tubule and collecting duct of the nephron. Loop diuretics act upon the Na/K/Cl channels, thiazide diuretics acts upon NaCl channels and dopamine acts upon the Na/H channels of the nephron to indirectly cause water excretion.

3. D

Thyroid storm, or sudden onset hyperthyroidism, is the most common endocrine cause of an elevated heart rate. Thyroid hormone, in additional to increasing heart rate, increases the body's metabolic rate resulting in weight loss, increases the speed of nerve transmission resulting in tremors and increases the speed of gastrointestinal motility resulting in diarrhea. Elevated estrogen levels results in feminization and increased risk of some cancers. Elevated growth hormone causes gigantism and acromegaly. Hypoaldosteronism leads to elevated potassium levels.

4. B

Thyroid hormone is an amino acid derivative but works similarly to steroid hormones in that it directly alters gene transcription in cells. It is responsible for increasing the basal metabolic rate and would therefore increase the rate at which genes are transcribed by affected cells in the body. Peptide hormones such as ADH and insulin exert effects on cells via a second messenger, namely cyclic AMP. Phosphodiesterase moderates the response of the second messenger pathway.

5. B

T_4 is the main product of the thyroid gland; it is converted to T_3 by removing an iodine atom. This is done by deiodinases found in target organs. Adequate iodine-intake ensures that the thyroid gland makes enough T_4 for the body. Thryoperoxidase is an enzyme in the thyroid gland which synthesizes T_3 and T_4. Thryoglobulin is a protein in the thyroid gland which carries tyrosine molecules to be iodinated and released as thyroid hormones.

6. A

Serum calcium levels negatively feedback on the C cells of the thyroid in order to tightly control calcium concentrations. A seven-transmembrane G-coupled protein senses serum calcium levels and stimulates calcitonin release when levels rise via an intracellular, calcium mediated pathway.

7. D

Insulin causes the recruitment of $GLUT_4$ transporters to the surface of cells. The symportation of sodium and glucose into cells helps to drive the sodium/potassium ATPase also located on the cell membrane. Thus, the net effect of glucose and insulin administration is to relocate potassium and glucose intracellularly, while displacing sodium extracellularly.

8. D

Following ovulation, estrogen levels continue to remain elevated in order to maintain the thickness of the endometrial cavity in anticipation of embryo implantation. Progesterone, secreted by the corpus luteum, stimulates gland production within the endometrial lining also in preparation for implantation. During this phase, FSH levels begin to drop and do not play a role in endometrial maturation.

9. C

Glucocorticoids are widely used in medicine to temper inflammatory responses by inhibiting leukocyte movement and blood flow to the sight of injury. In addition, glucocorticoids increase the metabolism of proteins, fats and carbohydrates in the body in order to prepare to fight off stress and/or infection. Thus, blood sugar levels increase in response to elevated glucocorticoid levels and exacerbate hyperglycemia in poorly controlled diabetics. Pancreatic beta cell destruction occurs early in type I diabetes via an autoimmune process. Increased muscle mass is a side effect of anabolic steroid administration.

10. D

Thyroid hormone is a permissive hormone, in that it allows normal cellular function to occur and regulates systemic parameters such as basal metabolic rate and energy utilization of cells. Growth hormone a hormone required for growth of individual tissues as well as the body during development and childhood and thus directs utilization of body fuels including glucose. Estrogen is a hormone necessary for development and maintenance of secondary female sex characteristics as well as female fertility. It does not have a direct effect on glucose utilization in the body.

11. C

Iodine is halogen commonly found in seawater, which gets concentrated in the thyroid and incorporated into thyroid hormone. Thus, radioactive iodine (which emits beta particles that destroy tissue) can be employed to reduce the number of cells producing thyroid hormone, effectively treating some forms of hyperthyroidism.

12. D

Norepinephrine is made in parts of the brain, as well as in the presynaptic terminals of sympathetic nerves and in the adrenal medulla in response to stress requiring a physiologic adaptation. It is mainly in the adrenal medulla where phenylethanolamine N-methyltransferase converts norepinephrine into epinephrine. This also occurs at a lesser extent in the synaptic terminals that rely on norepinephrine as a neurotransmitter. It is not synthesized in the brain.

13. B

Estrogen and progesterone made from the placenta after the first trimester negatively feeds back on the anterior pituitary and prevents FSH and LH from being secreted, thus preventing ovulation and menstruation. The placenta does not secrete testosterone. Beta-HCG from the fetus is responsible for maintaining the corpus luteum in the first trimester of pregnancy. The uterine lining does not secrete estrogen at any point.

14. A

Parkinson's disease is characterized by a lack of dopaminergic neurons in the substantia nigra, leading to difficulty with movement and balance. Symptoms can be mimicked by use of anti-dopaminergic drugs such as typical anti psychotic medications. Dopamine negatively regulates secretion of prolactin from the anterior pituitary so dopamine antagonism would result in unstimulated lactogenesis. Dopamine can also increase blood pressure and is commonly used in emergency resuscitation.

15. B

Hyperaldosteronism is the presence of elevated aldosterone levels that are resistant to a negative feedback mechanism, usually from a source outside of the adrenal cortex. Aldosterone is a potassium-wasting entity in that it stimulates sodium retention and potassium excretion in the kidney. Increased sodium retention causes reflexive water retention and a relative increase in blood pressure. Elevated aldosterone does suppress the renin-angiotensin system and so one would expect low levels of angiotensin II in response to hyperaldosteronism.

16. B

TRH is made by hypothalamus and acts on the anterior pituitary to secrete TSH. TSH acts on receptors in the thyroid gland to secrete T_4 and to a lesser extent, T_3, which exists as bound and free form in the blood. Primary hyperthyroidism (A) is an isolated increase in thyroid hormone (T_4 and/or T_3) which feeds back to the hypothalamus and diminishes TRH secretion. Secondary hyperthyroidism (B) is an elevation in TSH levels causing an increase in thyroid hormone. TRH is once again suppressed by the negative feedback mechanism. Tertiary hyperthyroidism (C) is characterized by an elevated secretion of TRH from the hypothalamus. Primary hypothyroidism (D) would be evidenced by depressed thyroid hormone levels.

17. C

Estrogen exposure in a pre pubertal female would result in premature breast development. Since androgens and progesterone are not yet being synthesized by the body, one is unlikely to have a menstrual period (stimulated by a combination of estrogen and progesterone), axillary hair (stimulated by androgens), or coordinated uterine contractions (stimulated by progesterone).

18. D

Long-term daily administration of progesterone suppresses the hypothalamic-pituitary-ovarian axis, and in most cases, prevents estrogen secretion and thus ovulation. Ovulation may still occur in some cases. Thus, progesterone's effect on cervical mucus and the endometrial lining provide its main contraceptive benefit. Much like progesterone secretion following ovulation in a normal cycle, progesterone thickens cervical mucus to prevent the migration of sperm and causes a thickened endometrium to prepare for implantation. Without estrogen, however, the endometrial lining is not hospitable to a developing embryo and would not allow implantation.

19. D

While PTH acts on many sites in the body to increase serum calcium levels, it primarily uses calcium stored in bone. Calcium is not stored in the mucosal cells of the intestines as it is absorbed from food. PTH secretion is triggered by low serum calcium levels and is inhibited via a negative feedback loop.

HIGH-YIELD SIMILAR QUESTIONS

Menstrual Cycle

1. FSH is inhibited early in the follicular phase in order to prevent the development of multiple follicles.

2. Early in the follicular phase estrogen has a negative feedback on the anterior pituitary and prevents the release of FSH and LH. Late in the follicular phase (around day 12) estrogen has a positive feedback effect on the anterior pituitary and stimulates FSH and LH. Estrogen stimulates the LH surge which results in ovulation.

3. Ovulation can be prevented by manipulating the hormones involved in the menstrual cycle.

Birth control pills keep estrogen and progesterone levels high so that FSH and LH are inhibited. Because of this inhibition a follicle does not develop and the LH surge does not occur therefore preventing ovulation.

CHAPTER 12: NERVOUS SYSTEM

1. B

The other choices are all functions of myelin.

2. A

There is much more sodium outside of the cell than in it, which explains why there's an influx of sodium when the voltage gated sodium channels are opened. Therefore, E would be positive. (B), (C), and (D) are thus wrong.

3. C

The postsynaptic potential initiated at the cell body does proceed in all directions, including down towards the dendrites. While it may be true that action potential propagation is typically unidirectional because of the refractory periods of action potentials, this is not true of postsynaptic potentials that initiate the action potential at the axon hillock. (A) is a true statement when defining a "requisite" amount to be sufficient for action potential (not postsynaptic potential) propagation. (B) is wrong because myelin only speeds up the signal with a minimal loss of signal at the axon.

4. C

Pupil constriction does not occur during a sympathetic, flight-or-fight response, while all the other answer choices do.

5. B

Redirection of blood from digestive tract to muscles is activated in a sympathetic response. The other answer choices are all parasympathetic responses.

6. D

Once you see that (D) is correct, you would have been able to eliminate (B) regardless of your knowledge of interneurons.

7. A

At the beginning of the ascent, voltage-gated sodium channels begin to open while potassium channels stay closed and open later after some delay. A little time before the peak, potassium channels begin to open as sodium channels begin to inactivate. During the descent, more potassium channels open to repolarize while more sodium channels are inactivated.

8. B

(A), (C), and (D) are all reasonable conclusions.

9. A

The neurotransmitter is packaged inside the vesicles of the presynaptic neuron before it is released after the action potential reaches the voltage-gated calcium channels. Then, the neurotransmitter is released from the vesicle and presynaptic neuron into the synaptic cleft, where it binds to the receptors of the postsynaptic neuron. The receptors determine the excitatory or inhibitory nature of the postsynaptic response.

10. C

The iris gives eyes their color.

11. C

The fovea is the most likely area of injury due to the fovea having the role of relaying acute vision input as well as because it is the area of the retina which contains mostly cones.

12. B

Because sodium channels open faster in cardiac muscle, the potential rises steeply. The potassium channels opening slower also accounts for the less dramatic repolarization/downward-sloping.

13. A

Schwann cells are glial cells that provide myelination to the neurons. They essentially wrap themselves around the axons. Astrocytes are phagocytic cells within the central nervous system. Lymphocytes are peripheral immunocytes. Leukocytes are the broader category of immunocytes that not only include lymphocytes, but also granulocytes.

14. C

The ectoderm gives rise to the central nervous system. Remember that the retina is also a component of the central nervous system, so defects in the ectoderm may led to defects in the retina.

15. B

TPA will inhibit the Na/K pump. This will not affect the influx of Na or the efflux of K in the neuron. However, it will inhibit and retard (possibly cease) the return to resting potential. Hence, once the neuron fires, exciting the muscle fiber and inducing contraction, there will be an inability to relax afterward.

HIGH-YIELD SIMILAR QUESTIONS

Action Potential

1. At the highest point of the curve.

2. An action potential is all or nothing and therefore the speed of an action potential cannot be increased. Information coded in action potentials can be altered by the frequency of action potentials, but not by altering the speed of one action potential.

3. When a membrane is hyperpolarized it is further from threshold and would require a larger stimulus to create an action potential. Therefore hyperpolarizing a membrane would be a way to inhibit an action potential. Action potentials are also inhibited during the absolute refractory period, which occurs during an action potential.

CHAPTER 13: GENETICS

1. C

The probability that the man is a carrier of the disease gene is 50 percent. Based on the information given, Tay-Sachs disease can be either X-linked or autosomal recessive. Tay-Sachs is actually autosomal recessive and, therefore, his dead brother was homozygous recessive. That means the dead brother received a copy of a recessive allele from each parent. It can be concluded that both parents are heterozygous because, first, they must both have one recessive allele given the homozygous recessive requirement of the disease, and second, they cannot be homozygous because they would not survive past age six to reproduce. During a mating of two heterozygous individuals, the probability of having a heterozygous child is 50 percent.

2. B

Crossing-over occurs during prophase I of the meiotic division, when homologous chromosomes attach at chiasma and can exchange genetic material. During anaphase I, chiasma disappear and homologus chromosomes are pulled to opposite poles of the cell. During telophase I, two haploid daughter cells are formed. During anaphase II, single chromatids are pulled towards the opposite poles of the cell.

3. A

The probability of crossing-over will increase the farther the genes are located on the chromosome. The other answer choices contradict this statement. The number of genes on a chromosome does not affect the rate of crossing-over.

4. C

The only way a type I (O) mother can have children with blood types II (A) and III (B) is if the father has a type IV (AB) blood type. That way, the father can pass an allele for antigen A or an allele for antigen B which would determine the blood type of a child. A father of blood type II (A) does not have an allele for antigen B and thus cannot have a child with blood type III. A father of blood type III (B) does not have an allele for antigen A and thus cannot have a child with blood type II.

5. C

The gene encoding the ABO blood system has three primary alleles (A, B, and O) which can combine in different combinations responsible for the four blood types.

6. D

A donor with type III (B) blood has antigen B and anti-A antibodies, while the receiver with blood type II (A) has antigen A and anti-B antibodies. The agglutination reaction occurs between the antigens of the donor and the antibodies of a receiver. In this case, antigens B will clump with anti-B antibodies.

7. A

Each birth is an independent event, so the probability of a boy is 50 percent no matter how many boys were born earlier.

8. C

The question is asking to identify a test cross represented by a mating of the subject being tested with a homozygous recessive individual. Then if the black dog is heterozygous, there would be a 50 percent chance of progeny with the recessive color of the coat (homozygous recessive). In mating with a homozygous dominant individual, 100 percent of the progeny would be black, not helping the verification. In mating with another heterozygote, there is only 25 percent probability of seeing a different color progeny if the dog is not purebred.

9. B

The question asks you to determine the probability of a phenotypically (homozygous dominant or heterozygous) healthy child if both parents are heterozygotes. According to Punnett square analysis the probability is 75 percent. Fifty percent is the probability of having only heterozygous children. Twenty-five percent is the probability of having homozygous dominant children.

10. A

Penetrance gives the fraction of individuals who, while having a disease allele, will develop the disease. Only (A) is consistent with this explanation.

11. D

(D) is correct because pleiotropy is the condition when one gene has multiple phenotypic effects, as in this case. Full penetrance would mean that 100 percent of the population carrying the defective allele develops the disease. Codominance means that heterozygotes display the in-between phenotype when compared to homozygous dominant and homozygous recessive individuals. Imprinting explains the differences in phenotypes depending whether the mutation is of maternal or paternal origin.

12. A

Trisomy 21 is a result of nondisjunction, a condition where homologous chromosomes do not separate during meiotic division, and one of the gametes receives an extra copy of a chromosome resulting in three instead of two chromosomes. Other causes of mutations generally refer to nucleotide addition-insertion, elimination-deletion, reverse nucleotide sequence-inversion, making other answer choices wrong.

13. D

If a homozygous recessive man marries a heterozygous woman there is a 50 percent chance that each child is affected. To find out the probability that all four children are affected, use the multiplication rule for statistical probability: $(1/2)^4 = 1/16$.

14. C

If sons are affected by the X-linked recessive disorder, they must have received the disease allele from the mother, because the father must have provided a Y-chromosome in order for the offspring to be a son. Thus the mother has to have at least one mutant allele, making (B) and (D) wrong. It is not possible exclude the possibility that 50 percent of boys would be affected. This is due to the fact that there are not enough children to rule out the possibility of a heterozygous mother. The best answer is (C).

15. B

The pedigree shows an autosomal recessive mode of inheritance because phenotypically normal parents (carriers) have about a 25 percent probability of an affected child. Generally, one generation is skipped. In an autosomal dominant mode of inheritance one would expect to see much more affected children. In the case of an X-linked recessive disorder, only males are generally affected, and on the pedigree shown none of the males are affected. Mitochondrial inheritance transmits the disease through the mother's alleles, and all the offspring of an affected mother would be affected, which is in a disagreement with the pedigree shown.

16. C

The daughter in generation two is affected and has to be heterozygous because her mother (generation I) was homozygous recessive. The father in generation II is normal and has to be homozygous recessive. As a result, the test cross in generation II of a heterozygous and a homozygous recessive individual results in a 50 percent chance of having an affected child (heterozygote).

17. C

In mitochondrial inheritance all offspring of affected females have a disorder due to the fact that there are no mitochondria passed to the children from their fathers, because the female egg contains the cytoplasm of the zygote, while the sperm provides only genetic material. Thus, condition I is correct. Part of the explanation depends on the cytoplasmic location of a mitochondrion; condition III is correct. There is no information provided to conclude that this is an X-linked condition; condition II is wrong.

18. D

A mother in generation I has to be a carrier to have two sons affected, because the disorder is X-linked recessive, affecting mostly males when both parents are phenotypically normal (mother is a carrier). The disorder cannot be dominantly X-linked because the mothers would be affected as well. This is not an autosomal recessive condition because one would not expect to see the predominance of either sex in the children affected, and the probability of children with the condition would be smaller (25 percent in the second generation). The father in generation II cannot be a carrier as the disorder is X-linked, and the father can either be affected or have a healthy genotype.

19. D

An extra chromosome 18 is an example of trisomy. It is a specific case of aneuploidy, a condition where the chromosomal number is not a multiple of 23. Triploidy refers to three full sets of chromosomes or 69 chromosomes. Polyploidy refers to numerous sets of chromosomes n × 23. Monosomy is a lack of one of the chromosomes in a pair.

20. C

The frequency of the disorder genotype is 1/10000. According to the Hardy-Weinberg principle, the frequency of the disease allele is the square root of 1/10000 or 0.01. Thus, the frequency of a healthy allele is 1 – 0.01 = 0.99.

HIGH-YIELD SIMILAR QUESTIONS

Genetics

1. Yes, as long as she had at least one child

2. 100%, 0%

3. 25%, 6.25% (presuming BO and AO genotypes)

CHAPTER 14: MOLECULAR GENETICS

1. B

A DNA primer is a short strand of DNA with a complementary sequence to a specific DNA sequence. Adenine matches with thymine, and guanine matches with cytosine. In the DNA double helix the strands are antiparallel, meaning they run in *opposite directions*. Standard notation requires writing from 5′ to 3′. Choice (B) is the only answer choice that obeys these rules. (A) is complementary to the sequence but not antiparallel. (C) is the same sequence as the target and is therefore not complementary.

2. D

RNA sequences can bind to specific complementary DNA sequences. However, in the case of RNA, thymine is replaced with uracil. Thefore, adenine matches with uracil, and guanine matches with cytosine. Just as with DNA primers, the RNA strand and its complementary DNA sequence will run antiparallel to each other. Given these rules, (D) is the only choice that fits. (A) describes the complementary DNA sequence. (B) and (C) are complementary but not antiparallel to the DNA sequence.

3. A

Point mutations exchange a single nucleotide for another. In the case of a point mutation in an intron, these mutations can usually have one of three possible effects: a nonsense mutation, a silent mutation, or a mutation that affects a splice site. Splicing, otherwise known as post-transcriptional processing, normally results in specific modifications to RNA products, usually involving the removal of introns and joining of exons. This process occurs in the cell's nucleus.

4. D

A point mutation results in the replacement of a single base nucleotide with another nucleotide. A frame-shift insertion involves the addition of one or more nucleotides, shifting the reading frame. A frame-shift deletion removes one or more nucleotides, shifting the reading frame. Each of these can introduce a premature stop codon.

5. C

Because host cell DNA polymerase is found only in the nucleus and mitochondrion, varicella virus, along with other DNA viruses that replicate in the cytoplasm, encodes for its own DNA polymerase.

6. D

While eukaryotic and prokaryotic DNA polymerases both have 3′ → 5′ polymerase activity, only Prokaryotic DNA polymerases have 5′ → 3′ exonuclease activity, a process used to remove primers. In eukaryotes, this is taken care of by specific RNase enzymes. Some eukaryotic DNA polymerases do have 3′ → 5′ exonuclease activity, which is used in proofreading and mismatch repair.

7. C

All eukaryotic DNA synthesis requires a primer. DNA synthesis involves the connection of the

5′ phosphate group to the 3′ hydroxyl group. DNA synthesis always occurs in the 3′ → 5′ direction.

8. A

The eukaryotic start codon codes for methionine. While some proteins undergo post-translation modification to remove the methionine, all proteins will have methionine as the first amino acid translated. The N-terminus is the beginning of a peptide chain and consists of a free amine group (–NH$_2$). The C-terminus is the end of a peptide chain and consists of a carboxyl group (–COOH)

9. C

Helicase is responsible for unwinding the DNA double helix, one of the first steps in initiating DNA synthesis. Topoisomerase acts to prevent tension from building up in the helix as it is unwound.

10. B

An insertion involves the addition of one or more basepairs to a sequence. A nonsense mutation A is a mutation that introduces a premature stop codon into a sequence. A frame-shift C changes the reading frame by adding or removing a multiple of one or two basepairs, shifting the reading frame. A silent mutation D involves the substitution of a basepair so that the sequence still codes for the same amino acid.

11. D

Ultraviolet ray exposure via sunlight can result in DNA damage (formation of pyramidine dimmers). Depending on the extent of the damage, a DNA repair pathway can be induced. Sunlight exposure can cause somatic cell DNA damage but does not result in germ cell damage.

12. D

Thymine and cytosine are pyramidines. Adenine and guanine are purines. The only purine-purine

or pyramidine-pyramidine substitution listed is cytosine to thymine.

13. A

Macrolide antibiotics interfere with ribosomal translocation, which is necessary for peptide elongation. (B), (C), and (D) occur prior to ribosomal translocation.

HIGH-YIELD SIMILAR QUESTIONS

DNA Transcription

1. 3′–UAGGGUACGUACCUA–5′

2. The following segments will be produced:
    5′–CUUAUGGUCAUCAUAAACG–3′
    5′–GCUACUGAUCAAUCG–3′
    5′–GCAAUCG–3′

DNA Replication

1. 5′–ACGAGCTATGCTACTATATG–3′ (the same as the original strand)

2. 25% posses an unlabeled strand from the original DNA sample.

CHAPTER 15: EVOLUTION

1. B

Darwin believed that random genetic mutation, in combination with natural selection, is the basis of evolution. He believed, then, that chance was a component of evolution. Lamark, conversely, believed that traits are actively acquired. He believed animals "acquired" traits by using them more than others, and not by chance.

2. A

Punctuated equilibrium is an evolutionary theory that states that most populations experience very little change throughout their histories, and when change does occur, it occurs in relatively short and rapid burst. Darwin's theory of evolution and natural selection states that genes that improve the reproductive success of the organism will increase in frequency over time. Lamark's theory of acquired characteristics states that the frequency of genes that organisms use often in their lifetime will increase over time. Differential reproduction states that gene frequencies in a population change over time as a result of certain individuals in a population producing offspring than other individuals in that population, therefore passing on their genes more often.

3. C

Radiometric dating works on the principle that a given radioisotope decays at a consistent rate, unaffected by environmental factors. Elements can have many different isotopes; that is, an identical number of protons but different number of neutrons. Radioisotopes are isotopes that spontaneously decay, or, in other words, transform into a different isotope. The half-life of a radioisotope is the rate at which this decay occurs. Carbon-14 dating is radiometric dating specific to living organisms. It works on the principle that while animals and plants are alive, they breathe in carbon-14 through CO_2 in the atmosphere. Because their bodies stop incorporating carbon-14 once they pass away, measuring the stage of decay of carbon-14 in organic remains can tell us how much time has passed since an organism died. The one caveat with carbon-14 dating is that carbon has a short half-life of only 5,730 years; therefore, it is useful to measure time for around only 60,000 years. In this example, the bird fossil has been dated to 200,000 b.c. through reliable stratigraphic analysis. Carbon-14 data is invalid in such cases.

4. A

Founder's effect refers to an evolutionary phenomenon in which a small number of individuals with rare genetic traits become isolated from their pop-

ulation, and their descendants form a population with a high concentration of those traits. The swallows on Tree Island and on Juvialand are the same species. Any sexual selection (B) should exert the same effects, rather than produce two starkly different populations. Likewise, any natural selection (C) for red feathers over black feathers is unlikely; if that were the case, one would expect the swallows on Juvialand to have higher concentrations of red feathers. Codominance (D) is used incorrectly in this context; it refers to a sharing of dominance between two gene phenotypes. Codominance between a red feather color gene and a black feather color gene, for instance, refers to equal and simultaneous expression of the genes, producing a mixture of both colors.

5. A

The Bottleneck effect simply refers to the general isolation of a number of individuals from a population, which results in a change of gene frequencies in that population. This isolation could be caused by any number of factors: death, movement, disease, environmental change, and so on. The Founder effect is a specific instance of this; it refers to a bottleneck event caused by displacement of a small group of the population. Genetic drift (D) is a chance change in allele frequencies from generation to generation, and not a genetic frequency change due to a specific event. Genetic drift does not cause a major change in the characteristics of an organism. Note the contrast with genetic *shift*, which can drastically alter the phenotypic characteristics of the organism, resulting, for instance, in increased virulence.

6. D

Analogous structures are similar structures found in two species that evolved in parallel due to similar environmental or evolutionary pressures. (Homologous structures, on the other hand, are similar structures found in two species that result from a common ancestral line and genetic background.) If the red bird is a descendant of the blue bird, then its wings are homologous to the blue bird's wings. In (A), (B), and (C), the two birds do not share a common ancestor and thus the characteristic would be considered analogous.

7. D

Polyphyletic groups are groups that do not include a common ancestor. The group composed of Z and B does not include a common ancestor. Monophyletic groups (B) include a common ancestor and all of its descendants. Paraphyletic groups (A) include a common ancestor but not all of the descendants of that ancestor. Parsimonious (C) means that when constructing a cladogram to represent evolutionary relationships between species, the simplest possible cladogram is also the most likely.

8. C

Natural selection would simultaneously select for very small gophers adept at hiding in small crevices, as well as very large gophers able to intimidate the squirrels. This would cause the gopher population to evolve into two opposite extremes for the size trait; this is called disruptive selection. Stabilizing selection (A) is the opposite; it refers to evolutionary forces that favor middle-of-the-road incarnations of a trait, preventing a population from moving toward either extreme of a trait. Directional selection (B) refers to evolutionary forces that move the population toward one gene extreme. Finally, Hardy-Weinberg equilibrium (D) refers to an environment in which gene frequencies and gene ratios are stable and remain constant.

9. B

The ratio of allele A and allele B should equal 100 percent, which means their frequencies should add up to 1.

10. B

Small populations (A) are less likely to remain in Hardy-Weinberg equilibrium because they are more susceptible to random variations in allele frequencies or genetic drift. Migration (C) means that the gene pool is not in a stable state. The different populations could, for instance, be under slightly different selective pressures, and migration between populations would prevent an equilibrium. If increased mating were associated with specific traits (D), that would confer a reproductive advantage on those traits, thus changing the gene frequency. Only (B) is correct: When all genes in a population offer the same reproductive advantage, then no gene will be favored by natural selection and frequencies will remain constant.

11. C

A monophyletic group is by definition a single species and all of its descendants. Thus, species A and species B must be descendants of a common ancestor. While it's likely both species' beaks are homlogous structures (A), we cannot determine this conclusively. It is possible that somewhere in the ancestral line between species A and B, beaks disappeared and re-appeared analogously. For this same reason, we cannot conclusively determine that (B) is true.

12. A

Simply based on condition iii, you can deduce that only (A) is possible. Monophyletic groups contain a single species and all its descendents. Only in species A is this true of condition iii. Furthermore, condition i is true for all answer choices except for (C). Paraphyletic refers to a group sharing common ancestors, but the group does not have to include all descendants. Polyphyletic refers to a group of individuals that do not share a common ancestor.

13. C

(A) is true: Even though the two species share a common ancestor, on the evolutionary path from species A to species M, the trait was lost and then regained. Thus, it was not genetically passed on as a common ancestory normally suggests. (B) is also true: I and A are direct descendants of one another and they both have the wing trait. (D) is also true: D and G share the no-wing trait as well as a common ancestor.

14. C

The founder effect results from the isolation of a genetically abnormal subset of a larger population, causing a population to evolve with starkly different genetic frequencies from the original population. The founder effect causes one species to evolve in different directions.

15. A

Adaptive radiation refers to a diversifying lineage in response to an increase in environmental and ecological diversity. The density of population (D) is irrelevant.

16. B

Assortative mating is a phenomenon in which individuals show a preference for mates who are similar to themselves in some respect: size, color, and so on. This phenomenon has the evolutionary effect of decreasing the range of variation or trait variance.

17. C

The bottleneck effect refers to an evolutionary event that causes a large proportion of a population to be killed off or isolated from the rest. Graph C best illustrates a drop in population.

18. C

The group selection theory states that certain individuals are altruistic and will act to the detriment of their own reproductive success for the benefit of the group's overall reproductive success. This theory has been invalidated and replaced by the theory of kin selection., which claims that when individuals act altruistically, it is in fact indirectly favorable to individual reproductive success. Individuals only sacrifice direct reproductive success when it significantly increases indirect reproductive success via their kin who share many of the same genes. Inclusive fitness (A) refers to the sum of an individual's direct and indirect fitness.

19. C

Hardy-Weinberg equilibrium is a state in which genotypic frequencies of the population are not changing. If p represents frequency of allele 1 and q represents frequency of allele 2, then the frequency of the AA genotype should be p^2, while the frequency of the aa genotype should be q^2. Finally, the frequency of the Aa genotype should be $q \times p$, and the frequency of the aA genotype should be $p \times q$. The frequencies of these three genotype frequencies of one gene should add up to one. Therefore, at Hardy-Weinberg equilibrium, the following formula is true:

$$p^2 + 2pq + q^2 = 1$$

In this question supposing p represents allele A, and q represents allele B, then it follows that $p = 80\% = 0.80$ and $q = 20\% = 0.20$.

The frequency of recessive homozygotes, then, is $q^2 = 0.20^2 = 0.04 = 4\%$.

The frequency of dominant heterozygotes, then, is $2pq = 2 \times 0.20 \times 0.80 = 32\%$.

HIGH-YIELD SIMILAR QUESTIONS

Hardy-Weinberg

1. frequency of the recessive allele = 0.021; frequency of the dominant allele = 0.979; number of heterozygotes in the population = 8305 people

2. frequency of XX = 0.04; frequency of Xx = 0.32; frequency of xx = 0.64

3. 84% of individuals are phenotypically normal (assuming that the phenotype coded for by the dominant allele is "normal")

PRACTICE SECTION 1

ANSWER KEY

1. A	19. D	36. A
2. D	20. D	37. B
3. A	21. A	38. A
4. C	22. D	39. D
5. C	23. A	40. D
6. B	24. D	41. C
7. C	25. B	42. C
8. C	26. B	43. B
9. A	27. D	44. B
10. B	28. C	45. D
11. A	29. A	46. B
12. B	30. D	47. D
13. B	31. D	48. B
14. D	32. A	49. C
15. D	33. B	50. A
16. B	34. B	51. A
17. A	35. A	52. A
18. B		

PASSAGE I

1. A

The null hypothesis is a hypothesis designed such that if it is refuted, then the actual hypothesis must be true. (B), (C), and (D) all present null hypotheses that if rejected, do not invalidate the actual hypothesis that hermit crab shell choice is influenced by color. If (B) is shown to be false, hermit crabs could prefer shells with the starkest color difference from their environment, and thus would still display color preference. If (C) is shown to be false, hermit crabs could prefer shells with the least color difference from their environment, and thus would still display color preference. If (D) is shown to be false, hermit crabs could prefer lighter-colored shells in certain instances, in which case color preference would still be an influence.

2. D

If the black paint was not actually black in practice, but a dark gray, this would not nullify the hypothesis that hermit crabs show shell preference based on color cues. There is still a color difference between the white shells and the dark-gray shells.

3. A

According to the data, the hermit crabs do choose the black shells over the white shells at a statistically significant rate, suggesting a preference for color. While in this particular experimental setup the hermit crabs always prefer the black shells, the experiment does not prove that this is always the case. For instance, the crabs could be choosing the black shells to stand out on the substrate such that their kin can find them easily. Perhaps on black substrate they would prefer white shells. It is also possible that they are choosing black shells because their natural environment is black. However, neither of these statements were proved conclusively in the experiment. It only demonstrates that a basic preference based on color.

4. C

(A), (B), and (D) present scenarios in which the visual cue—color—would affect hermit crab reproductive success. (C), however, presents a scenario in which color does not confer any advantage or disadvantage. Because hermit crabs show a preference for certain colors in the experiment, this suggests that certain colors confer reproductive advantages.

5. C

The experiment shows that crabs prefer dark-colored shells on white substrate, suggesting some kind of reproductive advantage for dark-colored shells in this environment. One would therefore expect evolutionary forces to select for crabs with dark shells in an environment of pure-white rocks, moving crabs in the direction of dark shells. Based on the experiment, one would also expect evolutionary forces to select for crabs with white shells in an environment of pure-black rocks. As evolutionary forces push the hermit crabs to fill different environmental niches, you will see selection in two opposite directions, also known as disruptive selection.

6. B

These findings do not strongly support the hypothesis that shell color affects hermit crab shell choice because the findings do not offer any indication as to why the crab population died out. Nor are the crabs in this population presented with a choice between different colored environments or shells. These findings do not conflict with the hypothesis either. Again, no evidence of preference or indifference to shell color is presented. Finally, the fact that the hermit crabs are not native to Jordan may suggest that the environment was likely suboptimal in many ways. However, it does not invalidate the fact that hermit crabs use color to help choose new shells.

7. C

Because these two species of hermit crabs are monophyletic, that means they share a common ancestor. As the species of hermit crabs used in the experiment show a strong preference for shells based on color, we can conclude that they are not colorblind. The trait must have arisen spontaneously in the second hermit crab species, or it must have been lost spontaneously in the first. In either case, because the trait is not shared between the two species, it can be neither analogous nor homologous. An analogous trait refers to a shared trait that arose separately through parallel evolutionary forces. A homologus trait refers to a shared trait that arose from shared genetic lines. (C), then, could be possible. The founder effect refers to new selective pressures affecting a population introduced to a new environment, which cause it to deviate from the rest of the species.

PASSAGE II

8. C

The disease allele is most likely recessive. While neither parent expresses the condition, one of the children is affected. In a dominant condition, one parent (at least) would need to be affected. There is no information in the text or pedigree to suggest codominance or a sex-linked trait. In the case of X-linked recessive inheritance, males are generally affected and that is not seen in this case.

9. A

If male 7, who is affected, marries a carrier, 50 percent of offspring would be affected and 50 percent would be carriers. A healthy noncarrier child cannot be born. It can be seen that male 7 is affected looking at the gel analysis. Male 7 has the same marker as an affected female 3 and no other marker to be heterozygous. It also makes sense as a smaller fragment with disease allele (due to deletion) migrates faster through the gel.

10. B

Expressivity, a term that refers to the degree of disease severity observed in affected individuals, varies according to the passage. It is mentioned that while some patients have mild respiratory difficulties, others have serious problems.

11. A

A mutation leading to cystic fibrosis can be classified as a deletion, as it results in a loss of three nucleotides. Inversion (C) would not change the number of nucleotides and would only affect their sequence. Insertion (D) would increase the number of nucleotides. Nondisjunction (B) refers to a failure of chromosomes to separate during meiosis; it does not deal with nucleotides.

12. B

Male 7 is homozygous recessive according to the gel electrophoresis results.

13. B

The fourth member alone is neither affected nor carrying a disease allele. On the gel, he has a larger fragment which migrated more slowly than the disease allele-containing fragment. It is the only fragment present, pointing to a homozygous condition.

14. D

A DNA fragment containing the disease allele would be shorter due to the deletion leading to cystic fibrosis; thus, it would move faster through the gel.

15. D

A mutation responsible for cystic fibrosis results in a deletion of three nucleotides. A nonsense mutation (B) introduces a stop code prematurely into the DNA sequence. A missense mutation (A) replaces one nucleotide with another, changing the peptide sequence of the encoded protein. A silent mutation (C) changes one of the nucleotides without affecting the type of amino acid in a sequence.

16. B

The frequency of the disease genotype is 1/100. The frequency of the disease allele, according to the Hardy-Weinberg principle, is the square root of 1/100 or 0.1.

17. A

Family member 5 is a carrier, as she has two types of DNA fragments: one for the wild type and one for the mutant allele. If member 5 marries another carrier, ¼ of their offspring on average will be affected.

QUESTIONS 18–21

18. B

(A) is a misuse of a detail; both rheumatic fever and type I diabetes occur initially in young populations, but co-occurence does not imply a similar etiology. (C) is a distortion; the specific hypersensitivity mechanism that causes rheumatic fever is cross-reactivity, where the immune system mistakes a body tissue for a foreign substance because they look similar. In an allergic reaction, the body has a response against a foreign substance that is too severe. In (D), although rheumatic fever causes a structural problem in the heart, the type of lesion mentioned in the passage occurs after infection, not at birth.

19. D

The question is intended to distract you with enzyme names that might seem intimidating. Nevertheless, the concept is simple: A kinase, when activated, phosphorylates its substrate. If the substrate is a metabolic enzyme, then this phosphorylation will take place at an allosteric site. Because this action activates PFK-1, the indicated process is an example of allosteric activation. (A) and (C) are wrong because the process causes an activation or agonistic effect, not an inactivation or antagonistic effect. Synergism (B) would require more than one enzyme with the same substrate to be present. This question presents two enzymes with different substrates.

20. D

The suffix kinase indicates that the function of the enzyme is to phosphorylate not isomerizes, thus eliminating (C). (A) is wrong because the indicated reaction does not occur. (B) is wrong because the indicated conversion would require two enzymes: an isomerase to convert glucose to fructose and a kinase to add the second phosphate group.

21. A

This question tests your ability to paraphrase the question and see the concept through the details. A good paraphrase is: Under what conditions does the breakdown of glucose stop with glycolysis and not proceed to form intermediates of the Krebs cycle? Since oxygen is the final electron acceptor of the electron transport chain, one could predict that low levels of oxygen would prevent aerobic metabolism. This is true and the accumulated pyruvate is converted to lactate under such conditions. (B) indicates a high concentration of oxidized substrates, implying an abundance of oxygen. (C) is wrong because while this would signal for an increase in the rate of glycolysis, it gives no information as to the oxygen levels of the cell and thus the ability of the cell to proceed into aerobic respiration. (D) is wrong because low levels of fructose-1,6-bisphosphate initiate the signal for gluconeogenesis, a separate metabolic pathway.

PASSAGE III

22. D

The passage describes that protons (H^+) are pumped across inner mitochondrial membrane into the intermembrane space making the intermembrane space more positive when compared to the matrix. pH drops in the intermembrane space as the proton concentration increases when compared to the matrix of mitochondria. (A) and (B) are only half right, and (C) is opposite the correct answer.

23. A

You're asked to choose one of the results that cannot be observed upon administration of antimycin A. According to the table, antimycin A blocks step 4 of the electron transport chain. The first figure shows that blocking step 4 will prevent the passage of electrons from cytochrome b to cytochrome c in the electron transport chain. As electrons don't travel further than cytochrome b, oxygen cannot remain the final acceptor of electrons (step 6 of ETC) and the transport is stopped at step 4 (choice A). (B) is wrong, as antimycin A indeed decreases the proton gradient, because when electrons travel only part of the transport chain less protons are pumped to the mitochondrial intermembrane space. This can be inferred from the passage that describes the buildup of proton gradient as electrons are passed from carrier to carrier. (C) is wrong: ATP synthesis is indeed stopped as the electrons never reach the final acceptor oxygen and the gradient would be lower than needed for ATP synthesis. This is inferred from the passage that mentions the specific gradient required. (D) is wrong as cytochrome b is indeed fully reduced and it can no longer pass its electrons to cytochrome c.

24. D

You're asked to use information in the passage and figures to determine which of the inhibitors will stop ATP synthesis without affecting the proton gradient. The table shows that oligomycin blocks the action of ATP synthase, which is responsible for ATP production. At the same time, as oligomycin does not affect any of the carriers in the chain, the electron gradient would be established and could not be dissipated as ATP synthase does not work (D). Choices (B) and (C) are wrong because both inhibitors interfere with electron transport along the chain, making the proton gradient less, even though ATP synthesis will come to a halt. (A) is wrong as 2, 4-dinitrophenol makes the inner mitochondrial membrane more permeable to protons that can escape from the intermembrane space back into the matrix without building up the gradient.

25. B

The question asks you to identify inhibitors that will interfere with the transport of electrons along the chain so that the final electron acceptor oxygen cannot receive electrons. Inhibitors listed in items II and III alone will interfere with the electron transport chain, while oligomycin does not disrupt the chain of carriers and blocks ATP synthase directly.

26. B

The question asks you to suggest what happens when the permeability of the inner mitochondrial membrane is increased. As the passage addresses the importance of building up a proton gradient across impermeable inner membrane, it can be inferred that if protons are allowed to pass, they will escape the intermembrane space—thus, decreasing the gradient. For (C), a lower proton gradient would decrease ATP synthesis, not increase ATP production.

27. D

The passage explains that, as protons pass through the ATP synthase into the mitochondrial matrix, ATP is made. As ADP and phosphates are needed for ATP production, it makes sense that they would

be present in mitochondrial matrix. (A) is wrong because, as per the passage, ATP synthase is a transmembrane enzyme complex and embedded into the membrane, and thus not in the mitochondrial matrix.

28. C

Rotenone will not produce a fully reduced cytochrome a, as rotenone disrupts step 2 of ETC and electrons don't go beyond FMN, leaving cytochrome a oxidized. (A), (B), and (D) interfere with step 6 preventing cytochrome a from passing its electrons to oxygen. Thus cytochrome a would be left fully oxidized.

PASSAGE IV

29. A

The presence of pre-existing lung disease could have a negative effect on the inspiratory reserve volume of the individuals in the study. A patient with asthma, an obstructive pulmonary disease, an asbestosis, or a restrictive lung disease would likely have different inspiratory reserve volumes. Tidal volume should not impact this experiment because the amount of drug delivered is the same in each case; we look for radioactivity, not a concentration-dependent phenomenon. Sex will make no difference; male lungs would generally be larger, but the measurements are made per unit of lung tissue. Bronchodilators with zero order kinetics are metabolized independently of their concentration. Because these medications are delivered directly to the lungs and do not undergo metabolism before contacting their target tissue, the kinetics of metabolism will have no bearing on the results.

30. D

IgE is formed as a result of exposure to an allergen. The first time the allergen is present, the body will form IgE, but there will be no signs of allergy.

IgE circulates and 'docks' or 'connects' to mast cells via the Fc region of the antibody. When the antibody comes in contact again with its antigen, a conformation change takes place in the antibody and the mast cell degranulates, resulting in histamine release and contributing to asthma attack.

31. D

The key to this question is knowing that acetylcholine is the primary neurotransmitter of the parasympathetic response. During the parasympathetic response the body is relaxed; the heart rate decreases and blood flow to the gut is increased. Remember parasympathetic is to 'rest and digest.' The sympathetic response, in contrast, comes into play when being chased by a tiger. The body will need great airflow to support running away. An asthma attack, then, is the opposite of a sympathetic response; it causes relative bronchoconstriction. The use of an anticholinergic medication will promote the sympathetic system to open the airways.

32. A

This question just requires summing the values for each column. The largest total will be the most effective, on average, at delivering medication to the lungs.

QUESTIONS 33–35

33. B

Chylomicrons transport fats from the intestines to the circulation. With that, one can predict that with low levels of chlyomicrons, the lipids will not enter circulation (eliminating (C) and (D)) but will pass out with the stool. While diarrhea (A) is always possible in a metabolic disorder, it is not specific to abetalipoproteinemia.

34. B

Replication errors are the least severe if chemical class of the base isn't changed. That is a mutation from a purine to a purine is less severe than a mutation from a purine to a pyrimidine. Using this, we can predict that (B) is true since (A) and (C) involve the change from a purine, A, to a pyrimidine, C or T. (D) is wrong for two reasons: first is, again, a purine change, and second, uracil is found only in RNA. Its inclusion in a strand of DNA would indicate a serious replication error.

35. A

The central dogma of molecular biology is that the genetic information contained in DNA is first transcribed to RNA and then translated to a linear sequence of amino acids which comprise the primary structure of a protein. The central dogma does not make claims to the details of transcription, only that is transferred information between DNA and RNA (B), nor does it tell of the flow of information or the organelle subserving this function (C) and (D).

PASSAGE V

36. A

There are multiple ways with which parietal cells are stimulated to release H^+. (A) G cells, located in antrum of the stomach, releases gastrin. Gastrin thereby will stimulate the cholecystokinin-B (CCKb) receptor. (B) Histamine can stimulate the release of H^+ by activating the H_2 receptors located on the parietal cells. (C) Postganglionic neurons release acetylcholine, which will activate the muscarinic (M3) receptors of the parietal cells, causing an increase in production of H^+. (D) Somatostatin inhibits H^+ secretion.

37. B

There are a few ways that Zollinger-Ellison syndrome can cause malabsorption of dietary lipids. One way is inactivation of pancreatic enzymes. Pancreatic enzymes are inactivated at acidic pH. With the overproduction of H^+ caused by an oversecretion of gastrin, pancreatic enzymes are inactivated, causing impairment of dietary lipid absorption. Zollinger-Ellison syndrome does not affect the liver's ability to create bile salts (A). Celiac disease is an autoimmune disease of the small intestine in reaction to gluten(C). One of the major causes of peptic ulcer disease (PUD) is *H. pylori*, a flagellated bacteria associated with duodenal and gastric ulcers (D).

38. A

Acetylcholine (Ach), Histamine, and Gastrin ((B), (C), and (D)) all bind to different receptors on parietal cells, all three leading to an increase in H^+ secretion. Ach is released from the vagus nerves, Histamine is released from mastlike cells in the gastric mucosa, and gastrin is released from G cells in the stomach's antrum. (A) GIP (gastric inhibitory peptide) causes pancreatic beta cells to secrete insulin. GIP also inhibits gastric H^+ secretion.

39. D

Gastrin is secreted by G cells located in the antrum of the stomach. It is secreted when food is ingested. Gastrin can also be stimulated to secretion by local vagal reflexes. Following an action potential, neurocrines (peptides synthesized in GI tract neurons) are released onto the G cells. These neurocrines are called gastrin-releasing peptides (GRP) or bombesin. Gastrin has two main functions: first, to stimulate H^+ secretion by gastric parietal cells, and second, to stimulate gastric mucosa growth. Cholecystokinin (CCK) promotes fat digestion and absorption (A). CCK also slows down/inhibits gastric emptying (B) and increases gastric emptying time. Secretin increases the secretion of pancreatic and biliary HCO_3^- (choice C).

40. D

In some cases of Zollinger-Ellison syndrome, diarrhea may be the only presenting symptom. This results from an oversecretion of gastrin and gastric acid production. The high acid content damages intestinal villi, leading to malabsorption and frequent diarrhea. Motilin, produced by intestinal M cells, increases GI motility (C). Some studies suggest that motilin release is stimulated by an alkaline pH in the duodenum.

41. C

The physiologic control of gastrin, the gastric G cells, are under negative feedback control. Once the gastric contents have been properly acidified, gastrin secretion is inhibited. But in Zollinger-Ellison syndrome the tumor does not respond to gastric pH and gastrin is produced regardless.

PASSAGE VI

42. C

The free energy of the reaction is the same whether it is catalyzed or uncatalyzed. It is the difference between the starting energy (here 45 kJ/mol) and the final reaction energy (here 10 kJ/mol), yielding 35 kJ/mol. (A) is the uncatalyzed activation energy—final energy. (B) is the catalyzed activation energy—final energy. (D) is wrong because the final energy is much lower than the initial value.

43. B

The activation energy for the uncatalyzed reaction is 80 kJ/mol, and the catalyzed is 55 kJ/mol. 80 − 55 = 25, and 25/85 ~ 32%. (A) is wrong because the enzyme by definition lowers the activation energy some amount. (C) is wrong because the activation energy required is still 66% of what it was originally; it only went down 33%. (D) is wrong because there is still clearly some activation energy required for the reaction to occur.

44. B

Estrogen is associated with conversion from fat to muscle, and therefore some of it is necessary in the body. In people with high fat content, however, the estrogen cannot 'keep up,' and its efficacy is reduced. (A) is wrong because velocity can never be higher than V_{max} in any individual. (C) is wrong because the aromatase is just as active (i.e., requires same activation energy) as in a healthy person, but is working over many more cells. (D) is wrong because the only thing that can make the enzyme structure change is an artificial chemical (i.e., drug), which is not the case here.

45. D

Noncompetitive inhibition is an irreversible form of inhibition where the inhibitor covalently binds to the enzyme and deactivates it permanently. No type of feedback mechanism would be effective here. (A) is wrong because there is no allosteric (remote) control in aromatase. (B) is wrong because there is no allosteric site and also because the enzyme is being inhibited, not activated. (C) is wrong because there is no feedback from the product (estrogen) in this type of inhibition.

46. B

Aromatase inhibition will decrease estrogen production, and therefore increase androgen availability. (A) is wrong because as the enzyme converts androgen to estrogen, activating aromatase will lead to even lower androgen counts. (C) is wrong because men do naturally have some aromatase in their bodies, and for the same reason as (A), androgen counts would decrease with artificial injection. (D) is wrong because aromatase (and the estrogen it produces) does affect men (by increasing libido, for instance) as well as women.

PASSAGE VII

47. D

It is impossible to ascertain what genotype the second sister (individual I-3) has; we can ascertain

that she has passed the MIDD form of diabetes to her children through her mitochondrial DNA, which cannot be represented through the typical autosomal alleles. This eliminates (B) and (C) (even though heterozygosity would be correct for the first sister). Even if we could determine both genotypes, (A) would be wrong because MODY is autosomal dominant, and if homozygous dominant, all the children would present with the disease.

48. B

The individual could present with type II diabetes or MIDD. The age of onset means that the individual could not present with type I (juvenile) diabetes. Type II is the most likely option given his age, but MIDD is also possible; we do not have any information on his mother, and as a male he would not pass on the disease to his children. One could also argue that MODY is possible; if he had MODY, his wife would be homozygous recessive since she did not present with the disease, but each of his children has a 50 percent chance of developing the disease. The likelihood of all three offspring not developing the disease is low ($1/8$), but not zero. However, item III with MODY is unambiguously wrong.

49. C

This requires the determination that the MODY form of diabetes is present on the bloodline containing individual IV-2, and that it has autosomal dominant inheritance (stated in the passage introduction). This means that the mother, who has the disease, is heterozygous (homozygous dominant is extremely rare for such diseases, but this can be confirmed to not be the case by looking at the previous generations). With this deduction, a Punnett square could be made as follows.

	Mother	
Father	M	m
m	Mm	mm
m	Mm	mm

From this, the answer is clearly 50 percent. (A) would require both parents to be homozygous recessive, and this is not the case since the mother had young-onset diabetes. (B) is typical of autosomal *recessive* conditions, and the passage stem said that MODY is autosomal dominant. (D) requires both parents to be heterozygous, and in this case the father would also have diabetes.

50. A

These two individuals have no risk of developing a genetically-inherited form of diabetes (the only types that come before age 40). Their father has MIDD, but since this disease is mitochondrial, it will not be passed through him. The mother can be assumed to have type II diabetes, due to the late age of occurrence. (B) would have assumed that both offspring would have had a 25 percent chance of getting the disease, as is typical with autosomal recessive. (C) would have assumed both offspring had a 50 percent chance of developing the disease, as would have been the case with autosomal dominant. (D) is simply the chance of one individual getting it if it had been autosomal dominant.

51. A

Penetrance is the likelihood that a certain genotype will be expressed in the phenotype. There are three nondiabetic offspring in generation 2. If each of these offspring fall within the 15 percent chance of nonpenetrance, the overall probability of this happening is $(.15)^3 = 0.03$. (B) is $(.15)^2$, which would be for only two of the offspring. (C) is the chance that *any one* of the nondiabetic children is a carrier. (D) is the rate of penetrance for those who have diabetes.

52. A

ADM, from the question stem, is not insulin-dependent. MIDD is, but because the individual's father has MIDD, it will not be passed on to him through mitochondrial DNA. Therefore, the

individual has no chance of developing insulin-dependent diabetes (and a 50 percent chance of developing ADM). (B) is the likelihood if one of the conditions was autosomal recessive. (C) would be correct if looking at the risk of developing any kind of diabetes. (D) is the chance if the mother, not the father, had MIDD.

PRACTICE SECTION 2

ANSWER KEY

1.	B	19.	D	37.	C
2.	C	20.	B	38.	A
3.	B	21.	B	39.	A
4.	B	22.	C	40.	B
5.	B	23.	C	41.	C
6.	C	24.	D	42.	B
7.	C	25.	D	43.	C
8.	B	26.	A	44.	A
9.	C	27.	D	45.	D
10.	C	28.	B	46.	A
11.	A	29.	A	47.	D
12.	D	30.	D	48.	A
13.	C	31.	A	49.	B
14.	C	32.	D	50.	C
15.	C	33.	C	51.	D
16.	D	34.	A	52.	C
17.	B	35.	A		
18.	A	36.	C		

PASSAGE I

1. B

The goal of this experiment, mentioned in the context of the two major classes of antiretroviral drugs that target reverse transcriptase, is to compare the two different mechanisms by which they act.

2. C

This question is asking which nucleotide pairs with adenine. The trick is to recognize that the parent strand in this case is RNA. Therefore, an adenine nucleotide (DNA) will pair with a uracil (RNA).

3. B

Drug C decreases the activity of the reverse transcriptase. This result, along with the information provided in the passage about drug mechanisms, means (B) is a possible mechanism (nonnucleoside reverse transcriptase inhibitor). (D) describes the mechanism of a nucleotide/nucleoside reverse transcriptase inhibitor, which based on the information in the passage, does not affect reverse transcriptase activity. (A) and (C) would not have any effect on reverse transcriptase activity.

4. B

The assay described in the passage is used to evaluate drugs that target reverse transcriptase. It is likely that drugs with other targets will not have an effect on the same variables as those examined in the assay used. Drug D is FDA approved and therefore should have an effect on the virus (A, C, and D).

5. B

Competitive inhibitors bind to the same active site that the substrate binds to, preventing the binding of the substrate. Noncompetitive inhibitors bind to the enzyme at a different site than the enzyme's active site. Given the description provided in the passage, non-nucleotide reverse transcriptase inhibitors act as noncompetitive inhibitors of reverse transcriptase.

6. C

As described in the passage, the mechanism of nucleoside/nucleotide reverse transcriptase inhibitors involves the early termination of transcription after their incorporation into the daughter DNA strand, implying that they cannot be removed. They do not affect translation (A). They are competitive inhibitors of reverse transcriptase (B). They act at the active site of reverse transcriptase (D).

7. C

Once a retrovirus integrates its DNA into the host DNA, it is called a provirus until its viral mRNA is transcribed. By definition, it will be found in the nucleus.

PASSAGE II

8. B

The most critical (and susceptible) stage of fetal development is considered to be the embryonic stage (weeks 3–8), when all organ morphogenesis is occurring. If the drug was ingested during fertizilation (C), the likely outcome would be termination of pregnancy before implantation. The later weeks (A) and (D) are considered less critical because all the organ systems have been formed.

9. C

Down syndrome is the excess of genetic code on the 21st chromosome. A typical human's karyotype is either 46 XY (typical male) or 46 XX (typical female). There are many ways for this to occur, via either a complete extra chromosome [trisomy 21 (47, XX, +21)] or a portion of (i.e., due to translocations). About 95 percent of Down syndrome is due to trisomy 21; in the majority of cases, nondisjunction occurs with the maternal gamete. Cystic fibrosis (A) is caused by a mutation in the CFTR (cystic fibrosis transmembrane conductance regulator) gene. Sickle cell disease (B) is an inherited blood disorder whereby red blood cells contain an abnormal type of hemoglobin. Polycythemia vera (D), a myeloproliferative disorder, is considered to be due to a mutation of the JAK2 protein, thereby allowing for unregulated control of blood cell production.

10. C

The first sign of gastrulation is the formation of the primitive streak, which arises from (C) epiblast cells, not (A) hypoblast cells. During normal embryonic development, the primitive streak will diminish in size and eventually become an insignificant structure that ultimately disappears by the end of the fourth week. But sometimes the remnants will persist and give rise to a sacrococcygeal teratoma. This is the most common tumor in newborns and most often occurs in females. Most of the tumors are benign, diagnosed on routine antenatal ultrasonography, and surgically removed. The prochordal plate (B) is composed of hypoblast cells that fused with epiblast cells to form a circular, midline thickening, and will be the future site of the mouth. The yolk sac is formed from a portion of the exocoelomic cavity (D), which is formed in part from hypoblast cells and the inner surface of the cytotrophoblast.

11. A

Medulloblastoma is a highly malignant primary brain tumor that originates in the cerebellum or posterior fossa. It manifests with increased intracranial pressure due to blockage of the fourth ventrcile. Craniopharyngioma (B) is a slow-growing tumor that develop from Rathke's pouch. It is the most common supratentorial tumor in childhood. The tumor may enlarge and compress the optic chiasm, resulting in blindness. Glioblastoma multiforme (C) is the most common primary brain tumor in adults. It is a rapidly growing, highly destructive tumor with death occurring within months. The tumor is associate with necrotic tissue because the tumor grows faster than new blood vessels can be developed to provide nourishment for the tumor cells. Optic nerve glioma (D) is the most common primary neoplasm of the optic nerve. Often diagnosed during childhood, about 10 percent of cases occur in association with neurofibromatosis type

I. It is a tumor of the visual system and has been known to involve the optic nerve, optic chiasm, and/or optic tract.

12. D

Gastroschisis is a result of a defect lateral to the median plane of the anterior abdominal wall. This defect allows the intestines and sometimes other organs to develop outside the fetal abdomen without involving the umbilical cord. No parietal peritoneum covers the organs. Omphalocele (B) is an anterior abdominal defect that does involve the umbilical cord. During the eighth week of development, the fetal midgut undergoes a physiologic umbilical herniation, in which the organs extend out into the extraembryonic celom, occupying the proximal segment of the umbilical cord. It is believed that an omphalocele occurs when the bowel fails to return into the abdomen. Meckel diverticulum (C) is a small outpouching of the small intestine that is present at birth. It is the vestigial remnant of the omphalomesenteric duct (vitelline duct) and is considered to be the most common gastrointestinal tract malformation. Myeloschisis (A) is considered to be the most severe form of spina bifida. The spinal cord in this area remains open due to lack of complete neural tube fusion.

13. C

Triploidy is an abnormal chromosomal condition usually resulting from fertilization of an oocyte by two sperms (dispermy). Most triplod fetuses are aborted spontaneously or are stillborns, and some die shortly after birth. (A) and (B) are aneuploidy, (C) triploidy, and (D) tetraploidy.

14. C

An ectopic pregnancy occurs when the blastocyst implants within an abnormal location. Oftentimes, the woman has a history of endometriosis or pelvic inflammatory disease. The most common site is the ampulla portion of the fallopian tube (80–90%), isthmic (5–10%); cornual (1–2%), abdominal (1–2%), and cervix (less than 1%).

15. C

Pelvic inflammatory disease/disorder (PID) is a general term applied to inflammation of the female reproductive system (uterus, fallopian tube, and/or ovaries) that has progressed to scarring and adhesions to nearby tissues and organs. PID is often associated with STDs (sexually transmitted diseases). With each episode of infection, the chance of infertility increases. (C) Chlamydia trachomatis and Neisseria gonorrhoeae are considered the leading causes of PID. Patients testing positive for one are often tested for the other, as the two are often both present. Syphillis (A) is an STD caused by the spirochete, treponema pallidum. Untreated syphilis can lead to systemic dissemination and damage—especially of the heart, brain, eyes, and bones—and has even been fatal in some. Human papilloma virus (HPV) (B) is considered to be the most common sexually transmitted disease in the United States. There are over 100 subtypes and some are known to cause cancer, primarily cervical, anal, vulvar, and penile cancers. Herpes (D) simplex virus (HSV) type 1 (HSV-1) and type 2 (HSV-2) are known to cause herpes simplex. Although in the past, genital herpes was considered to have been caused by HSV-2, the rate of genital HSV-1 infections has increased dramatically. Typical manifestations are painfully inflamed papules and vesicles on the outer genital surface, as well as the inner thigh, buttocks, or anus.

16. D

Fetal erythroblastosis (aka hemolytic disease of the newborn) occurs when small amounts of fetal blood pass through the placental membrane and enters the maternal blood. If the mother is Rh negative, and the fetus is Rh positive, the mother may have anti-Rh IgG antibodies which will enter fetal circulation and attack fetal red blood cells. If severe, the infant may be stillborn or die shortly after birth. Rubella (aka German measles) (A) is caused by the rubella virus. The disease is usually mild in children and adults, but if a mother is infected within the first 20 weeks of pregnancy, the child may be born with congenital rubella syndrome (CRS), and that can lead to developmental deafness, blindness, congenital heart defects, and even infant death. Sickle cell anemia occurs when there is a point mutation on the beta-globin chain of haemoglobin (B), when glutamic acid is substituted by valine. This causes red blood cells to lose their elasticity and become sickle-shaped during low oxygen conditions. Cystic fibrosis is caused by mutation of the CFTR gene (cystic fibrosis transmembrane conductance regulator gene) (C). This gene produces a chloride ion channel that is issential in sweat glands, digestive juices, and mucus production.

17. B

A partial hydatidiform mole usually results from an oocyte fertilized by two sperms. Most partial moles are triploid (contain three chromosome sets). The embryo usually dies, and the chorionic villi form into cystic swellings which resemble bunches of grapes. The moles will produce an abnormally high amount of human chorionic gonadotropin. Dizygotic twins (A) are the result of fertilization of two oocytes. The two zygotes may be of the same or different sexes.

QUESTIONS 18–21

18. A

Translation refers to the production of protein from mRNA. Though the conversion of DNA to RNA is discussed, the idea here is that one initial piece of information gives rise to other secondary pieces.

You can predict, then, that only eukaryotes have alternate splicing. Prokaryotic DNA is monocistronic. Although in transcription prokaryotes do have multiple reading frames (as do eukaryotes), this is not true in translation; their genes are organized in an operon and thus groups of proteins are produced en masse on one mRNA transcript in tandem fashion.

19. D

Gram-negative bacteria do not take up the gram stain because they have an outer cell wall which impedes the movement of any polar or large substance into the periplasmic space. This could also be a barrier to drugs. Capsids (A) are found in viruses, not bacteria. Bacteria are prokaryotes and thus have no membrane-bound organelles (B). All bacteria have an inner cell wall (C).

20. B

Only the endoplasmic reticulum is directly connected to the nucleus. The nucleolus (A) resides in the nucleus. Neither (C) nor (D) is continuous with the nucleus.

21. B

This is a straight recall question. Plasma cells (C) do not secrete hormones; they function in the immune system. Beta cells of the islets of Langerhans in the pancreas secrete insulin. Delta cells secrete somatostatin, which is also secreted by the D cells of the gastric antrum.

PASSAGE III

22. C

The destructive phase (A) is another name for the menstrual phase. It is named as such because during this period, the uterine lining is destroyed and discarded. The secretory phase (B) is another name for the luteal phase. It is named as such because

during this period, many hormones are secreted. The gestational phase (C) does not exist. Gestation refers to the period in which a woman carries an embryo in her womb. As menstruation refers to the cycle of events which lead up to gestation, it does not logically follow that one of its phases would occur during gestation. You may be thinking of the name *pregestational phase*, which is another name for the luteal phase. The proliferative phase (D) is another name for the follicular phase. It is called as such because during this period, follicules and the endometrium proliferate.

23. C

The passage tells us that the female menstrual cycle is a set of events which leads to ovulation. Ovulation is the release of ova into the uterus for fertilization. The chart shows us that Mary's menstrual cycle is 28 days long. This means that in a 365-day year, Mary would undergo 365/28 = 13 full menstrual cycles.

24. D

If fertilization fails to occur, the ovum is distentegrated through menses (A). It does not become the corpus luteum. The product of ovum and sperm fertilization is a zygote. The follicle before ovulation occurs is a follicle. It goes through different stages such as tertiary follicle and then Graafian follicle. What remains of the follicle following ovulation becomes the corpus luteum.

25. D

One would expect the conditions in (D) to increase the proportion of time a woman is susceptible to pregnancy, and in so doing, indirectly increase fertility. As for (A), about one-third of estrogen comes from fat. One needs very high levels of estradiol (an estrogen) to stimulate the LH surge necessary of ovulation. This is also why anorexic women often experience secondary ammenorhea. Progesterone (B) is actually used as a form of birth control. Low levels of estrogen (C) would exacerbate infertility, as explained in (A).

26. A

The combination pill is a mixture of progesterone and estradiol, in levels that mimic these hormones' levels during pregnancy. This tricks your body into believing it is pregnant, preventing the proliferative uterine phase and causing a lighter period.

27. D

The zygote is what is formed after the egg's fertilization by the sperm. If fertilization occurs, menses is prevented from occurring. Blood (A) is contained in menstrual discharge as a result of broken blood vessels in the endometrium. As the endometrium exits the body, it sloughs off some of the cells lining the vagina (B). The stratum functionalis (C) is the outer layer of the endometrium, and is the layer that is discharged.

28. B

FSH is inhibited by high estradiol levels. Estradiol levels increase until the midpoint of the follicular phase, and FSH increases until that time as well. FSH dips at the midpoint as a result of high levels of estradiol secreted by large follicles, inhibiting GnRH. GnRH from the hypothalamus controls FSH secretion by the pituitary.

29. A

In the beginning of the follicular phase, estradiol levels are low, and FSH and LH secretion is high due to the absence of negative feedback by estradiol on FSH and LH production. At about the middle of the follicular phase, estradiol levels are moderately high and begin to exert negative feedback on FSH and LH production. By the end of the follicular phase, very high estradiol levels are present, and at very high concentrations, estradiol stimulates FSH and LH production, resulting in an LH surge.

30. D

If you refer to the figure in the passage, you will see that (D) is true. The relationship between estradiol and progesterone levels controls gonadotropin release. Before the FSH and LH surge, there is high estradiol but low progesterone. After ovulation, there is high progesterone but low estradiol.

31. A

To prevent pregnancy, the couple needs to limit coitus in a way that prevents viable sperm from coming in contact with a viable ovum. We know from the passage that ova can remain viable for up to three days after ovulation (ovum disentegration typically begins 24 hours after ovulation but can begin as late as 72 hours later). We also know that male sperm can stay viable in the female reproductive tract for up to four days. A woman with the given menstrual cycle should limit coitus to three days after the basal temperature rise, and the following 21 days (four days before ovulation), choice (A).

PASSAGE IV

32. D

The experiment shows that the size of gene X in family 2 and the control group is the same. It is possible that there was a point mutation in gene X that affected its functional capability yet not the length of the gene. In mammals mtDNA encodes for 37 genes, so it is possible that the mtDNA mutation in family 2 affects one of the other genes. We know from the passage that family 2 has the clinical presentation of mitochondrial inheritance disorder, so item III is wrong. Items I and II are correct.

33. C

Since we know from the passage that gene X plays a role in aerobic respiration, we can predict the location of the gene X product. All proteins that play a role in aerobic respiration reside in the inner mitochondrial membrane and mitochondrial matrix. Because we know that the protein is a transmembrane protein, we can assume it is found in the inner membrane and not as a free protein in the matrix (D).

34. A

This question tests your ability to synthesize information from the passage with your knowledge about aerobic respiration. When oxygen is unavailable to accept electrons, pyruvate acts as the electron acceptor, forming lactic acid. It is unlikely that dysfunctions of aerobic respiration would cause an increase in phospholipids, alanine, or carbon dioxide.

35. A

As described in the passage and the subsequent experiment, mitochondrial inheritance disorders can take on multiple phenotypes (the visible appearance of a disease) and can be due to different mutations (different genotypes).

36. C

If a mitochondrial disorder were to be caused by a mutation in nuclear DNA, the mitochondria must rely somewhat on certain gene products from nuclear DNA. Mitochondria are only semi-autonomous and do not encode all their necessary genes in the mitochondrial DNA (D). Mitochondria are the only nonnuclear organelle to possess their own DNA (B).

37. C

Based on the passage and family tree illustration, we know that mitochondrial inheritance disorders have maternal inheritance of a mitochondrial genome that is separate from the nuclear genome. Maternal inheritance occurs because sperm cell mitochondria do not contribute to ova during fertilization. Items I, II, and III are correct.

38. A

Mitochondria have their own ribosomes separate from those made in the nucleus. Mitochondrial DNA is circular, but nuclear DNA is often found as linear chromosomes. mtDNA has maternal inheritance, whereas there are maternal and paternal inputs in nuclear DNA inheritance.

QUESTIONS 39–41

39. A

Lipase (B) breaks down fats, which are a different chemical class from polysccharides. Pepsin (D) is a hormone, not an enzyme. Trypsinogen (C) is a zymogen, not a hormone. The rationale for eliminating these answer choices is guided by the prediction, garnered from the question stem, that the answer must be an enzyme which is specific for starches.

40. B

For remembering RNA mutations, hint 1: Like DNA, changes within a base chemical class produce less severe mutation than changes between chemical classes. Hint 2: With RNA questions, eliminate any answer choice that includes T, as RNA only has U. Hint 3: Remember the wobble position! The third position in any codon is always most subject to variation due to the structure of the tRNA-mRNA interface. Thus, the genetic code has evolved to tolerate this variation without adverse consequences. Using this knowledge, one sees that (B) is correct because the mutation is both in the wobble position and changes a purine for a purine. (D) is wrong because, although the mutation is in the wobble position, AAT is not a valid RNA codon (AAU would be).

41. C

This question tests your ability to critically evaluate what some consider an inflammatory statement. (A) and (B) have no basis in genetics. (D) assumes that a longer time for procreation will result in increased progeny. (C) is true because male gametes have more genetic variation than female gametes and thus have a higher chance of containing a mutation encoding a sexually advantageous trait.

PASSAGE V

42. B

The voltage-gated sodium channels that are affected by carbamazepine are very likely to be implicated as a mediator for a kindling-like mechanism which is voltage-dependant in action. The sodium channel activity does not necessarily support excitotoxicity, which is based on the toxicity of certain neurotransmitters in the synapse.

43. C

Excitotoxicity, not the kindling model, deals primarily with the toxicity of neurotransmitters that are found at the synapse, so (A) is wrong. Moreover, even though lots of sub-threshold potentials are shot and culminate at the synapse (leading to excitability of downstream neurons), (A) is wrong because the excitotoxicity model does deal with processes at the synapse. The kindling model, albeit in most instances with electrical stimulation, may use chemical stimulation as well to cause sensitization, so (B) is wrong.

44. A

In light of the excitotoxicity view, extracellular administration of an enzyme which degrades glutamate (A) is a suitable method for normal treatment of a chronically epileptic patient. (B), (C), and (D) would exacerbate the seizures.

45. D

(A), (B), and (C) are not true of glutamate.

46. A

By cutting off blood flow, metabolic nutrients for the maintenance and production of various enzymes and carriers are impaired. Nothing in the passage leads you to believe reasonably that trauma to the brain would cause an increase in Brownian motion of neurotransmitters (B). Nor does the passage suggest any impact on action potential propagation (C) by trauma to the brain.

47. D

(A) is not plausible because the kindling model does not gradually increase the stimulus; moreover, the "epileptic threshold" is lowered, whereas the threshold stimulus is raised in accommodation. (B) and (C) are concerned as well with a raising of the threshold, and in the case of absolute refractory period, to an infinitely high one.

48. A

The cerebellum is responsible for balance.

PASSAGE VI

49. B

The sodium/potassium pump releases three sodium ions for every two potassium ions, creating a ratio of 1.5. This same ratio must be matched by the water concentration in the cell; hence, it is 60 percent water within the cell and 40 percent out of it. (This could also be determined from the figure by counting the 18 K^+ ions in the cell and 12 Na^+ ions outside the cell.) A 50/50 water concentration (A) would lead to too much water outside the cell (hypotonicity). A 75/25 concentration puts too much water inside the cell (hypertonicity).

50. C

ATP is the energy source for the sodium-potassium pump, which is necessary to control the sodium level in the cell. NaCl (table salt) is wrong because the sodium has no chemical effect until it is a separate positive ion. Glucose is actually a worsening factor because its presence would force some water into the cell. Urea plays no role within the cell; its function is to excrete sodium from the body.

51. D

Vasopressin is released when the body is dehydrated and causes the body to conserve water. It also controls the menstrual cycle and is highest at the time of ovulation. Vasopressin interferes with the sodium potassium pump, causing a "misinforming" such that the body thinks it is dehydrated when there's actually an excess of water. There is no evidence that women consume any more water than men (A); in fact, it is likely that they consume less because they sweat less. Brain mass (B) is determined by size, not gender (children do have a higher likelihood of hyponatremia for this reason, however). Although estrogen (C) does contribute to water storage, testosterone (another sex hormone also found in women) can actually block the effect of vasopressin.

52. C

The myelin sheath is a phospholipid layer that protects the neurons; this is the same function as the phospholipid bilayer of the cell membrane within the cell. The neuron has its own nucleus (called the same), choice (A). Animal cells do not have cell walls (B). The cytoplasm (D) is the fluid portion of the cell.

PRACTICE SECTION 3

ANSWER KEY

1.	A	19.	D	36.	C
2.	D	20.	E	37.	C
3.	C	21.	D	38.	B
4.	A	22.	A	39.	C
5.	D	23.	B	40.	D
6.	B	24.	D	41.	B
7.	B	25.	D	42.	C
8.	A	26.	B	43.	A
9.	D	27.	C	44.	A
10.	A	28.	C	45.	A
11.	A	29.	A	46.	C
12.	C	30.	A	47.	D
13.	C	31.	D	48.	B
14.	A	32.	A	49.	D
15.	A	33.	D	50.	D
16.	A	34.	B	51.	B
17.	A	35.	A	52.	C
18.	D				

PASSAGE I

1. A

(A) allows both hypotheses 1 and 2 to be valid and their data accepted. Tyrosinase levels are not correlated with melanin levels; they are correlated with melanin levels and thus skin color. A logical synthesis of the two hypotheses would be that somehow after translation of the gene for tyrosinase, the actual enzyme's activity is changed to become more active to produce darker colorations. Gene alterations (B) would mean gene products would correlate with melanin synthesis—that gene product could only be tyrosinase. (C) bears no relation to the relevance of the hypotheses.

2. D

The table shows that the cooler temperature correlates with more active melanin production and hence, tyrosinase activity level. A lower temperature (A) means more activity. The table shows varying activity levels with different group temperatures (B). A small percentage of coloration is detected at 5° (C).

3. C

The limb is the coolest region of the body, since it is the farthest from the body's core. Thus, it will have the highest activity rate at lower temperatures based on the passage results.

4. A

The active site (A) is most sensitive and involved in the activity of any enzyme. The other areas are either not as involved or not real areas of an enzyme.

5. D

At tertiary or quaternary levels, the active site emerges and is most delicate and susceptible to temperature changes.

6. B

Allosteric inhibitor (B) would alter enzymatic activity after translation of the gene and the activity level of tyrosinase. (A) and (C) apply to tyrosinase levels and would refute hypothesis 1 because it is pre-translational. (D) is simply about pH, which is an unknown variable based upon the passage.

7. B

There is some coloration at 10°C indicating some level of activity (B). There is no complete denaturing at any level (A) and (D). Choice (C) is a distracter because an allosteric site would enhance enzymatic activity if it were denatured, but in this case, activity is only moderate at 25°C so it's less plausible than (B).

8. A

pH is often a physical factor regulating enzymatic activity. Pressure is not generally an issue in living systems' enzymatic metabolism.

PASSAGE II

9. D

The passage states that the glomerular filtration rate is equal to the clearance of inulin, which is neither secreted nor reabsorbed. Glucose is normally always reabsorbed from the proximal convoluted tubules.

10. A

Less of the solute has been excreted than has entered the Bowman's capsule.

11. A

GFR is best approximated by a solute that is neither secreted nor reabsorbed in the glomerulus.

12. C

Inulin is a polysaccharide, as the passage states. Inulin would not be able to filter into the Bowman's capsule if it were bigger than an erythrocyte (red blood cell) or albumin (A) and (B), both of which cannot be filtered.

13. C

Approximately 90 percent of PAH which enters the kidneys, whether via the glomerular apparatus or nephron vasculature, is excreted. (A) and (B) are wrong because PAH would not be able to be filtered if it were bigger than an erythrocyte and albumin.

14. A

Clearance is a measurement of the excretion flow rate and GFR is a flow rate measurement of all the volume of fluid, including the solute, which filters through all the glomeruli in the body.

15. A

PAH clearance is equal to RPF, and if you look at the graph, a plasma creatinine concentration of 4 mg/dL corresponds to about 30 mL/min. Thus, using the filtration fraction equation, you get 30 mL/min/550 mL/min.

16. A

PAH is equal to RPF, and if one remembers that plasma is a component of blood, renal blood flow should be greater than renal plasma flow.

PASSAGE III

17. A

Interferons are messenger proteins that cause up-regulation of anti-infective genes in other cells. This means that the antiviral properties of interferons can be utilized only on pathogens located within the cell, such as viruses and a few bacteria. They have no effect on typical extracellular pathogens such as fungi and protozoa.

18. D

Interferon works to protect cells that have yet to be virally infected or which have yet to undergo viral uncoating inside the cell. Addition of interferon at this point in time would not be protective to the cells on the plate, and would thus cause the cytotoxic effect to clear the plate of viable cells.

19. D

Viral RNA is needed to produce proteins vital to viral proliferation, which includes the capsid protein. The viral envelope is obtained as the virus buds off of the infected cell and is not synthesized by genetic material contained in the virus. The cytotoxic burst is not a characteristic of every virus's replication cycle. Some viruses carry their own nucleic acid polymerase and thus do not need to penetrate the nucleus. The genetic material of the virus can be DNA or RNA; thus, the virus's inability to infect is not specific to the inhibition of viral RNA.

20. D

Stimulation of humoral, or B cell immunity, requires presentation of antigens to B cells, which then form antibodies specific to those antigens. Inflammation, phagocytosis, and histamine are mechanisms used by the non-specific and/or cell-mediated immune system. B lymphocytes may or may not be activated, depending on if they carry the immunoglobulin specific to the antigen being presented. Therefore, the most specific indication of B cell activation is the presence of immunoglobulins.

21. D

Cytotoxic T cells eliminate infected cells in three main ways: first, direct cytotoxicity via granzymes (B), second, indirect cytotoxicity via the FAS/FAS-L pathway (C), and third, interferon production, stimulating phagocytosis of the infected cell (D). Immunoglobulin production is a hallmark of the humoral immune system (A).

22. A

Recall that the thymus is the maturation site for T cells, the predominant lymphocyte in the bloodstream. Without this maturation process, T lymphocytes are quickly removed from circulation.

23. B

Oxygen is required for the synthesis of digestive enzymes used by macrophages. Poor perfusion leading to chronically hypoxic tissue tends to result in macrophages with a diminished ability to phagocytize foreign material and present antigens to stimulate the B cell response.

QUESTIONS 24–29

24. D

Insertional mutagenesis (A) describes site-directed mutagenesis. Nucleotide template-directed polymerization (B) describes the polymerase chain reaction (PCR). Plasmid-driven transcription (C) describes the creation of a knock-in mutant. This is a straight recall question.

25. D

This question requires that you recall the assumptions of the Hardy-Weinberg model. Rather than predicting an answer outright, it is easier to scan the answer choices and eliminate those that are not tenets of the model. (A) is a distortion because mating between species would introduce new genes into the pool and thus change the frequency of alleles in a population. However, you could be fooled by the phrase "set rate," which implies stability. (B) and (C) directly contradict the HW model.

26. B

This question requires you to reason through the renin-angiotensin-aldosterone (RAS) system. Renin is secreted by the juxtaglomerular apparatus (JGA) in response to low vascular volume (and hence low blood pressure). This causes the release of angiotensin, which in turn causes the release of aldosterone from the zona glomerulosa of the adrenal cortex. (A) causes the release of angiotensin. (C) is released in response to high serum calcium levels. (D) is released in response to TSH.

27. C

Stop: What do you have to know to answer this question? Think: How is the likelihood of inheritance of a trait determined? Predict: The second child's genotype is independent of the first. The genotype of the first child is unrelated to the odds of the second child having a given genotype. Using a Punnett square, with C as the normal gene and c as the gene for cystic fibrosis, the chances of the child inheriting the cc genotype, and thus having the disease, are 25 percent.

28. C

The formula for determining the number of genetically unique gametes for a given genotype with two possible alleles at each gene is 2^n, where $n = 3$. Therefore, there are a total of eight possible gametes.

29. A

Here you must know the role of the loop of Henle in the nephron. The question stem states that it maintains the osmotic gradient. It therefore allows the urine to become more concentrated, or hypertonic to the blood. (B) is wrong because a steeper osmotic gradient would allow more sodium to be excreted, not less. (C) is wrong because urine should be hypertonic to body fluids, to allow the body to clear waste without becoming dehydrated. (D) is wrong because the loop of Henle does not reabsorb blood proteins. In fact, blood proteins should not pass through the glomerulus at all; they are too large and their negative charge prohibits glomerular filtration.

QUESTIONS 30–36

30. A

(A) is correct because steroids are lipid-based and will pass into the cell readily. (B) is incorrect because peptides are generally negatively charged and thus would not move across the phospholipid membrane. (C) is incorrect because second messengers are molecules that work within the cell in response to activation from substance that bind to the cell membrane, rather than themselves originating from outside the cell. (D) is incorrect because glucose is a hydrophilic substance and a glucose analog would be unlikely to pass readily across the plasma membrane without a glucose transporter molecule.

31. D

Choice (A) is incorrect because there is no reason that the lungs would be uniquely suited to support the growth of mycobacteria. (B) is incorrect because although the lungs are the site for oxygen exchange, the digestive tract also has sufficient oxygen to support aerobic bacterial growth, such as the bacteria that causes stomach ulcers. (C) is incorrect because the bile salts are involved in fat emulsification, and would not likely prohibit bacterial growth. (D) is correct because it explains why the digestive tract is inhospitable to bacterial growth: most bacteria will not survive in the low pH of the stomach.

32. A

The question requires you to know that vasopressin (ADH) and oxytocin are the hormones released by the posterior pituitary gland. Because vasopressin increases fluid retention, a tumor causing increased vasopressin release could lead to hypertension. Plasma calcium levels are increased and decreased by parathyroid hormone and calcitonin, respectively, which are not related to the posterior pituitary, and thus choices (B) and (C) are incorrect. Choice (D), precocious puberty, can be triggered by a tumor forming on the anterior pituitary gland, which releases FSH and LH, but not the posterior gland.

33. D

To answer this question, you need to know that osteoclasts are responsible for reabsorbing bone into the blood. Choice (D), the macrophage, is a cell type that is also responsible for engulfing substances (such as infectious materials). Of choices (A), (B), and (C), red blood cells supply oxygen to the tissues, fibroblasts compose connective tissue and skin, and plasma cells produce antibodies as part of the immune response, but none of these cell types have roles in physiology analogous to that of an osteoclast.

34. B

(A) is incorrect because bronchiole constriction would decrease gas exchange, thus contributing to decreased running performance. Choice (B) is correct because increased surfactant would facilitate gas exchange by reducing surface tension on the alveoli, not reduce it. Choice (C) is incorrect because swollen epithelial linings would make it more difficult for gas exchange to occur. (D) is incorrect because these cilia normally beat continuously to remove excess fluids and foreign debris from the respiratory tract.

35. A

The question relies on your knowledge of the differences between prokaryotes and eukaryotes. Even if you do not remember which of the structures are found in prokaryotes such as bacteria, you can predict the answer based on your knowledge that prokaryotes lack membrane-bound organelles. Ribosomes lack membranes, so choice (A) is correct. (B), the mitochondrion, has the inner and outer membranes crucial to the electron transport chain. (C), the Golgi apparatus, has a single membrane. (D), the nuclear membrane, would not be present in a prokaryote, because it lacks a nucleus.

36. C

The question asks how coding for a functional protein could be retained in the presence of a genetic mutation. (A) is incorrect because mutations in DNA actually give rise to a wide array of illnesses. (B) is incorrect because codons are always the same size and would not expand to fill a gap; furthermore, there would be no physical gap to fill because the codons would still be linked normally in the DNA strand. (C) is correct because codons consist of three base pairs. If three base pairs were deleted, the reading frame would be conserved and a polypeptide would be created lacking one amino acid but otherwise normal; function might be retained. (D) is incorrect because back mutations resulting in restored function are extremely rare

PASSAGE IV

37. C

The bone marrow of centrally located bones such as the skull, sternum, vertebrae, and pelvis is primarily where hematopoiesis is located. The liver and spleen are sites of red cell production in the fetus, and occasionally in children and adults if the bone marrow is unable to keep up with demand for new red blood cells.

38. B

The kidney is the site of hydroxylation of vitamin D precursors into the most biologically active form, 1,25-dihydroxycholecalciferol. Folic acid and riboflavin (Vitamin B_2) are supplied by diet. Vitamin K is obtained from dietary sources as well as from the normal flora present in the large intestine.

39. C

EPO stimulates red blood cell formation in the bone marrow and is also thought to promote longevity of the red blood cell once it leaves the bone marrow. Thus lack of EPO would not result in abnormally sized or shaped cells unless an iron deficiency was also present. Schistocytes are the remnants of destroyed red blood cells in the circulation.

40. D

ELISA utilizes labeled antibodies which can be formulated to almost any moiety, including the manufactured sugars attached to exogenous EPO. Northern and Western blots are tests of RNA and protein expression, respectively. A peripheral smear would be used to examine the relative shapes and sized of blood cells. Spectrophotometry would not be sensitive in a blood sample.

41. B

Heme synthesis is dependent on iron stores in the body. Oxygen carrying capacity of red blood cells is dependent on the concentration of heme. Thus at chronically low states of oxygen, the body eventually loses the ability to compensate due to exhaustion of iron stores. At low oxygen states, one would expect elevated amounts of HIF, which the data confirms. Clumping of red blood cells would cause an increase in the expected red blood cell percentage.

42. C

HIF is thought to be an enhancer of EPO transcription in the cells of the kidney. Therefore a nonsense mutation would result in the loss of negative feedback regulation. HIF would not be hydroxylated and inactivated at high levels of oxygen. With this, one would expect that EPO production would remain constant at all levels of oxygen concentrations.

43. A

Red blood cells are anuclear—therefore, they do not reproduce by binary fission nor make proteins once they are matured and released into the bloodstream. The lack of a nucleus makes the cell particularly bendable, and thus able to navigate narrow capillaries. The structural proteins of the red blood cell allow it to fold down upon itself without losing its functional capacity to carry oxygen. The red blood cell membrane contains both cholesterol for structural stability and proteins to allow interactions with endothelial cells in capillaries.

44. A

HIF is active in its nonhydroxylated state to act as a transcription factor for EPO. The effect of EPO on erythropoiesis is mediated by the EPO receptor in the bone marrow. Heme precursors (amino acids and pyroxidine) become heme by a process dependent on iron stores. Increased red blood cell production leads to tissue oxygenation by improved oxygen carrying capacity of the blood per volume.

45. A

Epinephrine preferentially shunts blood away from the digestive and filtration systems of the body toward systems that facilitate escape from danger. The blood vessels supplying the kidneys vasoconstrict, thus exposing them to lower levels of oxygenated blood. In addition to increased EPO production, renin secretion also increases, as the vasoconstriction of the renal arterioles causes a sensation of volume depletion to the cells of the kidney. Epinephrine is normally regulated with a negative feedback mechanism. Prolonged exposure to exogenous epinephrine would shut down the body's normal production of it.

46. C

Methemoglobin reductase is responsible for converting Fe^{3+} back to Fe^{2+} in order to bind to oxygen. Fe^{3+} incorporated into heme is seen in 1–2 percent of molecules in a healthy individual. This percentage can increase with certain blood cell or metabolic diseases, leading to a chronic hypoxic state. The pneumonic OIL RIG (oxidation is loss, reduction is gain) can be used to remember how charges change.

PASSAGE V

47. D

Vitamin D is an important part of bone development. It can be synthesized from a precursor that is found in the skin. This precursor gets hydroxylated in the liver and again in the kidneys to become active. Vitamin D then acts at the kidney and intestine to increase reabsorption and absorption of calcium respectively. The development of the periosteum (A) will not be affected by a decrease in

sunlight. Vitamin C (B) is important to the hydroxylation and cross-linking of collagen fibrils, not for bone development. Slight changes in barometric pressure (C) will not impact bone development.

48. B

Osteoclasts are responsible for breaking down bone so it can be remodeled or so calcium can be released into the serum. Osteoclast function is opposed by osteoblasts which lay down bone matrix that is subsequently calcified (remember osteoBlast Builds). Overactivity of osteoclasts will cause bone loss, known clinically as osteoporosis. Overactivity of T and B cells (C) and (D) can cause a variety of problems including autoimmunity, leukemia, and hypergammaglobulinemia, but will not directly contribute to bone loss.

49. D

Secondary healing is responsible for most of bone healing. It involves the presence of a large hematoma that forms at the site of a bone break. This hematoma becomes a callus, which is subsequently vascularized. Collagen is laid down by mesechymal cells that migrate to the callus from the periosteum and surrounding soft tissue. Over time, the collagen that is laid down is replaced by calcified bone. Primary healing (C) is the direct deposition of bone at the site of a fracture without the step of collagen deposition that is subsequently replaced by bone. Membranous ossification (B) is a process of bone development that is responsible for the development of flat bones like the pelvis and bones of the cranium. In these instances, no collagen skeleton is present before bone is produced. Endochondral ossification (A) involves the deposition of collagen. (A) and (B) are processes of embryologic bone development, not bone healing.

50. D

Calcium is crucial to the functioning of nervous and muscle contraction. The key to this question is to know that the parathyroid glands and cells producing calcitonin are ensheathed with the thyroid. If the thyroid is removed, parathyroid must be retained to maintain calcium homeostasis. Calcitonin (B) does not contribute nearly as much to calcium homeostasis, so no effort is made to preserve those cells. In this case, lack of PTH (A) leaves the serum calcium relatively unchecked, and the patient will have calcium in excess producing her symptoms.

51. B

Vitamin D is one of four fat-soluble vitamins; A, K, and E are also stored in the fat. The other common vitamins are water-soluble and are lost in the urine if they aren't used at the time of ingestion.

52. C

The thymus is an organ in the neck which is very active during development and childhood. T cells in the thymus undergo a process of clonal deletion; if, for example a T cell "recognizes" or seeks to attack antigens naturally present on body tissues, that T cell will be eliminated by the thymus so it does not proliferate and go into the body to attack "self" tissues. Clonal deletion may lead to autoimmune attacks, in which T cells attack body tissue that they believe is foreign material; the problem is that the T cells think the foreign material must be neutralized and removed from the body.

INDEX